D1806977

EVOLVING CONSTITUTIONS OF INTERNATIONAL ORGANIZATIONS

International Law in Japanese Perspective

VOLUME 3

Series Editor
Shigeru Oda

The titles published in this series are listed at the end of this volume.

Evolving Constitutions of International Organizations

A Critical Analysis of the Interpretative
Framework of the Constituent Instruments
of International Organizations

by

TETSUO SATO
Faculty of Law
Hitotsubashi University
Japan

KLUWER LAW INTERNATIONAL
THE HAGUE / LONDON / BOSTON

A C.I.P. Catalogue record for this book is available from the Library of Congress.

ISBN 90-411-0202-7

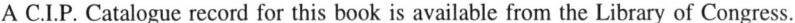

Published by Kluwer Law International,
P.O. Box 85889, 2508 CN The Hague, The Netherlands.

Sold and distributed in the U.S.A. and Canada
by Kluwer Law International,
675 Massachusetts Avenue, Cambridge, MA 02139, U.S.A.

In all other countries, sold and distributed
by Kluwer Law International,
P.O. Box 85889, 2508 CN The Hague, The Netherlands.

Printed on acid-free paper

Printed in the Netherlands

Table of Contents

Chapter Four Interpretative Procedures of Constituent Instruments
— Organs of International Organizations as Principal Interpreters of Constituent Instruments **161**

**Chapter Five   The Emerging Doctrine of Interpretation of
                  Constituent Instruments as the Constitutions of
                  International Organizations   227**

x

Preface

In the present book, I have advocated an emerging doctrine of the interpretative framework of constituent instruments as the constitutions of international organizations. I have argued that, under the influences of the inherent dynamism of international organizations, the interpretative framework of the constituent instruments of international organizations is not the same as that of ordinary treaties, and that the interpretation of the constituent instruments of international organizations deviates from the interpretative framework regulated by the law of treaties as codified by the Vienna Convention on the Law of Treaties. I have presented, as an alternative interpretative framework to that of ordinary treaties, a doctrine of constituent instruments as the constitutions of international organizations rather than as the (founding) treaties. In advocating this new doctrine of the interpretative framework, I have been careful not to attempt to construct a fragile house of cards. As the current doctrines and practices of States and international organizations do not support such a construction, the best way would be to construct a moderate but solid doctrine which could be sufficiently justified by actual practices and which could be further improved upon and refined, but even this has yet to be made.

In my opinion, the interpretative framework as constitutions differs from that as treaties in two respects: (1) on the quantitative aspect of the teleological extent admitted, in the sense that constituent instruments are interpreted within the teleological framework so that their efficient functioning and effective activities could be assured and promoted, and that predominant consideration is given to the "efficiency" and "effectiveness" of international organizations to the extent that the teleological reasoning deviates from the textual interpretative framework in the law of treaties; (2) on the qualitative aspect of legal significance possessed by the practice of the organs of international organizations, in the sense that the practice of international organizations affects, in feedback, the interpretations of constituent instruments so that it gives them an evolutionary nature, and that this "subsequent practice" of the organs is given the legal value which deviates qualitatively from the textual interpretative framework in the law of treaties. Certainly each of these two aspects has sometimes been referred to in different contexts by other writers. These two, however, have never been, with sufficient development and refinement, synthesized in this new doctrine of constituent instruments as the constitutions of international organizations.

xiii

In the field of international organizations where amendments of their constituent instruments are as exceptional as those of the United Nations, it is through the process of interpretation and application of constituent instruments that political evolutions and changes will be transformed into legal arguments. In this sense interpretation could be qualified as the "concept charnière (hinging concept)" between politics and the law.

We have seen that military enforcement measures were applied to Iraq in 1991 in a manner close to, if not the same as, that expected by the Charter. A series of "authorizations" of the use of force by peace keeping forces and/or Member States were allowed. An international tribunal to prosecute those responsible for serious violations of international humanitarian law were established both for former Yugoslavia and Rwanda. All of these activities were authorized under Chapter VII of the United Nations Charter. We must analyze and judge the legality of these activities in the light of the relevant provisions of Chapter VII. Here the possible conclusions reached are closely related to the position one might take in understanding the legal nature of Chapter VII and the Charter of the United Nations itself.

These and other similar activities will continue in the future in both the United Nations and other international organizations. We are expected to analyze and judge the legality of these activities in the light of the relevant provisions in their constituent instruments.

The emerging doctrine of the interpretative framework of constituent instruments as the constitutions of international organizations, which has gradually formed since 1950s and is now more or less established, will give a useful perspective in understanding the possible evolution of international organizations in the present and the future.

Tetsuo SATO

Kunitachi, Tokyo
October 1995

Acknowledgements

This monograph is a shortened, although somewhat revised, version of my book *Kokusai Soshiki no Sôzôteki Tenkai* (*Creative Evolution of International Organizations*) (Keiso Shobô, 1993) [in Japanese], which was submitted to Hitotsubashi University as a dissertation for the degree of Ph. D. in 1993.

I dedicate this monograph to two eminent professors of international law who both passed away several years ago: Professor Takeshi Minagawa of Hitotsubashi University and Professor Leo Gross of the Fletcher School of Law and Diplomacy. I owe much to them.

First of all, I would like to express my gratitude to His Excellency Shigeru Oda, Judge of the International Court of Justice and its Vice-President during 1991-1994 for recommending that my monograph be published as one of the new series under his general editorship, *International Law in Japanese Perspective*.

The idea of and the basis for the present monograph dates back to my Master's thesis submitted to Hitotsubashi University in 1980 under the supervision of Professor Minagawa. I later had the opportunity of studying as a Fulbright grantee at the Fletcher School of Law and Diplomacy, Tufts University during 1981-1983 under the supervision of Professor Leo Gross as well as Professor Alfred P. Rubin. After developing the original idea during these and later years, I published three articles on this issue in English: "Constituent Instruments of International Organizations and Their Interpretative Framework --- Introduction to the Principal Doctrines and Bibliography", 14 *Hitotsubashi Journal of Law & Politics* 1-22 (1986); "Status of Constituent Instruments of International Organizations in the Law of Treaties --- With Particular Reference to the Notion 'Relevant Rules of the Organization'", 16 *id.* 25-47 (1988); "An Emerging Doctrine of the Interpretative Framework of Constituent Instruments as the Constitutions of International Organizations", 21 *id.* 1-63 (1993). This idea was developed further in the article "Kokusai Soshiki Setsuritsu Bunsho no Kaishaku Purosesu (I), (II), (III)" ("Interpretation Process of Constituent Instruments of International Organizations (I), (II), (III)")[in Japanese], 16 *Hogaku Kenkyu* (*Law & Politics* (Hitotsubashi University Research Series)) 45-186 (1986), 19 *id.* 3-180 (1989), 21 *id.* 71-336 (1990). For this latter article, I was awarded the honor of the 24th (1991) Mine'ichiro Adachi Memorial Prize in Japan. The above-mentioned book in Japanese is based on this article.

In the course of the examination for the doctoral degree, I had the benefit of the invaluable advice of the three examiners, Professors Jun'ichi Akiba, Wakamizu Tsutsui and Yoshio Otani. I was also guided by the helpful suggestions of Professor Hisaji Uchida of Daito Bunka University in his excellent review of my book published in 93 *Kokusaiho Gaiko Zassi* (*The Journal of International Law and Diplomacy*) 194-99 (1994). Furthermore, Professors Jean Combacau of l'Université Paris - II and Aleth Manin of Paris - I (at that time) kindly read and commented on my English article during my period of research at l'Université Paris - II during 1990-1992. In gathering materials for my research, I was assisted by Ms. Y. Kamijo, research assistant of Hitotsubashi University, Professor Y. Saito of Asia University and Mr. Y. Kawamura in the Legal Office of the United Nations. The English in my monograph was greatly improved by the efforts of Professors Beverly I. Nelson, R. Siani and John Middleton of Hitotsubashi University.

I wish to thank sincerely all of the above and those whom I have failed to mention for their help and advice during the past fifteen or so years in developing the idea which originally came to me at the very beginning of my career as an international lawyer.

Finally, I am very pleased to record my deep gratitude to my parents, Shigeo and Tsuyako, and to my dear wife, Yoko, and two little daughters, Maori and Marumi.

T. S.

Abbreviations

ACC	Amazonian Cooperation Council
ADB	Asian Development Bank
AfDB	African Development Bank
A. F. D. I.	Annuaire Français de Droit International
ALADI	Latin American Integration Association
ARABSAT	Arab Corporation for Space Communications
ASEAN	Association of South East Asian Nations
BEU	Benelux Economic Union
CAEU	Council of Arab Economic Unity
CARICOM	Caribbean Community
CARIFTA	Caribbean Free Trade Association
CACEU	Central African Customs and Economic Union
CMEA	Council for Mutual Economic Assistance
COMECON	Council for Mutual Economic Assistance
EAC	East African Community
EC	European Communities
ECOWAS	Economic Community of the West-African States
ECR	Reports of the Court of Justice of the European Communities (European Court Reports)
EFTA	European Free Trade Association
ESA	European Space Agency
FAO	Food and Agricultural Organization of the United Nations
GATT	General Agreement on Tariffs and Trade
IAEA	International Atomic Energy Agency
IBRD	International Bank for Reconstruction and Development
ICAO	International Civil Aviation Organization
ICJ	International Court of Justice
IDA	International Development Association
IDB	Inter-American Development Bank
IFAD	International Fund for Agricultural Development
IFC	International Finance Corporation
ILC	International Law Commission
I. L. M.	International Legal Materials
ILO	International Labour Organisation
IMCO	Inter-Governmental Maritime Consultative Organization
IMF	International Monetary Fund
IMO	International Maritime Organization
INTELSAT	International Telecommunication Satellite Organization
INTERSPUTNIK	International System and Organization of Space Communications
INMARSAT	International Maritime Satellite Organization
ITO	International Trade Organization
ITU	International Telecommunication Union

LAES	Latin American Economic System
LAFTA	Latin American Free Trade Association
LAIA	Latin American Integration Association
LAS	League of Arab States
LN	League of Nations
NATO	North Atlantic Treaty Organization
OAS	Organization of American States
OAU	Organization of African Unity
OECD	Organization for Economic Co-operation and Development
Recueil des cours	Recueil des cours de l'Académie de droit international
R. G. D. I. P.	Revue Général de Droit International Public
UEAC	Union of Central African States
UN	United Nations
U. N. C. I. O.	United Nations Conference on International Organization (San Francisco, 1945)
UNESCO	United Nations Educational, Scientific and Cultural Organization
UNIDO	United Nations Industrial Development Organization
UPU	Universal Postal Union
WEU	Western European Union
WHO	World Health Organization
WIPO	World Intellectual Property Organization
WMO	World Meteorological Organization
WTO	Warsaw Treaty Organization *or* World Trade Organization

Note: As for the other abbreviations, this book generally conforms to the style of *A Uniform System of Citation* (15th ed. 1991) published by the Harvard Law Review Association.

Chapter One

Introduction

Section 1 The Problem

1. *Methodology of the interpretation of the constituent instruments of international organizations*[1] has been one of the central issues in disputes concerning the structures and activities of international organizations. This is primarily because international organizations are functional entities established by States on the basis of agreements (constituent instruments).[2] Since the purposes, functions, powers and competence, organizational structures, activities and all other important matters of international organizations are, in essence, provided in their constituent instruments, legal analyses of their structures and activities should, logically, start with analyses of, that is, interpretations of, their constituent instruments. In fact, many of the disagreements and disputes concerning their structures and activities, when discussed in the organs of international organizations or referred to the International Court of Justice (hereinafter also cited as the Court),

---

[1] *See*, for an introduction to the principal doctrines from the viewpoint of the notion "caractère constitutionnel," my article 'Constituent Instruments of International Organizations and Their Interpretative Framework', 14 *Hitotsubashi J. L. & Politics* 1, 2-10 (1986). The relevant part is summarized in our text (Section 2 The Doctrines). *See also*, Pollux, 'The Interpretation of the Charter,' 23 *Brit. Y. B. Int'l L.* 54 (1946); Hexner, 'Teleological Interpretation of Basic Instruments of Public International Organizations,' in *Law, State, and International Order, Essays in Honor of Hans Kelsen* 119 (S. Engel ed. 1964); Schachter, 'Interpretation of the Charter in the Political Organs of the United Nations,' *idem* at 269; Lang. 'Les régles d'interprétation codifiées par la Convention de Vienne sur le Droit des Traités et les divers types de traités,' 24 *Österreichische Zeitschrift für öffentliches Recht* 113 (1973); Ciobanu, 'Impact of the Characteristics of the Charter upon Its Interpretation', in *Current Problems of International Law: Essays on U.N. Law and the Law of Armed Conflict* 3 (A. Cassese ed. 1975); D. Simon, *L'interprétation judiciaire des traités d'organisations internationales* (1981); Skubiszewski, 'Remarks on the Interpretation of the United Nations Charter,' in *Völkerrecht als rechtsordnung, Internationale Gerichtsbarkeit, Menchenrechte: Festschrift für Herman Mosler* 891 (1983); Macdonald, 'The United Nations Charter: Constitution or Contract?', in *The Structure and Process of International Law* 889 (R. St. J. Macdonald & D. M. Johnston eds. 1983); E. McWhinney, 'The UN Charter: Treaty or Constitution?' in *Conflict and Compromise: International Law and World Order in a Revolutionary Age* 53 (1981); Sh. Rosenne, 'Is the Constituent Instrument of an International Organization an International Treaty?', in *Developments in the Law of Treaties 1945-1986* 181 (1989) [The original edition of this article was published in 12 *Comunicazione e Studi* 21 (1966).]. Sloan, 'The United Nations Charter as a Constitution', 1 *Pace Y. B. Int'l L.* 61 (1989).

[2] For the definition of international organizations, *see e.g.*, Virally, 'Definition and Classification of International Organizations: A Legal Approach', in *The Concept of International Organization* 50, 51 (G. Abi-Saab ed. 1981). The present article deals mainly with the United Nations and other universal international organizations. In this connection, Virally stated as follows (M. Virally, *L'organisation mondiale* 26 (1972)):
> "La raison d'être d'organisation internationale, comme de toute institution, est fonctionnelle. C'est la volonté, chez ses fondateurs, de disposer d'un instrument propre à la poursuite d'objectifs définis qui explique la création d'une organisation internationale. C'est la nature des activités nécessaires à la réalisation de cette fonction qui détermine la structure organique dont cette organisation est dotée par son acte constitutif. Il existe donc une relation dialectique entre les fonctions de l'organisation et ses éléments structurels: la relation entre la fin et les moyens."

See also Virally, 'La notion de fonction dans la théorie de l'organisation internationale', in *La communauté internationale: Mélange offerts à Charles Rousseau* 277 (1974); Chaumont, 'La signification du principe de spécialité des organisations internationales', in *Problème de droit des gens: Mélanges offerts à Henri Rolin* 55 (1964).

have been argued on the level of the interpretation of their constituent instruments.[3]

2.   The significance of the problem of methodology on this level of the interpretation of constituent instruments can be analyzed in the following manner.   On the one hand, international organizations are, as explained above, established on the basis of agreements which provide for their purposes, functions, and all other important matters; on the other hand, international organizations are required to function efficiently and perform effectively their given purposes and functions in changing world circumstances.[4]   Thus the point of issue is *how to reconcile or harmonize two conflicting demands: that of stability inherent in constituent instruments as agreements and that of dynamism inherent in the nature of international organizations.*   This point of issue has a profound importance, influencing almost every aspect of the structures and activities of international organizations both directly and indirectly.   In fact, this inherent confrontation between the stability of agreements and dynamism of international organizations corresponds to the phenomenon of a series of "crises" in international organizations which could be presented, essentially, as a confrontation between resistance and control by member States on the one hand and autonomy and dynamism of international organizations on the other.[5]

Section 2 The Doctrines

1.   This problem has been tackled by few scholars on the legal level, but perceived by many. It would be useful to trace briefly here the development among doctrines of the notion "caractère constitutionnel" of constituent instruments of international organizations.

        Classification of treaties has long occupied the minds of scholars.[6]   If there is any strain between the diversity of objects to be regulated and the identity of methods to regulate with --- namely, treaties --- the problem whether various kinds of treaties can be governed by the same

---

[3] *See*, in this connection, *e.g.*, Gordon, 'The World Court and the Interpretation of Constitutive Treaties', 59 *Am. J. Int'l L.* 794 (1965).

[4] For example, the Court, in the *Reparation* case (1949), confirmed the existence of the following famous legal principle (Advisory Opinion on Reparation for Injuries Suffered in the Service of the United Nations, [1949] I. C. J. 182):

> "Under international law, the Organization must be deemed to have those powers which, though not expressly provided in the Charter, are conferred upon it by necessary implication as being essential to the performance of its duties."

This principle of implied powers enunciated by the Court symbolizes the favorable attitude of the Court which has been shown in a series of later advisory opinions regarding the effectiveness of international organizations.   The concept of "necessity" indicated in this principle is a key criterion which could be applied, not only to the matter of powers, but also to all aspects of international organizations, in the interpretation of their constituent instruments.

[5] *See, e.g.*, Jacqué, 'Rapport général, Le Consta', in *Les organisations internationales contemporaines* 3, 8 (1988); Simon, 'Organisations internationales et politiques des Etats', *id.* at 107, 113.

[6] *See, e.g.*, Rapisardi-Mirabelli, 'La classification des traités internationaux', 4 *Revue de droit international et de législation comparée* 653 (1923); Kraus, 'Système et fonction des traités internationaux', 50 *Recueil des cours* 311 (1934).

system of "law of treaties" will continue to be at the root of different interpretations.

2.   Lord McNair pointed out and attempted to deal systematically with this problem. In his article 'The Functions and Differing Legal Character of Treaties' in 1930,[7] McNair classified treaties into four categories: (1) treaties having the character of conveyances, (2) treaties having the character of contracts, (3) law-making treaties ((a) treaties creating constitutional international law, (b) treaties creating or declaring ordinary international law, or pure law-making treaties) and (4) treaties akin to charters of incorporation. This attempt was based upon such criteria as the effect of war, use of *travaux préparatoires* as a means of interpretation,[8] opposability to non-parties, and lack of unanimity in their operations. McNair consequently concluded as follows:

> "My submission is that the task of deciding [disputes arising upon treaties] will be made easier if we free ourselves from the traditional notion that the instrument known as the treaty is governed by a single set of rules, however inadequate, and set ourselves to study the greatly different legal character of the several kinds of treaties and to frame rules appropriate to the character of each kind."[9]

3.   The establishment of "the supreme type of international organization"[10] --- the United Nations --- caused much concern among scholars with respect to the method of interpretation of the Charter.

Pollux, at the head of his article 'The Interpretation of the Charter'[11] which is an excellent treatment of this problem, pointed out succinctly the essential position:

> "The Charter, like every written Constitution, will be a living instrument. It will be applied daily; and every application of the Charter, every use of an Article, implies an interpretation; on each occasion a decision is involved which may change the existing law and start a new constitutional development. A constitutional customary law will grow up and the Charter itself will merely form the framework of the Organization which will be filled in by the practice of the different organs."[12]

It must be noted, however, that this kind of dynamic understanding of constituent instruments could be contrasted with a still persistent and not negligible traditional opinion favoring State sovereignty.[13]

---

[7] 11 *Brit. Y. B. Int'l L.* 100 (1930), *reprinted in* Lord McNair, *The Law of Treaties* 739 (1961).

[8] In this regard, McNair made an affirmative reference to the use or non-use of *travaux préparatoires* in accordance with whether a treaty concerned belongs to (2) or (3), which had been proposed by Q. Wright ('The Interpretation of Multilateral Treaties', 23 *Am. J. Int'l L.* 94 (1929)). *But see* Lord McNair, *The Law of Treaties* 366.

[9] Lord McNair, *The Law of Treaties* 754 (1961).

[10] Reparation for Injuries Suffered in the Service of the United Nations, [1949] I. C. J. 179.

[11] 23 *Brit. Y. B. Int'l L.* 54 (1946).

[12] *Id.*

[13] L. Kopelmanas, for example, stated as follows (*L'Organisation des Nations Unies* 294-95 (1947)):
"Les limitations que [les dispositions de la Charte des Nations Unies] apportent à la souveraineté des États membres, sont en effet établies au profit des compétences de l'Organisation. Ainsi en cas de doute sur leur signification, il n'y aura pas lieu de choisir entre deux interprétations, favorisant chacune une souveraineté

5

4.   The characteristics of the Charter, particularly in its interpretative framework, became the focus of attention in several early advisory opinions of the ICJ --- the *Reparation* Case (1949), *International Status of South West Africa* Case (1950) and *Effect of Awards* Case (1954).[14]

Based upon an analysis of the jurisprudence of the ICJ, Charles de Visscher acknowledged, although very cautiously, the speciality of interpretation method of constituent instruments. Starting from the position that "C'est du traité international que procèdent donc les organisations internationales. C'est un accord de volontés étatiques qui leur donne naissance. Jusqu'à quel point l'institution, qui celle-ci est née pour durer, peut-elle se détacher de la manifestation des volontés dont le texte est l'expression momentanée?"[15], de Visscher reached the following three conclusions:

"1) Il existe, dès à présent, un certain droit jurisprudentiel relatif l'interprétation des traités d'organisation internationals; droit que l'on peut considérer généralement comme tenant un juste milieu entre la tendance institutionnelle et l'interprétation contractuelle....

2)   La notion qui a été le mieux dégagée par nos décisions est celle du but, de l'objet, de la mission de l'Organisation elle-même et de ses organes en tant qu'elle transcende l'ordre de simple coordination ou juxtaposition entre Etats.

3)   Le problème essentiel que doit résoudre toute jurisprudence progressiste est celui d'une conciliation inéluctable entre les origines contractuelles de l'Organisation et son orientation irrésistiblement institutionnelle."[16]

étatique différente et par conséquent équivalentes en droit, mais entre l'interprétation favorable à la liberté de l'État et l'interprétation extensive des compétences de l'Organisation. Devant un tel choix, aucune hésitation ne semble possible. Les clauses portant limitation de la souveraineté étatique en faveur d'un organisme international, devront faire l'objet d'une interprétation stricte, de sorte que le manque de précision de leur termes jouerait automatiquement à l'encontre des compétences concédées à l'organisme international."
The general practice of the United Nations has apparently differed from what Kopelmanas expected. But it must also be noted that this realistic understanding of States' attitudes toward the United Nations is supported, clearly on some occasions, by the actual power politics among States.

[14]   Almost all of the cases concerning international organizations in the Court are related to the interpretation of constituent instruments, and references to the legal nature of constituent instruments can be found in many of the dissenting and separate opinions. See our analysis in Chapter Three.

Consequently it seems natural that this problem has drawn the attention of many scholars. *See, e.g.,* in addition to those listed in *supra* note 1, Engel, 'The Changing Charter of the United Nations', *Y. B. World Affairs* 71 (1953); Lachs, 'Les conventions multilaterales et les organisations internationales contemporaines', 2 *A. F. D. I.* 334 (1956); Lachs, 'Le développement et les fonctions des traités multilateraux', 92 *Recueil des cours* 229 (1957-II); Engel,'"Living International Constitutions and the World Court (the Subsequent Practice of International Organs under Their Constituent Instruments)', 16 *Int'l & Comp. L. Q.* 865 (1967).

[15]   'L'interprétation judiciaire des traités d'organiastion internationale', 41 *Rivista di diritto internazionale* 177, 181 (1958). "It is from the international treaty that the international organizations proceed. It is an agreement of States' wills which give birth to them. To what extent the institution, which was born to last, can it become detached from the manifestation of the wills, the text being their temporary expression." [Our translation]

[16]   *Id.* at 187. "1) It now exists a certain law of jurisprudence relating to the interpretation of treaties establishing international organizations; law which one can generally consider as occupying the exact middle between the institutional tendency and the contractual interpretation.... 2) The notion which has been best drawn by our decisions is that of purpose, of the objective, of the mission of the Organization itself and of its organs as far as it transcends the level of simple coordination or juxtaposition among States. 3) The essential problem that every progressive jurisprudence must

It should be noted that de Visscher, who held a realistic judgement towards the effectiveness of international organizations,[17] nevertheless, recognized the problem of conciliation between the contractual origin of the Organization and its institutional orientation to be ineluctable.[18]

5.   Whether constituent instruments of international organizations deserve a separate treatment, and, if so, what the characteristics are, were also studied to some extent by the fourth Special Rapporteur, H. Waldock, in his Report on the Law of Treaties. References to constituent instruments and international organizations in the draft articles ranged from simply mentioning them to entrusting important functions to their decisions.[19] The International Law Commission, in its discussions, decided, however, that these problems should be dealt with by the general reservation clause Article 5, which provides:

"The present Convention applies to any treaty which is the constituent instrument of an international organization and to any treaty adopted within an international organization without prejudice to any relevant rules of the organization."[20]

6.   Rosenne, who was a member of the International Law Commission, supported Waldock's treatment of these problems most strongly, and developed his observation in an article with the provocative title of 'Is the Constitution of an International Organization an International Treaty? Reflections on the Codification of the Law of Treaties'.[21]

The international treaty had its origins in the juristic conception of "contract" and the growth of the international law of treaties was closely influenced by private law theories of contract. With the invention of the multilateral treaty simultaneously performing a number of functions, however, it is becoming a matter of increasing urgency, said Rosenne, to liberate international legal theory from the restraints imposed by the historical background of the general notion of contract, and especially from experiences and concepts originating in domestic private

---

solve is that of inescapable conciliation between the contractual origins of the Organization and its irresistibly institutional orientation." [Our translation] *See also* Ch. de Visscher, *Problème d'interprétation judiciaire en droit international public* 140-53 (1963).

[17] *See also*, Ch. de Visscher, *Les effectivités du droit international public* 53-60, 159 (1967).

[18] *See also*, Ch. de Visscher, *Theory and Reality in Public International Law* 260-1 (Rev. ed. P. E. Corbett trans. 1968), *Théories et réalités en droit international public* 283-4 (4th ed.1970)

[19] For details on this point, *see* my article, 'Status of Constituent Instruments of International Organizations in the Law of Treaties --- With Particular Reference to the Notion "Relevant Rules of the Organization"', 16 *Hitotsubashi J. L. & Pol.* 25 (1988). Since the draft articles of Waldock dealt, to some extent, with the problem of treaty classification, the arguments in the Commission have drawn the attention of several scholars. *See, e.g.,* Dehaussy, 'Le problème de la classification des traités et le projet de convention établi par la Commission du Droit international des Nations Unies', in *Recueil d'études de droit international en hommage à Paul Guggenheim* 305 (1968); Virally, 'Sur la classification des traités à propos du projet d'articles de la Commission du droit international', 13 *Comunicazione e Studi* 15 (1969). With respect to the rules of interpretation, *see also* Lang, *supra* note 1.

[20] For our analysis of this provision, *see* Chap. 5, Sec. 2, (3).

[21] 12 *Comunicazioni e Studi* 21 (1966). *See also* 'La théorie de l'acte constitutif des organisations internationales', in Mme P. Bastid, *Cours de droit international public: Le droit des organisations internationales 50 (Les cours de droit, 1968-69).*

law.

Analyzing the various exceptions in the application of the law of treaties to constituent instruments, Rosenne stated as follows:

> "The fact that so many cardinal aspects relating to the very essence of the legal relationships created by membership in an international organization and participation in its constituent instrument are in practice governed by principles and rules fundamentally different from those applicable to the corresponding aspects of participation in multilateral treaties must raise serious doubts as to whether the constituent instruments of international organizations are of the same *genus*, in international law, as multilateral treaties."[22]

He further stated that the problems of the interpretation of international constituent instruments are "of a different order" from those normally found in the interpretation and application of treaties.

In answering the question posed in the title of his article, Rosenne came to the cautious conclusion that the question does not permit an unqualified answer, the reply depending on the circumstances in which the question is raised. For us, however, it is significant that Rosenne admitted the difference to be "one of kind, not of degree". He concluded his article with the following statement:

> "Since the law governing the constituent instruments of international organizations is developing along lines peculiar and appropriate to those instruments, and to them alone, without more than a superficial similarity with the law of treaties, and since the application of those instruments is dominated by the institutional element provided by the Organization, an element entirely missing for bilateral and multilateral treaties, it is deceptive to see in diplomatic and legal incidents concerning the constituent instruments ⟨precedents⟩ for the general law of treaties, and *vice versa*."[23]

7. It was R. Monaco who attempted to analyze the "caractère constitutionnel" itself of constituent instruments of international organizations. In so doing, Monaco presented the essence of his understanding as follows:

> "[L]'acte institutif d'une Organisation déterminée est bien un traité international, fondé, en tant que tel, sur la volonté des contractants et donc soumis, au moment de sa formation, à leur volonté, mais il est par ailleurs destiné à devenir la constitution, c'est-à-dire l'acte de fondation de l'Organisation, auquel celle-ci se rattache tout au long de son existence. On pourrait dire, par conséquent, que l'acte institutif revêt la forme du pacte mais possède la substance de la constitution: né sur la base d'une convention, il dépasse, avec le temps, son origine formelle, jusqu'à devenir une constitution de durée indéterminée dont le développement déborde le cadre à l'intérieur duquel elle avait été initialement conçue."[24]

---

[22] *Id.* at 66.

[23] *Id.* at 88.

[24] Monaco, 'Le caractère constitutionnel des actes institutifs d'Organisations internationales, in *La communauté internationale: Mélanges offerts à Charles Rousseau* 153, 154 (1974). ("The instituting act of a given Organization is indeed an international treaty founded as such on the will of the participants and therefore subject, at the moment of

8.   The interpretation method of constituent instruments is an important issue which has attracted the attention of, and has been studied by, various scholars.[25] It was D. Ciobanu who attempted to analyze systematically the interpretation process of constituent instruments --- here, the Charter of the United Nations --- in connection with their legal characteristics.

Ciobanu, in his article 'Impacts of the Characteristics of the Charter upon Its Interpretation'[26] in 1975, tackled the question "whether the methods, principles and rules usually applied in the process of treaty interpretation can without qualification be used for the interpretation of the Charter". He pointed out, among other things, the following: The Charter is the constituent instrument of the most important international political organization. The double character of the Charter --- as a general multilateral treaty and as a constitution of an international organization --- has important consequences, such as the existence of the law which presents "un particularisme irréductible au droit interne ou droit international", the voting procedure by which "in certain defined situations member States will be bound by a rule adopted by a specified majority even though they may have voted in the minority", and the amendment procedure --- Article 108 and 109 --- which does not need the consent of all the Member States. However, referring to the provision that the two-thirds majority required for the formal modification of the Charter must include all the permanent members of the Security Council, Ciobanu adds a caution that "it would be legally inadmissible and politically inadvisable to give the provisions of the Charter interpretations which amount to disguised modifications considered as such by a permanent Member".

9   D. Simon's *L'interprétation judiciaire des traités d'organisations internationales* is, although its analysis is limited to the jurisprudence --- judgments and advisory opinions --- of international courts, the most detailed study on this point up to the present. The theme of this voluminous book which exceeds 900 pages is described as "d'examiner si la méthods d'interprétation est influencée par les caractéristiques propres des traités créateurs de structures d'organisation".

Based upon a comprehensive analysis of jurisprudence in the first part, Simon concluded that the judge seems to base its reasoning on the same fundamental principle:

---

its formation, to their will, but it is in other respects destined to become the constitution, namely the act of foundation of the Organization, with which the Organization is connected throughout its existence. One could say that the institutive act is clothed with the form of a pact but possesses the substance of a constitution: born on the basis of a convention, it exceeds, with time, its formal origin until it becomes a constitution of indeterminate duration the development of which oversteps the bounds within which the Organization had been initially conceived." [Our translation])

   See also J. Rideau, *Juridictions internationales et contrôle du respect des traités constitutifs des organisations internationales* 2-39 (1969).

[25] *See, e.g.*, B. V. Cohen, *The United Nations: Constitutional Developments, Growth, and Possibilities* (1961); Mushkat, 'De quelques problèmes relatifs à l'interprétation de la Charte et aux transformations de structure des Nations-Unies', 17 *Revue hellénique de droit international* 240 (1964); Gordon, *supra* note 3; Morawiecki, 'Les fonctions des Nations Unies et leur efficacité', 4 *Polish Y. B. Int'l L.* 69 (1971); for an excellent analysis of the decisions of international tribunals, *see* Lauterpacht, 'The Development of the Law of International Organization by the Decisions of International Tribunals', 152 *Recueil des cours* 379 (1976).

[26] Ciobanu, *supra* note 1.

"[I]l s'agit, dans tous les cas, de donner aux stipulations conventionnelles relatives aux compétences de l'organisation, ou aux pouvoirs des organes, la signification la plus favorable à l'élargissement des attributions des institution mises en place par la charte."[27]

But at the same time,

"pour déterminer le sens et la portée des conventions 'constitutionnelles', le juge international fait preuve d'un remarquable éclectisme quant au choix des moyens d'interprétation qu'il est appelé à utiliser, et n'hésite pas à mêler méthodes extensives et restrictives, les differents procédés à sa disposition étant sélectionnés et combinés en fonction du résultat qu'il se propose d'atteindre."[28]

According to Simon, "s'il est vrai que les chartes constitutives, malgré leur contenu constitutionnel, restent fortement teintée d'interétatique, il arrive également que les traités qualifiés d'ordinaires comporte, au-delà d'un échange synallagmatique de prestations, certain germes d'institutionalisation"[29], and this "interpénetration réciproque" is expressed by the "éclectisme" of interpretation methods. From these considerations, Simon deduced the following observation:

"[L]'interprétation des conventions 'constitutionnelles' presente, par rapport à celle des conventions 'ordinaires', une difference de degré et non de nature, ou si l'on préfère, une spécificité d'ordre quantitatif plus que qualitatif."[30]

---

[27] D. Simon, L'interprétation judiciaire des traités d'organisations internationales --- Morphologie des conventions et fonction juridictionnelle 308 (1981). "It concerns, in all cases, to give to the conventional stipulations related to the competence of the organization, or to the powers of the organs, the meaning most favorable to the enlargement of the competence of the institutions established by the charter." [Our translation]

[28] Id. at 456. "In order to determine the meaning and the scope of the 'constitutional' conventions, the international judge showed a remarkable eclecticism with regard to the choice of interpretation methods that it is invited to use, and does not hesitate to mix extensive and restrictive methods, the different methods at its disposal being selected and combined in accordance with the result that it intends to reach." [Our translation]

[29] Id. at 476. "If it is true that the constitutive charters, despite their constitutional content, remain strongly tinted with inter-statism, it equally happens that the treaties qualified for being ordinary comprise, beyond a synallagmatic exchange of benefits, certain germs of institutionalization." [Our translation]

[30] Id. at 477. "The interpenetration of the 'constitutional' conventions present, in comparison with the 'ordinary' conventions, a difference of degree and not of nature, or if one prefers, a specificity of quantitative rather than qualitative level." [Our translation] This position taken by Simon is opposed to that of Rosenne who admitted the difference to be "one of kind, not of degree". Simon elaborated this position (with which we also *disagree*) as follows (id. at 478):

"[L]e critère décisif dans le choix des méthodes d'interprétation n'est pas en réalité un critère 'organique', opposant les conventions créant une organisation internationale et les conventions dites ordinaires, mais un critère complexe, que nous proposons d'appeler le degré d'intégration du système conventionnel en cause, étant entendu que ce critère ne conduit pas à une classification rigide des traités, mais à une gradation continue des instruments conventionnels, selon la part restrictive de l'institution et du contrat dans l'économie d'ensemble de l'accord."

"The decisive criterion in the choice of interpretation methods is not in reality an 'organic' criterion opposing the conventions creating an international organization to the so-called ordinary conventions, but a complex criterion, that we propose to call the degree of integration of the conventional system in question, it being understood that this criterion does not lead to a rigid classification of the treaties, but to a continuous gradation of the conventional instruments, according to the restrictive part of the institution and of the contract in the entire structure of the agreement." [Our translation]

10.   The problem of the interpretation process from the viewpoint of the legal nature of constituent instruments has continued to draw attention among international lawyers.[31] It could be concluded, however, that the doctrines remain relatively elementary in the sense that, although they begin to recognize the double aspects (treaty and constitution) of constituent instruments,[32] they are far from presenting an interpretative framework.[33] To the contrary, there still seems to be a tendency, among doctrines in general, to consider that the interpretation of constituent instruments could be explained, despite their constitutional aspect, within the interpretative framework in the law of treaties. One can summarize the current doctrinal level by referring to the above-quoted passage of Monaco which is one of the best descriptions of this problem, but which still remains introductory. This is the starting point of our present study.

Section 3 The Purpose and Constitution of the Present Book

1.   **The purpose of the present book** is to analyze and clarify the law-creating process of the interpretation of constituent instruments, and to advocate *an emerging doctrine of the interpretative framework of constituent instruments as the constitutions of international organizations.*[34] We will argue that, *under the influence of the inherent dynamism of*

---

[31] For recent articles on this point, *see, e.g.*, Skubiszewski, Macdonald, McWhinney, Rosenne and Sloan listed in *supra* note 1.

[32] It is generally admitted in France that constituent instruments have a double nature of treaty and constitution. *See, e.g.*, H. Thierry, J. Combacau, S. Sur & Ch. Vallée, *Droit international public* 703 (5th ed. 1986); N. Q. Dinh, P. Daillier & A. Pellet, *Droit international public* 560 (5th ed. 1994); M. Bettati, *Le droit des organisations internationales* 61-2 (Que sais-je?, 1987); P.-M. Dupuy, *Droit international public* 105 (2d ed. 1993); J. Combacau & S. Sur, *Droit international public* 718 (1993).

[33] The importance of this question with respect to interpretation is pointed out, but not developed, by Goodrich as follows (Goodrich, 'The Changing United Nations', in *Transnational Law in a Changing Society, Essays in Honor of Philip C. Jessup* 259, 260 (W. Friedmann et al. ed. 1972)):

> "*The Charter, it is often stated, is not only a treaty but also a constitution.* The importance of this characterization lies in the fact that, as a treaty to which two or more states are parties, it might be thought of as an instrument defining the rights and obligations of the parties and therefore subject to restrictive interpretation. As a constitutional document, on the other hand, the Charter not only defines the rights and duties of members but also determines the functions, powers, and responsibilities of organs which are established for the purpose of giving effect to the aims of the Organization. In this respect, the Charter is similar to the constitution of a state, and particularly of a federal state such as the United States, which defines the functions and powers of organs and provides the legal basis for the development of the powers of the central government to meet the demands which changing circumstances may create. *Its interpretation raises questions that do not arise in the case of an ordinary treaty.*" [Italics ours]

[34] In the sphere of international law and the law of international organizations, the expressions "constitution" and "constitutional (constitutionnel)" have often been used but in different meanings. For these usages, *see, e.g.*, Opsahl,' An "International Constitutional Law"'?, 10 *Int'l & Comp. L. Q.* 760 (1961); Ganshof van der Meersch, 'L'ordre juridique des Communautés européennes et le droit international', 148 *Recueil des cours* 21-3 (1975); Suy, 'The Constitutional Character of Constituent Treaties of International Organizations and the Hierarchy of Norms', in *Recht zwischen*

international organizations, the interpretative framework of the constituent instruments of international organizations is not the same as that of ordinary treaties, and that the interpretation of the constituent instruments of international organizations deviates from the interpretative framework regulated by the law of treaties as codified by the Vienna Convention on the Law of Treaties. We will advocate, as the alternative interpretative framework to that of ordinary treaties, a doctrine of constituent instruments as the constitutions of international organizations rather than as the (founding) treaties. In advocating this new doctrine of the interpretative framework, it is important not to attempt to construct a fragile house of cards. As the current doctrines and practices of States and international organizations do not support such a construction, the best way would be to construct a moderate but solid doctrine which could be sufficiently justified by actual practices and which could be further improved upon and refined, but even this has yet to be made.

2.   **The structure of the present book:** In our opinion, the interpretative framework as constitutions differs from that as treaties in two respects: *(1) on the quantitative aspect of the teleological extent admitted, in the sense that constituent instruments are interpreted within the teleological framework so that their efficient functioning and effective activities could be assured and promoted, and that predominant consideration is given to the "efficiency" and "effectiveness" of international organizations to the extent that the teleological reasoning deviates from the textual interpretative framework in the law of treaties; (2) on the qualitative aspect of legal significance possessed by the practice of the organs of international organizations, in the sense that the practice of international organizations affects, in feedback, the interpretations of constituent instruments so that it gives them an evolutionary nature, and that this "subsequent practice" of the organs is given the legal value which deviates qualitatively from the textual interpretative framework in the law of treaties.* Certainly each of these two aspects has sometimes been referred to in different contexts by other writers. These two, however, have never been, with sufficient development and refinement, synthesized in this new doctrine of constituent instruments as the constitutions of international organizations.

It would be logically more persuasive to develop the later analysis by contrasting the interpretative framework as constitutions and that as treaties in accordance with the differences on two aspects respectively. In the present book, however, the structure of our analysis is, because of the quantity of pages necessary for each chapter and for analytical convenience, as follows.

In "Chapter Two: Treaty Interpretation and Constituent Instruments", we will first analyze

---

Umbruch und Bewahrung, Festschrift für Rudolf Bernhardt 267 (U. Beyerlin et al. eds. 1995).

Here in this article, we define the expression "constitution" as those provisions that provide for the legal foundations and frameworks for structures and activities of international organizations, as is pointed out later in the text. It differs, for example, from the usage of Friedmann in his "constitutional approach" (in the sense of providing the legal and institutional framework which will be competent to deal with the various aspects of the organized life of mankind) in contrast to "functional approach." W. Friedmann, *Changing Structure of International Law* 275-7 (1964).

"The Legal Nature of the Rules of Treaty Interpretation" in Section 1. We will then analyze the provisions related to interpretation (Articles 31 and 32) in the Vienna Convention of the Law of Treaties in "Section 2: The Framework of Treaty Interpretation" and conclude that a teleological reasoning could be used only within the four corners of the text interpreted by the textual approach codified in this Convention, and that subsequent practice mentioned in Paragraph 3 (b) of Article 31 (General Rule of Interpretation) includes only such practice as to signify an implied consent of all the relevant States parties. In "Section 3: An Overview of Principal Doctrines of the Interpretative Framework of Constituent Instruments", we will classify current principal doctrines on this problem and draw attention to the fact that there exist, inter alia, two conflicting interpretative frameworks: Strict Framework of the Law of Treaties which emphasize the treaty aspect of constituent instruments, and Functional Framework Based upon the Law of Treaties which pays due attention to the functional necessity of international organizations.

In "Chapter Three: An Analysis of the Jurisprudence of the International Court of Justice", we will analyze and clarify, from the viewpoint of the characteristics of constituent instruments *vis-à-vis* ordinary treaties, the Court's approach to the issue: its reasoning, method of interpretation and value judgment. Purpose of our analysis will be most reasonably achieved by examining the differences and confrontations between the majority opinion and individual opinions.

In "Chapter Four: Interpretative Procedures of Constituent Instruments ----- Organs of International Organizations as Principal Interpreters of Constituent Instruments", we will analyze the legal effects attributed to the interpretations of constituent instruments by the organs of international organizations and the institutional mechanism through which different and conflicting interpretations are to be unified. Since a value judgment of the interpreter is always involved, problems of who is to interpret and apply a norm is inevitably combined with how to interpret it in the actual process of determining the content of the norm concerned.

In "Chapter Five: The Emerging Doctrine of Interpretation of Constituent Instruments as the Constitutions of International Organizations", we will first explain the concept and characteristics of "constitutions" and develop the two differences mentioned above in "Section 1: Constituent Instruments as the Constitutions of International Organizations". The second difference of qualitative aspect is particularly taken up in "Section 2: The Legal Significance of the Practice of International Organizations". We will seek the theoretical foundations of this emerging doctrine in the various legal theories and materials in "Section 3: In Search of the Theoretical Foundations of the Interpretative Framework as the Constitutions of International Organizations". These legal theories and materials, although sometimes mentioned as suggestive by different writers, have never been systematically analyzed and appreciated. We will also attempt to point out some important elements for establishing this new interpretative framework in "Section 4: Toward the Determination of the Interpretative Framework as the Constitutions of International Organizations".

Section 4 Possible Contributions for the Future

It has already been pointed out in 1958 that a large number of the provisions of the United

Nations Charter were, more or less, transformed from their original meaning in the actual operation of the Organization.[35] We also know, for example, that a series of arguments have been presented with regard to the legal foundations of the peace keeping operations, and that the Court acknowledged in 1971 that Article 27 (3) with respect to the procedure of the Security Council had been transformed as a result of the "general practice" of the United Nations. It is quite reasonable to expect that similar phenomena will occur with respect to these and other provisions as the United Nations continues to adapt itself to the ever-changing international political environment.

In the field of international organizations where amendments of their constituent instruments are as exceptional as those of the United Nations, it is through the process of interpretation and application of constituent instruments that political evolutions and changes will be transformed into legal arguments. In this sense interpretation could be qualified as the "concept charnière (hinging concept)" between the politics and the law.[36]

To give a typical example, the attitude of east European communist States toward international organizations has, inevitably, changed markedly since the late 1980s when the Soviet Union disintegrated and they abandoned their ideological and political positions. We have already seen that unprecedented military enforcement measures, except the case of the Korean War, were applied to Iraq in 1991 in a manner close to, if not the same as, that expected by the Charter. A series of "authorizations" of the use of force by peace keeping forces and/or Member States were allowed. An international tribunal to prosecute those responsible for serious violations of international humanitarian law has been established both for former Yugoslavia and Rwanda. All of these activities have been authorized under Chapter VII of the United Nations Charter.[37] We must analyze and judge the legality of these activities in the light of the relevant provisions of Chapter VII.[38] Here the possible conclusions reached are closely related to the position one might take in

---

[35] Robinson, 'Metamorphosis of the United Nations', 94 *Recueil des cours* 493 (1958).

[36] S. Sur, *L'interprétation en droit international public* 85, 130 (1974).

From a global viewpoint, the attitudes of various States to the interpretation of constituent instruments could be briefly summarized as follows: (1) The attitude of the western States, which was initially favorable to the institutional evolution when they occupied the majority, changed to a reserved and consensus-oriented one as they lost their advantaged position; (2) The attitude of Afro-Asian States is, with their majority position, fundamentally favorable to the institutional evolution; (3) The attitude of the socialist States was, with their constantly minority position, always negative to the institutional evolution, but became more flexible since 1960s with a change of international political configuration and with a policy of peaceful coexistence; after the 1980s it was expected that their attitude would become closer to that of western States. *See e.g.*, *The Concept of International Organization* 20-3, 171-245 (G. Abi-Saab ed. 1981).

The significance of this global analysis is, of course, limited because of the recent phenomenon of international political multipolarization (*see* for example the critique of Simon, *supra* note 6, at 111-3). However, it certainly signifies the important status that methodology of the interpretation of constituent instruments has occupied in the history of international organizations.

[37] *See, e.g.*, Dupuy, 'Editorial: Sécurité collective et organisation de la paix', 97 *R. G. D. I. P.* 617-27 (1993).

[38] *See, e.g.*, M. Bedjaoui, *The New World Order and the Security Council, Testing the Legality of its Acts* (1994).

understanding the legal nature of Chapter VII and the Charter of the United Nations itself.

The emerging doctrine of the interpretative framework of constituent instruments as the constitutions of international organizations, which has gradually formed since 1950s and is now more or less established, will give a useful perspective in understanding the possible evolution of international organizations in the present and the future.[39]

---

[39] A position taken by Blum (Y. Blum, *Eroding the United Nations Charter* (1993)) contrasts markedly with ours. Kirgis appropriately commented (Book review by Kirgis, 88 *Am. J. Int'l L.* 552, 553 (1994)) that Blum's approach is unduly rigid and that it fails to allow for inevitable and natural development in the interpretation of a constituent instrument to keep pace with changing demands.

Chapter Two

Treaty Interpretation

and

Constituent Instruments

Section 1 The Legal Nature of the Rules of Treaty Interpretation

1. Legal interpretation is not a cognition. It inevitably involves the value judgment of an interpreter. Treaty interpretation also involves the value judgment of an interpreter.[1] Rules of

---

[1] Kelsen, in this connection, pointed out as follows (H. Kelsen, *Pure Theory of Law* 351 (2d ed. trans. by M. Knight, 1967). *See also* H. Kelsen, *The Law of the United Nations: A Critical Analysis of Its Fundamental Problems* xvi (1950).):

"[T]he law to be applied constitutes only a frame within which several applications are possible, whereby every act is legal that stays within the frame.

If 'interpretation' is understood as cognitive ascertainment of the meaning of the object that is to be interpreted, then the result of a legal interpretation can only be the ascertainment of the frame which the law that is to be interpreted represents, and thereby the cognition of several possibilities within the frame. The interpretation of a statute, therefore, need not necessarily lead to a single decision as the only correct one, but possibly to several, which are all of equal value, though only one of them in the action of the law-applying organ (especially the court) becomes positive law. The fact that a judicial decision is based on a statute actually means only that it keeps inside the frame represented by the statute; it does not mean that it is *the* individual norm, but only that it is one of those individual norms which may be created within the frame of the general norm.

Traditional jurisprudence, however, ... will have us believe that the statute, applied to the concrete case, can always supply only *one* correct decision and that the positive-legal 'correctness' of this decision is based on the statute itself. This theory describes the interpretive procedure .... as if by a purely intellectual activity, among the various existing possibilities only one correct choice could be made in accordance with positive law."

Lauterpacht, a follower of Kelsen, however, dissented on this point as follows (Lauterpacht, 'Restrictive Interpretation and the Principle of Effectiveness in the Interpretation of Treaties', 26 *Brit. Y. B. Int'l L.* 48, 81-82 (1949)):

"[The judicial function of interpretation], far from being limited to discovering the meaning of a text, may legitimately impart to it a meaning by reference to the paramount principle of the completeness and the rational development of the law and of the requirements of justice in the light of the purpose of the treaty viewed as a whole. This does not mean that the judgment thus given is based on 'political' considerations and that when confronted with a variety of possible interpretations the judicial decision is in the last resort a political act. For although there are many possible interpretations of a disputed provision there is in theory --- in what is believed to be the accurate legal theory --- only one correct interpretation of the law.... [T]o say that in every case there are a number of *equally* correct legal interpretations and that the choice between them is --- legitimately, avowedly, and consciously --- the result of a political decision and of political predilections of the judge is to put forward an assertion which denies the very essence of the judicial function in a society under the rule of law. Undoubtedly, the judicial choice of the standard of interpretation may be influenced by a variety of factors seemingly extraneous to the text. But these factors --- such as considerations of justice, canons of fairness and good faith, and, in proper cases, an equitable reconciliation of the interests at stake --- are of legitimate legal relevance. They do not obliterate the border line between the function of the judge and the powers of the legislator."

Against this position of Lauterpacht, Stone pointed out as follows (Stone, 'Non Liquet and the Function of Law in the International Community', 35 *Brit. Y. B. Int'l L.* 124, 133 (1959). See also Stone, 'Fictional Elements in Treaty Interpretation --- A Study in the International Judicial Process', 1 *Sydney L. Rev.* 344 (1955), *reprinted in* J. Stone, *Of Law and Nations: Between Power Politics and Human Hopes* 167 (1974).):

"In one sense Sir Hersch seems to mean, by the 'completeness' of international law which excludes *non liquet*, the potential elaboration of the existing principles of international law, and of the general principles of law as a part thereof.... But it is a juristic commonplace that the main judicial problem springs from the fact that opposed decisions can usually be attached to different principles; and, indeed, often to the same principle by reason of its ambiguity, circuity or indeterminacy. Nothing in these competing starting-points themselves can direct the court which of them is the correct one, that is, the correct principle or version of a principle to choose for the instant case. That choice finally is the court's choice, a law-creating choice, however much it be concealed

19

interpretation in the law of treaties, however, could restrain the scope of a judgment *within a certain framework*.

2.	The utility and even the existence of rules of international law governing the interpretation of treaties are sometimes questioned.[2] The first two Special Rapporteurs (Brierly and Lauterpacht) on the law of treaties also expressed doubts as to the existence in international law of any general rules for the interpretation of treaties. These doubts were aptly explained by the following statement.

> *"The process of interpretation, rightly conceived, cannot be regarded as a mere mechanical one of drawing inevitable meanings from the words in a text, or of searching for and discovering some pre-existing specific intention of the parties with respect to every situation arising under a treaty....* In most instances ... interpretation involves giving a meaning to a text --- not just any meaning which appeals to the interpreter, to be sure, but a meaning which, in the light of the text under consideration and of all the concomitant circumstances of the particular case at hand, appears in his considered judgement to be one which is logical, reasonable, and most likely to accord with and to effectuate the larger general purpose which the parties desired the treaty to serve. This is obviously a task which calls for investigation, weighing of evidence, judgement, foresight, and a nice appreciation of a number of factors varying from case to case. *No canons of interpretation can be of absolute and universal utility in performing such a task, and it seems desirable that any idea that they can be should be dispelled.*"[3] [Italics ours]

3.	Other jurists, although they express reservations as to the obligatory character of certain of the so-called canons of interpretation, showed less hesitation in recognizing the existence of some general rules for the interpretation of treaties. In fact, Fitzmaurice, the third Rapporteur on the law of treaties, deduced six principles from the jurisprudence of the Permanent Court of International Justice and the International Court of Justice[4]; the "Institut de droit international", in 1956, adopted a resolution in which it formulated two articles containing a small number of basic principles of interpretation[5]; and the Convention on the Law of Treaties drafted by the International Law Commission contains three provisions codifying the rules of interpretation.

4.	Consequently, the problem on this point is related rather to *the legal nature of the rules of treaty interpretation*. The Commission stated the majority view on this point as follows.

> "[The principles and maxims of treaty interpretation in international practice] are, for the

---

by the form of logical deduction from the principle finally chosen. In so far as it is the court's decision, it is proper to expect the court to bring its full wisdom to bear in making this legal determination, and to hold the court responsible for the justness and wisdom of the content of the resulting legal rule."

[2] Report of the International Law Commission to the General Assembly (hereinafter cited as ILC Report), [1966] 2 *Y. B. Int'l L. Comm'n* 169, 218, U. N. Doc. A/6309/Rev. 1.

[3] Harvard Law School, 'Research in International Law', 29 *Am. J. Int'l L. Supp.* 946 (1935).

[4] *See infra* note 9.

[5] 46 *Annuaire de l'Institut de Droit International* 358-59, 364-65 (1956).

most part, principles of logic and good sense valuable only as guides to assist in appreciating the meaning which the parties may have intended to attach to the expressions that they employed in a document. Their suitability for use in any given case hinges on a variety of considerations which have first to be appreciated by the interpreter of the document.... Even when a possible occasion for their application may appear to exist, their application is not automatic but depends on the conviction of the interpreter that it is appropriate in the particular circumstances of the case. In other words, recourse to many of these principles is discretionary rather than obligatory and the interpretation of documents is *to some extent an art, not an exact science.*"[6] [Italics ours]

5.   Finally, it is to be noted that the Commission, despite its position explained above, considered it desirable to formulate general rules for the interpretation of treaties by the following reasons.[7]

(1) The interpretation of treaties in good faith and according to law is essential if the *pacta sunt servanda* rule is to have any real meaning.

(2) Having regard to the divergent opinions concerning methods of interpretation, it seemed desirable that the Commission should take a clear position with regard to *the role of the text in treaty interpretation.*

(3) A number of articles adopted by the Commission contain clauses which distinguish between matters expressly provided in the treaty and matters to be implied in it by reference to the intention of the parties; and clearly, the operation of such clauses can be fully appreciated and determined only in the light of *the means of interpretation admissible for ascertaining the intention of the parties.*

(4) *The establishment of some measure of agreement in regard to the basic rules of interpretation* is important not only for the application but also for the drafting of treaties.

6.   Having been adopted in the Vienna Convention on the Law of Treaties, the rules of interpretation in Articles 31 to 33 now seem to represent customary rules on this point. The European Court of Human Rights, in the *Golder* case, stated as follows:

"The Court is prepared to consider ... that it should be guided by Articles 31 to 33 of the Vienna Convention of 23 May 1969 on the Law of Treaties. That Convention has not yet entered into force and it specifies, at Article 4, that it will not be retroactive, but its Articles 31 to 33 enunciate in essence generally accepted principles of international law to which the Court has already referred on occasion....

In the way in which it is presented in the 'general rule' in Article 31 of the Vienna Convention, the process of interpretation of a treaty is a unity, a single combined operation; this rule, closely integrated, places on the same footing the various elements enumerated in the four paragraphs of the Article."[8]

---

[6] ILC Report, *supra* note 2, at 218.

[7] *Id.* at 219.

21

Section 2   The Framework of Treaty Interpretation
----- An Analysis of Articles 31 and 32 of
the Vienna Convention on the Law of Treaties

(1)   The General Rule of Interpretation

1.   As is quite well known, there are today *three main schools of thought on the theory of interpretation*,[9] which are the "intentions of the parties" approach, the textual approach and the teleological approach.   These three approaches are not necessarily exclusive of one another, and theories of treaty interpretation normally comprise all three.   However, each tends to confer primacy on one particular aspect of treaty interpretation, if not to the exclusion, certainly to the subordination of the others.[10]

---

[8] 57 *Int'l L. Rep.* 200, 213-14 (1980). *But see* I. Sinclair, *The Vienna Convention on the Law of Treaties* 131 (2d ed. 1984).

[9] Among the vast literature on treaty interpretation, *see, e.g.*, Fitzmaurice, 'The Law and Procedure of the International Court of Justice: Treaty Interpretation and Certain Other Treaty Points', 28 *Brit. Y. B. Int'l L.* 1 (1951)(hereinafter cited as Fitzmaurice, 1951); ditto, 'The Law and Procedure of the International Court of Justice 1951-4: Treaty Interpretation and Other Treaty Points', 33 *Brit. Y. B. Int'l L.* 203 (1957)(hereinafter cited as Fitzmaurice, 1957); Jacobs, 'Varieties of Approach to Treaty Interpretation: With Special Reference to the Draft Convention on the Law of Treaties Before the Vienna Diplomatic Conference', 18 *Int'l & Comp. L. Q.* 318 (1969); 'Report of the International Law Commission to the General Assembly', [1966] 2 *Y. B. Int'l L. Comm'n* 169, 218, U.N. Doc. A/6309/Rev. 1; I. Sinclair, *The Vienna Convention on the Law of Treaties* 114 (2d ed. 1984).

[10] Fitzmaurice, 1951, *supra* note 9, at 1. *See also* V. D. Degan, *L'Interprétation des accords en droit international* 67-148 (1963).
        On the one hand, the teleological approach might be reduced to a variant of one of the other two approaches. In so far as it relies on the objects and purposes of the treaty as they are expressed in the text (the preamble or the treaty as whole), it could be a variant of the textual approach.   In so far as it goes beyond the text and seeks to ascertain the original aims of the parties by reference to the entire course of negotiations and the other circumstances, it could be that of the subjective approach.   It is said that recent developments in the teleological approach, particularly with respect to the constituent instruments of international organizations, would justify its inclusion as a separate category.   Jacobs, *supra* note 9, at 319-20. *See also* I. Voïcu, *De l'interprétation authentique des traités internationaux* 32 (1968).
        On the other hand, a dominant approach in the United States has been such a teleological approach as to give much discretion to an interpreter in concrete cases by listing various sources of interpretation without establishing any order of priority among them (for example, the Draft Convention on the Law of Treaties prepared in 1935 as part of the Harvard Research in International Law, the Restatement of the Foreign Relations Law of the United States (1965), and the amendment submitted by the U.S.A. (Mr. McDougal) in the U.N. Conference on the Law of Treaties (1968)).   This kind of teleological approach could easily lead to the justification of what an interpreter would regard as "objects and purposes" in his subjective judgment, which is quite convenient for a powerful State like the U.S.A.   This approach is not accepted in the current international society as is shown by the fact that the amendment was rejected by an overwhelming majority. *See*, for this approach, McDougal, 'The International Law Commission's Draft Articles upon Interpretation: Textuality redivivus', 61 *Am. J. Int'l L.* 992 (1967); Rosenne, 'Interpretation of Treaties in the Restatement and the International Law Commission's Draft Articles: A Comparison', 5 *Colum. J. Transnat'l L.* 205, 229 (1966).

2.   The traditional controversies have been fought between the "intentions of the parties" approach and the textual approach. No one seriously denies that the aim of treaty interpretation is to give effect to the intentions of the parties, and the question is how is the desired end to be achieved and where is the authentic expression of these intentions primarily to be looked for. In other words, the question is a choice between what meaning is to be attributed to the text *in the light of the intentions of the parties* or what the intentions of the parties must be presumed to have been *in the light of the meaning of the text* they drew up.[11]

The predominant place has been occupied by *the textual approach*.[12] This is, in fact, proved by the fact that Article 32 provides for recourse to the preparatory works of the treaty and other circumstances, and is entitled "supplementary means of interpretation." The word "supplementary" emphasizes that Article 32 does not provide for alternative, autonomous, means of interpretation, but only for means to aid an interpretation governed by the principles contained in Article 31.[13]

3.   Article 31, paragraph 1 stipulates as follows:

"A treaty shall be interpreted in good faith in accordance with the ordinary meaning to be given to the terms of the treaty in their context and in the light of its object and purpose."

This paragraph is understood to include three principles: (1) Interpretation in good faith which flows directly from the rule *pacta sunt servanda*; (2) The parties are to be presumed to have that intention which appears from the ordinary meaning of the terms used by them; (3) The ordinary meaning of a term is not to be determined in the abstract but in the context of the treaty and in the light of its object and purpose.[14]

4.   Article 31, paragraph 2 defined such elements, in addition to the text, including its preamble and annexes, as to be considered as the context for the purpose of the interpretation of a treaty. Article 31, paragraph 3 specified such elements as to be taken into account together with the

---

[11] Fitzmaurice, 1957, *supra* note 9, at 204-7. *See also* G. Haraszti, *Some Fundamental Problems of the Law of Treaties* 28 (1973).

[12] In the International Law Commission, for example, the majority emphasized the primacy of the text as the basis for the interpretation of a treaty, while at the same time giving a certain place to extrinsic evidence of the intentions of the parties and to the objects and purposes of the treaty as means of interpretation. According to the commentary (ILC Report, *supra* note 2, at 220, para. 11),

"[Article 31] is based on the view that the text must be presumed to be the authentic expression of the intentions of the parties; and that, in consequence, the starting point of interpretation is the elucidation of the meaning of the text, not an investigation ab initio into the intentions of the parties."

[13] The arguments on treaty interpretation in the Commission and the diplomatic conferences were mainly concerned with the status to be given to the preparatory works as means of treaty interpretation. As a consequence, criticisms against the Commission's draft articles are mainly concerned with the adequacy of the status given to the preparatory work in Articles 31 and 32. *See, e.g.,* Sharma, 'The ILC Draft and Treaty Interpretation with Special Reference to Preparatory Works', 8 *Indian J. Int'l L.* 367 (1968); Mehrish, 'Travaux Préparatoires as an Element in the Interpretation of Treaties', 11 *Indian J. Int'l L.* 39 (1971).

[14] ILC Report (1966), *supra* note 2, at 221, para. 12. *See also* J. F. O'Connor, *Good Faith in International Law* 108-11 (1991).

context. According to the commentary,

"The elements of interpretation in [Article 31] all relate to the agreement between the parties *at the time when or after it received authentic expression in the text. Ex hypothesi* this is not the case with preparatory work which does not, in consequence, have the same authentic character as an element of interpretation, however valuable it may sometimes be in throwing light on the expression of the agreement in the text."[15] [Italics original]

5.   A problem in connection with the constituent instrument of an international organization (usually a multilateral treaty) is whether the *travaux préparatoires* of a multilateral treaty may be invoked as against States which did not participate in the negotiations, but which subsequently acceded to the treaty.

The Permanent Court of International Justice, in the *Territorial Jurisdiction of the International Commission of the River Oder* case, did not take into consideration the *travaux préparatoires* of certain provisions of the Treaty of Versailles on the ground that three of the States before the Court had not participated in the conference which prepared the Treaty; it did not distinguish between published and unpublished documents either.[16]

Waldock doubted, however, the rationality of this ruling.[17] The commentary also pointed out as follows:

"The Commission doubted, however, whether this ruling reflects the actual practice regarding the use of *travaux préparatoires* in the case of multilateral treaties that are open to accession by States which did not attend the conference at which they were drawn up. Moreover, the principle behind the ruling did not seem to be so compelling as might appear from the language of the Court in that case. A State acceding to a treaty in the drafting of which it did not participate is perfectly entitled to request to see the *travaux préparatoires*, if it wishes, before acceding. Nor did the rule seem likely to be practically convenient, having regard to the many important multilateral treaties open generally to accession. These considerations apply to unpublished, but accessible, *travaux préparatoires* as well as to published ones.... Accordingly, the Commission decided that it should not include any special provision in the article regarding the use of *travaux préparatoires* in the case of multilateral treaties."[18]

The jurisprudence of tribunals on this point does not seem to be settled.[19] The doctrines,[20]

[15] ILC Report, *supra* note 2, at 220, para.10.

[16] Order of August 20th, 1929, Territorial Jurisdiction of the International Commission of the River Oder, [1929] P. C. I. J., ser. A. No. 23, 41-43.

[17] Waldock, Third Report on the Law of Treaties, [1964] 2 *Y. B. Int'l L. Comm'n* 58-59, para. 21, U. N. Doc. A/CN. 4/167 and Add. 1-3. *See also* the supporting statement of Rosenne on this point ([1966] 1-II *Y. B. Int'l L. Comm'n* (872d mtg.) 200-1, para. 34.

[18] ILC Report, *supra* note 2, at 223, para. 20.

[19] The admissibility of invoking the *travaux préparatoires* against an acceding State which had not participated in the negotiation of the treaty in question was an issue in the *Young Loan* case: The Kingdom of Belgium, the French

however, are considered to be in accordance with the position of the above commentary. In the context of our study, we should note the following two points,[21] which would apply to constituent instruments as far as they are multilateral treaties.

(1)   Recourse to *travaux préparatoires* does not depend on the participation in the drafting of the text of the State against whom the *travaux* are invoked. To hold otherwise would disrupt the unity of a multilateral treaty, since it would imply that two different methods of interpretation should be employed, one for States who participated in the *travaux préparatoires* and another for States who did no so participate.

(2)   *The travaux préparatoires* should be in the public domain so that States which have not participated in the drafting of the text should have the possibility of consulting them. *Travaux préparatoires* which are kept secret by the negotiating States should not be capable of being invoked against subsequently acceding States.

(2) The Principle of Effectiveness

1.   *In general*: Apart from an extreme teleological interpretation, methods of more or less teleological interpretations have been called by various names such as liberal interpretation, extensive interpretation, principle of effectiveness (*l'effet utile, l'efficacité*), and *ut res magis valeat quam pereat*. These names do not seem to have been clearly defined and distinguished from one another.[22]

In the first place, liberal or extensive interpretation could be analyzed in relation to the corresponding strict or restrictive interpretation. On a superficial level, it could be pointed out that neither extensive nor restrictive interpretation can be admitted; because the purpose of interpretation of treaties is the elucidation of the intentions of the contracting parties and their authentic expression is the text of treaties, it cannot be permitted by definition either to extend nor to restrict the text of treaties; extensive or restrictive interpretation is only the outcome of the interpreters' activities applying the various methods of interpretation.[23] However, it is on those occasions when various methods do not lead to the confirmed common will of the parties, leaving

---

Republic, the Swiss Confederation, the United Kingdom and the United States of America v. The Federal Republic of Germany, 59 *Int'l L. Rep.* 494, 544-45, 564 (1980). *See also* the discussion by Rosenne concerning the *Aerial Incident* case, Rosenne, 'Notes, Travaux Préparatoires', 12 *Int'l & Comp. L. Q.* 1378 (1963).

[20] *See, e.g.,* Yasseen, 'L'interprétation des traités d'après la Convention de Vienne sur le droit des traités', 151 *Recueil des cours* 1, 89-90 (1976-III); Sinclair, *supra* note 9, at 142-44; Haraszti, *supra* note 11, at 122-24.

[21] Sinclair, *supra* note 9, at 144. *See also* H. Lauterpacht, *The Development of International Law by the International Court* 136-37 (1958).

[22] Gutiérrez Posse, 'La maxime ut res magis valeat quam pereat (Interprétation en fonction de l'"effet utile'), Les Interprétation "extensives'"et "restrictives"', 23 *Österreichische Zeitschrift für öffentliches Recht* 229 (1972); Lord McNair, *The Law of Treaties* 383 (1961).

[23] Ch. de Visscher, *Problème d'interprétation judiciaire en droit international public* 87-8 (1963); Haraszti, *supra* note 11, at 151-3.

25

two or more interpretations of similar reasonableness that the principle of extensive or restrictive interpretation is put forward. In other words, these principles are important as a guiding principle for selection on these occasions.[24]

Secondly, it could be argued that principle of effectiveness or *ut res magis valeat quam pereat* simply means that treaties have to be interpreted so that they become effective in practice rather than invalid or null and are, therefore, nothing more than an interpretation in good faith.[25] However, the choice is not between full effectiveness and utter frustration of the purpose of the treaty, but usually between a higher and a lower degree of effectiveness.[26] These principles are understood to suggest that as far as not clearly incompatible with the text of treaty provisions, an interpretation giving a higher degree of effectiveness should be chosen. In sum, teleological interpretations such as extensive interpretation or principle of effectiveness should be understood as suggesting that, if the intentions of parties cannot be clearly confirmed and leave different reasonable interpretations, that interpretation giving a higher degree of effectiveness to the treaty provisions concerned should be chosen.

2. *The relationship between the principle of restrictive interpretation and the principle of effectiveness* has been exhaustively analyzed by Lauterpacht. On the one hand, the main explanation of the prominence of the rule of restrictive interpretation is that, because States are sovereign, restrictions upon the sovereignty of States cannot reasonably be presumed. On the other hand, however, Lauterpacht contended, the purpose of treaties is to limit the sovereignty of States in the particular sphere concerned and to lay down rules regulating conduct by restricting the freedom of action of States. If the parties, in a freely accepted treaty, go to the length of inserting a provision, it must be presumed that they intended that provision to be fully effective and its operation unhampered by restrictive rules.[27]

---

[24] *See, e.g.*, Haraszti, *id.* at 154-5.

[25] *Id.* at 166-7. In the same way, Degan explained as follows (Degan, 'Attempts to Codify Principles of Treaty Interpretation and the South-West Africa Case', 8 *Indian J. Int'l L.* 9, 21 (1968)):

> "Effective interpretation is not the same as extensive interpretation or construction. The opposite of an extensive interpretation is a restrictive one; and the opposite of effectiveness is non-effectiveness. The two ideas are quite different. Non-effectiveness is much more dangerous to the basic principle pacta sunt servanda than an extensive interpretation.
>
> To give full effect to a treaty provision does not mean its broad interpretation. It means respect for the rights and obligations of the contracting parties, and consequently respect for the principle, pacta sunt servanda."

[26] Lauterpacht, 'Restrictive Interpretation and the Principle of Effectiveness in the Interpretation of Treaties', 26 *Brit. Y. B. Int'l L.* 48, 69-70 (1949).

[27] *Id.* at 57-8, 60-1. In the same way, Bernhardt contended as follows:

> "The restrictive interpretation of treaty obligations with regard to State sovereignty is, in my opinion, even now no longer a generally accepted principle, and so it is rightly not to be found among the primary rules of interpretation."

Bernhardt, 'Interpretation and Implied (Tacit) Modification of Treaties, Comments on Arts. 27, 28, 29 and 38 of the ILC's 1966 Draft Articles on the Law of Treaties', 27 *Zeitschrift für auslandisches öffentliches Rechts und Völkerrecht* 491, 504 (1967).

Scholars in socialist countries had generally taken a stand in favor of the absolute priority of a restrictive interpretation from the viewpoint of respecting the sovereignty of States.[28]

The jurisprudence of the Court might not necessarily have been clear on this point. However, it is said, the combination of the recognition of the principle of restrictive interpretation with the refusal to apply it in individual cases on the ground that the treaty is clear or that restrictive interpretation can be resorted to only if all other methods of interpretation have failed is a frequent feature of the jurisprudence of the Court.[29]

3.　　　The problem in the present context is *the degree of teleological reasoning* in applying the principle of effectiveness which has been explicitly or implicitly resorted to in treaty interpretation. In other words, *what is the relationship between the principle of effectiveness and the textual approach adopted as the general rule of interpretation ?* The answer is that *a teleological reasoning could be used only within the four corners of the text interpreted by the textual approach.*

This problem can be clarified through the analysis of the drafting process of the relevant provision of the Vienna Convention on the Law of Treaties. Here, the special rapporteur, Waldock, contrary to the preceding rapporteurs, always kept in mind the problems posed by constituent instruments, and made reference to them in a suggestive manner. In his third report, Waldock proposed the following article.[30]

> "Article 72. Effective interpretation of the terms
> (ut res magis valeat quam pereat)
> In the application of articles 70 and 71 [the general rules of interpretation based upon the textual approach] a term of a treaty shall be so interpreted as to give it the fullest weight and effect consistent:
> (a) with its natural and ordinary meaning and that of the other terms of the treaty; and
> (b) with the objects and purposes of the treaty."

Waldock explained, in the commentary, that he hesitated for two reasons to propose the inclusion of the principle of "effective" interpretation among the general rules. First, there is some tendency to equate and confuse "effective" with "extensive" or "teleological" interpretation, and

---

[28] Haraszti, *supra* note 11, at 156-7, 163-4.

[29] Lauterpacht, *supra* note 26, at 61.

　　See, for the argument supporting the application of the restrictive interpretation, Speech by M. de Lapradelle, Advisory Opinion on Competence of the International Labour Organisation in the Matter of the Regulation of Conditions of Work of Persons Employed in Agriculture, [1922] P.C.I.J., ser. C, No. 1, at 174-5; The S. S. "Wimbledon," [1923] P.C.I.J., ser. A, No. 1, at 37; The S. S. "Lotus," [1927] P.C.I.J., ser. A, No. 10, at 18.

　　See, for the argument cautious in applying this approach, The S. S. "Wimbledon," [1929] P.C.I.J., ser. A, No. 1, at 24-5; Territorial Jurisdiction of the International Commission of the River Oder, [1929] P.C.I.J., ser. A, No. 23, at 26.

[30] Waldock, 'Third Report on the Law of Treaties', [1964] 2 *Y. B. Int'l L. Comm'n* 52-3, U.N. Doc. A/CN. 4/167 and Add. 1-3.

to give it too large a scope. Secondly, "effective" interpretation, correctly understood, may be said to be implied in interpretation made in good faith. Properly limited, it does not call for "extensive" or "liberal" interpretation in the sense of an interpretation going beyond what is expressed or necessarily implied in the terms.[31]

On balance, however, Waldock thought it desirable to include the principle, proper limited, in the draft articles. He thought it desirable for two reasons to formulate it in a separate article.

"The first is that the principle has special significance as the basis upon which it is justifiable to imply terms in a treaty for the purpose of giving efficacy to an intention necessarily to be inferred from the express provisions of the treaty. The second is that in this sphere --- the sphere of implied terms --- there is a particular need to indicate the proper limits of the application of the principle if too wide a door is not to be opened to purely teleological interpretations. *The point is of particular consequence in the interpretation of constituent treaties of international organizations and although those treaties, by their functional nature, may legitimately be more subject to teleological interpretations, there is evidently some limit to what may be deduced from them and still be considered 'interpretation.'*[32] [Italics ours]"

It was in the light of these considerations that draft article 72 had been formulated so as to make the principle of effectiveness subject to (a) the natural and ordinary meaning of the terms and (b) the objects and purposes of the treaty. This formulation, Waldock thought, while containing the principle of effectiveness within the four corners of the treaty, still leaves room for such measure of teleological interpretation as can legitimately be considered to fall within the legal boundaries of interpretation.[33]

Draft article 72 was unpopular among the members of the Commission and was ultimately deleted.[34] It seems, therefore, that Waldock's intention indicated in the commentary was not well appreciated by the members. The final draft articles contained the expression "in the light of its object and purpose" in the article of general rule of interpretation. The attitude of the Commission on this point can be found in the commentary of the final draft articles:

"Properly limited and applied, the maxim does not call for an 'extensive' or 'liberal' interpretation in the sense of an interpretation going beyond what is expressed or necessarily to be implied in the terms of the treaty. Accordingly, it did not seem to the Commission that there was any need to include a separate provision on this point. Moreover, to do so might encourage attempts to extend the meaning of treaties

---

[31] *Id.* at 60, para. 27.

[32] *Id.* at 61, para. 29.

[33] *Id.* at para. 30.

[34] Summary Records of the 766th Meeting, [1964] 1 *Y. B. Int'l L. Comm'n* 288-91, paras. 69-120.

illegitimately on the basis of the so-called principle of 'effective interpretation.'"[35]

4.   This status of the principle of effectiveness --- the degree of its teleological reasoning and the relationship with the textual approach --- indicated in the above analysis is fundamentally confirmed by the jurisprudence of the Court. It seems that the Court has subordinated the principe of effectiveness to that of the textual and natural meaning, in the sense that it is never legitimate, even with the object of giving maximum effect to a text, to interpret it in a manner actually contrary to, or not consistent with, its plain meaning.[36]

It was in the *Peace Treaties* case (2d Phase) that the Court, after stating that it was "the duty of the Court to interpret the Treaties, not to revise them," went on:

"The principle of interpretation expressed in the maxim: ut res magis valeat quam pereat, often referred to as the rule of effectiveness, cannot justify the Court in attributing to the provisions for the settlement of disputes in the Peace Treaties a meaning which ... would be contrary to their letter and spirit."[37]

Judge Read did not think that the interpretation he favored would do violence to the terms of the Peace Treaties, and argued in his dissenting opinion that, of the two technically possible constructions, that one should be adopted which would give the treaty its maximum effect, or at any rate prevent it from being deprived of due effect.[38] It was, however, by an overwhelming

---

[35] ILC Report, *supra* note 2, at 219, para. 6.

It is quite natural, in this connection, that Schreuer mentioned the "preponderant inclination towards the objective method" of the Vienna Convention and pointed out as follows (Schreuer, 'The Interpretation of Treaties by Domestic Courts', 45 *Brit. Y. B. Int'l L.* 255, 274, 279 (1971)):

"[The effect of the 'object and purpose' doctrine is] very much restricted by their being linked with the provision concerning the ordinary meaning of the terms in their context, which is then defined in the subsequent paragraph very narrowly."

[36] Fitzmaurice, 1957, *supra* note 9, at 223. He specifically pointed out as follows (Fitzmaurice, 1951, *supra* note 9, at 19):

"The main problem with regard to the principle of effectiveness is to keep it within bounds, to prevent it from leading to judicial legislation (its natural tendency being teleological), and to preserve a due proportion between it and the textual principle. The Court has shown itself aware of this necessity, and has indicated the limits of the principle of effectiveness, and its subordination, in case of conflict, to that of the natural meaning."

[37] Advisory Opinion on Interpretation of Peace Treaties with Bulgaria, Hungary and Romania (Second Phase), [1950] I. C. J. 229.

[38] *Id.* at 236-45.

In this connection, the following opinion of McNair (Lord McNair, *The Law of Treaties* 383-4 (1961)) is suggestive as indicating that the application of the principle of effectiveness is limited within the framework of the general rule of interpretation mainly based upon the textual approach.

"Many treaties fail --- and rightly fail --- in their object by reason of the words used, and tribunals are properly reluctant to step in and modify or supplement the language of the treaty....

No doubt the general object of the parties to these treaties was to provide some arbitral machinery for the solution of disputes but --- either inadvertently or because the parties were unable to agree --- they had not inserted in the treaties the provision which would have been necessary to make the arbitration obligatory."

It should be pointed out in this connection that even Lauterpacht who emphasized the importance of the principle of effectiveness recognized in the same way the limit of application of this principle by saying (Lauterpacht, *supra* note 26, at 83-4):

majority of eleven votes to two that the Court rejected the contention by Judge Read.

(3) Subsequent Practice

1.　　It is widely recognized that subsequent practice of the parties in the application of the treaty is important as an element of interpretation because it constitutes objective evidence of the understanding of the parties as to the meaning of the treaty.[39] This point is well recognized by the Court as well.[40]

The probative value of subsequent practice varies accordingly as it shows the common understanding of the parties as to the meaning of the terms. It is said, however, that the practice of an individual State may have special cogency when it relates to the performance of an obligation which particularly concerns that State.[41]

2.　　Waldock kept in mind the constituent instruments of international organizations in connection with this principle. Waldock drew attention to the problem, but did not attempt to analyze it as this is a question outside the law of treaties. He stated:

> "Certain of the cases in which the Court has had recourse to subsequent practice have concerned the interpretation of the constitutions of international organizations. The most notable is its recent Opinion on Certain Expenses of the United Nations, in which the Court made a large use of the subsequent practice of organs of the United Nations as a basis for its findings on a number of points. The problem of the effect of the practice of organs of an international organization upon the interpretation of its constituent instrument raises an important constitutional issue as to how far individual Member States are bound by the practice. Although the practice of the organs as such may be consistent, it may have been opposed by individual Members or by a group of Members which have been outvoted. This special problem appears to relate to the law of international organizations rather than to the general law of treaties...."[42]

It is Waldock's idea, therefore, that, in the interpretation of the constituent instruments of international organizations, the subsequent practice of State parties has probative value in relation to them, whereas the relationship between the subsequent practice of the organs and the constituent instruments will not be prejudiced by the Convention on the Law of Treaties.[43]

"[The principle of effectiveness] is a principle which can give life and vigour to an intention which is controversial, hesitant, or obscure. It cannot be a substitute for intention; it certainly cannot claim to replace it."

[39] *See, e.g.*, McNair, *supra* note 38, at 424; Harvard Law School, 'Research in International Law', 29 *Am. J. Int'l L.*, *Supp.* 966 (1935); De Visscher, *supra* note 23, at 121-7; 46 *Annuaire de l'Institut de Droit International* 359, 365 (1956).

[40] *See, e.g.*, Advisory Opinion on Competence of the International Labour Organisation in Regard to International Regulation of the Condition of Labour of Persons Employed in Agriculture, [1922] P.C.I.J., ser. B, No. 2, at 39; Corfu Channel case, [1949] I. C. J. 25.

[41] Waldock, *supra* note 30, at 59, para. 24. *See* International Status of South-West Africa, [1950] I. C. J. 135-6.

[42] Waldock, *supra* note 30, at 59-60, para. 24a.

[43] Some members emphasized that, in the interpretation of constituent instruments, subsequent practice, if not of the

3.   The process of amendment through subsequent practice is legally quite different from that of interpretation, although the line between them may be sometimes blurred. As pointed out by Waldock,[44] however, subsequent practice when it is consistent and embraces all the parties would appear to be decisive of the meaning to be attached to the treaty. Here subsequent practice as an element of treaty interpretation and that in the formation of a tacit agreement overlap and the meaning derived from the practice becomes an authentic interpretation established by agreement. Furthermore, if the interpretation adopted by the parties diverges from the natural and ordinary meaning of the terms, there may be a blurring of the line between the interpretation and the amendment of a treaty by subsequent practice.[45]

Waldock dealt with interpretation in his draft article 71 and amendment in article 73, as he thought the two should be distinguished. In the discussion of the Commission, most of the members thought that article 73 dealt with the modification of treaties and should not be placed in the section concerning the interpretation of treaties.[46] This provision was redrafted as such and adopted in the final draft articles as "Article 38. Modification of treaties by subsequent practice"[47] which stipulated as follows:

"A treaty may be modified by subsequent practice in the application of the treaty establishing the agreement of the parties to modify its provisions."[48]

In the diplomatic conference in 1968, however, this draft article was deleted after some discussion,[49] which does not seem to clarify this point.[50]

---

organs but of the individual member States, has great significance. For de Luna, *see* Summary Records of the 766th Meeting, *supra* note 34, at 285, para. 39. Lachs stated (*id.* at 286, para. 46):

> "[I]n international organizations, changes could be brought about by way of practice and interpretation in such a manner as to give certain provisions of the constituent instrument a meaning which was very remote from that envisaged by the parties at the time of signature.... It was also worth remembering that the original parties to the Charter were now outnumbered by the States that had acceded to the Charter since 1945. It would be going too far to claim that the original signatories had a greater say in the interpretation of the Charter than the majority. The burden of the operation of a treaty, in the light of the realities of international relations, fell upon all its signatories; there was therefore no reason for giving a higher standing to the intentions of the original parties in the matter of interpretation."

[44]   Waldock, *supra* note 30, at 60, para. 25.

[45]   *See* Decision of the Arbitration Tribunal Established Pursuant to the Arbitration Agreement Signed on January 22, 1963, between the United States of America and France, Decided at Geneva on December 22, 1963, 3 *Int'l Legal Materials* 668, 713 (1964). Here the Tribunal found that the Agreement had been modified in a certain respect by subsequent practice.

[46]   Summary Records of the 766th Meeting, *supra* note 34, at 291, 296-8, paras. 121-2, 134-59.

[47]   *Id.* at 309, para. 3, and 318, para. 49.

[48]   ILC Report, *supra* note 2, at 236.

[49]   United Nations Conference on the Law of Treaties, First Session, Vienna, 26 March - 24 May 1968, UNOR 207-15, 215, para. 60 (1969).

[50]   Jacobs, in this connection, contended as follows (Jacobs, *supra* note 9, at 332):

> "[W]hile the failure to give subsequent practice a prominent position in the rules of interpretation would effectively have precluded its use in a case to which the Convention applies, the omission of an article providing for modification by subsequent practice will not preclude a party from relying on a general rule of international

4.   Based upon these considerations, some comments could be added.

The first point is related to the nature of subsequent practice. The subsequent practice in Paragraph 3 (b) of Article 31 (General Rule of Interpretation) is "concordant subsequent practice common to all the parties,"[51] in other words, an implied consent.[52] A subsequent practice which does not fall within this narrow definition would constitute a supplementary means of interpretation within the meaning of Article 32.

The second point is whether the intention of the parties clarified through their subsequent practice is that at the time of the conclusion of the treaty, in other words whether subsequent practice could be relied upon only in so far as it reflects the original intention of the parties at the conclusion of the treaty or not.

This may be answered in the affirmative.[53]   In fact, the Permanent Court, in the *Interpretation of the Treaty of Lausanne* case (1925), stated:

"The facts subsequent to the conclusion of the Treaty of Lausanne can only concern the Court in so far as they are calculated to throw light on the intention of the parties at the time of the conclusion of that treaty."[54]

In this regard, however, it is pointed out that the school which would search for the original intention of the parties, considering that all the negotiators concluded is to be found in the treaty and that the function of the interpreter is limited to the elucidation of the original intention of the parties, is now in regression, and that the jurisprudence relating to the subsequent practice refers to the original meaning only as lip service.[55]   It is at least to be noted that subsequent practice mentioned in Paragraph 3 (b) of Article 31 (General Rule of Interpretation) includes only such practice as to signify the above-mentioned implied consent, and that, to that extent, it will not be relevant to the question of the possible legal effect of this practice whether the implied consent

---

customary law recognizing such modification, as evidenced by State practice and the decisions of international tribunals."

See also Yasseen, *supra* note 20, at 51.

[51] I. Sinclair, *The Vienna Convention on the Law of Treaties* 138 (2d ed. 1984).

[52] Yasseen, who was a member of the Commission, stated that subsequent practice in Paragraph 3 (b) of Article means "a tacit authentic interpretation" and that it includes, as an element of the general rule of interpretation, not subsequent practice in general, but only those subsequent practice which are not only concordant, but also common to all the parties and of a certain constance. Yasseen, *supra* note 20, at 48, 52. This is supported by the following Commentary (ILC Report, *supra* note 2, at 222, para. 15):

"The text provisionally adopted in 1964 spoke of a practice which 'establishes the understanding of all the parties'. By omitting the word 'all' the Commission did not intend to change the rule. It considered that the phrase 'the understanding of the parties' necessarily means 'the parties as a whole'. It omitted the word 'all' merely to avoid any possible misconception that every party must individually have engaged in the practice where it suffices that it should have accepted the practice."

[53] Haraszti, *supra* note 11, at 143-4.

[54] Advisory Opinion on Interpretation of Article 3 (2) of the Treaty of Lausanne, [1925] P.C.I.J., ser. B, No. 12, at 24.

[55] Cot, 'La conduite subséquente des parties à un traité', 70 *R.G.D.I.P.* 632, 647, 651-3 (1966). *See also* Jacobs, *supra* note 9, at 329.

consent signified in subsequent practice is not compatible with the text, it goes out of "interpretation" and into "modification" through subsequent practice provided in the draft article 38. At any rate, the existence of an implied consent will be a conclusive element in the determination of a meaning given to the provision concerned.

Thirdly, there remains the question of what effect a subsequent practice which does not signify an implied consent of the parties as a whole would have. This will become an important issue in the interpretation of constituent instruments particularly in relation to the appreciation of the subsequent practice of organs.

In this connection, Fitzmaurice has proposed the theory of 'emergent purpose'.[56] According to this theory, the notion of object or purpose is itself not a fixed and static one, but is liable to change, or rather develop as experience is gained in the operation and working of the convention. At any given moment, the convention is to be interpreted not so much, or not merely, with reference to what its object was when entered into, but with reference to what that object has since become and now appears to be. It is important to note, however, that this is a question of modification through subsequent practice, rather than of interpretation.[57]

Section 3   An Overview of Principal Doctrines of the Interpretative Framework of Constituent Instruments[58]

1.   Current principal doctrines upon the interpretative framework of the constituent instruments of international organizations could, for analytical convenience, be classified into the following *three categories* in accordance with Fitzmaurice.[59]

(i)   International organizations prima facie have the powers expressly conferred on them by their constituent instruments, and only have such additional or implied powers as are necessary for the accomplishment of these expressed powers and no others.

(ii)   International organizations must, in addition to the powers mentioned under (i), be deemed

---

[56] Fitzmaurice, 1957, *supra* note 9, at 208. *See also* Fitzmaurice, 1951, *supra* note 9, at 8, n. 2.

[57] Fitzmaurice stated as follows (*id.* at 225):

   "[I]f ... it is, in the language of the Court, the duty of a tribunal 'to interpret treaties, not to revise them', it is equally the duty of a tribunal to interpret them as revised, and to give effect to any revision arrived at by the parties. In the last analysis, it seems to be a matter chiefly of the nature and weight of the evidence required to establish the existence of such a revision, whether it results from writing or from practice. Looked at in this way, a legitimate place can be found for the doctrine of 'emergent purpose' ... not as a theory of interpretation, but as a substantive rule of treaty law affecting the revision of treaties ...."

[58] *See*, for details of this "Section 2: An Overview of Principal Doctrines of the Interpretative Framework of Constituent Instruments", my article 'Constituent Instruments of International Organizations and Their Interpretative Framework', 14 *Hitotsubashi J. L. & Pol.* 1, 11-21 (1986).

[59] Fitzmaurice, 'The Law and Procedure of the International Court of Justice: International Organizations and Tribunals', 29 *Brit. Y. B. Int'l L.* 1, 6 (1952), *reprinted in* Sir Gerald Fitzmaurice, I *The Law and Procedure of the International Court of Justice* 75 (1986).

by implication to have the ancillary powers necessary to enable them to carry out their functions and fulfill their objects and purposes as laid down in their constituent instruments.

(iii)   International organizations are not limited to what is expressed in or follows by implication from their constituent instruments, but must be regarded as having all such powers as are necessary to enable them to 'develop' in accordance with the requirements of international life.

Various doctrines would be located upon the continuum between the extreme first position and the extreme third position. The majority of scholars in western countries seem to be in the second category.

2.   The first category could be named *Strict Framework of the Law of Treaties*. Doctrines in this category would, emphasizing the treaty aspect of the constituent instruments, understand the functions and powers of international organizations restrictively as only being deduced from the treaties (constituent instruments) within the strict framework of textual treaty interpretation. Here included are most of the scholars in the socialist countries (probably up to the 1970s or 1980s) such as Tunkin, Prandler[60] and Haraszti,[61] as well as Kelsen[62] and Hackworth.[63]

Tunkin, for example, based upon the understanding that a constituent instrument is "the result and an expression of the coordinated wills of participating States," criticized the Court's formulation of the legal principle of implied powers as alleging a rule of international law to the effect that additional powers "essential" for the performance of the duties of an international organization are always implied. Tunkin contended:

"[T]he 'implied competence' of an international organization may be admitted in each particular case only to the extent to which it may be considered as actually implied in the provisions of the statute of the organization but not on the basis of a specific rule of international law on the implied competence."[64]

3.   The third category could be named *Liberal Position Free from the Law of Treaties*. Doctrines in this category would, focusing upon the evolutionary aspect of international organizations, understand their functions and powers only from the viewpoint of their efficient and effective functioning rather than from that of their being controlled by their constituent instruments. Here included are Alvarez and Seyersted, and not many.

Alvarez, in his individual opinion in the advisory opinions with respect to the *Conditions of Admission* case (1948) and the *Competence of the General Assembly* case (1950), developed

---

[60] Prandler, 'Competence of the Security Council and the General Assembly', in *Questions of International Law* 153 (G. Haraszti ed. 1977).

[61] Haraszti, *supra* note 11, at 171-3.

[62] H. Kelsen, *The Law of the United Nations, A Critical Analysis of its Fundamental Problems* 329-30 (1950). *But see* ditto, *Recent Trends in the Law of the United Nations* 911-2 (1951).

[63] *See infra* 'Dissenting Opinion of Judge Hackworth' (*Reparation* case & *Effect of Awards* case in Chap. 3, Sec. 2).

[64] Tunkin, 'The Legal Nature of the United Nations', 119 *Recueil des cours* 25 (1966). *See also* G. Tunkin, *Theory of International Law* 325 (W. E. Butler trans. 1974).

his idea of "New International Law"[65] and contrasted the "New System of Interpretation" with the "Old System of Interpretation."[66] From these considerations, the legal nature of international organizations was presented as follows:

"[A]n institution, once established, acquires a life of its own, independent of the elements which have given birth to it, and it must develop, not in accordance with the views of those who created it, but in accordance with the requirements of international life."[67]

Seyersted, on the other hand, advocated the theory of inherent powers of international organizations based upon their various kinds of practice such as organic jurisdiction, capacity to conclude treaties, territorial jurisdiction and other international acts.[68] He contended:

"[I]ntergovernmental organizations, like States, have an inherent legal capacity to perform any 'sovereign' or international acts which they are in a practical position to perform."[69]

4.   The second category could be named *Functional Framework Based upon the Law of Treaties*. Most of the current doctrines in the western countries would belong to this category. While basing the functions and powers of international organizations upon their constituent instruments, they give a great role to the functional necessity caused by the inherent dynamism of international organizations.   Bowett, for example, contended:

"It was a fairly common view during the early tentative days of the United Nations, that it could only exercise powers specifically granted to it under its constitution. The constitution was a finite instrument which contained the full total of powers delegated by the founding sovereign States to the international organization. While this static view has been persisted in by a minority of jurists, it has generally come to be acknowledged that international constitutional instruments are to be interpreted dynamically, and that the powers of an international organization may go beyond those specifically allocated to it."[70]

The guiding principle in interpreting the Charter of the United Nations has evolved from the static to the dynamic (at least in Western countries). It is noted, however, that there are still different groups in terms of level of flexibility in this category --- the question whether one can imply only such powers as arise by necessary intendment from the constitutional provisions or

---

[65] Advisory Opinion on Conditions of Admission of a State to Membership in the United Nations (Article 4 of the Charter), [1948] I. C. J. 69-70. *See also* A. Alvarez, *Le droit international nouveau dans ses rapports avec la vie actuelle des peuples* (1959); Johnson, 'Review of Books: Le Droit international nouveau dans ses rapports avec la vie actuelle des peuples. By Alejandro Alvarez', 35 *Brit. Y. B. Int'l L.* 274 (1959).

[66] Advisory Opinion on Competence of the General Assembly for the Admission of a State to the United Nations, [1950] I. C. J. 16-8.

[67] *Conditions of Admission* case, *supra* note 65, at 68.

[68] Seyersted, 'United Nations Forces, Some Legal Problems', 37 *Brit. Y. B. Int'l L.* 351, 448-53 (1961).

[69] Seyersted, 'Objective International Personality of Intergovernmental Organizations, Do Their Capacities Really Depend upon the Conventions Establishing Them?', 34 *Nordisk Tidsskrift for International Ret, Acta Scandinavica Juris Gentium* 1, 28 (1964).

[70] D. Bowett, *United Nations Forces, A Legal Study of United Nations Practice* 307-8 (1964). *See also* L. Goodrich, *The United Nations* 68-74 (1960); *Ditto, The United Nations in a Changing World* 36 (1974).

whether a more liberal approach is permissible so that powers relating to the purposes and functions specified in the constitution can be implied.[71]

5.   Now *some comments upon these doctrines* could be presented as follows.

The first comment is with respect to the Liberal Position. Alvarez's argument based upon "New International Law" is, although suggestive on the level of idea, unable to be applied to actual cases as an argument *lex lata*. In the *Competence of the General Assembly* case (1950), Alvarez claimed that the General Assembly may still determine whether or not the right of veto has been abused and, if the answer is in the affirmative, it can proceed with the admission without any recommendation by the Security Council. This view was, however, specifically criticized by the Court.[72] Thus, his argument is, in its concrete application, more an argument *de lege ferenda*, or, in Samore's stern expression, "a house of cards."[73]

The theory of inherent powers advocated by Seyersted cannot be accepted without reservation either. It is, among others, because constituent instruments are drawn not only in terms of purposes but also of functions, and States thereby establish a principle of the limitation of the functional means.[74] This is what the Court has pronounced in several cases.[75]

6.   The second comment is with respect to the Strict Framework. It is certainly not easy to ignore the following statement based upon the realistic recognition of the actual political structure.

"It was clear from the beginning that the United Nations as an inter-State organization and as an organization of peaceful coexistence of States belonging to different social and economic systems might be effective and might successfully develop only on the basis of consensus among member States and first of all that of the great powers.

---

[71] D. Bowett, *The Law of International Institutions* 337-8 (4th ed. 1982).

Some of the various doctrines could be classified in the following way.

(1) Those scholars who base themselves upon the reasoning of "logical presupposition" would be relatively closer to the strict position: H. Schermers, *International Institutional Law* 208-9 (1980); McMahon, 'The Court of the European Communities Judicial Interpretation and International organizations', 37 *Brit. Y. B. Int'l L.* 320 (1961).

(2) Many scholars would be content with reiterating the reasoning and framework used by the Court in the Reparation case: R. Kahn, *Implied Powers of The United Nations* 33 (1970); *see also* G. Weissberg, *The International Status of the United Nations* 24 (1961), and B. Rouyer-Hameray, *Les compétences implicites des organisations internationales* 68 (1962).

(3) Those scholars who give more considerations to the practice of international organizations would be closer to the liberal position: Vallat, 'The Competence of the United Nations General Assembly', 97 *Recueil des cours* 203, 249-50 (1959); Bowett, *supra* note 71, at 338; ditto, *supra* note 70, at 309.

[72] *Competence of the General Assembly* case, *supra* note 66, at 9.

[73] Samore, 'The New International Law of Alejandro Alvarez', 52 *Am. J. Int'l L.* 41, 54 (1958).

[74] *See, e.g.*, Rama-Montaldo, 'International Legal Personality and Implied Powers of International Organizations', 44 *Brit. Y. B. Int'l L.* 111, 119-20 (1970); Seidl-Hohenveldern, 'The Legal Personality of International and Supranational Organizations', 21 *Revue égyptienne de droit international* 35, 41-2 (1965).

[75] *See, e.g.*, Advisory Opinion on Reparation for Injuries Suffered in the Service of the United Nations, [1949] I. C. J. 180; Advisory Opinion on Certain Expenses of the United Nations (Article 17, Paragraph 2, of the Charter), [1962] I. C. J. 168 (1962)

The tendency to impose upon the United Nations certain practices in violation of the basic provisions of the Charter ... have caused great tensions and brought the Organization to the verge of a breakdown."[76]

On the other hand, there is some room for criticism of this position.[77] Among others, it is not evident to what extent Tunkin would accept as constitutional the various kinds of practice of international organizations which Seyersted mentioned above. In any event, those scholars in the ex-socialist countries are expected, in accordance with the changing attitude of their countries toward international organizations, to come closer to the position of the second category.

7.   The third comment is with respect to the Functional Framework. As was pointed out, the doctrines in this category are also divided among themselves in terms of their levels of flexibility. This would originate in the various judgments with respect to the relative weights to be assigned respectively to the treaty aspect and the constitutional aspect of constituent instruments.[78] It seems, however, fair to conclude on the whole that *these doctrines in this category of the functional framework would, in contrast to the doctrines in the strict framework, deviate from the textual interpretative framework of the law of treaties, which subordinates the principle of effectiveness to that of the text and natural meaning by restricting the scope of the principle of effectiveness within the four corners of the text.* The doctrine in the strict framework represented by Tunkin now occupies a small minority in the whole world, and the United Nations and other universal organizations are operated, based upon the majority voting rule although modified by the recent practice of consensus, in *the functional interpretative framework.*

---

[76] Tunkin, *supra* note 64, at 28.

[77] Kelsen's argument, for example, has been criticized by Schachter. Schachter, 'Review, The Law of the United Nations', 60 *Yale L. J.* 189, 192-3 (1951).

[78] The Commission, in its commentary attached to the draft articles on the law of treaties, pointed out the importance of this judgment by saying (ILC Report, *supra* note 2, at 218, para. 4 (1966)):

"[Principles and maxims of treaty interpretation] are, for the most part, principles of logic and good sense valuable only as guides to assist in appreciating the meaning which the parties may have intended to attach to the expressions that they employed in a document. Their suitability for use in any given case hinges on a variety of considerations which have first to be appreciated by the interpreter of the document.... Even when a possible occasion for their application may appear to exist, their application is not automatic but depends on the conviction of the interpreter that it is appropriate in the particular circumstances of the case. In other words, recourse to many of these principles is discretionary rather than obligatory and the interpretation of documents is to some extent an art, not an exact science."

Chapter Three

An Analysis of the Jurisprudence

of

the International Court of Justice

Section 1   The Method of Analysis

1.   **The Importance of the Jurisprudence of the International Court of Justice**[1] as materials for our analysis must be emphasized. Firstly, States do their best in the Court to prove their claims; based upon these arguments, the judges, supposedly the most highly qualified lawyers, representing the main forms of civilization and the principal legal systems of the world (Article 9 of the Statute), give their decision. Secondly, therefore, it can reasonably be assumed that, although various interpretations and evaluations would be possible on a certain issue, those which are sufficiently persuasive are represented in the majority opinion and individual opinions of the Court. Thirdly, interpretations of constituent instruments of international organizations have frequently been a legal issue in the Court's jurisprudence. Consequently, they are important materials for our analysis.[2]

2.   **The Purpose of our Analysis** is not to pass judgment on whether a judgment by the Court on a certain concrete issue was appropriate or not, but to analyze and clarify, from the viewpoint of the characteristics of constituent instruments *vis-à-vis* ordinary treaties, the Court's approach to the issue: its reasoning, method of interpretation and value judgment.

3.   **The Method of our Analysis** is a comparison of the majority opinion with individual ones (separate opinions and dissenting opinions). The purpose of our analysis will be most reasonably achieved by examining the differences and confrontations between the majority opinion and individual ones. Although there exist various arguments[3] as to whether individual opinions should be allowed to be made public, "it is often the case, particularly with difficult or controversial questions, that a decision can only properly be appreciated in the light of a contrary view."[4] Rosenne stated as follows:

"For a full understanding of the real implications of any judgment or advisory opinion in terms of the rule of law applied, not merely the pleadings, which will indicate how the

---

[1] For the relevant bibliography on the jurisprudence of the International Court of Justice as a whole, *see, e.g.,* H. Lauterpacht, *The Development of International Law by the International Court* (1958); *Hanrei Kenkyu Kokusaishihosaibansho (The Jurisprudence of the International Court of Justice)* (Y. Takano ed.1965); J. H. W. Verzijl, *The Jurisprudence of the World Court*, 2 vols. (1965 & 1966); G. Fitzmaurice, *The Law and Procedure of the International Court of Justice*, 2 vols. (1986); E. S. Yambrusic, *Treaty Interpretation* (1987).

[2] *But see* W. M. Reisman & A. R. Willard, *International Incidents, The Law That Counts in World Politics* 3-24, esp. 13 (1988). *See,* for a persuasive criticism of this approach, Bowett, 'International Incidents: New Genre or New Delusion?', 12 *Yale J. Int'l L.* 386 (1987).

[3] *See, e.g.,* Hambro, 'Dissenting and Individual Opinions in the International Court of Justice', 17 *Zeitschrift für ausländiches öffentliches Recht und Völkerrecht* 229 (1956-57); Anand, 'The Role of Individual and Dissenting Opinions in International Adjudication', 14 *Int'l & Comp. L. Q.* 788 (1965); I. Hussain, *Dissenting and Separate Opinions at the World Court* 1-9 (1984).

[4] Fitzmaurice, 'The Law and Procedure of the International Court of Justice: General Principles and Substantive Law', 27 *Brit. Y. B. Int'l L.* 1,2 (1950), *reprinted in* G. Fitzmaurice, 1 *The Law and Procedure of the International Court of Justice* 2 (1986).

parties presented the issues, but also the individual opinions appended to the judgment, which will illustrate the main lines of the discussion in the Court when it withdrew to deliberate on the case, must be consulted."[5]

4. **Objectivity in the Analysis** requires that the materials to be analyzed be comprehensive. One tends to construct his theory by collecting only those parts in those judgments of the Court which are favourable to his theory. This must be avoided. In this chapter, all the cases in which constituent instruments were at issue[6] will not only be dealt with, but also the reasoning as a whole, and the framework of judgment, in addition to the rationale on individual points of issue, will be analyzed as far as possible.

Section 2 Questions Relating to the Structures and Activities of the United Nations

1 Conditions of Admission of a State to Membership in theUnited Nations (Article 4 of the Charter) [1948] [7]

The question adopted by the General Assembly in 1947 was as follows: "Is a Member of the United Nations which is called upon, in virtue of Article 4 of the Charter, to pronounce itself by its vote, either in the Security Council or in the General Assembly, on the Admission of a State to membership in the United Nations, juridically entitled to make its consent to the admission dependent on conditions not expressly provided by paragraph 1 of the said Article?" The Court, in the present advisory opinion, reached a negative conclusion by 9 votes[8] to 6. Both Judges

---

[5] Sh. Rosenne, *The Law and Practice of the International Court* 597 (2nd rev. ed. 1985).

[6] The present study is confined to the jurisprudence of the International Court of Justice, and that of the Permanent Court of International Justice will not be dealt with here. As to the cases before the ICJ, Advisory Opinion on Interpretation of Peace Treaties with Bulgaria, Hungary and Romania (Second Phase)(1950) was already briefly analyzed (*supra* at Chapter Two, Section 1, (2), 4); Case concerning Northern Cameroons (1963), Advisory Opinion on Applicability of the Obligation to Arbitrate under Section 21 of the United Nations Headquarters Agreement of 26 June 1947 (1988) and Advisory Opinion on Applicability of Article VI, Section 22, of the Convention on the Privileges and Immunities of the United Nations (1989) will not be dealt with because they are considered not to be sufficiently relevant in the present context of our study. Advisory Opinion on Application for Review of Judgement No. 333 of the United Nations Administrative Tribunal will not be dealt with either because the three cases dealt with in the text will suffice for the point of issue in these cases. Case concerning Questions of Interpretation and Application of the 1971 Montreal Convention arising from the Aerial Incident at Lockerbie (Provisional Measures)(1992) is potentially relevant, but should be analyzed together with its Judgment on the Merits to be given at some future date.

[7] For the relevant bibliography on the present advisory opinion, *see, e.g.*, Liang, 'Notes on Legal Questions Concerning the United Nations', 43 *Am. J. Int'l L.* 288 (1949); Humber, 'Admission to the United Nations', 24 *Brit. Y. B. Int'l L.* 90 (1947); Berlia, 'Admission d'un État aux Nations Unies (Charte art. 4)', 53 *R. G. D. I. P.* 481 (1949), Gross, 'Progress towards Universality of Membership in the United Nations', 50 *Am. J. Int'l L.* 791 (1956), *reprinted in* L. Gross, 2 *Essays on International Law and Organization* 607 (1984).

[8] The nine judges were Guerrero (President), Alvarez, Fabela, Hackworth, de Visscher, Klaestad, Badawi Pasha, Hsu Mo and Azevedo.

Alvarez and Azevedo appended a statement of their individual opinion. Judges Basdevant (Vice-President), Winiarski, McNair and Read appended a statement of their joint dissenting opinion. Both Judges Zoričić and Krylov appended a statement of their dissenting opinion. The reasoning of the majority opinion and that of the joint dissenting opinion will be analyzed here.

(1) The Reasoning of the Majority Opinion

1. The majority opinion, after making some preliminary remarks upon such points as delimitation of the question and jurisdiction of the Court, recalled, first of all, the five conditions required, under paragraph 1 of Article 4, of an applicant for admission ----- an applicant must (1) be a State; (2) be peace-loving; (3) accept the obligations of the Charter; (4) be able to carry out these obligations; and (5) be willing to do so. Then it pointed out that all these conditions are subject to the judgment of the Organization: the judgment of the Security Council and the General Assembly, and, in the final analysis, that of its Members.

2. The majority opinion reached a negative conclusion by fundamentally basing itself upon *the textual approach.* The core of its reasoning is as follows:

"Having been asked to determine the character, exhaustive or otherwise, of the conditions stated in Article 4, *the Court must in the first place consider the text of that Article....*

The terms 'Membership in the United Nations is open to all other peace-loving States which....' and 'Peuvent devenir Membres des Nations unies tous autres États pacifiques', *indicate that States which fulfil the conditions stated have the qualifications requisite for admission. The natural meaning of the words used leads to the conclusion that these conditions constitute an exhaustive enumeration and are not merely stated by way of guidance or example. The provision would lose its significance and weight, if other conditions, unconnected with those laid down, could be demanded.* The conditions stated in paragraph 1 of Article 4 must therefore be regarded not merely as the necessary conditions, but also as the conditions which suffice.

Nor can it be argued that the conditions enumerated represent only an indispensable minimum, in the sense that political considerations could be superimposed upon them, and prevent the admission of an applicant which fulfils them. *Such an interpretation would be inconsistent with the terms of paragraph 2 of Article 4,* which provide for the admission of *'tout État* remplissant ces conditions' --- *'any* such State'. It would lead to conferring upon Members an indefinite and practically unlimited power of discretion in the imposition of new conditions. Such a power would be inconsistent with the very character of paragraph 1 of Article 4 which, by reason of the close connexion which it establishes between membership and the observance of the priciples and obligations of the Charter, clearly constitutes a legal regulation of the question of the admission of new States. *To warrant an interpretation other than that which ensues from the natural meaning of the words, a decisive reason would be required which has not been established.*

Moreover, the spirit as well as the terms of the paragraph preclude the idea that considerations extraneous to these principles and obligations can prevent the admission of a State which complies with them. If the authors of the Charter had meant to leave Members free to import into the application of this provision considerations extraneous to the conditions laid down therein, they would undoubtedly have adopted a different wording.

The Court considers that the text is sufficiently clear; consequently, it does not feel that it should deviate from the consistent practice of the Permanent Court of International Justice, according to which there is no occasion to resort to preparatory work if the text of a convention is sufficiently clear in itself.

The Court furthermore observes that Rule 60 of the Provisional Rules of Procedure of the Security Council is based on this interpretation."[9]   [Italics ours]

(2) The Reasoning of the Dissenting Opinion of Judges Basdevant, Winiarski, McNair and Read

1.   The dissenting judges, after making some preliminary remarks on their differences from the majority opinion, state their starting point as follows:

"The reason why the question stated has been submitted to the Court is that the relevant provisions did not seem to be clear enough to provide a simple and unambiguous answer to the question. Such, at any rate, was the view of the General Assembly and we share it. Accordingly, in our opinion, we are confronted with a question of interpretation and therefore we must aplpy the rules generally recognized in regard to the interpretation of treaties."[10]

Thus, it is pointed out that the relevant provision of paragraph 1 of Article 4 should be interpreted in its entire legal context as supplied by the other provisions, paragraph 2 of Article 4 in particular, of the Charter and the principles of international law.

2.   Within this general framework of interpretation, a primary consideration is given to the distinction between a system of accession clause by virtue of which a declaration of accession made by a third State involves automatically the acquisition of membership of the union by that State, and a system of admission which the Charter has adopted. In the working of this latter system, the Charter requires the intervention of the two principal political organs of the United Nations. This is an important point in the reasoning of the dissenting judges, and the core of the point is as follows:

"The resolutions which embody either a recommendation or a decision in regard to admission are decisions of a political character; they emanate from political organs; by general consent they involve the examination of political factors, with a view to deciding

---

[9]   Advisory Opinion on Conditions of Admission of a State to Membership in the United Nations (Article 4 of the Charter), [1948] I. C. J. 62-63.

[10]   *Id.* at 83.

44

whether the applicant State possesses the qualifications prescribed by paragraph 1 of Article 4; ... The admission of a new Member is pre-eminently a political act, and a political act of the greatest importance.

The main function of a political organ is to examine questions in their political aspect, which means examining them from every point of view. It follows that the Members of such an organ who are responsible for forming its decisions must consider questions from every aspect, and, in consequence, are legally entitled to base their arguments and their vote upon political considerations. That is the position of a member of the Security Council or of the General Assembly who raises an objection based upon reasons other than the lack of one of the qualifications expressly required by paragraph 1 of Article 4."[11]

3.   The dissenting judges admitted that the Member States are bound to respect paragraph 1 of Article 4, and, in consequence, bound not to admit a State which fails to possess the conditions required in this paragraph. But is there any other legal restriction consisting in a prohibition to oppose an application for admission on grounds foreign to the qualifications required by paragraph 1 of Article 4 ? Here it is pointed out that there is a rule of interpretation frequently applied by the Permanent Court of International Justice, when confronted with a rule or principle of law, to the effect that no restriction upon this rule or principle can be presumed unless it has been clearly established, and that in case of doubt it is the rule or principle of law which must prevail. They state that there is no treaty provision which establishes such a restriction in the present case.

The effect of paragraph 1 of Article 4 is, it is said, that certain qualifications therein enumerated are essential; but there is no express and direct statement that these qualifications are sufficient and that once they are fulfilled admission must of necessity follow. The language of Article 4 is permissive in tone, not obligatory, and this provision contains no evidence of any definite intention to deprive the Member States of the legal right possessed by them of giving effect to other considerations.

The dissenting judges stated that this view accords with the intentions of the framers of the Charter and pointed out as follows:

"Without wishing to embark upon a general examination and assessment of the value of resorting to *travaux préparatoires* in the interpretation of treaty, it must be admitted that if ever there is a case in which this practice is justified it is when those who negotiated the treaty have embodied in an interpretative resolution or some similar provision their precise

---

[11] *Id.* at 85.

The majority opinion specifically criticized this view by stating as follows (*id.* at 64):

"The political character of an organ cannot release it from the observance of the treaty provisions established by the Charter when they constitute limitations on its powers or criteria for its judgment. To ascertain whether an organ has freedom of choice for its decisions, reference must be made to the terms of its constitution. In this case, the limits of this freedom are fixed by Article 4 and allow for a wide liberty of appreciation. There is therefore no conflict between the functions of the political organs, on the one hand, and the exhaustive character of the prescribed conditions, on the other."

intentions regarding the meaning attached by them to a particular article of the treaty. This is exactly what was done with respect to paragraph 2 of Article 4."[12]

Consequently, they examine the Minutes of the San Francisco Conference and reach the conclusion that "[i]n our opinion, while the Charter makes the qualifications specified in paragraph 1 of Article 4 essential, it does not make them sufficient. If it had regarded them as sufficient, it would not have failed to say so. The point was one of too great importance to be left in obscurity."[13]

4.   For these reasons, the answer by the dissenting judges was as follows:

"A Member of the United Nations which is called upon, in virtue of Article 4 of the Charter, to pronounce itself by its vote, ... on the admission of a State which possesses the qualifications specified in paragraph 1 of that Article, is participating in a political decision and is therefore legally entitled to make its consent to the admission dependent on any political considerations which seem to it to be relevant. In the exercise of this power the Member is legally bound to the Purposes and Principles of the United Nations and to act in such a manner as not to involve any breach of the Charter." [14]

(3) Some Comments

1.   As is clear from the previous quotation, the majority opinion is fundamentally based upon the textual approach. But it was not appropriate that it "consider[ed] that the text is sufficiently clear" and declined to resort to preparatory work. In fact, since the judges were largely divided and the joint dissenting judges reached the opposite conclusion, the majority opinion should have examined the preparatory work and shown that it did not support the dissenting judges. It is reasonably pointed out that a method of interpretation which, with reference to an essential aspect of a basic international instrument, confines itself to a deduction from the natural meaning of words runs the danger of unduly simplifying the difficult process of interpretation.[15]

2.   It is also pointed out that the majority opinion is apparently opposite to the joint dissenting opinion, but that, essentially, the difference between these two opinions is one of emphasis, not of substance.[16] While, on the one hand, the dissenting opinion held that the Member States were, in participating in a political decision, legally bound to have regard to the principle of good faith, to give effect to the Purposes and Principles of the United Nations and to act in such a manner as not to involve any breach of the Charter, the majority opinion, on the other, admitted a substantial degree of elasticity by saying as follows:

"Article 4 does not forbid the taking into account of any factor which it is possible reasonably and in good faith to connect with the conditions laid down in the very wide and

---

[12] *Id.* at 87.

[13] *Id.* at 90.

[14] *Id.* at 92.

[15] H. Lauterpacht, *The Development of International Law by the International Court* 55 (1958).

[16] *Id.* at 150-51. Ch. de Visscher, *Problème d'interprétation judiciaire en droit international public* 149 (1963)

very elastic nature of the prescibed conditions; no relevant political factor ----- that is to say, none connected with the conditions of admission ----- is excluded."[17]

3.   Based upon the above analysis, could some observations with regard to the interpretation method of constituent instruments be deduced? Some indeed refer to the specific characteristics of the Charter; Hudson, for example, commented as follows:

"The Charter is not an ordinary treaty. It is the basic constitutional instrument of the organized community of states. As such, its interpretation is not necessarily to be approached along merely traditional lines. The Charter was not framed solely with a view to Members of the Organization.... Hence the interpretation of the Charter should be approached in such a way as to give effect to the community character of the instrument."[18]

It is not clear what he meant by this. However, judging from the fact that Hudson is favorable to Judges Alvarez[19] and Azevedo,[20] he seems to emphasize the importance of the principle of universality[21] although this principle closely connected with an automatic accession was denied at the San Francisco Conference.

Simon is more straightforward on this point. After quoting a portion of the majority opinion criticizing the joint dissenting opinion, he stated:

"[C]ette limitation du pouvoir discrétionnaire des États ne peut guère s'expliquer, au-delá des arguments de texte invoqués par la Cour, que par la prise en considération d'un principe jugé essentiel à l'efficacité des Nations Unies, et qui se retrouve en filigrane tout au long de

---

[17] *Conditions of Admission* case, *supra* note 9, at 63.

[18] Hudson, 'Admission to the United Nations: Advisory Opinion of World Court as to Conditions', 34 *Am. B. A. J.* 652, 653 (1948).

Feinberg also referred to the notion that "un instrument international qui, à l'instar du Pacte de la Société des Nations, peut être considéré comme la charte constitutionnelle du monde appelée à transformer la communauté internationale anarchique en une société juridiquement organisée". Feinberg, 'L'admission de nouveaux Membres à la Société des Nations et à l'Organisation des Nations Unies', 80 *Recueil des cours* 293, 346 (1952).

[19] Judge Alvarez devoted a large portion of his separate opinion to the general observation mentioned above (*supra* at Chapter Two, Section 2, 3), and then dealt with the present question. After having recognized that the conditions in Article 4 (1) were exhaustive, he stated that "having regard to the nature of the universal international society, the purposes of the United Nations Organization and its mission of universality, it must be held that all States fulfilling the conditions required by Article 4 of the Charter have a *right* to membership in that Organization." *Conditions of Admission* case, *supra* note 9, at 71.

[20] According to Judge Azevedo, "[o]nce it is admitted that a State has proved that it has all the required qualifications, a refusal to accept its application might be considered tantamount to a violation, not only of an interest, but of a right ...". *Id.* at 81.

[21] While universality will not ensure the solution of major problems of international politics, it has great significance for the development of international law. Gross stated in this connection as follows (Gross, 'Election of States to United Nations Membership', *in* L. Gross, 1 *Essays on International Law and Organization* 585, 605 (1984)):

"[I]f it is true, as I believe it is, that the development of international law is bound up with that of international organization, the achievement of universality would mean the transformation of the present decentralized and rudimentary society of nations into a relatively more centralized society, and equally, the transformation of the United Nations into organs of that society.... Universality of membership is an important, but not a decisive, element in this process."

l'avis: il s'agit de la vocation de l'ONU à l'universalité."[22]

It could not probably be denied that *there was a substantive value judgment in favour of promoting the universality of the United Nations behind the fundamentally textual approach of the majority opinion.* However, it is going too far to say that, as Simon says, "l'interprétation juridictionnelle des traités constitutifs tend effectivement privilègier le développement des finalités institutionnelles, à la fois en tendant le contenu matériel des compétences de l'organisation et en limitant la portée des compétences retenues des États-membres."[23] More suggestive would be the following statement of Judge de Visscher who was a member of the majority opinion:

"[L]a Cour s'est appliquée à concilier les fins de l'Organisation internationale avec le respect des textes, à favoriser son développement sans porter atteinte à ses bases conventionnelles.... Dans un égal souci des buts et principes institutionnels et du respect des textes, une saine interprétation veille l'équilibre des volontés dont les traités sont l'expression."[24]

2 Competence of the General Assembly for the Admission of a State to the United Nations [1950]

In 1949, the General Assembly requested the ICJ to give an advisory opinion on the question: "Can the Admission of a State to membership in the United Nations, pursuant to Article 4, paragraph 2, of the Charter, be effected by a decision of the General Assembly when the Security Council has made no recommendation for admission by reason of the candidate failing to obtain the requisite majority or of the negative vote of a permanent Member upon a resolution so to recommend?" The Court reached a negative conclusion by 12 votes[25] to 2.[26] The reasoning of the majority opinion and that of the dissenting opinion by Judge Alvarez will be analyzed here.

(1) The Reasoning of the Majority Opinion

The majority opinion, at the beginning, rejected the objections based upon the grounds

---

[22] D. Simon, *L'interprétation judiciaire des traités d'organisations internatinales* 193 (1981). "[T]his limitation of the discretionary power of States cannot be explained, beyond the textual arguments invoked by the Court, except by taking into consideration a principle thought essential for the effectiveness of the United Nations, and which is found like filigree all through the opinion: it concerns the vocation of the U.N. for the universality." [Our translation]

[23] *Id.* at 194. "the jurisdictional interpretation of the constitutive treaties tends in reality to privilege the development of the institutional finalities both by stretching the material content of the competences of the Organization and by limiting the scope of the retained competences of the Member States." [Our translation]

[24] de Visscher, *supra* note 16, at 150. "[T]he Court has made a serious effort to reconcile the ends of the Organization with the respect of texts, to favor its development without undermining its conventional basis.... With an equal concern for the institutional purposes and principles and the respect of texts, a sound interpretation attends to an equilibrium of the wills of which the treaties are the expression." [Our translation]

[25] The twelve judges were Basdevant (President), Guerrero (Vice-President), Hackworth, Winiarski, Zoričić, de Visscher, Sir Arnold McNair, Klaestad, Badawi Pasha, Krylov, Read and Hsu Mo.

[26] The two judges were Alvarez and Azevedo.

relating to non-competence to interpret the provisions of the Charter and alleged political character of the question. It then stated, *based upon the textual approach*, as follows:

"The Court has no doubt as to the meaning of this text. It requires two things to effect admission: a 'recommendation' of the Security Council and a 'decision' of the General Assembly. It is in the nature of things that the recommendation should come before the decision. The word 'recommendation', and the word 'upon' preceding it, imply the idea that the recommendation is the foundation of the decision to admit, and that the latter rests upon the recommendation. Both these acts are indispensable to form the judgment of the Organization to which the previous paragraph of Article 4 refers. The text under consideration means that the General Assembly can only decide to admit upon the recommendation of the Security Council; it determines the respective roles of the two organs whose combined action is required before admission can be effected: in other words, the recommendation of the Security Council is the condition precedent to the decision of the Assembly by which the admission is effected.

In one of the written statements placed before the Court, an attempt was made to attribute to paragraph 2 of Article 4 a different meaning. The Court considers it necessary to say that *the first duty of a tribunal which is called upon to interpret and apply the provisions of a treaty, is to endeavour to give effect to them in their natural and ordinary meaning in the context in which they occur. If the relevant words in their natural and ordinary meaning make sense in their context, that is an end of the matter.* If, on the other hand, the words in their natural and ordinary meaning are ambiguous or lead to an unreasonable result, then, and then only, must the Court, by resort to other methods of interpretation, seek to ascertain what the parties really did mean when they used these words."[27] [Italics ours]

In the present case, the majority opinion finds no difficulty in ascertaining the natural and ordinary meaning of the words in question and no difficulty in giving effect to them; it considers, furthermore, that its conclusions are fully confirmed by the structure of the Charter, and particularly by the relations established by it between the General Assembly and the Security Council, stating as follows:

"To hold that the General Assembly has power to admit a State to membership in the absence of a recommendation of the Security Council would be to deprive the Security Council of an important power which has been entrusted to it by the Charter. It would almost nullify the role of the Security Council in the exercise of one of the essential functions of the Organization. It would mean that the Security Council would have merely to study the case, present a report, give advice, and express an opinion. This is not what

---

[27] Advisory Opinion on Competence of the General Assembly for the Admission of a State to the United Nations, [1950] I. C. J. 7-8.

49

Article 4, paragraph 2, says."[28]

(2) The Reasoning of the Dissenting Opinion of Judge Alvarez

Judge Alvarez, using a major portion of his dissenting opinion, developed a general observation (particularly method of interpretation) advocating "New International Law." He then dealt with the present problem in the following way. Two situations are distinguished; (a) the State seeking admission has failed to obtain the requisite number of votes in the Security Council; (b) the State seeking admission has obtained the requisite number of votes in the Council, but one of the permanent Members has made use of the veto. In the opinion of Judge Alvarez, "[the latter] is the case which we must specially consider. I think that the General Assembly may appraise the veto."[29] When the right of veto was created, he stated, the only objects in view were matters concerning the maintenance of peace and international security. The text of Article 27, which established this right, is clear, if taken in isolation; but it is no longer clear if we have regard to the nature and objects of the United Nations Organization. Thus:

"Even if it is admitted that the right of veto may be exercised freely by the permanent Members of the Security Council in regard to the recommendation of new Members, the General Assembly may still determine whether or not this right has been abused and, if the answer is in the affirmative, it can proceed with the admission without any recommendation by the Council."[30]

This solution, he added, is not only consistent with the spirit of the Charter by the terms of which the U.N.O. has a universal role, with the consequence that all members of the international community which fulfil the conditions laid down in Article 4 have a right to be admitted, but also consistent with the requirement of common sense because it would be an absurdity that a single vote would be able to frustrate the votes of all the other Members of the United Nations.[31]

(3) Some Comments

1.   What is interesting in the present case is that the six judges who dissented in the *Condition of Admission* case have followed a basically similar reasoning with that of the majority opinion in that case, and that "a practically unanimous Court"[32] has adopted a textual approach. In this connection, the majority opinion specifically stated as follows:

---

[28] *Id.* at 9.

[29] *Id.* at 19.

[30] *Id.* at 20.

[31] *Id.* at 21.

    For a similar conclusion of Judge Azevedo, but based upon his unique understanding of the term "decision" in the Charter, *see id.* at 34. In general, for the discussion of these judges, *see* Fitamaurice, 'The Law and Procedure of the International Court of Justice: International Organizations and Tribunals', 29 *Brit. Y. B. Int'l L.* 28-31 (1952), *reprinted in* G. Fitzmaurice, 1 *The Law and Procedure of the International Court of Justice* 97-100 (1986).

[32] Lauterpacht, *supra* note 15, at 122.

"When the Court can give effect to a provision of a treaty by giving to the words used in it their natural and ordinary meaning, it may not interpret the words by seeking to give them some other meaning. In the present case the Court finds no difficulty in ascertaining the natural and ordinary meaning of the words in question and no difficulty in giving effect to them. Some of the written statements submitted to the Court have invited it to investigate the *travaux préparatoires* of the Charter. Having regard, however, to the consideration above stated, the Court is of the opinion that it is not permissible, in this case, to resort to *travaux préparatoires*."[33]

2.   In the context of our study, attention is drawn to the point that the majority opinion has based its reasoning upon *the consistent practice of an organ as a legal ground supporting its conclusion.* It stated as follows:

"The organs to which Article 4 entrusts the judgment of the Organization in matters of admission have consistently interpreted the text in the sense that the General Assembly can decide to admit only on the basis of a recommendation of the Security Council. In particular, the Rules of Procedure of the General Assembly provide for consideration of the merits of an application and of the decision to be made upon it only 'if the Security Council recommends the applicant State for membership' (Article 125). The rules merely state that if the Security Council has not recommended the admission, the General Assembly may send back the application to the Security Council for further consideration (Article 126). This last step has been taken several times...."[34]

3.   It has been rejected in the "practically unanimous" vote by the Court to take the position, as Judge Alvarez does, that the General Assembly prevails over the Security Council in the matter of admission. It is pointed out that the relationship between the General Assembly and the Security Council in the present matter is "une espèce de balancement de pouvoirs," which is "un des traits caractèristiques de la Charte,"[35] and that the Court has refused to upset "l'équilibre organique de l'organisation en détruisant le balancement égalitaire Assemblée-Conseil et en déplaçant le centre de gravité de l'organisation au profit de l'Assemblée générale" as not in conformity with the Charter even if it might promote the universality of the United Nations.[36] Verzijl, in a similar way, stated as follows:

"The conclusion [of Judge Alvarez] is in my view totally unacceptable under the actual provisions of the Charter, however much one may regret that those provisions are as they are. It is not for a Court of Justice to amend the law. For, an amendment it would undoubtedly be."[37]

---

[33] *Competence of the General Assembly* case, *supra* note 27, at 8.

[34] *Id.* at 9.

[35] Exposé de M. Georges Scelle, I. C. J. Pleadings 163 (1950).

[36] J. Rideau, *Juridictions internationales et contrôle du respect des traités constitutifs des organisations internationales* 220 (1969).

[37] J. H. W. Verzijl, 2 *The Jurisprudence of the World Court* 21 (1966).

3 Reparation for Injuries Suffered in the Service of the United Nations [1949][38]

In 1948, the General Assembly decided to submit two legal questions to the ICJ for an advisory opinion, the first of which is as follows: "In the event of an agent of the United Nations in the performance of his duties suffering injury in circumstances involving the responsibility of a State, has the United Nations, as an Organization, the capacity to bring an international claim against the responsible *de jure* or *de facto* government with a view to obtaining the reparation due in respect of the damage caused (a) to the United Nations, (b) to the victim or to persons entitled through him ?" The Court reached an affirmative conclusion upon (a) unanimously, and upon (b) by 11 votes[39] against 4.[40]

(1) The Reasoning of the Majority Opinion[41]

1.   In responding to the above question, the majority opinion divided it into three parts: (1) whether, in general, the characteristics of the Organization do, or do not, include for the Organization a right to present an international claim; (2) whether the sum of the international rights of the Organization comprises the right to bring the kind of international claim described in the Request of this Opinion; (3) whether the Organization has the capacity to bring an international claim even against a State that is not a member of the Organization. It is understood that the first is a question of legal personality, the second a question of relationship between the objects of the Organization and its functions, and the third a question of opposability.

2.   With regard to the first question of legal personality, the majority opinion set its starting point as follows:

"To answer this question, which is not settled by the actual terms of the Charter, we must consider what characteristics it was intended thereby to give to the Organization."[42]

Following this approach, the majority opinion points out that the Charter has not been content to make the Organization merely a center for harmonizing the actions of nations in the attainment of the common ends (Article 1, para. 4), but has equipped that center with organs, given it special tasks, and defined the position of the Members in relation to the Organization. After further pointing out that practice, in particular the conclusion of conventions to which the

---

[38] For the relevant bibliography on the present advisory Opinion, *see, e.g.*, Liang, 'Notes on Legal Questions Concerning the United Nations, Reparation for Injuries Suffered in the Service of the United Nations', 43 *Am J. Int'l L.* 460 (1949); G. Weissberg, *The International Status of the United Nations* 170-200 (1961); Eagleton, 'International Organization and the Law of Responsiblity', 76 *Recueil des cours* 319 (1950).

[39] The eleven judges were Basdevant (President), Guerrero (Vice-President), Alvarez, Fabela, Zoričić, de Visscher, Sir Arnold McNair, Klaestad, Read, Hsu Mo and Azevedo.

[40] The four judges were Hackworth, Badawi Pasha, Krylov and Winiarski.

[41] For an excellent analysis of the majority opinion, *see* Rama-Montaldo, 'International Legal Personality and Implied Powers of International Organizations', 44 *Brit. Y. B. Int'l L.* 111, 124-31 (1970).

[42] Advisory Opinion on Reparation for Injuries Suffered in the Service of the United Nations, [1949] I. C. J. 178.

Organization is a party, has confirmed this character of the Organization, it "has come to the conclusion that the Organization is an international person." [43] In other words,:

"In the opinion of the Court, the Organization was intended to exercise and enjoy, and is in fact exercising and enjoying, functions and rights which can only be explained on the basis of the possession of a large measure of international personality and the capacity to operate upon an international plane.... [I]t could not carry out the intentions of its founders if it was devoid of international personality. It must be acknowledged that its Members, by entrusting certain functions to it, with the attendant duties and responsibilities, have clothed it with the competence required to enable those functions to be effectively discharged." [44]

3.   The majority opinion, after giving an affirmative answer to the first question of legal personality, proceeded to the second question.

In respect of "the damage caused (a) to the United Nations," that is, exclusively damage caused to the interests of the Organization itself, to its administrative machine, to its property and assets, and to the interests of which it is the guardian, the majority opinion quickly admitted it by simply saying that "[i]t is clear that the Organization has the capacity to bring a claim for this damage." [45]

4.   The reasoning of the majority opinion in respect of "the damage caused ... (b) to the victim or persons entitled through him" is the most important part in the present context.

The majority opinion, first of all, denies the relevancy of the analogy of the traditional rule of diplomatic protection of nationals abroad. On the one hand, it does not involve the giving of a negative answer in the light of the difference of the subjects (a State *vis-à-vis* the Organization), the existence of exceptions to this rule, and the similarities of the bases of two cases. On the other hand, it does not justify in itself an affirmative reply either because it is not possible to assimilate the legal bond which exists, under Article 100 of the Charter, between the Organization on the one hand, and the Secretary-General and the staff on the other, to the bond of nationality. Thus the majority opinion set its starting point as follows:

"The Court is here faced with a new situation. The questions to which it gives rise can only be solved by realizing that the situation is dominated by the provisions of the Charter considered in the light of the principles of international law." [46]

It, first of all, developed an approach to the Charter interpretation on a general theoretical level by saying:

"The Charter does not expressly confer upon the Organization the capacity to include, in its claim for reparation, damage caused to the victim or to persons entitled through him.

---

[43] *Id.* at 179.

[44] *Id.*

[45] *Id.*

[46] *Id.* at 182.

The Court must therefore begin by enquiring whether the provisions of the Charter concerning the functions of the Organization, and the part played by its agents in the performance of those functions, imply for the Organization power to afford its agents the limited protection that would consist in the bringing of a claim on their behalf for reparation for damage suffered in such circumstances. *Under international law, the Organization must be deemed to have those powers which, though not expressly provided in the Charter, are conferred upon it by necessary implication as being essential to the performance of its duties.* This princiciple of law was applied by the Permanent Court of International Justice to the International Labour Organization in its Advisory Opinion No. 13 of July 23rd, 1926 (Series B., No. 13, p. 18), and must be applied to the United Nations."[47] [Italics ours]

It, then, applied this principle of law to the United Nations and admitted the capacity of the Organization to exercise a measure of functional protection of its agents by the following reasoning:

"Having regard to its purposes and functions already referred to, the Organization may find it necessary, and has in fact found it necessary, to entrust its agents with important missions to be performed in disturbed parts of the world. Many missions, from their very nature, involve the agents in unusual dangers to which ordinary persons are not exposed. For the same reason, the injuries suffered by its agents in these circumstances will sometimes have occurred in such a manner that their national State would not be justified in bringing a claim for reparation on the ground of diplomatic protection, or, at any rate, would not feel disposed to do so. *Both to ensure the efficient and independent performance of these missions and to afford effective support to its agents, the Organization must provide them with adequate protection.*

This need of protection for the agents of the Organization, as a condition of the performance of its functions, has already been realized, and the Preamble to the Resolution of December 3rd, 1948, shows that this was the unanimous view of the General Assembly.

For this purpose, the Members of the Organization have entered into certain undertakings, some of which are in the Charter and others in complementary agreements. The content of these undertakings need not be described here; but the Court must stress the importance of the duty to render to the Organization 'every assistance' which is accepted by the Members in Article 2, paragraph 5, of the Charter. It must be noted that the effective working of the Organization --- the accomplishment of its task, and the independence and effectiveness of the work of its agents --- require that these undertakings should be strictly observed. For that purpose, it is necessary that, when an infringement occurs, the Organization should be able to call upon the responsible State to remedy its default, and in particular, to obtain from the State reparation for the damage that the default

---

[47] *Id.* at 182-83.

may have caused to its agent.

In order that the agent may perform his duties satisfactorily, he must feel that this protection is assured to him by the Organization, and that he may count on it. *To ensure the independence of the agent, and consequently, the independent action of the Organization itself, it is essential that in performing his duties he need not have to rely on any other protection than that of the Organization (save of course for the more direct and immediate protection due from the State in whose territory he may be). In particulr, he should not have to rely on the protection of his own State. If he had to rely on that State, his independence might well be compromised, contrary to the principle applied by Article 100 of the Charter.* And lastly, it is essential that --- whether the agent belongs to a powerful or to a weak State; to one more affected or less affected by the complications of international life; to one in sympathy or not in symathy with the mission of the agent --- he should know that in the performance of his duties he is under the protection of the Organization. This assurance is even more necessary when the agent is stateless.

Upon examination of the character of the functions entrusted to the Organization and of the nature of the missions of its agents, it becomes clear that the capacity of the Organization to exercise a measure of functional protection of its agents arises by necessary intendment out of the Charter.[48] [Italics ours]

5.   The third question of opposability will not be dealt with here.

(2) The Reasoning of the Dissenting Opinion of Judge Hackworth

1.   Judge Hackworth concurred, but for different reasons, in the conclusion of the majority opinion on Question (a), and could not concur on Question (b).

2.   On Question (a), Judge Hackworth reached *an affirmative answer by an application of the doctrine of implied powers, which was not the case for the majority opinion.* After referring to Article 104, paragraphs 1 and 2 of Article 105 and the Convention on Privileges and Immunities, he stated as follows:

"[I]f the Organization is to make contracts, to acquire and dispose of property, to institute legal proceedings, and to claim the benefits of the privileges and immunities to which it is entitled, it must be able to carry on negotiations with governments as well as with private parties. It must therefore be able to assert claims in its own behalf. No other conclusion consistent with the specified powers and with the inherent right of self-preservation could possibly be drawn. The Organization must have and does have ample authority to take needful steps for its protection against wrongful acts for which Member States are responsible. Any damage *suffered by the Organization* by reason of wrongful acts committed against an agent, while in the performance of his duties, would likewise be

---

[48]   *Id.* at 183-84.

within its competence.

This is a proper application of the doctrine of implied powers."[49] [Italics original]

3. As to Question (b), Judge Hackworth stated, "a different situation is presented."[50] "In giving our answer, we must look to the traditional international practice of nations with respect to private claims, and to the express treaty stipulations as regards the Organization." "As to international practice, we find at once that heretofore only States have been regarded as competent to advance such international claims." "As to the Oganization, ... there is no specific provision in the Charter, nor is there provision in any other agreement ... conferring upon the Organization authority to assume the role of a State." "I am equally convinced that there is no implied power to be drawn upon for this purpose."[51]

In the light of the above understanding, Judge Hackworth criticized the reasoning of the majority opinion based upon the doctrine of implied powers, by saying:

"It is stated in the majority opinion that the Charter does not expressly provide that the Organization should have capacity to include, in 'its claim for reparation', damage caused to the victim or to persons entitled through him, but the conclusion is reached that such power is conferred by necessary implication. This appears to be based on the assumption that, to ensure the efficient and independent performance of missions entrusted to agents of the Organization, and to afford them moral support, the exercise of this power is necessary.

The conclusion that power in the Organization to sponsor private claims is conferred by 'necessary implication' is not believed to be warranted under rules laid down by tribunals for filling lacunae in specific grants of power.

There can be no gainsaying the fact that the Organization is one of delegated and enumerated powers. It is to be presumed that such powers as the Member States desired to confer upon it are stated either in the Charter or in complementary agreements concluded by them. Powers not expressed cannot freely be implied. Implied powers flow from a grant of expressed powers, and are limited to those that are 'necessary' to the exercise of powers expressly granted. No necessity for the exercise of the power here in question has been shown to exist. There in no impelling reason, if any at all, why the Organization should become the sponsor of claims on behalf of its employees, even though limited to those arising while the employee is in line of duty. These employees are still nationals of their respective countries, and the customary methods of handling such claims are still available in full vigour. The prestige and efficiency of the Organization will be safeguarded by an exercise of its undoubted right under point [(a)]. Even here it is necessary to imply power, but, as stated above, the necessity is self-evident. *The exercise*

---

[49] *Id.* at 196-97.

[50] *Id.* at 197.

[51] *Id.* at 198.

of an additional extraordinary power in the field of private claims has not been shown to be necessary to the efficient performance of duty by either the Organization or its agents."[52] [Italics ours]

For these reasons, an analogy between functions of a State in the protection of its nationals and functions of the Organization in the protection of its employees, Judge Hackworth pointed out, "transcend, by far, anything to be found in the Charter of the United Nations, as well as any known purpose entertained by the drafters of the Charter.... Capacity of the Organization to act in the field here in question must rest upon a more solid foundation."[53]

4.   Judge Hackworth also differed from the majority opinion in the interpretation of Article 100 which provides for the international status of the staff. According to Judge Hackworth, this article (similar articles are also found in the constituent instruments of many other international organizations such as ICAO, IMF, IBRD, and ILO) is only designed to place service with the United Nations on a high plane of loyalty and fidelity and to require Member States to respect this status. Since, he pointed out, the privileges and immunities inure to the benefit of the United Nations and not to the benefit of the individuals, any claim based upon a breach of them should be in favor of the Organization and would fall to be dealt with under [(a)] above ,and not under [(b)]. The only remedy known to international law in a claim on behalf of the individual is through the government of the State of which the claimant is a national.

"International law on this subject is well settled, and any attempt to engraft upon it, save by international compact, a theory, based upon supposed analogy, that organizations, not States and hence having no nationals, may act as if they were States and had nationals, is, in my opinion, unwarranted."

If it desires to go further, he added, and to espouse claims on behalf of employees, he conventional method is open.[54]

(3) Some Comments

1.   As to the question of the international legal personality of the United Nations, no doubt was expressed in the proceedings before the ICJ, though there were different opinions on this point in the discussion in the Six (Legal) Committee of the General Assembly. The Court, as was indicated above, gave an affirmative answer unanimously.

2.   What is most important in the present study is the reasoning followed by the majority opinion regarding the capacity of the Organization to bring an international claim for the damage suffered by staff --- Question (b) --- in the service of the United Nations, in other words, the capacity of the Organization to exercise a measure of functional protection over its agents. Only in the written statement of the United States was the capacity to claim reparation with respect to

---

[52] *Id.*

[53] *Id.* at 199. For Krylov's criticism, *see id.* at 217-18.

[54] *Id.* at 203. For Badawi Pasha's criticism, *see id.* at 211.

damage suffered by its agent disputed because "[t]he basis of an internaional claim is, in theory, an injury to, or loss suffered by, the State of which the claimant is a national."[55] All the other statements both written and oral were affirmative on this point, and the majority opinion could be said to have synthesized these arguments.[56]

Opinions differ on this point. On the one hand, some present doubts,[57] like Judge Hackworth, as to whether an invocation of the implied powers for the necessity of effective performance of the task would be sufficient for the Court to admit that the Organization possesses the capacity to exercise a functional protection over its agents. On the other hand, it is pointed out that the view of Judge Hackworth loses sight of the fact that agents who perform duties for the Organization may be stateless persons or persons who possess the nationality of the defended State and that it would, in that case, deprive individual claimants of a remedy which would give

---

[55] Letter of the United States of America, I. C. J. Pleadings 22 (1949).

[56] Arguments on this point were as follows. In the first place, it was pointed out that the Organization possessed certain implied powers. For example, Mr. Feller, as counsel for the Secretary-General of the United Nations, stated as follows (Statement by Mr. Feller, I. C. J. Pleadings at 76; *See also* Exposé de M. Kaeckenbeck, I. C. J. Pleadings at 98, and Statement by Mr. Fitzmaurice, id, at 116-17):

"In essence, our position at this point is that the United Nations, in addition to its rights under the Charter or express international agreement, possesses those substantive rights of general international law which are necessary and proper for the exercise of its functions."

In the second place, the point of issue in Question (b) was analyzed by Fitzmaurice in an excellent manner (*id.* at 122-23)

"[T]he simple relationship of master and servant between the United Nations Organization and its employees would not, of itself, do more than enable the Organization to make a claim in respect of the loss caused to itself by the injury to its servant; and this relationship would not, *per se*, enable the Organization to make a claim on behalf of the injured party or his dependents. Where a State is legally entitled to make a claim on behalf of the victim himself and in respect of the damage caused to him, it is because of the existence of a special relationship between them, namely, nationality, and it would seem, on the same reasoning, that if the United Nations Organization is to be able to make a similar claim, it must equally be because of the existence of some special relationship of an analogous character between it and its servants, over and above the ordinary relationship of master and servant ....

... [Here we reach the heart of the difficulty.] We have to find a basis, other than the mere relationship of master and servant *per se*, which will enable us to conclude that the Organization has the capacity to make a direct claim on behalf of the individual concerned, not only despite the absence of any nationality link between him and the Organization, but even in spite of the presence of that very link between him and another international entity, his own national State, which is perfectly entitled to make the claim, and whose right to do so continues to exist and to be valid."

Fitzmaurice found this requisite basis in such considerations as a special relationship of international allegiance between the Organization and its servants provided for in Article 100 and essentiality to the good and effective functioning of the Organization and adequate performance of its functions. This position was adopted by the majority opinion.

Various problems could arise in the actual exercise by the Organization of this capacity of functional protection of its agents. *See in general* Hardy, 'Claims by International Organizations in Respect of Injuries to Their Agents', 37 *Brit. Y. B. Int'l L.* 516 (1961).

[57] Ogawa, 'The International Court of Justice and Law-making (1) [in Japanese]', 15 (4) *J. L. & Pol. (Hotoseiji)* 619, 635-36 (1964).

them rights commensurate with the duties they have to perform.[58]

On this question of the applicablity of the doctrine of implied powers, Wright gave a following judgment:

"*Fundamentally, the Court and the dissenting judges differed in the liberality with which they were willing to construe international instruments and international law.* The Court held that powers of the United Nations could be implied from necessity and convenience in carrying out the purposes stated in the Charter; that the agents and interests of, and injuries to, the United Nations should be liberally construed; and generally that analogy, general principles of law, the legal conscience of the peoples, and the exigencies of contemporary international life must be considered in determining rights and powers under international law. *The Court manifested the tendency, displayed by Chief Justice Marshall in dealing with the American Constitution and by the Permanent Court of International Justice in dealing with the League of Nations Covenant, to construe the rights and powers of the Organization with which the Court was connected broadly enough to permit that Organization to function and to achieve its purposes.* International laywers who recognize that, if stability is to be restored, international law and international institutions must be continually adapted to the changing conditions of the world and the changing aspirations of its people will welcome this tendency of the Court. In a world, shrinking but inadequately regulated, interdependent but imperfectly aware of its condition, it is probably safer to treat the claims of the international society liberally, even if such treatment, restricting the traditional sovereignty of states, involves some danger of stimulating revolt by the states least aware of the situation."[59]

4 Effect of Awards of Compensation Made by the United Nations Administrative Tribunal [1954]

In 1953, considering the awards made by the U. N. Administrative Tribunal, the General Assembly decided to submit two legal questions to the ICJ for an advisory opinion, the first of which is as follows: "Having regard to the Statute of the United Nations Administrative Tribunal and to any other relevant instruments and to the relevant records, has the General Assembly the right on any grounds to refuse to give effect to an award of compensation made by that Tribunal in favour of a staff member of the United Nations whose contract of service has been terminated without his assent?" The Court reached a negative conclusion by 9 votes[60] against 3. Judges

---

[58] Honig, 'The International Court of Justice 1947-50', *Zeitschrift für ausländisches öffentliches Recht und Völkerrecht* 497, 528-29 (1952).

[59] Wright, 'The Jural Personality of the United Nations', 43 *Am. J. Int'l L.* 509, 515-16 (1949).

[60] The nine judges were Sir Arnold McNair (President), Guerrero (Vice-President), Winiarski, Klaestad, Badawi, Read, Hsu Mo, Armand-Ugon and Kojevnikov.

Alvarez, Hackworth and Levi Carneiro appended their dissenting opinions. Here we will analyze the reasoning of the dissenting opinion of Judge Hackworth as well as that of the majority opinion.

(1) The Reasoning of the Majority Opinion

1.   The majority opinion consistes of two parts, the first part being a direct answer to the question of the General Assembly and the second an examination of main arguments of the States as well as its criticism against them.

2.   In the first part, the majority opinion, at the outset, clarified the meaning of the question of the General Assembly and set the question as "whether the Tribunal is established either as a juridical body, or as an advisory organ or a mere subordinate committee of the General Assembly."

It was by *the textual approach* that the majority opinion constructed its reasoning in answering this question, which occupied a major part of the opinion. The core of this reasoning is as follows:

> "[Article 1, 2 and 10] and the terminology used are evidence of the judicial nature of the Tribunal.   Such terms as 'tribunal', 'judgment', competence to 'pass judgment upon applications', are generally used with respect to judicial bodies.   The above-mentioned provisions of Articles 2 and 10 are of an essentially judicial character and conform with rules generally laid down in statutes or laws issued for courts of justice, such as, for instance, in the Statute of the International Court of Justice, Article 36, paragraph 6, Article 56, paragraph 1, Article 60, first sentence.   They provide a striking contrast to Staff Rule III.I of the United Nations ...
>
> ... The independence of its members is ensured by Article 3, paragraph 5 ...   These provisions prescribe both in the original and in the amended text that the Tribunal shall, if it finds that the application is well founded, order the rescinding of the decision contested or the specific performance of the obligation invoked.   As the power to issue such orders to the chief administrative officer of the Organization could hardly have been conferred on an advisory organ or a subordinate committee, these provisions confirm the judicial character of the Tribunal...
>
> This examination of the relevant provisions of the Statute shows that the Tribunal is established, not as an advisory organ or a mere subordinate committee of the General Assembly, but as an independent and truly judicial body pronouncing final judgments without appeal within the limited field of its functions."[61]

3.   In the second part, the majority opinion, this time, resorted to *the teleological or functional approach*, the core of which is as follows:

> "The legal power of the General Assembly to establish a tribunal competent to render judgments binding on the United Nations has been challenged.   Accordingly, it is necessary to consider whether the General Assembly has been given this power by the Charter.   There

---

[61] Advisory Opinion on Effect of Awards of Compensation Made by the United Nations Administrative Tribunal, [1954] I. C. J. 51-53.

is no express provision for the establishment of judicial bodies or organs and no indication to the contrary. However, in its Opinion --- *Reparation for Injuries suffered in the Service of the United Nations,* Advisory Opinion: I. C. J. Reports 1949, p. 182 --- the Court said:

'Under international law, the Organization must be deemed to have those powers which, though not expressly provided in the Charter, are conferred upon it by necessary implication as being essential to the performance of its duties.'

The Court must therefore begin by enquiring whether the provisions of the Charter concerning the relations between the staff members and the Organization imply for the Organization the power to establish a judicial tribunal to adjudicate upon disputes arising out of the contracts of sevice.

[Reference was made to some provisions of Chapter XV, particularly Article 101.]

It would, in the opinion of the Court, hardly be consistent with the expressed aim of the Charter to promote freedom and justice for individuals and with the constant preoccupation of the United Nations Organization to promote this aim that it should afford no judicial or arbitral remedy to its own staff for the settlement of any disputes which may arise between it and them.

In these circumstances, the Court finds that the power to establish a tribunal, to do justice as between the Organization and the staff members, was essential to ensure the efficient working of the secretariat, and to give effect to the paramount consideration of securing the highest standards of efficiency, competence and integrity. Capacity to do this arises by necessary intendment out of the Charter."[62] [Italics ours]

(2) The Reasoning of the Dissenting Opinion of Judge Hackworth

1.   Judge Hackworth disagreed with the majority opinion upon all such points as legal nature of the Administrative Tribunal, who the parties to a case coming before the Administrative Tribunal are, and budgetary authority of the General Assembly. Here we, however, focus upon the question of the legal nature of the Administrative Tribunal --- whether to find it as a subsidiary organ of the General Assembly or as a judicial tribunal --- and the concept of implied powers which lied behind the question.

2.   Judge Hackworth also adopted the textual approach. The statement "in accordance with the present Charter" in Article 7, paragraph 2 of the Charter which states "[s]uch subsidiary organs as may be found necessary may be established in accordance with the present Charter" is given definite expression Article 22 which provides: "The General Assembly may establish such subsidiary organs as it deems necessary for the performance of its functions." In the light of these provisions, he pointed out as follows:

"It must be concluded, therefore, that when the General Assembly approved the Statute

---

[62] *Id.* at 56-58.

creating the Administrative Tribunal it did so in the exercise of its authority under Article 22. Nowhere else in the Charter is any such authorization to be found. And nowhere else in the Charter can there be found any authorization, express or implied, for the establishment by the General Assembly of any other kind of organ be it judicial, *quasi* judicial or non-judicial....

... There is, therefore, no point to saying that the Statute of the Tribunal is based on Article 101 of the Charter, as has been argued, and as so based is relieved of the consequences of Article 22. That argument must be dismissed as without legal justification.

The reasonable deduction, then, is that the Administrative Tribunal is a subsidiary organ of the General Assembly, created by an act of the Assembly, pursuant to the authorization in Article 22."[63]

Judge Hackworth elaborated on the meaning of the expression "such subsidiary organs as it deems necessary for the performance of its functions" as follows. A "subsidiary organ" means an auxiliary or inferior organ and it cannot bind the principal organ. The principal organ must have the authority to accept, modify, or reject the acts or recommendations of the subordinate organs, and it cannot reassign any of its functions to a subsidiary organ in such a manner as to relinquish its control over the subject-matter.

3. Judge Hackworth also criticized the point that the majority opinion, in admitting the power of the General Assembly to establish the Administrative Tribunal, relied upon certain implied powers under the Charter, and in particular the power to implement Article 101, paragraph 3, concerning the maintenance of a high standard of efficiency, etc.

"*The doctrine of implied powers is designed to implement, within reasonable limitations, and not to supplant or vary, expressed powers.* The General Assembly was given express authority by Article 22 of the Charter to establish such subsidiary organs as might be necessary for the performance of its function, whether those functions should relate to Article 101 or to any other article in the Charter. *Under this authorization the Assembly may establish any tribunal needed for the implementation of its functions. It is not, therefore, permissible, in the face of this express power, to invoke the doctrine of implied powers to establish a tribunal of a supposedly different kind, nor is there warrant for concluding that such a thing has resulted.*"[64] [Italics ours]

(3) Some Comments

1. While the majority opinion was based upon the analysis of the Statute of the Administrative Tribunal, Judge Hackworth's was based upon that of the express provisions of the Charter and claimed that the authority of the General Assembly to establish organs was limited to the establishment of subsidiary organs and that, therefore, the Administrative Tribunal was a

---

[63] *Id.* at 78-79.

[64] *Id.* at 80-81.

subsidiary, inferior organ whose decision could not bind the General Assembly which had established it.

The majority opinion specifically criticized this view as follows:

"This view assumes that, in adopting the Statute of the Administrative Tribunal, the General Assembly was establishing an organ which it deemed necessary for the performance of its own functions. But the Court cannot accept this basic assumption. *The Charter does not confer judicial functions on the General Assembly and the relations between staff and Organization come within the scope of Chapter XV.... By establishing the Administrative Tribunal, the General Assembly was not delegating the performance of its own functions: it was exercising a power which it had under the Charter to regulate staff relations.* In regard to the Secretariat, the General Assembly is given by the Charter a power to make regulations, but not a power to adjudicate upon, or otherwise deal with, particular instances."[65] [Italics ours]

Behind the above confrontation over the legal nature of the Administrative Tribunal exists a difference of opinion regarding the authority of the General Assembly to establish such a tribunal. In the light of the decisive role played by the different concepts of implied powers in this difference of opinion, we could consider that *the conclusion of this opinion was dependent upon the different concepts of implied powers, that is, either to admit implied powers, like Judge Hackworth, only within the strict framework of textual treaty interpretation, or to acknowledge the doctrine of implied powers, like the majority opinion, as a legal principle in the function framework based upon the constituent instrument.*

It is submitted that the majority opinion followed the same reasoning and invoked the concept of implied powers in the same way as in the *Reparation* case,[66] and that the contrast and confrontation with the reasoning followed by, and the limited concept of implied powers invoked by, Judge Hackworth was once again made clear.

2.   It will be useful to look at the responses given by the majority opinion to some of the arguments made by States based upon the limited concept of implied powers.

Firstly, it was contended that there was no need to establish a tribunal with authority to make decisions binding on the General Assembly itself, and that an implied power can only be exercised to the extent that the particular measure under consideration could be regarded as absolutely essential.

The majority opinion responded simply as follows:

"There can be no doubt that the General Assembly in the exercise of its power could have set up a tribunal without giving finality to its judgments. In fact, however, it decided, after long deliberation, to invest the Tribunal with power to render judgments which would be

---

[65] *Id.* at 61.

[66] de Visscher, *supra* note 16, at 145.

'final and without appeal', and which would be binding on the United Nations. The precise nature and scope of the measures by which the power of creating a tribunal was to be exercised, was a matter for determination by the General Assembly alone."[67]

Here in this portion, the majority opinion neither supports nor rejects the expression "absolutely",[68] but rather entrusts the judgment to the General Assembly. This is certainly a problem. Elihu Lauterpacht, in connection with the restraint of judicial review, reached a following conclusion:

"[T]he restraint demonstrated by the Court appears to accord with the idea that *the Organization is the best judge of what circumstances require* and to this extent, therefore, the Court's restraint is directed towards *the more effective fulfilment of the objectives of the Organization.*"[69] [Italics ours]

3.   Secondly, it was also contended that an implied power to impose legal limitations upon the General Assembly's express Charter powers is not legally admissible. It was argued that the establishment of a tribunal competent to make an award of compensation to which the General Assembly was bound to give effect would divest the General Assembly of the power conferred by paragraph 1 of Article 17 of the Charter and would, therefore, contravene the provisions relating to the budgetary power.

Although this argument was supported by the dissenting judges,[70] the majority opinion replied as follows:

"But the function of approving the budget does not mean that the General Assembly has an absolute power to approve or disapprove the expenditure proposed to it; for some part of that expenditure arises out of obligations already incurred by the Organization, and to this extent the General Assembly has no alternative but to honour these engagements."[71]

4.   Thirdly, it was also contended that the implied power of the General Assembly to establish a tribunal could not be carried so far as to enable the tribunal to intervene in matters falling within the province of the Secretary-General. The majority opinion also rejected this argument by stating as follows:

"The General Assembly could at all times limit or control the powers of the Secretary-General in staff matters, by virtue of the provisions of Article 101. Acting under powers confered by the Charter, the General Assembly authorized the intervention of the Tribunal

---

[67] *Effect of Awards* case, *supra* note 61, at 58.

[68] When we recall that the confrontation between the majority opinion and Judge Hackworth in the *Reparation* case was based upon the different content (more flexible one or rather rigid one) given to the doctrine of implied powers, it is clear that the majority opinion did not consider that the degree of "necessity" must be "absolutely necessary". On this point, *see also* H. Lauterpacht, *supra* note 15, at 276-77.

[69] E. Lauterpacht, 'The Development of the Law of International Organization by the Decisions of International Tribunals', 152 *Recueil des cours* 379, 430 (1976).

[70] *Effect of Awards* case, *supra* note 61, at 75 (Alvarez), 85 (Hackworth) and 96 (Levi Carneiro).

[71] *Id.* at 59.

to the extent that such interventiion might result from the exercise of jurisdiction conferred upon the Tribunal by its Statute."[72]

In conclusion, we could understand that *the majority opinion did not adopt the view that an implied power cannot impose legal limitations upon express powers.*[73]

5. Certain Expenses of the United Nations (Article 17, Paragraph 2, of the Charter) [1962][74]

In 1961, the General Assembly decided to request that the ICJ give an advisory opinion on the following question: Do the expenditures authorized in General Assembly resolutions relating to the United Nations operations in the Congo (ONUC) and the operations of the United Nations Emergency Force (UNEF) constitute 'expenses of the Organization' within the meaning of Article 17, paragraph 2, of the Charter of the United Nations? The Court reached an affirmative conclusion by 9 votes[75] to 5.[76] Judge Spiropoulos made a declaration. Judges Sir Percy Spender, Sir Gerald Fitzmaurice and Morelli appended statements of their Separate Opinions. President Winiarski and Judges Basdevant, Moreno Quintana, Koretsky and Bustamante y Rivero appended statements of their Dissenting Opinions.

(1) The Reasoning of the Majority Opinion

1. The majority opinion could be, for convenience, divided into three parts: (1) rejection of the objection to the power of the Court to give an advisory opinion, and another preliminary point relating to the French amendment; (2) meaning of "expenses of the Organization" in Article 17, paragraph 2, of the Charter; (3) whether the expenditures of ONUC and UNEF constitute

---

[72] *Id.* at 60.

[73] H. Lauterpacht, *supra* note 15, at 277.

[74] For the relevant bibliography on the present advisory opinion, *see, e.g.*, Amerasinghe, 'The United Nations Expenses Case --- A Contribution to the Law of International Organization', 4 *Indian J. Int'l L.* 177 (1964); Gross, 'Expenses of the United Nations for Peace-Keeping Operations: The Advisory Opinion of the International Court of Justice', 17 *Int'l Organization* 1 (1963); Hogg, 'Peace-Keeping Costs and Charter Obligations --- Implications of the International Court of Justice Decision on Certain Expenses of the United Nations', 62 *Colum. L. Rev.* 1230 (1962); Jackson, 'The Legal Framework of United Nations Financing: Peacekeeping and Penury', 51 *California L. Rev.* 79 (1963); Meron, 'Budget Approval by the General Assembly of the United Nations: Duty or Discretion ?', 42 *Brit. Y. B. Int'l L.* 91 (1967); Pharand, 'Analysis of the Opinion of the International Court of Justice on Certain Expenses of the United Nations', 1 *Canadian Y. B. Int'l L.* 272 (1963); Rama Rao, 'The Expenses Judgment of the International Court of Justice --- A Critique', 12 *Indian Y. B. Int'l Aff.* 134 (1963); Russell, 'United Nations Financing and "The Law of the Charter"', 5 *Colum. J. Transnational L.* 68 (1966); Simmonds, 'The UN Assessments Advisory Opinion', 13 *Int'l & Comp. L. Q.* 854 (1964); Thierry, 'Avis consultatif de la Cour International de Justice de 20 juillet 1962, Certaines dépenses des Nations Unies (Article 17 paragraphe 2 de la Charte)', 8 *A. F. D. I.* 247 (1962).

[75] The nine judges were Alfaro (Vice-President), Badawi, Wellington Koo, Spiropoulos, Sir Percy Spender, Sir Gerald Fitzmaurice, Tanaka, Jessup and Morelli.

[76] The five judges were Winiarski (President), Basdevant, Moreno Quintana, Koretsky and Bustamante y Rivero.

"expenses of the Organization". In the context of our study, we will deal only with (2) and (3).

2.   In dealing with the meaning of "expenses of the Organization" of Article 17, paragraph 2, the majority opinion set *its basic attitude to the interpretation of the United Nations Charter* as follows:

"Turning to the question which has been posed, the Court observes that it involves an interpretation of Article 17, paragraph 2, of the Charter. On the previous occasions when the Court has had to interpret the Charter of the United Nations, *it has followed the principles and rules applicable in general to the interpretation of treaties*, since it has recognized that *the Charter is a multilateral treaty, albeit a treaty having certain special characteristics*. In interpreting Article 4 of the Charter, the Court was led to consider 'the structure of the Charter' and 'the relations established by it between the General Assembly and the Security Council'; a comparable problem confronts the Court in the instant matter. The Court sustained its interpretation of Article 4 by considering the manner in which the organs concerned 'have consistently interpreted the text' in their practice (*Competence of the General Assembly for the Admission of a State to the United Nations, I.C.J. Reports 1950, pp. 8-9).*"[77] [Italics ours]

3.   That part of the majority opinion which considered the meaning of "expenses of the Organization" of Article 17, paragraph 2, of the Charter could be divided into the following three portions:[78] (1) definition of the scope of this question; (2) interpretation of "expenses of the Organization" in the context of the text of Article 17; (3) interpretation of "expenses of the Organization" in the context of the general structure and scheme of the Charter. Suffice it to deal with (2) and (3) here.

The majority opinion, after deciding the scope of the question but before proceeding to the consideration of the meaning of "expenses of the Organization" --- (2) and (3) mentioned above --- set *its approach in the reasoning* as follows:

"The text of Article 17, paragraph 2, refers to 'the expenses of the Organization" without any further explicit definition of such expenses. It would be possible to begin with a general proposition to the effect that the 'expenses' of any organization are the amounts paid out to defray the costs of carrying out *its purposes*, in this case, the political, economic, social, humanitarian and other purposes of the United Nations. The next step would be to examine, as the Court will, whether the resolutions authorizing the operations here in question were *intended to carry out the purposes of the United Nations* and whether the expenditures were incurred in furthering these operations....

It is perhaps the simple identification of 'expenses' with the items included in a budget, which has led certain arguments to link the interpretation of the word 'expenses' in

---

[77] Advisory Opinion on Certain Expenses of the United Nations (Article 17, Paragraph 2, of the Charter), [1962] I. C. J. 151, 157.

[78] Pharand, *supra* note 73, at 273.

paragraph 2 of the Article 17, with the word 'budget' in paragraph 1 of that Article; in both cases, it is contended, the qualifying adjective 'regular' or 'administrative' should be understood to be implied. Since no such qualification is expressed in the text of the Charter, it could be read in, only if such qualification must necessarily be implied from the provisions of the Charter considered as a whole, or from some particular provision thereof which makes it unavoidable to do so in order to give effect to the Charter."[79]

4.	The majority opinion, based upon the above statement, proceeded to *the interpretation of "expenses of the Organization" in the context of the text of Article 17* --- (2) mentioned above ---. Here it distinguished paragraphs 1 and 2. In considering *paragraph 1 of Article 17*, the majority opinion rejected the argument that "regular expenses" should be understood to mean "administrative expenses", firstly in the light of the drafters' intention of the Charter and, secondly in the light of the practice the Organization. With regard to *the drafters' intention*, it pointed out as follows:

"In the first place, concerning the word 'budget' in paragraph 1 of Article 17, it is clear that the existence of the distinction between 'administrative budgets' and 'operational budgets' was not absent from the minds of the drafters of the Charter, nor from the consciousness of the Organization even in the early days of its history. In drafting Article 17 ... [i]f it had been intended that pragraph 1 should be limited to the administrative budget of the United Nations organization itself, the word 'administrative' would have been inserted in paragraph 1 as it was in paragraph 3. Moreover, had it been contemplated that the Organization would also have had another budget, different from the one which was to be approved by the General Assembly, the Charter would have included some reference to such other budget and to the organ which was to approve it."[80]

With regard to *the practice of the Organization*, which is an important point of issue in the present context of our study, the majority opinion elaborated as follows:

"Similarly, at its first session, the General Assembly in drawing up and approving the Constitution of the International Refugee Organization, provided that the budget of that Organization was to be divided under the headings 'administrative', 'operational' and 'large-scale resettlement'; but no such distinctions were introduced into *the Financial Regulations of the United Nations which were adopted by unanimous vote in 1950, and which, in this respect, remain unchanged.* These regulations speak only of 'the budget' and do not provide any distinction between 'administrative' and 'operational'.

In subsequent sessions of the General Assembly, including the sixteenth, there have been numerous references to the idea of distinguishing an 'operational' budget.... But these discussions have not resulted in the adoption of two separate budgets based upon such a distinction.

---

[79] *Certain Expenses* case, *supra* note 77, at 158-59.

[80] *Id.* at 159.

Actually, *the practice of the Organization is entirely consistent with the plain meaning of the text.* The budget of the Organization has from the outset included items which would not fall within any of the definitions of 'administrative budget' which have been advanced in this connection. Thus, for example, prior to the establishment of, and now in addition to, the 'Expanded Programme of Technical Assistance' and the 'Special Fund', both of which are nourished by voluntary contributions, the annual budget of the Organization contains provision for funds for technical assistance.... Although during the Fifth Committee discussions there was a suggestion that all technical assistance costs should be excluded from the regular budget, the items under these heads were all adopted on second reading in the Fifth Committee *without a dissenting vote.* The 'operational' nature of such activities so budgeted is indicated by the explanations in the budget estimates ....

It is *a consistent practice of the General Assembly* to include in the annual budget resolutions, provision for expenses relating to the maintenance of international peace and security. Annually, since 1947, the General Assembly has made anticipatory provision for 'unforeseen and extraordinary expenses' arising in relation to the 'maintenance of peace and security'.... These annual resolutions on unforeseen and extraordinary expenses were *adopted without a dissenting vote in every year from 1947 through 1959,* except for 1952, 1953 and 1954, when the adverse votes are attributable to the fact that the resolution included the specification of a controversial item --- United Nations Korean war decorations.

It is notable that the 1961 Report of the Working Group of Fifteen on the Examination of the Administrative and Budgetary Procedures of the United Nations, while revealing wide differences of opinion on a variety of propositions, records that the following statement was *adopted without opposition*:

'22. Investigations and observation operations undertaken by the Organization to prevent possible aggression should be financed as part of the regular budget of the united Nations.'"[81] [Italics ours]

In connection with *paragraph 2 of Article 17*, the majority opinion reached the same conclusion.

5.   The majority opinion proceeded from the text of Article 17 to *its place in the general structure and scheme of the Charter* --- (3) mentioned above. Here it considered and rejected the argument that those expenses resulting from operations for the maintenance of international peace and security were not "expenses of the Organization" within the meaning of Article 17, paragraph 2, of the Charter but were dealt with exclusively by the Security Council through agreements negotiated in accordance with Article 43 of the Charter. The legal grounds of the majority opinion on this point are the following three:

Firstly, the responsibility conferred upon the Security Council for the maintenance of international peace and security is "primary" --- Article 24 --- not exclusive, except "coercive or

---

[81] *Id.* at 159-61.

enforcement action" under Chapter VII.

Secondly, the General Assembly may, based upon Articles 14, 35 and others, and with the consent of the States concerned, recommend and organize those measures which are short of coercive or enforcement actions --- peace-keeping operations. The "action" in Article 11, paragraph 2 is a coercive action.[82]

Thirdly, the argument that Article 43 constitutes a particular rule, a *lex specialis*, which derogates from the general rule in Article 17 --- the allocation of costs of such enforcement actions as might be taken by direction of the Security Council must be made through agreements concluded under Article 43 --- cannot be applied to UNEF and ONUC which were not enforcement actions within the compass of Chapter VII of the Charter.[83]

6.　The majority opinion, after thus having considered the meaning of "expenses of the Organization" in the context of the text of Article 17 on the one hand, and in the context of the general structure and scheme of the Charter on the other, next proceeded to the examination of the expenditures enumerated in the request: *whether the expenditures of UNEF and ONUC constitute "expenses of the Organization"*. That part of the reasoning of the majority opinion relating to this examination consists of three portions: (1) general consideration; (2) specific examination of the expenditures of UNEF; and (3) specific examination of the expenditures of ONUC.

7.　In *the general consideration*, the majority opinion set its approach in the light of *their relevancy to the objectives of the United Nations*.

"In determining whether the actual expenditures authorized constitute 'expenses of the Organization whithin the meaning of Article 17, paragraph 2, of the Charter', the Court agrees that *such expenditures must be tested by their relationship to the purposes of the United Nations in the sense that if an expenditure were made for a purpose which is not one of the purposes of the United Nations, it could not be considered an 'expense of the Organization".*[84] [Italics ours]

Consequently, the majority opinion developed its reasoning in the light of the conformity with the objectives of the United Nations. It, however, contained a controversial problem of "presumption".

---

[82] The majority opinion supplemented this point by adding as follows (*id.* at 165):

"*The practice of the Organization* throughout its history bears out the foregoing elucidation of the term 'action' in the last sentence of Article 11, paragraph 2." [Italics ours]

[83] The grounds of this argument were, firstly that the operations known as UNEF and ONUC were not *enforcement* actions within the compass of Chapter VII of the Charter; secondly, that it would be impossible to envisage all potential expenses of actual enforcement actions in such agreements concluded perhaps long in advance; and thirdly, that an argument which insists that all measures taken for the maintenance of international peace and security must be financed through agreements concluded under Article 43, would exclude the possibility that the Security Council might act under some other Article of the Charter, but Articles of Chapter VII refers to the power of the Security Council to police the situation.

[84] *Certain Expenses* case, *supra* note 77, at 167.

"[W]hen the Organization takes action which warrants the assertion that it was appropriate for the fulfilment of one of the stated purposes of the United Nations, the presumption is that such action is not *ultra vires* the Organization....

In the legal systems of States, there is often some procedure for determining the validity of even a legislative or governmental act, but no analogous procedure is to be found in the structure of the United Nations. Proposals made during the drafting of the Charter to place the ultimate authority to interpret the Charter in the International Court of Justice were not accepted; the opinion which the Court is in course of rendering is an *advisory* opinion. As anticipated in 1945, therefore, each organ must, in the first place at least, determine its own jurisdiction. If the Security Council, for example, adopts a resolution purportedly for the maintenance of international peace and security and if, in accordance with a mandate or authorization in such resolution, the Secretary-General incurs financial obligations, these amounts must be presumed to constitute 'expenses of the Organization'."[85] [Italics original]

8.   Although the majority opinion pointed out that the general reasoning just developed and applied to the relevant resolutions "might suffice as a basis for the opinion of the Court", it found it appropriate to take into consideration other arguments advanced and proceeded to the examination of the expenditures of UNEF and ONUC.

With regard to *the expenditures of UNEF*, the majority opinion, firstly in order to analyze the functions of UNEF, considered the relevant resolutions *adopted by the General Assembly without a dissenting vote* and concluded as follows: the Force was not used for purposes of enforcement and the operations were undertaken to fulfil a prime purpose of the United Nations; consequently, the Secretary-General properly exercised the authority given him to incur financial obligations of the Organization and expenses resulting from such oblgations must be considered "expenses of the Organization within the meaning of Article 17, paragraph 2".

Secondly, the majority opinion, in order to examine the expenditures of UNEF, considered the relevant resolutions *adopted by the requisite two-thirds majority* and concluded as follows: "The Court concludes that, from year to year, the expenses of UNEF have been *treated by the General Assembly* as expenses of the Organization within the meaning of Article 17, paragraph 2, of the Charter."[Italics ours]

9.   With regard to *the expenditures of ONUC*, the majority opinion, firstly in order to analyze the functions of ONUC, considered the relevant resolutions *adopted by theGeneral Assembly without a dissenting vote* and concluded as follows: the operations of ONUC did not include a use of armed force against a State which the Security Council, under Article 39, determined to have committed an act of aggression or to have breached the peace; financial obligations which, in accordance with the clear and reiterated authority of both the Security Council and the General

---

[85] *Id.* at 168.

Assembly, the Secretary-General incurred on behalf of the United Nations, constitute obligations of the Organization.

Secondly, the majority opinion, in order to examine the expenditures of ONUC, considered the relevant resolutions and concluded that the General Assembly decided that the expenses concerned were "expenses of the Organization" to be apportioned in accordance with the power granted to the General Assembly by Article 17, paragraph 2, of the Charter.

(2) The Reasoning of the Separate Opinion of Judge Sir Percy Spender

1.   The separate opinion of Judge Spender consists of, after a brief introduction, three parts: (1) interpretation of Article 17; (2) general observations on the interpretation of the Charter; (3) practice within the United Nations --- its effect on or value as a criterion of interpretation. Here we will deal with (2), leaving (3) to be dealt with in Chapter V of our study.

2.   "General Observations on the Interpretation of the Charter" dealt squarely with the subject of our study. The reasoning of this part consists of three portions: (a) interpretation in general; (b) interpretation of constituent instruments of international organizations; and (c) interpretation of the Charter of the United Nations.

With regard to *interpretation in general*, Judge Spender noted the existence of the cardinal rule of interpretation that words are to be read, if they may so be read, in their ordinary and natural sense. He also noted, however, that this injunction is sometimes a counsel of perfection: the ordinary and natural sense of words may at times be a matter of considerable difficulty to determine; what is their ordinary and natural sense to one may not be so to another; moreover, the intention of the parties at the time when they entered into an engagement will not always --- depending upon the nature and subject-matter of the engagement --- have the same importance. In this connection, the following point is important:

> "In particular in the case of a multilateral treaty such as the Charter the intention of its original Members, except such as may be gathered from its terms alone, is beset with evident difficulties. Moreover, since from its inception it was contemplated that other States would be admitted to membership so that the Organization would, in the end, comprise 'all other peace-loving States which accept the obligations contained in the Charter' (Article 4), *the intention of the framers of the Charter appears less important than intention in many other treaties where the parties are fixed and constant and where the nature and subject-matter of the treaty is different. It is hardly the intention of those States which originally framed the Charter which is important except as that intention reverals itself in the text.* What is important is *what the Charter itself provides*; what --- to use the words of Article 4 --- is 'contained in ... the Charter'."[86] [Italics ours]

Thus he concluded that "the meaning of words, however described, depends upon subject-matter and the context in which they are used".

---

[86] *Id.* at 184-85.

3.   Judge Spender, however, pointed out that, in *the interpretation of constituent instruments of international organizations*, "there are particular considerations to which regard should ... be had". Since this portion contains quite important suggestions, it should be cited here.

"In the interpretation of a multilateral treaty such as the Charter which establishes a permanent international mechanism or organization to accomplish certain stated purposes there are *particular considerations* to which regard should, I think, be had.

Its provisions were of necessity expressed in broad and general terms. It attempts to provide against the unknown, the unforeseen and, indeed, the unforeseeable. Its text reverals that *it was intended --- subject to such amendments as might from time to time be made to it --- to endure, at least it was hoped it would endure, for all time. It was intended to apply to varying conditions in a changing and evolving world community and to a multiplicity of unpredictable situations and events. Its provisions were intended to adjust themselves to the ever changing pattern of international existence.* It established international machinery to accomplish its stated purposes.

It may with confidence be asserted that *its particular provisions should receive a broad and liberal interpretation* unless the context of any particulr provision requires, or there is to be found elsewhere in the Charter, something to compel a narrower and restricted interpretation.

The stated purposes of the Charter should be the prime consideration in interpreting its text.

Despite current tendencies to the contrary the first task of the Court is to look, not at the *travaux préparatoires* or the practice which hitherto has been followed within the Organization, but at the terms of the Charter itself."[87] [Italics ours]

Judge Spender, in this way, excluded the *travaux préparatoires* and the practice of the Organization on the one hand, and asserted *a teleological interpretation based upon general terms of the provisions* on the other.

4.   Judge Spender then applied the above consideration relating to the constituent instruments to *the Charter of the United Nations*. The relevant portion should also be cited:

"The purpose pervading the whole of the Charter and dominating it is that of maintaining international peace and security and to that end the taking of effective collective measures for the prevention and removal of threats to the peace.

Interpretation of the Charter should be directed to giving effect to that purpose, not to frustrate it. If two interpretations are possible in relation to any particular provision of it, that which is favourable to the accomplishment of purpose and not restrictive of it must be preferred.

---

[87] *Id.* at 185.

A general rule is that words used in a treaty should be read as having the meaning they bore therein when it came into existence. *But this meaning must be consistent with the purposes sought to be achieved.* Where, as in the case of the Charter, the purposes are directed to saving succeeding generations in an indefinite future from the scourge of war, to advancing the welfare and dignity of man, and establishing and maintaining peace under international justice for all time, *the general rule above stated does not mean that the words in the Charter can only comprehend such situations and contingencies and manifestations of subject-matter as were within the minds of the framers of the Charter* (cf. *Employment of women during the Night*, P.C.I.J., Series A/B, No. 50, p. 377).

The wisest of them could never have anticipated the tremendous changes which politically, militarily, and otherwise have occurred in the comparatively few years which have elapsed since 1945.... All that the framers of the Charter reasonably could do was to set forth the purposes the organization set up should seek to achieve, establish the organs to accomplish these purposes and confer upon these organs powers in general terms. Yet *these general terms, unfettered by man's incapacity to foretell the future, may be sufficient to meet the thrusts of a changing world.*

The nature of the authority granted by the Charter to each of its organs does not change with time. *The ambit or scope of the authority conferred may nonetheless comprehend ever changing circumstances and conditions and embrace, as history enfolds itself, new problems and situations which were not and could not have been envisaged when the Charter came into being.* The Charter must *accordingly* be interpreted, whilst in no way deforming or dislocating its language, so that *the authority conferred upon the Organization and its various organs may attach itself to new and unanticipated situations and events.*"[88] [Italics ours]

5. "Practice within the United Nations --- Its effect on or value as a criterion of interpretation" is the best part of the dissenting opinion of Judge Spender. Because we think that this point is closely related to the core of the problem in our study, we will analyze this part of his opinion later by examining this point in a theoretical perspective. Here we just note that Judge Spender criticized the majority opinion relying on the practice within the United Nations and stated as follows:

"I find difficulty in accepting the proposition that a practice pursued by an *organ* of the United Nations may be equated with the subsequent conduct of *parties* to a bilateral agreement and thus afford evidence of intention of the parties to the Charter (who have constantly been added to since it came into force) and in that way or otherwise provide a criterion of interpretation. Nor can I agree with a view sometimes advanced that a common practice pursued by an organ of the United Nations, though *ultra vires* and in point of fact

---

[88] *Id.* at 186-87.

having the result of amending the Charter, may nonetheless be effective as a criterion of interpretation."[89] [Emphasis original]

(3) The Reasoning of the Dissenting Opinion of Judge Winiarski

1. The dissenting opinion of Jugde Winiarski referred, in addition to a brief introduction, to such points as the necessity of examining the conformity of the resolutions concerned with the Charter, who has the power to make an authoritative interpretation of the Charter, methods of interpretation, the problem of nullity and the difference between binding decisions and recommendations. Here we will look at his observations upon methods of interpretation.

2. Judge Winiarski criticized the teleologinal reasoning followed by the majority opinion, and this is considered to be based upon his different understanding of the legal nature of the Charter as a multilateral treaty.

"The [Majority] Opinion attaches great importance to the purposes of the Organization as set forth in Article 1 of the Charter. Indeed, it has been asserted that these purposes and in particular the maintenance of international peace and security may provide a legal justification for certain decisions, even if these are not in conformity with the Charter, and that in any event a consideration of the purposes must furnish guidance as to the interpretation of the Charter. In the case before the Court, however, this argument certainly has not the importance which there is a temptation to attribute to it; on the contrary, care must be taken not to draw conclusions too readily from it.

The Charter has set forth the purposes of the United Nations in very wide, and for that reason *too indefinite, terms*. But ... it does not follow, far from it, that the Organization is entitled to seek to achieve those purposes by no matter what means. The fact that an organ of the United Nations is seeking to achieve one of those purposes does not suffice to render its action lawful. *The Charter, a multilateral treaty which was the result of prolonged and laborious negotiations, carefully created organs and determined their competence and means of action.*

The intention of those who drafted it was clearly to abandon the possibility of useful action rather than to sacrifice the balance of carefully established fields of competence, as can be seen, for example, in the case of the voting in the Security Council. *It is only by such procedures, which were clearly defined, that the United Nations can seek to achieve its purposes.* It may be that *the United Nations is sometimes not in a position to undertake action which would be useful for the maintenance of international peace and security or for one or another of the purposes indicated in Article 1 of the Charter, but that is the way in which the Organization was conceived and brought into being.*

The same reasoning applies to the rule of construction known as the rule of

---

[89] *Id.* at 189-90.

effectiveness (*ut res magis valeat quam pereat*) and, perhaps less strictly, to the doctrine of implied powers."[90] [Italics ours]

3.   Judge Winiarski was also negative in relying upon the practice of the Organization. "Reliance has been placed upon practice as providing justification for an affirmative answer to the question submitted to the Court. The technical budgetary practice of the Organization has no bearing upon the question, which is a question of law. From strictly legal point of view, it is difficult to find here anything that would justify a firm conclusion... In the present case the controversy arose practically from the beginning in 1956 ....

It is therefore difficult to assert, in the case before the Court, either that practice can furnish a canon of construction warranting an affirmative answer to the question addressed to the Court, or that it may have contributed to the establishment of a legal rule particular to the Organization, created *praeter legem*, and, still less, that it can have done so *contra legem*."[91] [Italics original]

(4) Some Comments

1.   This advisory opinion has widely been regarded as probably both the most difficult and the most significant of its series of opinions on the interpretation and implementation of the Charter.[92] In fact, the opinion dealt with, in addition to the interpretation of "expenses of the Organization" in Article 17 (2) of the Charter, many problems including the competence of the Court to give advisory opinions, interpretation of the Question, powers of the Security Council and the General Assembly, the problem of *ultra vires* and methods of interpretation.[93] Here we will make some observations about methods of interpretation in accordance with the context of our study.

2.   It was Thierry who made an excellent analysis of this opinion in the light of the method of interpretation. Suffice it to cite the following part of his analysis as a general observation upon the method of interpretation:

"*La Charte en effet est un instrument juridique suffisamment vaste et complexe pour se prêter, notamment en ce qui concerne les développements juridiques qui n'ont pu être envisagés lors de son établissement, à des interprétations diverses voire opposées...*

On peut concevoir *une interprétation conservatrice de la Charte*, fondée sur une exégèse inspirée par les travaux préparatoires et la recherche de la volonté des rédacteurs de ce traité multilatéral. On peut au contraire se montrer favorable à *une interprétation plus ≪dynamique≫* qui se prévaut de ≪l'esprit du traité des exigences supérieures de l'Organisation≫.

En fait le choix entre plusieurs interprétations possibles dépend de deux facteurs: le

---

[90] *Id.* at 230.

[91] *Id.* at 230-32.

[92] Simmonds, *supra* note 74, at 854.

[93] *See* on this point, for example, Amerasinghe, *supra* note 74.

premier est en quelque sorte subjectif: c'est *la tendance de l'interprète*. À ce point de vue il y a lieu de constater que la Cour par sa composition n'est pas nécessairement animée d'un esprit hostile à l'Assemblée générale. Le second est objectif: c'est *la méthode d'interprétation*. L'appréciation qui est portée sur des faits ou des situations juridiques nouvelles dépend directement des critères choisis en vue de cette appréciation.... Il y a lieu de noter à ce sujet l'importance que la Cour a attachée aux raisonnements fondés sur *la considération des buts de l'Organisation*, sur *la pratique juridique suivie par celle-ci*, et sur *les exigences de son fonctionnement*.

Les opinions émises par la Cour dans son Avis découlent en premier lieu de l'importance attachée par la Haute juridiction aux considérations tirées des *buts des Nations Unies* et de la concordance des actes accomplis par les organes de l'Organisation avec ceux-ci. La Cour s'est attachée à ce critère à plusieurs reprises dans le cours de son Avis aussi bien au sujet des dépenses de la F.U.N.U. et de l'O.N.U.C. qui ≪doivent être appréciées d'après leur rapport avec les buts des Nations Unies≫ qu'en ce qui concerne les opérations elles-mêmes.

Il n'est pas excessif d'affirmer qu'il résulte de l'Avis de la Cour que celle-ci a accordé une priorité aux raisonnements fondés sur les buts de l'institution pour n'admettre qu'en seconde ligne ceux qui ont trait aux compétences des organes....

En second lieu, il convient de constater l'importance juridique que la Cour a attribuée à *la pratique des Nations Unies*. Cell-ci est évoquée un grand nombre de fois dans l'Avis du 20 juillet. La Cour s'est par exemple longuement étendue sur la pratique budgétaire de l'Organisation pour montrer que le budget des Nations Unies a comporté des dépenses opérationnelles aussi bien que des dépenses administratives. Les Résolutions de l'Assemblée autorisant les dépenses de la F.U.N.U. et de l'O.N.U.C. ont été analysées notamment à la lummière des déclarations du Secrétaire général, avec le souci de faire apparaître pour chacune d'entre elles quelle a été l'intention de l'Assemblée, son opinion quant à la nature juridique de ces dépenses....

Dans chacun de ces cas la Cour n'a pas cité la pratique des organes seulement au point de vue historique, elle a attaché une valeur juridique à celle-ci. Lorsqu'une attitude de l'un des organes de l'Organisation lui apparaît comme suffisamment continue et fondée sur des votes répétés et unanimes, la Cour voit dans cette continuité et dans ces votes une présomption de validité....

Le souci de la Cour enfin, en tant qu'organe judiciaire principal des Nations Unies, de prendre en considération les conditions de fait qui sont à la base de l'évolution institutionnelle de l'Organisation nous paraît enfin évident. La Cour s'est efforcée de tenir compte en interprétant la Charte des *exigences du fonctionnement de l'Organisation* dans les circonstances concrètes où celle-ci est placée. En présence de deux solutions juridiques possibles, la Cour, comme elle l'a fait au sujet du fondement de la F.U.N.U., choisit ou tout au moins n'écarte pas, celle qui permet à l'Organisation d'assurer ses responsabilités eu égard aux buts qui lui ont été impartis par la Charte."[94] [Italics mostly ours]

3.   Clearly there is a difference of opinion regarding the applicability of teleological method of interpretation to the Charter of the United Nations: the majority opinion and Judge Spender *versus* Judge Winiarski. While the majority opinion relied on the teleological reasoning pointed out by Thierry, Judge Spender elaborated on the reason why such an approach should be taken.

---

[94] Thierry, *supra* note 73, at 269-72.

"The Charter is indeed a legal instrument vast and complex enough to lend itself, particularly with regard to the legal developments which could not be envisaged at its establishment, to diverse and even opposite interpretations...

One can conceive a conservative interpretation of the Charter, based upon an exegesis inspired by the *travaux préparatoires* and the search of the will of the authors of this multilateral treaty. One can on the contrary turn out to be favorable for a more '*dynamic*' interpretation which avails itself of 'the spirit of the treaty of the superior demands of the Organization'.

As a matter of fact the choice between several possible interpretations depends on two factors: the first is in a way subjective: this is *the tendency of the interpreter*. From this viewpoint there is ground for finding that the Court is by its composition not necessarily animated by a spirit hostile to the General Assembly. The second is objective: this is *the method of interpretation*. The appreciation which is given on the legal new facts or situations depends directly on the criteria chosen in view of this appreciation... There is ground for noting on this matter the importance that the Court has attached to the reasonings based upon *the consideration of the purposes of the Organization*, upon *the legal practice followed by it*, and *the demands of its functioning*.

The opinions expressed by the Court in its Opinion proceed in the first place from the importance attached by the High Jurisdiction to the considerations drawn from *the purposes of the United Nations* and from the concordance of the acts achieved by the organs of the Organization with them. The Court has paid particular attention to this criterion several times in the course of its Opinion on the matter of the expenses of the U.N.E.F. and of the O.N.U.C. which 'must be tested by their relationship to the purposes of the United Nations' as well as with regard to the operations themselves.

It is not excessive to affirm that it follows from the Opinion of the Court that it has given a priority to the reasonings based upon the purposes of the institution, admitting only secondarily those related to the competences of the organs....

In the second place, it is advisable to note the legal importance that the Court has conferred upon *the practice of the United Nations*. This is evoked many times in the Opinion of July 20. The Court has for example dwelt at length upon the budgetary practice of the Organization to show that the budget of the United Nations has comprised operational expenses as well as administrative expenses. The Resolutions of the Assembly authorising the expenses of the U.N.E.F. and of the O.N.U.C. have been analyzed particularly in the light of the declarations of the Secretary General, with a view to make appear for each of them what has been the intention of the Assembly, its opinion as to the legal nature of these expenses....

In each of these cases the Court has not cited the practice of the organs only from the historical viewpoint, it has attached a legal value to it. When the attitude of one of the organs of the Organization appears to it to be sufficiently continuous and based upon repeated and unanimous votes, the Court sees in this continuity and in these votes a presumption of validity....

Finally the preoccupation of the Court, as the principal judicial organ of the United Nations, to take into consideration the factual conditions which are at the basis of the institutional evolution of the Organization seems evident to us. The Court has, in interpreting the Charter, made every effort to take into account *the demands of the functioning of the Organization* in the concrete circumstances in which it is placed. Faced with two possible legal solutions, the Court will, as it has done with regard to the foundation of the U.N.E.F., choose or at least not exclude that which permits the Organization to secure its responsibilities in consideration of the purposes which have been given to it by the Charter." [Our translation]

77

The approach of Judge Spender excluded resort to the *travaux préparatoires* as well as the practice of the Organization and relied heavily upon the terms of the Charter itself, which were of necessity expressed in broad and general terms. Here is an understanding that *the drafters' intention expected that the Organization would continue to function effectively in the changing international relations*, or that *it should be so presumed*.

The approach of Judge Winiarski, however, although he also admitted the Charter being drafted in very wide and general ("too indefinite" according to his expresseion) terms, put emphasis rather upon the aspect that the Charter was also nothing but the result of political and realistic negotiations based upon the interests among the founding States. Here is an understanding that *the drafters' intention expected that the United Nations could seek to achieve its purposes only by such procedures clearly defined in the Charter*. Judge Koretsky similarly stated as follows:

"I am prepared to stress the necessity of the strict observation and proper interpretation of the provisions of the Charter, its rules, without limiting itself by reference to the purposes of the Organization; otherwise one would have to come to the long ago condemned formula: 'The ends justify the means'."[95]

4.   Another important question pointed out by some judges is what legal significance the practice of an organ of the United Nations could possibly have in the interpretation of the Charter. While the majority opinion gave to the practice a legal value as a criterion of interpretation of the Charter, Judges Spender and Winiarski criticized this reasoning. As was explained above, we will examine this point later in a theoretical perspective. Here we simply cite an observation of Gross to bring the issue into bold relief as follows:

"If the brilliant reasoning of the Court does not convince one fully, this may be explained by the fact that in order to find an answer to the Assembly's question, the Court relied heavily on the words used by the Assembly in the resolutions which were put in question by the request for the advisory opinion. The impression seems inescapable that the Court's reasoning was addressed not primarily to the question put to it but to another question which, to make the point clear, might be formulated as follows: Do the expenses authorized in a number of General Assembly resolutions relating to UN operations in the Congo ... and ... to operations of the UN Emergency Force ... *constitute in the view of the General Assembly* expenses of the Organization ? This question, however, was not before the Court; yet a great deal of the Court's reasoning and of the argument by governments appears to have been addressed to it....

... [T]he problem posed by it might have been better approached from a legal point of view if the resolutions themselves had been disregarded. In other words, if the question which indeed arose in 1956, and again in 1960, had been submitted, as ideally it should have been, to the Court for an opinion *before* the first financial resolutions on UNEF and

---

[95] *Certain Expenses* case, *supra* note 77, at 268.

ONUC were adopted or immediately after they were adopted, or as soon as it was established that Members were in arrears, there would not have been an impressive series of resolutions before the Court, but one or none. The question then would clearly have been whether the expenses which it was proposed to incur, or which in fact had been incurred on a provisional basis, could be regarded legally as coming within the budgetary powers of the Assembly under paragraphs 1 or 2, or both, of Article 17. The Court then would not have been able to rely on a string of resolutions and to attach probative value to them, but would have been bound to search for a criterion of 'expenses of the Organization' in the Charter independent of the *ipse dixit* of the General Assembly repeated over a period of time amidst persistent controversy."[96] [Italics original]

5. There was also another question of who has the power to interpret (authoritatively) the Charter of the United Nations. The various positions of judges, for convenience, omitting the details, could be classified into the following three categories.

(1) The interpretation by the General Assembly (at least of Article 17) is final and binding. (Judges Spender and Morelli)[97]

(2) The resolutions clearly for the fulfilment of one of the stated purposes of the United Nations are presumed to be valid and constitutional. (Majority Opinion and Judge Fitzmaurice)[98]

(3) Strong denial of the power of the General Assembly to make an authoritative interpretation of the Charter. (Judge Winiarski)[99]

Because we think that this point is also closely related to the core of the problem in our study, we will examine it later (Chapter Four) in a larger perspective.

Section 3 Questions Relating to South West Africa

1 International Status of South-West Africa [1950][100]

In 1949, the General Assembly decided to submit the following questions to the ICJ for an advisory opinion: "What is the international status of the Territory of South-West Africa and what are the international obligations of the Union of South Africa arising therefrom, in particular: (a) Does the Union of South Africa continue to have international obligations under the Mandate for South-West Africa and, if so, what are those obligations? ; (b) Are the provisions of Chapter XII of the Charter applicable and, if so, in what manner, to the Territory of South-West Africa ? ; (c)

---

[96] Gross, *supra* note 74, at 17-18.

[97] *Certain Expenses* case, *supra* note 77, at 183, 224.

[98] *Id.* at 168.

[99] *Id.* at 229.

[100] For the relevant bibliography on the present advisory opinion, *see, e.g.*, J. Dugard, *The South West Africa / Namibia Dispute* (1973); S. Slonim, *South West Africa and the United Nations: an International Mandate in Dispute* (1972); Zacklin, 'The Problem of Namibia in International Law', 171 *Recueil des cours* 227 (1981).

Has the Union of South Africa the competence to modify the international status of the Territory of South-West Africa ... ?"

(1) The General Question and Question (a)

The Court came to the conclusion on the General Question, unanimously, that "South-West Africa is a territory under the international Mandate assumed by the Union of South Africa, and the conclusion on Question (a), by 12 votes[101] to 2, that "the Union of South Africa continues to have the international obligations stated in Article 22 of the Covenant of the League of Nations and in the Mandate for South-West Africa as well as the obligation to transmit petitions from the inhabitants of that Territory, the supervisory functions to be exercised by the United Nations, to which the annual reports and the petitions are to be submitted ..." Here we will analyze the majority opinion and the Separate Opinions of Judges McNair and Read (these were dissenting opinions on this point).

(1) The Reasoning of the Majority Opinion

1.   The majority opinion began at once with an examination of Question (a) because it considered that an examination of the three particular questions would furnish a sufficient answer to this general question and that it was not necessary to consider the general question separately.

The majority opinion pointed out, at the beginning, that an international régime, the Mandates System, created by Article 22 of the Covenant of the League of Nations, was to give effect to two principles: the principle of non-annexation and the principle that the well-being and development of such peoples form "a sacred trust of civilization". It, then, admitted that this Mandates System had created an international status by stating as follows:

> "*The object of the Mandate regulated by international rules far exceeded that of contractual relations regulated by national law.* The Mandate was created, in the interest of the inhabitants of the territory, and of humanity in general, *as an international institution with an international object — a sacred trust of civilization.* It is therefore not possible to draw any conclusion by analogy from the notions of mandate in national law or from any other legal conception of that law. *The international rules regulating the Mandate constituted an international status for the Territory recognized by all the Members of the League of Nations, including the Union of South Africa.*"[102] [Italics ours]

2.   According to the majority opinion, the international obligations assumed by the Union of South Africa were of two kinds. One kind was directly related to the administration of the Territory, and corresponded to the sacred trust of civilization referred to in Article 22 of the Covenant. Th. other related to the machinery for implementation, and was closely linked to the supervision and control of the League and corresponded to the "securities for the performance of this trust" referred to in the same article.

---

[101] The twelve judges were Basdevant (President), Guerrero (Vice-President), Alvarez, Hackworth, Winiarski, Zoričić, de Visscher, Klaestad, Badawi Pacha, Krylov, Hsu Mo and Azevedo.

[102] Advisory Opinion on International Status of South-West Africa, [1950] I. C. J. 132.

"[The first-mentioned group of] obligations represents the very essence of the sacred trust of civilization. Their *raison d'être* and original object remain. Since their fulfilment did not depend on the existence of the League of Nations, they could not be brought to an end merely because this supervisory organ ceased to exist. Nor could the right of the population to have the Territory administered in accordance with these rules depend thereon."[103]

This view was stated to be confirmed by the following three points: the first was Article 80, paragraph 1, of the Charter presupposing, as far as mandated territories were concerned, that the rights of States and peoples should not lapse automatically on the dissolution of the League of Nations; the second was the Resolution of the League of Nations on the termination of the League's existence which did not say that the Mandates themselves came to an end but, on the contrary, manifested its understanding that the Mandates were to continue in existence until "other arrangements" were established; the third was the statements of the Union of South Africa acknowledging the continuance of its obligations.

3.   Particularly important in the context of our study is the reasoning followed by the majority opinion with regard to the above-mentioned *second group of obligations*. Since the Council disppeared by the dissolution of the League, the question here arises whether the supervisory functions are to be exercised by the new international organization created by the Charter, and whether the Union of South Africa is under an obligation to submit to a supervision by this new organ and to render annual reports to it. And *it was by the teleological method of interpretation relying upon the necessity for supervision that the majority opinion reached an affirmative answer*. The majority opinion, after stating that "there seem to be decisive reasons for an affirmative answer to the above-mentioned question", developed *its teleological reasoning* as follows:

"The obligation incumbent upon a mandatory State to accept international supervision and to submit reports is an important part of the Mandates System. When the authors of the Covenant created this system, they considered that the effective performance of the sacred trust of civilization by the mandatory Powers required that the administration of mandated territories should be subject to international supervision. The authors of the Charter had in mind the same necessity when they organized an International Trusteeship System. *The necessity for supervision continues to exist despite the disappearance of the supervisory organ under the Mandates System. It cannot be admitted that the obligation to submit to supervision has disappeared merely because the supervisory organ has ceased to exist, when the United Nations has another international organ performing similar, though not identical, supervisory functions.*

These general considerations are confirmed by *Article 80, paragraph 1, of the*

---

[103] *Id.* at 133.

Charter, as this clause has been interpreted above.... The purpose must have been to provide a real protection for those rights; but no such rights of the peoples could be effectively safeguarded without international supervision and a duty to render reports to a supervisory organ.

The Assembly of the League of Nations, in its Resolution of April 18th, 1946, gave expression to a corresponding view.... This resolution presupposes that the supervisory functions exercised by the League would be taken over by the United Nations.

The competence of the General Assembly of the United Nations to exercise such supervision and to receive and examine reports is derived from the provisions of *Article 10 of the Charter*, which authorizes the General Assembly to discuss any questions or any matters within the scope of the Charter and to make recommendations on these questions or matters to the Members of the United Nations. This competence was in fact exercised by the General Assembly in Resolution 141 (II) [1947], and in Resolution 227 (III) [1948]
...

For the above reasons, the Court has arrived at the conclusion that the General Assembly of the United Nations is legally qualified to exercise the supervisory functions previously exercised by the League of Nations with regard to the administration of the Territory, and that the Union of South Africa is under an obligation to submit to supervision and control of the General Assembly and to render annual reports to it."[104]
[Italics ours]

(2) The Reasoning of the Separate Opinion of Judge McNair

1.   Judge McNair considered, on the one hand, that the legal nature of the Mandates System was based upon Article 22 of the Covenant and that what rights and duties the Mandatory possessed in regard to the area of territory being administered by it depended upon the Mandate, an international agreement. He, on the other hand, admitted the objective character of Article 22 of the Covenant by saying as follows:

"From time to time it happens that a group of great Powers, or a large number of States both great and small, assume a power to create by a multipartite treaty some new international régime or status, which soon acquires a degree of acceptance and durability extending beyond the limits of the actual contracting parties, and giving it an objectiv existence. This power is used when some public interest is involved, and its exercise often occurs in the course of the peace settlement at the end of a great war."[105]

He referred, as examples, to the status of demilitarization of the Aaland Islands and the régime of an international waterway of the Kiel Canal, and asserted that "[t]he Mandates System seems to me to be an *a fortiori* case".

Judge McNair further explained that the provisions of the Mandate were in part contractual

---

[104] *Id.* at 136-37.
[105] *Id.* at 153.

and in part "dispositive" and that, in addition to the personal rights and obligations, they also created certain "real" rights and obligations. "[T]he Mandate transferred to the Mandatory, or created and recognized in the hands of the Mandatory, certain rights of possession and government (administrative and legislative) which are valid *in rem* --- *erga omnes*, that is, against the whole world . " Thus he pointed out that the Mandate created a status for South West Africa, and that "[t]his status --- valid *in rem* --- supplies the element of permanence which would enable the legal condition of the Territory to survive the disappearance of the League, even if there were no surviving personal obligations between the Union and other former Members of the League."

2. Judge McNair, with the above understanding of the legal nature of the Mandates System, then proceeded to the effect of the dissolution of the League. On the one hand, because the Mandate for South-West Africa was never formally terminated despite the dissolution of the League, he concluded, firstly that "[t]he obligations owed to the League itself have come to an end", secondly that "[t]he obligations owed to former Members of the League ... subsist, except in so far as their performance involves the actual co-operation of the League", and thirdly that "the international status created for South-West Africa ... subsists".

On the other hand, he noted that the Mandate provided two kinds of machinery for its supervision. The first was a judicial supervision and the compulsory jurisdiction under Article 7 of the Mandate was expressly preserved by means of Article 37 of the Statute of the ICJ. The second was an administrative supervision by the Council of the League. This latter, however, was stated to have lapsed.

> "This supervision has lapsed because the League and its Council and Permanent Mandates Commission --- the organs which were designated (i) to receive the reports, (ii) to be satisfied with them and (iii) to examine and advise upon them --- no longer exist, so that it has become impossible to perform this obligation."[106]

(3) The Reasoning of the Separate Opinion of Judge Read

1. The reasoning of Judge Read was based upon the traditional principles of treaty law. He concurred in the part of the majority opinion which related to the continued substantive international obligations of the Union of South Africa arising under the Mandate. He was, however, unable to concur in the part which was concerned with accountability to, and supervision by, the United Nations or in the reasons by which it was justified.

Judge Read recognized three kinds of obligations under the Mandetes System: the first were obligations designed to secure and protect the well-being of the inhabitants (a sacred trust of civilization); the second comprised those due to, and enured to, the benefit of the Members of the League, e.g., in respect of missionaries and nationals; the third comprised the legal duties concerned with the supervision and enforcement of the first and the second. He, then, pointed out that these obligations had one point in common that each Member of the League had a legal interest, *vis-à-vis* the Mandatory Power, in matters "relating to the interpretation or the application

---

[106] *Id.* at 159.

of the provisions of the Mandate". And, in this connection, he stated as follows:

"It is a principle of international law that the parties to a multilateral treaty, regardless of their number or importance, cannot prejudice the legal rights of other States. The United Nations, by signing and ratifying the Charter, could and did establish the competence of the Organization to perform functions in relation to the mandated territories. *They could not, in law, transfer functions from the League to the Organization, without the consent and authority of the League, or of Members of the League whose legal rights would thus be impaired.* Consequently, while the Charter had come into force and the organization of the United Nations had come into being before the dissolution of the League, the legal rights of many States, which were not members of the new Organization, as regards the mandated territories including South-West Africa, remained in full force and vigor."[107] [Italics ours]

2.   Starting from the above-mentioned principle, Judge Read differed from the majority opinion on two points: the first was the survival of the rights and legal interests of the Members of the League; and the second related to the third kind of obligations mentioned above concerning the supervision and enforcement. With this latter point, he stated, no problem existed as regards the compulsory jurisdiction of the PCIJ, which was transferred to the ICJ; however, the obligations in relation to report and accountability to, and supervision by, the League presented more difficulty, because, while the discharge of these obligations directly involved the participation of the Council and the Permanent Mandates Commission, the League, by its Resolution in 1946, recognized "that, on the termination of the League's existence, its functions with respect to the mandated territories will come to an end". Consequently, he concluded that "[i]t was no longer possible for the Union [of South Africa] to send reports to a non-existent Council, or to be accountable to, or supervised by, a non-existent Permanent Mandates Commission".[108]

(2) Question (b)

As to the former part of Question (b), the Court, unanimously, gave an affirmative answer that "the provisions of Chapter XII of the Charter are applicable to the Territory of South-West Africa in the sense that they provide a means by which the Territory may be brought under the Trusteeship System.

The latter part of Question (b) asked whether the Charter imposes upon the Union of South Africa an obligation to place the Territory under the Trusteeship System by means of a Trusteeship Agreement. It is this part which is important in the context of our study. While the majority opinion gave a negative answer by a textual approach, Judges de Visscher, Krylov and Alvarez appended statements of their dissenting opinions and Judges Guerrero, Zoričić and Badawi Pasha in general shared the views of **Judge de Visscher** The majority opinion refuted the dissenting opinions. Here we will analyze the argument of **Judge de Visscher** as representing the dissenting

---

[107] *Id.* at 165.

[108] *Id.* at 166.

opinions.

(1) The Reasoning of the Majority Opinion

The majority opinion based its reasoning upon *the textual approach* as follows:

"Articles 75 and 77 show, in the opinion of the Court, that this question must be answered in the negative. The language used in both articles is permissive ("as may be placed thereunder"). Both refer to subsequent agreements by which the territories in question may be placed under the Trusteeship System. An "agreement" implies consent of the parties concerned, including the mandatory Power in the case of territories held under Mandate (Article 79). The parties must be free to accept or reject the terms of a contemplated agreement. No party can impose its terms on the other pary. Article 77, paragraph 2, moreover, presupposes agreement not only with regard to its particular terms, but also as to which territories will be brought under the Trusteeship System."[109]

(2) The Argument of Judge de Visscher and the Refutation of the Majority Opinion

1.   The argument of Judge de Visscher was that the provisions of Chapter XII did not impose on the Union of South Africa a legal obligation to conclude a Trusteeship agreement, but that they imposed on it *an obligation to take part in negotiations with a view to concluding an agreement.*

At the beginning, Judge de Visscher indicated a rule of interpretation to which he had recourse.

"It is an acknowledged rule of interpretation that treaty clauses must not only be considered as a whole, but must also be interpreted so as to avoid as much as possible depriving one of them of practical effect for the benefit of others. This rule is particularly applicable to *the interpretation of a text of a treaty of a constitutional character like the United Nations Charter,* above all *when,* as in this case, *its provisions create a well-defined international régime,* and for that reason may be considered as complementary to one another."[110] [Italics ours]

2.   Judge de Visscher stated that Article 80, paragraph 2, was clearly a direction to the mandatory Powers to be ready, at the earliest opportunity, to negotiate with a view to concluding such agreements and that what it intended to prevent was that a mandatory Power, while invoking on the one hand the disappearance of the League of Nations, should refuse on the other hand to consider submitting itself to the only régime contemplated in the Charter, namely the Trusteeship System. The above rule of interpretation, he stated, would lead to the following conclusion:

"The wording of Articles 75, 77 and 79 is permissive in the sense that the placing under Trusteeship is contingent upon the conclusion of subsequent agreements, the mandatory Power being free to accept or to reject the terms of a proposed agreement.... It is impossible, however, to reconcile these permissive provisions with Article 80, paragraph 2, and with the clear intent of the authors of the Charter to substitute the Trusteeship

---

[109] *Id.* at 139.

[110] *Id.* at 187.

System for the Mandates System, without admitting that *the mandatory Power, while remaining free to reject the particular terms of a proposed agreement, has the legal obligation to be ready to take part in negotiations and to conduct them in good faith with a view to concluding an agreement.*"[111] [Italics ours]

3.   This conclusion was considered to be supported by the following factors.

The first was the psychological value of the opening of negotiations. When the object of the negotiations was only to apply in practice principles forming part of a pre-established international régime, the opening of such negotiations was often a decisive step toward the conclusion of an agreement.

The second was the word "voluntarily" which appeared in Article 77 only in respect of territories in category (c). This provision, which was so clearly in contrast with the absence of any similar indication regarding territories in categories (a) and (b), must have been inserted with some definite purpose.

Thirdly, the international system which the Charter created would never have had more than theoretical existence if the mandatory Powers had considered themselves under no obligation to negotiate agreements to convert their Mandates into Trusteeship Agreements. In this connection, Judge de Visscher made the following suggestive statement.

"The obligation to be ready to negotiate with a view to concluding an agreement represented the minimum of international co-operation without which the entire régime contemplated and regulated by the Charter would have been frustrated. In this connection one must bear in mind that *in the interpretation of a great international constitutional instrument, like the United Nations Charter, the individualistic concepts which are generally adequate in the interpretation of ordinary treaties, do not suffice.* Under Article 76 of the Charter, 'the basic objectives of the Trusteeship System' conform to 'the purposes of the United Nations laid down in Article 1 of the present Charter'. In recognizing its obligation to be ready to negotiate with a view to concluding a Trusteeship Agreement, a mandatory Power, without thereby jeopardizing its freedom to accept or refuse the terms of such an Agreement, co-operates in a particularly important field in the attainment of the highest objectives of the United Nations."[112] [Italics ours]

4.   *The refutation made by the majority opinion* against the above explained argument of Judge de Visscher was also *textual*. It, for example, pointed out: "[The word 'voluntarily'] alone cannot, however, override the principle derived from Articles 75, 77 and 79 considered as a whole. An obligation for a mandatory State to place the Territory under Trusteeship would have been expressed in an direct manner."[113] It also pointed out that, while Article 80, paragraph 2, referred not merely to territories held under Mandate but also to the territories mentioned in Article 77 (b)

---

[111] *Id.* at 187-88.

[112] *Id.* at 189-90.

[113] *Id.* at 139.

and (c), it was evident that there could be no obligation to enter into negotiations with a view to concluding Trusteeship Agreement for those territories.[114] This prudent attitude of the majority opinion on this point is clear in the following statement:

> "It is true that, while Members of the League of Nations regarded the Mandates System as tho bost mothod for discharging the sacred trust of civilization provided for in Article 22 of the Covenant, the Members of the United Nations considered the International Trusteeship System to be the best method for discharging a similar mission. It is equally true that the Charter has contemplated and regulated only a single system, the International Trusteeship System. It did not contemplate or regulate a co-existing Mandates System. It may thus be concluded that it was expected that the mandatory States would follow the normal course indicated by the Charter, namely, conclude Trusteeship Agreements. *The Court is, however, unable to deduce from these general considerations any legal obligation for mandatory States to conclude or to negotiate such agreements. It is not for the Court to pronounce on the political or moral duties which these considerations may involve.*"[115] [Italics ours]

(3) Question (c)

The Court, unanimously, concluded that the Union of South Africa acting alone has not the competence to modify the international status of the Territory of South-West Africa, and that the competence to determine and modify the international status of the Territory rests with the Union of South Africa acting with the consent of the United Nations.

(4) Some Comments

1. As to the former part of Question (a), it is important that *the Mandate was created as an international institution with an international object of a sacred trust of civilization, and that it constituted an international status recognized by all the Members of the League of Nations.* Fitzmaurice understood this point as follows:

> "Although the point was not perhaps very explicitly stated in the opinion of the Court itself, the *South-West Africa* case is authority for the proposition that certain types of international régimes or systems, while having their origin in instruments contractual in form, are not themselves of a contractual character but rather have, or acquire, an essentially objective, self-contained character, a status independent of the instrument that created them, so that their existence is not affected by the lapse of that instrument, material

---

[114] *Id.* at 140.

[115] *Id.* at 140.

changes in its terms, or the disappearance of one of the parties to it."[116]

It is suggestive that, in a similar way, Judge McNair, well known as an authority in the treay law field, also admitted the objective character of an international institution although from a somewhat different angle.[117]

2.   What is most important in the context of our study is the confrontation, as to the latter part of Question (b), between the majority opinion and the dissenting opinions of Judges McNair and Read.

The majority opinion, based upon the substantive reason of the continuing necessity for supervision, interpreted the Charter of the United Nations and the resolution dissolving the League of Nations, and recognized the supervisory competence of the General Assembly. We could find *an application of the docrine of implied powers* in this part of the reasoning,[118] as was pointed out, for example, by Rideau:

"Par l'utilisation de la méthode des compétences implicites, on déduit de l'existence d'obligations la nécessité de la survivance d'un système de surveillance et de contrôle."[119]

Against this teleological reasoning were presented criticisms by not only Judges McNair[120] and Read,[121] but also by others,[122] one of whom, Taijudo, pointed out that the supervisory

---

[116] Fitzmaurice, 'The Law and Procedure of the International Court of Justice: General Principles and Substantive Law', 27 *Brit. Y. B. Int'l L.* 1,8 (1950), *reprinted in* G. Fitzmaurice, 1 *The Law and Procedure of the International Court of Justice* 8 (1986).

[117] With respect to this view of Judge McNair, Taijudo expressed a prudent position by saying that this view, although very interesting, needs further proof for its total affirmation. Taijudo, 'International Status of South-West Africa --- A Study of an Advisory Opinion by the International Court of Justice [in Japanese]', 64(1) *Hogaku Ronso (Kyoto L. Rev.)* 88, 99 (1958).

[118] Uchida, 'International Status of South-West Africa [in Japanese]', in *Hanrei Kenkyu Kokusaishihosaibansho (The Jurisprudence of the International Court of Justice)* 332 (Y. Takano ed. 1965). *See also* Lauterpacht, *supra* note 1, at 278-79.

[119] Rideau, *supra* note 36, at 261. "By utilizing the method of implied competences, one deduces from the existence of obligations the necessity of the survival of a system of supervision or of control." [Our translation]

[120] Judge McNair, after criticizing each of the alleged legal grounds for admitting an obligation on the Union of South Africa to accept the administrative supervision of the Mandate by the United Nations, concluded as follows (*International Status of South-West Africa* case, *supra* note 102, at 161-62):

"In these circumstances, I cannot find any legal ground on which the Court would be justified in replacing the Council of the League by the United Nations for the purposes of exercising the administrative supervision of the Mandate and the receipt and examination of reports. It would amount to imposing a new obligation upon the Union Government and would be a piece of judicial legislation."

[121] Judge Read denied the possibility of the United Nations to succeed to the functions, powers and responsibilities of the League in respect of Mandates from the consensual viewpoint of international law, and concluded as follows (*id.* at 172):

"[Such a succession] could not be based on implications or inferences drawn from the nature of the League and the United Nations or from any similarity in the functions of the organizations. Such a successtion could not be implied, either in fact or in law, in the absence of consent, express or implied by the League, the United Nations and the Mandatory Power."

[122] *See, e.g.,* Fitzmaurice, 'Judicial Innovation --- Its Uses and Its Perils --- as Exemplified in Some of the Work of the

competence of the General Assembly had to be more clearly demonstrated because this teleological reasoning would not be compatible with a contrary reasoning used in rejecting the obligation to take part in negotiations with a view to concluding an agreement, because the Union of South Africa would have the obligation to submit to its supervision, and because the drafters' intention to that effect could be found neither in the League of Nations' resolution nor in the United Nations' resolution.[123]

Having explained the confrontation of opinion on this problem, we would like to note two points.   Firstly, while some consider it a question of succession between international organizations,[124] it would be better to consider it a question of different approaches of interpretation among the judges to the relevant international instruments because the majority opinion dealt with it as a question of treaty interpretation.[125]

The second point is the significance given to the confrontation among the judges in the light of the different approaches of interpretation. Two Judges (particularly Judge Read) and others considered that there was a logical jump in the reasoning of the majority opinion (it stepped out of the limit of teleological reasoning) because, it seems to us, they analyzed the role of the necessity for supervision within the context of *the Mandate as an internatinal treaty*, or within *the traditional framework of ordinary treaty interpretation*.[126] On the other hand, the majority opinion considered that the international object of "a sacred trust of civilization" which implied the necessity for supervision far exceeded that of contractual relations and that it constituted *an international institution possessing an international objective status*. Consequently, we must adopt an appropriate reasoning within the framework, not of an ordinary treaty, but of a different *treaty establishing an international status or institution.*[127] Within this framework, it is submitted, the majority opinion considered it possible and necessary to apply *the doctrine of implied powers* in order to admit an international supervision necessary for the effective performance of the sacred

---

International Court of Justice during Lord McNair's Period of Office', in *Cambridge Essays in International Law, Essays in Honour of Lord McNair* 24, 37-38 (1965).

[123]   Taijudo, *supra* note 117, at 96-97.

[124]   Lauterpacht, *supra* note 1, at 279; Chiu, 'Succession in International Organizations', 14 *Int'l & Comp. L. Q.* 83 (1965).

[125]   Kahn, 'The International Court's Advisory Opinion on the Internatinal Status of South-West Africa', 4 *Int'l L. Q.* 78, 90 (1951). *See also* Advisory Opinion on Admissibility of Hearings of Petitioners by the Committee on South West Africa, [1956] I. C. J. 33 (Declaration by Judge Winiarski) and 66 (Joint Dissenting Opinion by five judges).

[126]   For example, Kahn supported the views of Judges McNair and Read (Kahn, *id.* at 91), and Uchida also stated that, from the standpoint of positive law, the approach of Judge Read should be supported (Uchida, *supra* note 118, at 333).

[127]   Judge de Visscher wrote elsewhere (de Visscher, *supra* note 16, at 146) as follows:

"L'efficacité des organisations internationales ne dépend pas seulement de l'étendue de leurs pouvoirs, mais également de la continuité de leur action, surtout quand celle-ci est représentée par un régime juridique qui peut se réclamer de buts hautement humains et civilisateurs. C'est l'idée de la continuité du droit qui a inspiré l'avis consultatif de la Cour internationale de Justice du 11 juillet 1950 relatif au *Statut international du Sud-Ouest africain.*"

trust of civilization, and approved the supervisory competence of the United Nations.

3.   Another interesting point is the confrontation of opinion among the judges over a legal obligation to be ready to negotiate with a view to concluding an agreement. Some claimed that it would be a "fundamental weakness" to end up with admitting an obligation to negotiate on the part of "other territories" in Article 80(2).[128] It would certainly not be possible to admit, like Judge Alvarez, an obligation to conclude an agreement.[129] When we see, however, a strong teleological reasoning in the latter part of Question (a), it does not necessarily seem impossible to admit a legal obligation to be ready to negotiate with a view to concluding an agreement. We could conclude that Judge de Visscher advocated an application of the principle of *effet utile* in "the interpretation of a great international constitutional instrument", but that the Court abstained from stepping out of the textual approach by a narrow margin of 8 votes to 6.

2 Voting Procedure on Questions relating to Reports and Petitions concerning the Territory of South-West Africa [1955]

In 1954, the General Assembly requested the ICJ to give an advisory opinion on the question whether Rule F on the voting procedure to be followed by the General Assembly in taking decisions on questions relating to reports and petitions, which adopted a two-thirds majority rule based upon Article 18, paragraph 2, of the Charter, is a correct interpretation of the 1950 advisory opinion. The Court, unanimously,[130] gave an affirmative answer. Judges Basdevant, Klaestad and Lauterpacht appended statements of their separate opinions.

(1) The Reasoning of the Majority Opinion

1.   The majority opinion analyzed the question by dividing into two parts the following passage of the 1950 advisory opinion:

"The degree of supervision to be exercised by the General Assembly should not therefore exceed that which applied under the Mandates System, and should conform as far as possible to the procedure followed in this respect by the Council of the League of Nations."

2.   *The first question* was whether the former part of the passage might properly be construed as including the system of voting to be followed by the General Asembly. The majority opinion seem to have relied upon *the textual approach*.

"The function of supervision exercised by the General Assembly generally takes the form

---

[128] Kahn, *supra* note 125, at 95.

[129] Judge Alvarez, after developing his doctrine of new international law, stated that the obligation of the Union of South-Africa to negotiate and conclude an agreement with the United Nations "derives from the spirit of the Charter, which leaves no place for the future co-existence of the Mandates System and the Trusteeship System" (*International Status of South-West Africa* case, *supra* note 102, at 183).

[130] The judges were Hackworth (President), Badawi (Vice-President), Guerrero, Basdevant, Winiarski, Zoričić, Klaestad, Read, Hsu Mo, Armand-Ugon, Kojevnikov, Sir Muhamad Zafrulla Khan, Lauterpacht, Moreno Quintana and Córdova.

of action based on the reports and observations of the Committee on South-West Africa, whose functions are analogous to those exercised by the Permanent Mandates Commission. The words 'the degree of supervision' relate to the extent of the substantive supervision thus exercised, and not to the manner in which the collective will of the General Assembly is expressed.

Accordingly, these words, if given their ordinary and natural meaning, should not be interpreted as relating to procedural matters. They relate to the measure and means of supervision."[131]

The majority opinion, by stating that "[t]his interpretation of the words used is confirmed by an examination of the circumstances which led to their use", proceeded to the analysis of the relevant circumstances of the 1950 opinion to further support its conclusion.

3.   *The second question* was whether Rule F was in accord with the latter part of the passage. The latter part was stated to relate to the way in which supervision is to be exercised, a matter which is procedural in character. The majority opinion, after stating that "[t]he voting system of the General Assembly was not in contemplation" when the Court stated it, pointed out:

"The constitution of an organ usually prescribes the method of voting by which the organ arrives at its decisions. The voting system is related to the composition and functions of the organ. It forms one of the characteristics of the constitution of the organ. Taking decisions by a two-thirds majority vote or a simple majority vote is one of the distinguishing features of the General Assembly, while the unanimity rule was one of the distinguishing features of the Council of the League of Nations. These two systems are characteristic of different organs, and one system cannot be substituted for the other without constitutional amendment. To transplant upon the General Assembly the unanimity rule of the Council of the League would not be simply the introduction of a procedure, but would amount to a disregard of one of the characteristics of the General Assembly. Consequently the question of conformity of the voting system of the General Assembly with that of the Council of the League of Nations presents insurmountable difficulties of a juridical nature."[132]

For these reasons which were presented, as above, in the form of a general rule in the law of international organization, the majority opinion concluded that "the voting system of the General Assembly must be considered as not being included in the procedure which the General Assembly should follow in exercising its supervisory functions".

4.   It seems to be clear, the majority opinion pointed out, that the General Assembly was proceeding upon the assumption that the word "procedure", as used in the second part of the passage in question, includes the voting system. According to the majority opinion, there was, even in this case, equally no incompatibility between Rule F and the previous Opinion.

"[T]he authority of the General Assembly to exercise supervision over the administration

---

[131] Advisory Opinion on Voting Procedure on Questions relating to Reports and Petitions concerning the Territory of South-West Africa, [1955] I. C. J. 72.

[132] *Id.* at 75.

of South-West Africa as a mandated Territory is based on the provisions [Article 10] of the Charter. While, in exercising that supervision, the General Assembly should not deviate from the Mandate, its authority to take decisions in order to effect such supervision is derived from its own constitution.

... It is from the Charter that the General Assembly derives its competence to exercise its supervisory functions; and it is within the framework of the Charter that the General Assembly must find the rules governing the making of its decisions in connection with those functions. It would be legally impossible for the General Assembly, on the one hand, to rely on the Charter in recieving and examining reports and petitions concerning South-West Africa, and, on the other hand, to reach decisions relating to these reports and petitions in accordance with a voting system entirely alien to that prescribed by the Charter."[133]

The majority opinion, furthermore, pointed out that the Court was indicating that, in the nature of things, the General Assembly would operate under an instrument different from that which governed the Council of the League of Nations, and, consequently, concluded that the expression "as far as possible" was designed to allow for adjustments and modifications necessitated by legal or practical considerations.

(2) Some Comments

1.   One of the problems in this opinion is whether, as to the first question, the relevant passage of the 1950 opinion was really as clear as the majority opinion thought it to be. The majority opinion relied on *the textual approach having recourse to the natural and ordinary meaning*, and confirmed it by the examination of the relevant circumstances of the 1950 opinion.

On the other hand, Judge Lauterpacht pointed out, in his separate opinion, that, although it was "possible" to answer the question in the way the majority opinion did, it was, in his view, "essential" that the opinion should contain an answer to the legal issues relevant to the case relied upon especially by South Africa. The expression "degree of supervision" has two meanings: firstly, the means of supervision and secondly, the method of deciding whether the administering authority has complied with them and what steps it ought ot take with that object in view. The procedure of voting determines the degree of supervision and accepted usage includes voting within matters of procedure. Thus Judge Lauterpache concluded as follows:

"For these reasons I am reluctant to admit that the ordinary and natural meaning of words excludes the method of voting from the notion of degree of supervision. There is no ordinary and natural meaning of the term 'degree of supervision' in the abstract.... [I]t is relative to the situations and problems with which the Court is concerned....

It is, of course, possible that the question of voting was not before the mind of the Court when it gave the Opinion in 1950. This does not mean that the procedure of voting is not an essential element in the situation. On the contrary, it is for this Court, confronted

---

[133] *Id.* at 76.

as it is with an apparent gap in the Opinion of the Court of 1950 with respect to a situation which calls for clarification, to fill the lacuna by all available means of interpretation."[134]

2.	Judge Lauterpacht also disagreed with the majority opinion as to the question whether the General Assembly had the power to proceed by a voting procedure other than that laid down in Artilce 18 of the Charter. Principle would seem to demand, Judge Lauterpacht stated, that whenever the basic instrument of a corporate political body prescribed the matter in which its collective will was to be formed and expressed, that basic instrument was in this respect paramount and overriding, and that it would be so in the case of a function accepted under some extraneous instrument such as a treaty. In the League of Nations, however, there were opposing considerations both of practice and principle. (In the 12th advisory opinion, the PCIJ stated that the Council could undertake to give decisions by a majority in specific cases, if express provision was made for this power by treaty stipulations. And many treaties adopted subsequent to the Peace Treaties including the "Minorities Treaties" contained provisions allowing the Council to proceed by a majority of votes.) Thus Judge Lauterpacht concluded that "it cannot be said, by way of an absolute rule, that in no circumstances may the General Assembly act by a system of voting other than that laid down in the Charter".[135]

When we compare these reasons based upon by Judge Lauterpacht and the statement made by the majority opinion in the form of a general rule in the law of international organization, we could share the following opinion of Rideau:

"En invoquant la nécessité du respect de la Charte, la Cour donne une interprétation de l'avis de 1950 favorable aux compétences de l'O.N.U...."[136]

---

[134] *Id.* at 95-96. *See also* Verzijl, *supra* note 37, at 229.

For Judges Klaestad and Lauterpacht who examined the substantive issues of the claims by the Union of South Africa, the grounds for their affirmative answers to the question were as follows. When the Union of South Africa, by a concurrent vote in the Council, gave an expression of its acceptance of a Resolution concerning reports or petitions relating to the Territory of South-West Africa, the Union Government became, by reason of that acceptance, legally bound to comply with the Resolution. On the contrary, recommendations by the General Assembly of the United Nations adopted by virtue of Article 10 concerning reports and petitions relating to the Territory of South-West Africa are not legally binding on the Union of South Africa in its capacity as Mandatory Power, although they might have "effects ... of a moral or political character" (Klaestad: *id.* at 88) or "some legal obligation" (Lauterpacht: *id.* at 118) to give due consideration in good faith. Because the decisions of the General Assembly in the meaning of Rule F do not possess a degree of legal authority equal to that of the decisions of the Council of the League of Nations, they, although adopted through a less stringent voting procedure of two-thirds majority, cannot be held to involve a degree of supervision exceeding that which obtained under the Mandate System.

[135] *Id.* at 111.

[136] Rideau, *supra* note 36, at 265. *See also* Simon, *supra* note 22, at 198.

However, we should keep in mind the folloing view critical on this point. Jennings, after citing a passage by Judge McNair in the 1950 Opinion to the effect that there could be no legal ground for replacing the Council of the League by the United Nations (*see* the quotation in *supra* note 121), stated as follows (Jennings, 'The International Court's Advisory Opinion on the Voting Procedure on Questions Concerning South-West Africa', 42 *Transactions of the Grotius Society* 85, 97 (1957)):

"The attempts of the 1955 Judges to discover that 'legal ground' and then to compare in terms of degree, supervision by two bodies utterly dissimilar in kind, seems to me only to demonstrate the soundness and the

3 Admissibility of Hearings of Petitioners by the Committee on South West Africa [1956]

In 1955, the General Assembly requested the ICJ to give an advisory opinion on the following question: Is it consistent with the 1950 advisory opinion for the Committee on South West Africa to grant oral hearings to petitioners on matters relating to the Territory of South West Africa? The Court gave an affirmative answer by 8 votes[137] to 5.[138] Judges Winiarski and Kojevnikov, while voting in favour of the opinion, made brief declarations. Judge Lauterpacht appended a long statement of his separate opinion. Judges Badawi, Basdevant, Hsu Mo, Armand-Ugon and Moreno Quintana appended the joint statement of their dissenting opinion.

(1) The Reasoning of the Majority Opinion

1.	The majority opinion consists of two parts: its own answer to the question and its refutation against the objections to its answer. Here we will consider the former part.

2.	The majority opinion, at the outset, defined the meaning of the question as whether it would be consistent with the 1950 opinion for the General Assembly to authorize the Committee on South West Africa to grant oral hearings to petitioners. It then pointed out the gist of the operative part of the 1950 opinion: the obligations of the Mandatory continue unimpaired with the difference of the supervisory organs; the General Assembly is legally qualified to carry out an effective and adequate supervision of the administration of the Mandated Territory. The majority opinion, then, set its starting point as follows:

> "In determining the question whether in these circumstances it would be consistent with the Opinion of the Court of 11 July 1950 for the Committee on South West Africa to grant oral hearings to petitioners, the Court must have regard to the whole of its previous Opinion and its general purport and meaning."[139]

The majority opinion, after explaining that the 1950 opinion pointed out that the obligations of the Mandatory could not be extended but also that the necessity for supervision continued to exist, manifested *its teleological attitude* by stating as follows:

> "The general purport and meaning of the [1950 Opinion] is that the paramount purpose underlying the taking over by the General Assembly of the United Nations of the supervisory functions in respect of the Mandate for South West Africa formerly exercised by the Council of the League of Nations was to safeguard the sacred trust of civilization through the maintenance of effective international supervision of the administration of the Mandated Territory.

---

wisdom of the 1950 dissents."

[137] The eight judges were Hackworth (President), Winiarski, Klaestad, Read, Kojevnikov, Sir Muhammad Zafrulla Khan, Sir Hersch Lautrpacht and Córdova.

[138] The five judges were Badawi (Vice-President), Basdevant, Hsu Mo, Armand-Ugon and Moreno Quintana.

[139] Advisory Opinion on Admissibility of Hearings of Petitioners by the Committee on South Africa, [1956] I. C. J. 27.

Accordingly, in interpreting any particular sentences in the [1950 Opinion], *it is not permissible, in the absence of express words to the contrary, to attribute to them a meaning which would not be in conformity with this paramount purpose or with the operative part of that Opinion.*"[140] [Italics ours]

3.   Here a brief reference was made to the way in which the question of the grant of oral hearings to petitioners had been dealt with during the regime of the League of Nations: the Permanent Mandates Commission had this question under consideration, but it never made a definite recommendation to the Council; after obtaining the views of the Mandatory Powers, all of whom were opposed to the granting of oral hearings, the Council decided that there was no occasion to modify the procedure theretofore followed by the Commission; in his Report to the Council, the Rapporteur stated that, in any particular case, the Council could decide on such exceptional procedure as might seem appropriate and necessary. Consequently, the majority opinion admitted that "[i]t is clear that oral hearings were not granted to petitioners by the Permanent Mandates Commission at any time during the regime of the League of Nations". The majority opinion, however, reached the following conclusion in the next paragraph:

> "The right of petition was introduced into the Mandates System by the Council of the League on January 31st, 1923, and certain rules relating to the matter were prescribed. This was an innovation designed to render the supervisory function of the Council more effective. *The Council having established the right of petition, and regulated the manner of its exercise, was, in the opinion of the Court, competent to authorize the Permanent Mandates Commission to grant oral hearings to petitioners, had it seen fit to do so.*"[141] [Italics ours]

(2) The Reasoning of the Separate Opinion of Judge Lauterpacht

1.   Judge Lauterpacht, at the outset, dealt with a preliminary issue which was primarily responsible for the division of the Court and which was connected with the exercise of its advisory function: although the request for an advisory opinion was stated in apparently general terms, it was clear from the documents submitted that the General Assembly was referring to a specific question as it resulted from a particular situation (the Union of South Africa declined to accept the 1950 opinion and refused to comply with its obligations); consequently, the Court ought to answer in relation both to the specific situation underlying the request and to the general question. The conclusion of Judge Lauterpacht was, in a nutshell, as follows: it was not consistent with the 1950 opinion to grant oral hearings to petitioners in circumstances in which there was present the requisite co-operation on the part of the Mandatory complying with his obligation; it was, however, consistent with it whenever, owing to the absence of such co-operation on the part of the Mandatory, the Committee felt constrained to other sources of information.

---

[140] *Id.* at 28.

[141] *Id.* at 29.

2.   Judge Lauterpacht frankly admitted that normally, i.e., so long as there were available the regular sources of information through annual reports and petitions transmitted by the Union of South Africa, the grant of oral hearings to petitioners would exceed the degree of supervision applied during the Mandate System and that it would not conform to the 1950 opinion. In this connection, it is worth citing the following passage which criticized the reasoning of the majority opinion:

> "Neither have I found it possible to rely to any substantial extent on the view that although the Council of the League did not permit and that although it expressly rejected the procedure of oral hearings, it was *entitled* to grant oral hearings by virtue of its inherent powers in the matter of supervision ... Any devolution of powers [from the Council of the League of Nations to the General Assembly of the United Nations] in this respect could take place only subject to the governing rule as laid down in that Opinion, namely, that the degree of supervision by the General Assembly should not exceed that applied under the Mandates System. I find it difficult to accept as a substantial ground for the present Opinion of the Court an interpretation which construes that qualifying rule as referring not necessarily to the system which actually applied but to one which could or might have been applied in certain circumstances. *The doctrine of implied powers of the Council might, if resorted to, render meaningless — to a large extent — the rule that there must be no excess of supervision. As the Council of the League, in the exercise of its alleged inherent powers, could introduce any means of supervision not patently inconsistent with the mandate, no means of supervision thus introduced by the General Assembly could conceivably be in excess of the supervision 'applied' under the Mandates System.* I cannot accept any such interpretation of the Advisory Opinion of 1950 which may go a long way towards reducing its principal qualifying provision to a mere form of words."[142] [Italics ours]

3.   On the other hand, Judge Lauterpacht considered that, in answering the question against the background of the fact that the two basic provisions of the operative part of the 1950 opinion were in abeyance owing to the attitude adoted by the Union of South Africa, the Court had to be guided by established principles of interpretation and the applicable general principles of law.

Firstly, the 1950 opinion must be read as a whole. Then, it is impossible, without destroying its effect, to maintain fully and literally provisions qualifying the operation of a system whose main characteristics have become inoperative. If the degree of supervision is in danger owing to the attitude of the Government of South Africa, it is fully consistent with the 1950 opinion that in some respects that supervision should become more stringent provided that it can be said that the total effect is not such as to increase the degree of supervision as previously obtaining.

Secondly, the status of South West Africa — a régime in the nature of an objective law which is legally operative irrespective of the conduct of the Union of South Africa — must be

---

[142] *Id.* at 40.

given effect in terms of its general purpose, having regard to the attitude adopted by the Union. It is a sound principle of law that whenever a legal instrument of continuing validity cannot be applied literally owing to the conduct of one of the parties, it must, without allowing that party to take advantage of its own conduct, be applied in a way approximating most closely to its primary object.

Thirdly, it is a rule of common sense and good faith not to permit a party which repudiates an instrument to rely literally on it. May the Court replace one means of supervision by another? This is not the way in which courts normally proceed in the matter of contracts between individuals. Judge Lauterpacht developed a suggestive statement as follows:

"However, this is not a case of a contract or even of an ordinary treaty anologous to a contract.... [T]his is a case of the operation and application of multilareral instruments, as interpreted by the Court in [the 1950 opinion], creating *an international status --- an international régime --- transcending a mere contactual relation*. The essence of such instruments is that their validity continues notwithstanding changes in the attitudes, or the status, or the very survival of individual parties or persons affected. Their continuing validity implies their continued operation and the resulting legitimacy of the means devised for that purpose by way of judicial interpretation and application of the original instrument. *The unity and the operation of the régime created by them cannot be allowed to fail because of a breakdown or gap which may arise in consequence of an act of a party or otherwise....* It is just because the régime established by them cnstitutes a unity that, in relation to instruments of this nature, the law --- the existing law as judicially interpreted --- finds means for removing a clog or filling a lacuna or adopting an alternative device in order to prevent a standstill of the entire system on account of a failure in any particular link or part. This is unlike the case of a breach of the provisions of an ordinary treaty --- which breach creates, as a rule, a right for the injured party to denounce it and to claim damages."[143] [Italics ours]

4.   Next, Judge Lauterpacht enquired to what extent the situation with which the General Assembly were confronted called for and permitted the application of the principles of law as above outlined. Because of the non co-operation of the Mandatory, the annual report of the Mandatory disappeared; the degree of supervision diminished and a gap was created here; the written petition sent by the inhabitants lost its effectiveness. In these circumstances, were oral hearings not fundamentally inconsistent with the 1950 opinion and one of the means necessary to give effect to its essential purpose ? To this question answered Judge Lauterpacht in the affirmative.

(3) The Reasoning of the Joint Dissenting Opinion
1.   The five dissenting judges emphasized that it was a compatibility with the 1950 opinion of

---

[143] *Id.* at 48-49.

a decision to grant hearings to petitioners which was to be appraised, and nothing else. The Court should seek the elements for its reply in the 1950 opinion, not in factual or legal considerations outside the scope of that opinion, in particular in the attitude of the Union of South Africa; these facts were subsequent in date to the 1950 opinion and they cannot therefore constitute factors to be considered in ascertaining the meaning and scope of that opinion. They continued as follows:

"It may furthermore be observed that it is only if it should be found that a proper interpretation of the Opinion of 1950 leads to the conclusion that the hearing of petitioners is not consistent with that Opinion, that the question may arise whether the refusal of the Union of South Africa to submit to the exercise of supervision constitutes a new element such as nevertheless to justify such a hearing. That would be neither to have regard to the meaning of the Opinion of 1950 nor to ascertain whether the hearing of petitioners is or is not consistent with that Opinion, which is a purely legal question and, as such, one suitable for submission to the Court. It would be to enquire whether that refusal constitutes a ground justifying the supervising authority in departing in this respect from observance of the Opinion of 1950. *Such a question might be asked, but the considerations upon which a reply to it might be based would go beyond the scope of legal considerations and would involve political elements the appraisal of which is not within the domain of the Court, and such a question has not been put to it.*"[144] [Italics ours]

2.   According to these five judges, the spirit of the 1950 opinion confirmed the continuity of the Mandate and of the international obligations of the Union of South Africa which resulted therefrom. What was the meaning of this continuity, of this maintenance of the *status quo*? The analysis of the 1950 opinion and other circumstances confirmed, they stated, that the opinion intended to maintain the former practice and not to refer to powers which might subsequently be held to have belonged to the Council, although the latter never exercised them. Consequently they concluded as follows:

"Since the Opinion of 1950 made reference to the former practice and since the Permanent Mandates Commission did not have recourse to the hearing of petitioners, we are compelled to take the view that such hearings by the Committee on South West Africa would not be consistent with the Opinion given by the Court in 1950."[145]

(4) Some Comments

1.   The core of the issue in this opinion was related to the way of accepting the question: whether the Court should reply without considering the context or background of the question, or it may formulate its answer in such a manner as to make its advisory opinion effective and useful by considering these factors.[146] In this connection, comparison with the case in the 1955 opinion

---

[144] *Id.* at 62.

[145] *Id.* at 70.

[146] Uchida, *supra* note 118, at 346.

would be suggestive, as Uchida pointed out as follows: what draws our attention is that, in the present case, the Court, unlike in the 1955 opinion, replied to the question not in the abstract but by taking into consideration the concrete circumstatnces (the Union of South Africa's refusal to co-operate with the United Nations) although not to the extent that Judge Lauterpacht did; this way of approaching the question was adopted by Judge Lauterpacht in his Separate Opinion in 1955 while the joint dissenting judges followed the approach similar to the majority opinion in the 1955 opinion.[147]

When we consider the above-mentioned comparison and the fact that the majority opinion in the 1956 opinion heavily relied upon "the general purport and meaning of the [1950 Opinion]", that is, "to safeguard the sacred trust of civilization through the maintenance of effective international supervision", we would be compelled to admit that *a teleological reasoning played an important role in the present opinion*. Rideau pointed out as follows:

> "On retrouve là encore la méthode d'interprétation de la Cour qui, pour aborder une situation non prévue par la Charte, fait appel à la théorie de l'effet utile, sous une forme ou sous une autre, pour accorder aux organes de l'organisation des compétences non prévues par les traités constitutifs."[148]

2.   In the context of our study, we should note that Judge Lauterpacht, while he did not admit an application of the docrine of implied powers on the general level, did admit, in relation to the specific situation underlying the question, the characteristic feature of multilateral instruments creating an international status, an international régime transcending a mere contractual relation.

4   South West Africa Cases [1962 and 1966]

In 1960, Ethiopia and Liberia, relating to "the continued existence of the Mandate for South West Africa and the duties and performance of the Union [of South Africa], as Mandatory, thereunder", instituted proceedings against the Union, relying on Article 7 [149] of the Mandate and

---

[147]   Uchida, *id.* at 347-48. In this connection, Zacklin also stated as follows (Zacklin, *supra* note 100, at 264):
"Although the request for the opinion was virtually identical in nature to that of 1955 the Court did not approach its task in the same way. In contrast to its narrow approach in the 1955 opinion, the Court now opted for a broad examination of its 1950 opinion and decided that the answer to the General Assembly's request could only be given by reference to 'its general purport and meaning', namely, the safeguarding of the sacred trust of civilization through the maintenance of effective international supervision."
See also Slonim, *supra* note 100, at 158.

[148]   Rideau, *supra* note 36, at 267. "One finds here again the method of interpretation of the Charter which, in order to approach a situation not anticipated by the Charter, appeals to the theory of effectiveness, under one form or another, in order to allow the organs of the organization competences not anticipated by the constitutive treaties." [Our translation]

[149]   Paragraph 2 of Article 7 provided as follows:
"The Mandatory agrees that, if any dispute whatever should arise between the Mandatory and another Member of the League of Nations relating to the interpretation or application of the provisions of the Mandate, such dispute, if it cannot be settled by negotiation, shall be submitted to the Permanent Court of International Justice provided for by Article 14 of the Covenant of the League of Nations."

Article 37 of the Statute of the Court. The Applicants demanded the Court to declare (1) that the Mandate was a treaty in force, (2) that the Union, in administering the Territory, violated the obligations of the Mandate and of Article 22 of the Covenant, (3) the Union violated the obligation to submit to the supervision and control of the General Assembly with regard to the exercise of the Mandate. The respondent, the Republic of South Africa, made preliminary objections and claimed (1) that, by reason of the dissolution of the League of Nations, the Mandate for South West Africa was no longer a 'treaty or convention in force' within the meaning of Article 37 of the Statute (a) with respect to the Mandate Agreement as a whole, (b) with respect to Article 7, (2) that neither of the Applicants was 'another Member of the League of Nations', as required for *locus standi* by Article 7 of the Mandate, (3) that the conflict or disagreement alleged by the Applicants to exist between them and the Republic of South Africa, was by reason of its nature and content not a 'dispute' as envisaged in Article 7 of the Mandate, particularly in that no material interests of the applicants or of their nationals were involved therein or affected thereby, (4) the alleged conflict or disagreement was as regards its state of development not a 'dispute' which 'cannot be settled by negotiation' within the meaning of Article 7. The Court, in its judgment in 1962, found, by 8 votes to 7[150], that it had jurisdiction to adjudicate upon the merits of the dispute. On the other hand, the Court, in its judgment in 1966, decided, by the President's casting vote --- the votes being equally divided[151], to reject the claims of the Applicants by holding that the Applicants did not possess any right on the present claim. Since the reasoning of the 1966 judgment is considered to be based upon the joint dissenting opinion of Judges Fitzmaurice and Spender in the 1962 judgment, we will analyze the reasonings both of the 1962 judgment and of the 1966 judgment in the light of the method of interpretation.

(1) The Reasoning of the 1962 Judgment

1.   The majority opinion, at the outset, confirmed the existence of a dispute between the parties, and gave a brief account of the origin, nature and characteristics of the Mandates System established by the Covenant.

"The essential principles of the Mandates System consist chiefly in the recognition of certain rights of the peoples of the underdeveloped territories; the establishment of a regime of tutelage for each of such peoples to be exercised by an advanced nation as a 'Mandatory' 'on behalf of the League of Nations'; and the recognition of 'a sacred trust of civilisation' laid [u]pon the League as an organized international community and upon its Member States....

... The rights of the Mandatory in relation to the mandated territory and the inhabitants

---

[150] The eight judges were Alfaro (Vice-President), Badawi, Moreno Quintana, Wellington Koo, Koretsky, Bustamante Y Rivero, Jessup and Sir Louis Mbanefo. The seven judges were Winiarski (President), Basdevant, Spiropoulos, Sir Percy Spender, Sir Gerald Fitzmaurice, Morelli and van Wyk.

[151] The eight votes were cast by Sir Percy Spender (President), Winiarski, Spiropoulos, Sir Gerald Fitzmaurice, Morelli, Gros and van Wyk. The seven votes were cast by Wellington Koo (Vice-President), Koretsky, Tanaka, Jessup, Padilla Nervo, Forster and Sir Louis Mbanefo.

have their foundation in the obligations of the Mandatory and they are, so to speak, mere tools given to enable it to fulfil its obligations. The fact is that each Mandate under the Mandates System constitutes a new international institution, the primary, overriding purpose of which is to promote 'the well-being and development' of the people of the territory under Mandate."[152]

2.   The majority opinion, then, proceeded to the examination of the four preliminary objections.

As to the first objection. The majority opinion, by examining the Mandate and other relevant instruments, rejected the claims that the Mandate was not a treaty but an executive action, that the Mandate was described as a Declaration, that the Mandate was not registered in accordance with Article 18 of the Covenant. The Court in the 1950 opinion, it pointed out, was unanimous on the finding that Article 7 of the Mandate was still in force, and "[t]he unanimous holding of the Court in 1950 ... continues to reflect the Court's opinion today".

3.   As to the second objection. Against the contention that since all Member States of the League necessarily lost their membership and its accompanying rights when the League itself ceased to exist, there could no longer be "another Member of the League of Nations", the majority opinion stated as follows:

"This contention is claimed to be based upon *the natural and ordinary meaning* of the words employed in the provision. But *this rule of interpretation is not an absolute one. Where such a method of interpretation results in a meaning incompatible with the spirit, purpose and context of the clause or instrument in which the words are contained, no reliance can be validly placed on it.*"[153] [Italics ours]

Firstly, the administrative supervision by the League constituted a normal security to ensure full performance by the Mandatory of the "sacred trust" toward the inhabitants of the mandated territory, but the specially assigned role of the Court was even more essential, since it was to serve as the final bulwark of protection by recourse to the Court against possible abuse or breaches of the Mandate.

Secondly, the right to implead the Mandatory Power before the Court was the most reliable procedure of ensuring protection by the Court.

Thirdly, an agreement was reached among all the Members of the League at the Assembly session in 1946 to continue the different Mandates as far as it was practically feasible or operable with reference to the obligations of the Mandatory Powers and therefore to maintain the rights of the Members of the League, notwithstanding the dissolution of the League itself.

4.   As to the third objection. The majority opinion stated as follows:

"The question which calls for the Court's consideration is whether the dispute is a 'dispute' as envisaged in Article 7 of the Mandate and within the meaning of Article 36 of the Statute of the Court.

---

[152]   South West Africa Cases, Preliminary Objections, [1962] I. C. J. 329.

[153]   *Id.* at 336.

101

The Respondent's contention runs counter to *the natural and ordinary meaning* of the provisions of Article 7 of the Mandate, which mentions 'any dispute whatever' arising between the Mandatory and another Member of the League of Nations 'relating to the interpretation or the application of the provisions of the Mandate'. *The language used is broad, clear and precise; it gives rise to no ambiguity and it permits of no exception....* [T]he manifest scope and purport of the provisions of this Article indicate that the Members of the League were understood to have a legal right or interest in the observance by the Mandatory of its obligations both toward the inhabitants of the Mandated Territory, and toward the League of Nations and its Members."[154] [Italics ours]

The contention based upon the fact that Article 22 did not provide for the Mandatory's submission to the Court in regard to its observance of the Mandate was also rejected because Article 7, paragraph 2, was clearly in the nature of implementing one of the "securities for the performance of this trust" and that Article 7 reads: "The Mandatory agrees that ...".

5.   As to the fourth objection. The majority opinion stated as follows:

"The fact that a deadlock was reached in the collective negotiations in the past and the further fact that both the written pleadings and oral arguments of the Parties in the present proceedings have clearly confirmed the continuance of this deadlock, compel a conclusion that no reasonable probability exists that further negotiations would lead to a settlement.

... [Although the Respondent contended that the collective negotiations in the United Nations were one thing and direct negotiations between it and the Applicants were another,] it is not so much the form of negotiation that matters as the attitude and views of the Parties on the substantive issues of the question involved. So long as both sides remain adamant, and this is obvious even from their oral presentations before the Court, there is no reason to think that the dispute can be settled by further negotiations between the Parties."[155]

For these reasons, the majority opinion found that the Court had jurisdiction to adjudicate upon the merits of the dispute.

(2) The Reasoning of the 1966 Judgment

1.   The judgment consists of two parts, the first part being the reasoning itself of the majority opinion leading to the rejection of the Applicants' claims, the second refutation to the criticisms against the reasoning.

2.   The majority opinion set its starting point as follows:

"[T]here was one matter that appertained to the merits of the case but which had an antecedent character, namely the question of the Applicants' standing in the present phase of the proceedings, --- not, that is to say, of their standing before the Court itself, which

---

[154] *Id.* at 343.

[155] *Id.* at 345-46.

was the subject of the Court's decision in 1962, but the question, as a matter of the merits of the case, of their legal right or interest regarding the subject-matter of their claim, as set out in their final submissions." [156]

The majority opinion, before dealing with the question, referred to the structure characterizing the Mandate for South West Africa. Their substantive provisions may be regarded as falling into two main categories: "conduct" provisions defining the mandatory's powers and its obligations in respect of the inhabitants of the territory and towards the League and its organs, and "special interests" provisions conferring in different degrees, according to the particular mandate or category of mandate, certain rights (e.g., freedom for missionaries) relative to the mandated territory, directly upon the members of the League as individual States, or in favour of their nationals.

"In the present case", stated the majority opinion, "the dispute between the Parties relates exclusively to the former of these two categories of provisions, and not to the latter." Consequently, "the question is whether the various mandatories had any direct obligation towards the other members of the League individually, as regards the carrying out of the 'conduct' provisions of the mandates."[157]

3.   The majority opinion, in dealing with this question, set its approach as follows:

"16.   It is in their capacity as former members of the League of Nations that the Applicants appear before the Court.... Accordingly, in order to determine [whether the Applicants' rights include any right individually to call for the due execution of the 'conduct' provisions], *the Court must place itself at the point in time when the mandates system was being instituted, and when the instruments of mandate were being framed.* The Court must have regard to the situation as it was at that time, which was the critical one, and to *the intentions of those concerned as they appear to have existed, or are reasonably to be inferred, in the light of that situation....* Only on this basis can a correct appreciation of the legal rights of the Parties be arrived at.... [T]he meaning of a juridical notion in a historical context, must be sought by reference to the way in which that notion was understood in that context.

17.   It follows that any enquiry into the rights and obligations of the Parties in the present case must proceed principally on the basis of considering, in the setting of their period, the texts of the instruments and particular provisions intended to give juridical expression to the notion of the 'sacred trust of civilization' by instituting a mandates system.

18.   The enquiry must pay no less attention to the juridical character and structure of the institution, the League of Nations, within the framework of which the mandates system was organized, and which inevitably determined how this system was to operate, --- by what

---

[156] South West Africa Cases, Second Phase, [1966] I. C. J. 18.

[157] *Id.* at 22.

methods, --- through what channels, --- and by means of what recourses."[158] [Italics ours]

4.   The majority opinion, based upon this approach, examined the Covenant, the Mandate and the structure of the League, within the framework of which the mandates system functioned, and reached the following conclusion:

> "[T]he Court considers that even in the time of the League, even as members of the League when that organization still existed, the Applicants did not, in their individual capacity as States, possess any separate self-contained right which they could assert, independently of, or additionally to, the right of the League, in the pursuit of its collective, institutional activity, to require the due performance of the Mandate in discharge of the 'sacred trust'. This was vested exclusively in the League, and was exercised through its competent organs."[159]

5.   Next, the majority opinion proceeded to the examination of the criticisms against its reasoning. Here we will look at, among others, the refutations against the arguments based upon "humanitarian considerations" and "necessity".

As to the former, the majority opinion stated as follows:

> "[I]t has been suggested ... that humanitarian considerations are sufficient in themselves to generate legal rights and obligations ... The Court does not think so. *It is a court of law, and can take account of moral principles only in so far as these are given a sufficient expression in legal form....*
>
> 50.   *Humanitarian considerations may constitute the inspirational basis for rules of law,* just as, for instance, the preambular parts of the United Nations Charter constitute the moral and political basis for the specific legal provisions thereafter set out. *Such considerations do not, however, in themselves amount to rules of law.... [T]he existence of an 'interest' does not of itself entail that this interest is specifically juridical in character.*
>
> ... [Even if all civilized nations have an interest in seeing that a 'sacred trust of civilization' is carried out,] in order that this interest may take on a specifically legal character, the sacred trust itself must be or become something more than a moral or humanitarian ideal. *In order to generate legal rights and obligations, it must be given juridical expression and be clothed in legal form.*"[160] [Italics ours]

6.   The latter, the argument of "necessity" was summarized by the majority opinion as follows: since the Council had no means of imposing its views on the mandatory, and since no advisory opinion it might obtain from the Court would be binding on the latter, the mandate could have been flouted at will. *Hence* it was essential, as an ultimate safeguard or security for the performance of the sacred tust, that each member of the League should be deemed to have a legal right or interest in that matter and, in the last resort, be able to take direct action relative to it.

---

[158] *Id.* at 23.

[159] *Id.* at 29.

[160] *Id.* at 34-35.

The majority opinion criticized this argument of "necessity" as understood above, in the following way: in relation to the "conduct" provisions of the mandates, it was never the intention that the Council should be able to impose its views on the various mandatories --- the system adopted was one which deliberately rendered this impossible; in the international field, the existence of obligations that cannot in the last resort be enforced by any legal process, was always the rule rather than the exception; acceptance of the Applicants' contention would involve acceptance of the proposition that even if the Council of the League should be perfectly satisfied with the way in which a mandatory was carrying out its mandate, any individual member of the League could independently invoke the jurisdiction of the Court in order to have the same conduct declared illegal. Consequently, the majority opinion concluded as follows:

"89.   The Court feels obliged in conclusion to point out that *the whole 'necessity' argument appears, in the final analysis, to be based on considerations of an extra-legal character, the product of a process of after-knowledge.... [T]hat necessity, if it exists, lies in the political field. It does not constitute necessity in the eyes of the law.* If the Court, in order to parry the consequences of these events, were now to read into the mandates system, by way of, so to speak, remedial action, *an element wholly foreign to its real character and structure as originally contemplated when the system was instituted*, it would be engaging in an *ex post facto* process, exceeding its functions as a court of law....

91.   It may be urged that the Court is entitled to engage in a process of 'filling in the gaps', in the application of a teleological principle of interpretation, according to which instruments must be given their maximum effect in order to ensure the achievement of their underlying purposes.... [I]t is clear that it can have no application in circumstances in which the Court would have to go beyond what can reasonably be regarded as being a process of interpretation, and would have to engage in a process of rectification or revision. *Rights cannot be presumed to exist merely because it might seem desirable that they should.*"[161]
[Italics ours]

(3) Some Comments

The judgments in 1962 and 1966 were related to various problems and issues.[162] In the context of our study, however, questions in the light of the method of interpretation could be considered to have been properly analyzed by the dissenting opinion of Judge Tanaka. Here we will look at, among others, two points: the survival of the Mandate as an international institution despite the dissolution of the League, and the refutation to the criticism against the argument of "necessity".

1.   As to *the survival of the Mandate as an international institution despite the dissolution of the League*, Judge Tanaka considered that the following three characteristics would distinguish

---

[161] *Id.* at 47-48.

[162] For these points, *see, e.g.*, J. Dugard, *supra* note 100, at 264-75, 332-74; S. Slonim, *supra* note 100, at 278-309.

the Mandate from other kinds of treaties. Firstly, the aims and purposes of the Mandate were, unlike those of commercial treaties, a realization of identical aims (a "sacred trust of civilization"), and similar to law-making treaties. Secondly, the long-term nature of the mandate agreement was what characterized it from the other contracts. This character derived from the nature of the purposes of the mandates system, namely the promotion of material and moral well-being and social progress of the mandated territories, which could not be realized instantaneously or within a foreseeable space of time. Thirdly, the mandate agreement required from the Mandatory a strong sense of moral conscience and was of the nature of a bona fide contract; the weight of the mandates system should be put on the obligations of the Mandatory rather than on its rights. Thus, Judge Tanaka stated:

"From the nature and characteristics of the mandates system and the mandate agreement, indicated above, we can conclude that, *although the existence of contractual elements in the Mandate cannot be denied, the institutional elements predominate over the former.* We cannot explain all the contents and functions of the mandates system from the contractual, namely the individualistic, and subjective viewpoint, but *we are required to consider them from the institutional, namely collectivistic, and objective viewpoint also.*"[163] [Italics ours]

Based upon the above understanding of the mandates system, Judge Tanaka gave the following suggestive statement on the question of the survival of the Mandate as an international institution despite the dissolution of the League:

"The controversy concerning the survival or lapse of the Mandate on the dissolution of the League, and accordingly of rights and obligations created by it, may be, in its final instance, attributed to the fundamental difference of methods existing in regard to the interpretation of law, namely the antagonism between *voluntarism* and *objectivism.* Controversies present themselves as to *whether law cannot attribute certain effects to a treaty or a convention --- which the parties did not or could not foresee at the moment of its inception --- or whether law, on the contrary through its interpretation may be expected to play the function of filling the lacuna of juridical acts by creating certain legal effects uncovered by the original intent of the parties.*

From the point of view of *purely juridical formalism,* there is the conclusion that, so far as the Mandate is conceived as a contract between the two parties, namely the League of Nations on the one hand and the Mandatory on the other, the dissolution of the League would produce, as a necessary consequence, the absolute extinction of the Mandate with all its legal vincula and that nothing remains thereafter. This is the fundamental standpoint upon which the arguments of the Respondent are based....

... *The essential viewpoint of the [1950] Opinion, however, is based on the idea of*

---

[163] *Id.* at 267-68. Similar reference to the characteristics of the mandates system was made by Judge Bustamante (South West Africa Cases, Preliminary Objections, [1962] I. C. J. 356-58).

'international institution with international object --- a sacred trust of civilization', not much on consensual elements.

... The Mandate as an institution is the starting point of the Opinion and the most influential reason to justify the survival of the Mandate notwithstanding the dissolution of the League."[164] [Italics ours]

"The recognition of the institutional side of the Mandate beside its contractual side by the 1950 Advisory Opinion and the 1962 Judgment can confer on the mandates system *a durability beyond the life of the League and an objective existence independent of the original or ulterior intent of the parties.* This recognition is nothing else but a product of a scientific method of interpretation of the mandates system, in which the consideration of spirit and objectives as well as social reality of this system play important roles. This method of interpretaion may be called *sociological* or *teleological,* in contrast with strict juristic formalism. Relying on the concept of the Mandate as an institution of a sociological nature, we take a step forward out of traditional conceptional jurisprudence, which would easily assert the lapse of the Mandate on the dissolution of the League.

What has been said about the question of the survival of the Mandate can be applied to the continuation of international supervision and the replacement by the United Nations of the Council of the League. The solution of the latter question is to be found in the same direction as the former. *The continuation of international supervision of the Mandate by the United Nations is a logical conclusion of the survival of the Mandate as an international institution.*"[165] [Italics ours]

2.   As to *the refutation to the criticism against the argument of "necessity"*[166], Judge Tanaka also gave the following suggestive statement:

"It is argued tht the Court's Opinion on the existence of international supervision, namely the Respondent's accountability to the United Nations, is based on the doctrine of

---

[164] *Id.* at 269.

[165] *Id.* at 276. Zacklin, in this connection, stated as follows(Zacklin, *supra* note 100, at 286):

"It is this clash between Judges Spender and Fitzmaurice, on the one hand, and Judge Jessup, on the other, which points most clearly to the differences in philosophy and judicial approach which shaped the outcome of the South West Africa cases."

It is also to be noted that Judge *ad hoc* Van Wyk asserted that the principle of effectiveness could not override the clear natural meaning of a text and must be understood restrictively (South West Africa Cases, Preliminary Objections [1962] I. C. J. 575-91), and that, on the contrary, Judge Nervo asserted that the interpretation of the Mandate and the obligations of the Respondent, is to be made, taking into account, besides the text and spirit of the relevant instruments, the circumstances existing now in 1966, not only those which prevailed in 1920 (South West Africa Cases, Second Phase [1966] I. C. J. 456, 463-64). *See also,* Dissenting Opinion of Judge Jessup (Treaty Interpretation), *id.* at 352-56.

[166] It is quite suggestive that when Judges Spender and Fitzmaurice, in their joint dissenting opinion in 1962, ciriticized the argument of "necessity" in the same manner, they described the controversy on this point as "the heart of the present case". South West Africa Cases, Preliminary Objections [1962] I. C. J. 518-26.

'necessity', and that the Court cannot exceed the limitation incumbent upon it as a court of law.

Undoubtedly a court of law declares what is the law, but does not legislate. In reality, however, where the borderline can be drawn is a very delicate and difficult matter. Of course, judges declare the law, but they do not function automatically. We cannot deny the possibility of some degree of creative element in their judicial activities. What is not permitted to judges, is to establish law independently of an existing legal system, institution or norm. What is permitted to them is to declare what can be logically inferred from the *raison d'être* of a legal system, legal institution or norm. In the latter case the lacuna in the intent of legislation or parties can be filled.

So far as the continuance of international supervision is concerned, the above-mentioned conclusion cannot be criticized as exceeding the function of the Court to interpret law. The Court's Opinion of 1950 on this question is not creating law simply for the reason of necessity or desirability without being founded in law and fact. *The survival of the Mandate despite the dissolution of the League, the importance of international supervision in the mandates system, the apearance of the United Nations which, as the organized international community, i[s] characterized by political and social homogeneity with the defunct League of Nations, particularly in respect of the 'sacred trust' for peoples who have not yet attained a full measure of self-government, and the establishment of the international trusteeship system, the Respondent's membership in the United Nations, and, finally, the refusal by the Respondent to conclude a trusteeship agreement as expected by the Charter: these factors, individually and as a whole, are enough to establish the continuation of international supervision by the United Nations.*

Consideration of the necessity that the paralysis of mandate without supervision must be avoided, can by no means be denied. But we are not going to deduce the above-mentioned conclusion from mere necessity or desirability but from the *raison d'être* and the theoretical construction of the mandates system as a whole.

We, therefore, must recognize that social and individual necessity constitutes one of the guiding factors for the development of law by the way of interpretation as well as legislation....

Such attitude of interpretation has been known as a method of 'libre recherche scientifique' or 'Freirecht', mainly in civil-law countries for three-quarters of a century as emancipating judges from the rigid interpretation of written laws and emphasizing the creative role in their judicial activities. *There is no reason to believe that the same method should be denied in the field of international law except the opposing tendency of strong voluntarism derived from the concept of soverignty and not being in conformity with the concept of law which attributes to law an objective and independent existence from the will and intention of those to whom law is addressed.*

In short the difference of opinions on the questions before us is in the final instance attributed to *the difference between two methods of interpretation: teleological or sociological and conceptional or formalistic.*"[167] [Italics ours]

5 Legal Consequences for States of the Continued Presence of South West Africa in Namibia (South West Africa) notwithstanding Security Council Resolution 276 (1970) [1971][168]

While the General Assembly, in 1966, decided to terminate South Africa's mandate and to assume direct responsibility for the territory, the Security Council declared, in resolution 276 (1970), that "the continued presence of the South African authorities in Namibia is illegal and that consequently all acts taken by the Government of South Africa on behalf of or concerning Namibia after the termination of the Mandate are illegal and invalid". And the Security Council, in resolution 284 (1970), decided to submit the following question to the ICJ for an advisory opinion: "What are the legal consequences for States of the continued presence of South Africa in Namibia, notwithstanding Security Council resolution 276 (1970) ?". The Court gave the opinion, by 13[169] votes to 2[170], (1) that, the continued presence of South Africa in Namibia being illegal, South Africa was under an obligation to withdraw its administration from Namibia immediately and thus put an end to its occupation of the Territory; by 11 votes to 4[171], (2) that States Members of the United Nations were under obligation to recognize the illegality of its presence and to refrain from any dealings with the Government of South Africa, and (3) that it was incumbent upon Non-Member States to give assistance, within the scope of subparagraph (2) above, in the action taken by the United Nations. President Sir Muhammad Zafrulla Khan made a declaration; Vice-President Ammoun and Judges Padilla Nervo, Petrén, Onyeama, Dillard and de Castro appended separate opinions; Judges Sir Gerald Fitzmaurice and Gros appended dissenting opinions.

---

[167] South West Africa Cases, Second Phase, [1966] I. C. J. 276-78.

[168] For the relevant bibliography on the present advisory opinion, *see*, in addition to those cited in the footnotes, the following: Jaqué, 'L'avis de la Cour International du Justice du 21 Juin 1971', 76 *R. G. D. I. P.* 1046 (1972); Dugard, 'The Opinion on South West Africa (Namibia): the Teleologists Triumph', 88 *South African L. J.* 467 (1971); Dugard, 'Namibia (South West Africa): The Court's Opinion, South Africa's Response, and Prospects for the Future', 11 *Columbia J. Transna'l L.* 14 (1972); Lissitzyn, 'International Law and the Advisory Opinion on Namibia', *id.* at 50; Rovine, 'The World Court Opinion on Namibia', *id.* at 203; Gordon, 'Old Orthodoxies amid New Experiences: The South West Africa (Namibia) Litigation and the Uncertain Jurisprudence of the International Court of Justice', 1 *Denver J. Int'l L. & Policy* 65 (1971).

[169] The thirteen judges were Sir Muhammad Khan (President), Ammoun (Vice-President), Padilla Nervo, Forster, Bengzon, Petrén, Lachs, Onyeama, Dillard, Ignacio-Pinto, de Castro, Morozov and Jiménez de Aréchaga.

[170] The two judges were Sir Gerald Fitzmaurice and Gros.

[171] The four judges were Sir Gerald Fitzmaurice, Gros, Petrén and Onyeama.

(1) The Reasoning of the Majority Opinion

1.   The majority opinion could be, for convenience, divided into three parts: the first part dealt with the preliminary objections by the Government of South Africa; the second related to the main issues of the question; the third dealt with, based upon the conclusions reached above, the legal consequences arising for States. We will focus upon the second part in the context of our study.

2.   The second part related to several important issues. In the first issue, which is the most important point in the context of our study, the majority opinion examined, as the issues underlying the question, the substance and scope of Article 22 of the League Covenant and the nature of "C" mandates. Against the view of the Government of South Africa that "C" mandates were in their practical effect not far removerd from annexation, the majority opinion, after referring to Article 22 of the Covenant and Articles of the Mandate, concluded as follows:

> "In sum the relevant provisions of the Covenant and those of the Mandate itself preclude any doubt as to the establishment of definite legal obligations designed for the attainment of the object and purpose of the Mandate.
>
> ... [T]he final outcome of the negotiations [preceding the adoption of the final version of Article 22 of the League Conenant], however difficult of achievement, was a rejection of the notion of annexation. It cannot tenably be argued that the clear meaning of the mandate institution could be ignored by placing upon the explicit provisions embodying its principles a construction at variance with its object and purpose."[172]

What is quite important is the following reason given to support the above conclusion.

> "51.   Events subsequent to the adoption of the instruments in question should also be considered. [Reference was made to the practice of the Allied and Associated Powers.]
>
> 52.   Furthermore, the subsequent development of international law in regard to non-self-governing territories, as enshrined in the Charter of the United Nations, made the principle of self-determination applicable to all of them....
>
> 53.   All these considerations are germane to the Court's evaluation of the present case. *Mindful as it is of the primary necessity of interpreting an instrument in accordance with the intentions of the parties at the time of its conclusion, the Court is bound to take into account the fact that the concepts embodied in Article 22 of the Covenant --- 'the strenuous conditions of the modern world' and 'the well-being and development' of the peoples concerned --- were not static, but were by definition evolutionary, as also, therefore, was the concept of the 'sacred trust'. The parties to the Covenant must consequently be deemed to have accepted them as such.* That is why, viewing the institutions of 1919, the Court must take into consideration the changes which have occurred in the supervening half-century, and *its interpretation cannot remain unaffected by the subsequent development of law,* through the Charter of the United Nations and by

---

[172] Advisory Opinion on Legal Consequences for States of the Continued Presence of South Africa in Namibia (South West Africa) notwithstanding Security Council Resolution 276 (1970), [1971] I. C. J. 30.

way of customary law. Moreover, *an international instrument has to be interpreted and applied within the framework of the entire legal system prevailing at the time of the interpretation.* In the domain to which the present proceedings relate, the last fifty years, as indicated above, have brought important developments. These developments leave little doubt that the ultimate objective of the sacred trust was the self-determination and independence of the peoples concerned. In this domain, as elsewhere, the *corpus iuris gentium* has been considerably enriched, and this the Court, if it is faithfully to discharge its functions, may not ignore."[173] [Italics mostly ours]

In the light of the foregoing, the Court was unable to accept any construction which would attach to "C" mandates an object and purpose different from those of "A" or "B" mandates.

3.   Secondly, the majority opinion examined the situation which had arisen on the demise of the League and with the birth of the United Nations. Based upon the continuing necessity for supervision upon which the 1950 opinion relied, the majority opinion stated as follows:

"[T]he League of Nations was the international organization entrusted with the exercise of the supervisory functions of the Mandate. Those functions were an indispensable element of the Mandate. But that does not mean that the mandates institution was to collapse with the disappearance of the original supervisory machinery. To the question whether the continuance of a mandate was inseparably linked with the existence of the League, the answer must be that *an institution established for the fulfilment of a sacred trust cannot be presumed to lapse before the achievement of its purpose.* The responsibilities of both mandatory and supervisor resulting from the mandates institution were complementary, and the disppearance of one or the other could not affect the survival of the institution....

57.   *It would have been contrary to the overriding purpose of the mandates system to assume that difficulties in the way of the replacement of one regime by another designed to improve international supervision should have been permitted to bring about, on the dissolution of the League, a complete disappearance of international supervision.*"[174] [Italics ours]

The majority opinion supported the above conclusion by interpreting Article 80 of the Charter of the United Nations, a resolution of the Assembly of the League, the practice of the South African Government and the practice of the United Nations. The fact, however, that these elements were in principle included in the 1950 opinions is clear from the expression by the majority opinion of "this brief *summary* of the events preceding the present request for advisory opinion".[175]

4.   Thirdly, the majority opinion dealt with various objections concerning the General Assembly

---

[173]   *Id.* at 31-32.

[174]   *Id.* at 32-33.

[175]   *Id.* at 45.

resolution or Security Council resolutions. Here we will draw attention to the reasons given by the majority opinion to reject the objections on the following two points.

In the first place, against the contention that the Covenant of the League of Nations did not confer on the Council of the League power to terminate a mandate for misconduct of the mandatory, the majority opinion stated as follows:

"For this objection to prevail it would be necessary to show that the mandates system, as established under the League, excluded the application of *the general principle of law that a right of termination on account of breach must be presumed to exist in respect of all treaties , except as regards provisions relating to the protection of the human person contained in treaties of a humanitarian character (as indicated in Art. 60, para. 5, of the Vienna Convention)*. The silence of a treaty as to the existence of such a right cannot be interpreted as implying the exclusion of a right which has its source outside of the treaty, in general international law, and is dependent on the occurrence of circumstances which are not normally envisaged when a treaty is concluded."[176] [Italics]

In the second place, as to the scope of the binding decisions by the Security Council based upon Articles 24 and 25 of the Charter, the majority opinion, resorting to the textual approach (here the context), stated as follows:

"113. It has been contended that Article 25 of the Charter applies only to enforcement measures adopted under Chapter VII of the Charter. It is not possible to find in the Charter any support for this view. Article 25 is not confined to decisions in regard to enforcement action but applied to 'the decisions of the Security Council' adopted in accordance with the Charter. Moreover, that Article is placed, not in Chapter VII, but immediately after Article 24 in that part of the Charter which deals with the functions and powers of the Security Council. If Article 25 had reference solely to decisions of the Security Council concerning enforcement action under Articles 41 and 42 of the Charter, that is to say, if it were only such decisions which had binding effect, then Article 25 would be superfluous, since this effect is secured by Articles 48 and 49 of the Charter."[177]

(2) The Reasoning of the Dissenting Opinion of Judge Fitzmaurice

1.   Judge Fitzmaurice, at the outset, pointed out that the majority opinion was based upon an unsubstantiated assumption that the survival of the Mandate *necessarily* entailed the supervisory role of the United Nations, and presented his fundamental position by saying as follows:

"My reading of the situation is based --- in orthodox fashion --- on what appears to have been *the intentions of those concerned at the time*. The Court's view, the outcome of a different, and to me alien philosophy, is based on *what has become the intentions of new*

---

[176] *Id.* at 47.

[177] *Id.* at 52-53.

112

and different entities and organs fifty years later."[178] [Italics ours]

2.   Firstly, in connection with the survival of the reporting obligation, Judge Fitzmaurice pointed out as follows:

> "Holding that the reporting obligation was an essential part of the mandates system, and
> must survive if the system itself survived, the Court went on to hold that *therefore* it
> survived as an obligation to report specifically to the Assembly of the United Nations. This
> last leg of the argument not only lacked all logical rigour and necessity but involved an
> obvious fallacy, --- which was the reason for the dissenting views expressed by Judges Sir
> Arnold McNair (as he then was) and Read --- dissenting views with which I agree."[179]

Judge Fitzmaurice, after examining Articles 10 and 80, reached the following conclusion based upon *the textual approach*:

> "It comes to this therefore, that there is absolutely nothing in Article 80 to enable it to be
> read as if it said 'The League is still in being, but if and when it becomes extinct, all
> mandatories who are Members of the United Nations will thereupon owe to the latter
> Organization their obligations in respect of mandated territories'. *That* of course ... is
> precisely what (or something like it) the Charter ought to have stated, in order to bring
> about the results which --- (once it had become clear that SW. Africa was not going to be
> placed under the United Nations trusteeship system) --- it was then attempted to deduce
> from such provisions as Articles 10 and 80. But the Charter said no such thing, and these
> Articles, neither singly nor together, will bear the weight of such a deduction."[180]

3.   Secondly, in responding negatively to the question whether the League had any power of unilateral revocation of mandates, Judge Fitzmaurice showed his *restrictive understanding of the doctrine of implied powers* when he said:

> "Where a sovereign State is concerned, and where also it is not merely a question of
> pronouncing on the legal position, but of ousting that State from an administrative role
> which it is physically in the exercise of , it is not possible to rely on any theory of implied
> or inherent powers. It would be necessary that these should have been given concrete
> expression in whatever are the governing instruments....
>
> 72.   In consequence, within a jurisprudential system involving sovereign independent States
> and the major international organizations whose membership they make up, there must be
> a natural presumption *against* the existence of any such drastic thing as a power of
> unilaterally displacing a State from a position or status which it holds."[181]

4.   Thirdly, in indicating the limit of the competence and powers of the United Nations, Judge Fitzmaurice referred to the scope of the implied powers of the General Assembly and the legal

---

[178] *Id.* at 223.

[179] *Id.* at 234.

[180] *Id.* at 239.

[181] *Id.* at 267-68.

value of the practice of the Organization. *The Assembly had,* he stated, *no implied powers except those purely domestic, internal, and procedural executive powers without which such a body could not function,* e.g., to elect its own officers; fix the dates and times of its meetings; determine its agenda; appoint standing committees and *ad hoc* ones; establish staff regulations; decide to hold a diplomatic conference under United Nations auspices, and so on. All its powers, whether they be executive or recommendatory, were precisely formulated in the Charter and there was no residuum.[182]

Certainly, Judge Fitzmaurice admitted that naturally any organ must be deemed to have the powers necessary to enable it to perform the specific functions it was invested with. Here he cited the formula of the doctrine of implied powers that the Court presented in the *Reparation* case. It must be noted, however, that Judge Fitamaurice added the following explanation:

> "This is acceptable if it is read as being related and confined to existing and specified duties; but it would be quite another matter, by a process of implication, to seek to bring about an extension of functions, such as would result for the Assembly if it were deemed (outside of Articles 4, 5, 6 and 17) to have a non-specified power, not only to discuss and recommend, but to take executive action, and to bind."[183]

Judge Fitzmaurice was also negative on *the legal value given to the practice of the Organization,* and stated as follows:

> "In the same way, whereas the practice of an organization, or of a particular organ of it, can modify the manner of exercise of one of its functions (as for instance in the case of the veto in the Security Council which is not deemed to be involved by a mere abstention), such practice cannot, in principle, modify or add to the function itself. Without in any absolute sense denying that, through a sufficiently steady and long-continued course of conduct, a new *tacit agreement* may arise having a modificatory effect, the presumption is against it, --- especially in the case of an organization whose constituent instrument provides for its own amendment, and prescribes with some particularity what the means of effecting this are to be."[184]

(3) Some Comments

1.   The most important point in the context of our study is, as was pointed out above in the reasoning of the majority opinion, the method of interpretation of international instruments. As was acknowledged by the majority opinion, the international instrument here in question was a mandate, a special type of instrument which was not only an international agreement having a

---

[182] *Id.* at 281.

[183] *Id.* at 282.

[184] *Id.*

nature of treaty, but also was composite in nature and instituted a novel international régime.[185] Consequently what was in question was a method of interpreting a special type of treaty having an institutional character.[186]

The specificity of this method of interpretation will be clear when we compare the present majority opinion with the dissenting opinion of Judge Fitzmaurice or with the majority opinion in 1966 judgment. *While the latter aimed at seeking the intentions of the parties at the time when the treaty was concluded, the former, although it also pointed out such a necessity, gave greater weight to the circumstances at the time of interpretation.* If we carefully read the relevant portion of the majority opinion, we could distinguish two points.[187]

The first point is that *the concepts embodied in Article 22 were not static, but were by definition evolutionary.* While it was Article 22 of the Covenant and the Mandate which were in question, the same consideration would, it can be asserted, apply to *the constituent instrument of an international organization*; the constituent instrument, in principle, does not provide in a contractual manner for respective rights and obligations of the parties like ordinary treaties, but establishes an international organization which could be reasonably expected to adapt itself to the changing circumstances and to continue to efficiently function and effectively perform its activities; for this reason, *it comprises a lot of provisions which are not static but are by definition evolutionary.*

The second point is that *an international instrument has to be interpreted and applied within the framework of the entire legal system prevailing at the time of the interpretation.* As is clear from the expression, this statement applies not only to the mandate and the constituent instrument of an international organization, but also to all international instruments. Here the contrast with the opposing philosophy of the 1966 judgment was clearly demonstrated.[188]

---

[185] The majority opinion stated as follows (*id.* at 46):

"94. In examining this action of the General Assembly it is appropriate to have regard to the general principles of international law regulating termination of a treaty relationship on account of breach. For even if the mandate is viewed as having the character of an institution, as is maintained, it depends on those international agreements which created the system and regulated its application. As the Court indicated in 1962 'this Mandate, like practically all other similar Mandates' was 'a special type of instrument composite in nature and instituting a novel international régime. It incorporates a definite agreement ...' (*I. C. J. Reports 1962*, p. 331). The Court stated conclusively in that judgment that the Mandate '... in fact and in law, is an international agreement having the character of a treaty or convention' (*I. C. J. Reports 1962*, p. 330)."

[186] Hirose, 'The Right of Self-Determination of Peoples and the Powers of the United Nations [in Japanese] ', 204 *Meiji Gakuin L. Rev.* 1, 45 (1973).

[187] Bollecker, 'L'avis consultatif du 21 Juin 1971 dans l'affaire de la Namibie (Sud-Est Africain), 17 *A. F. D. I.* 281, 290-94 (1971).

[188] *See also* Hevener, 'The 1971 South-West African Opinion, A New International Judicial Philosophy', 24 *Int'l & Comp. L. Q.* 791 (1975).

In this connection, the following statement of Simon (D. Simon, *supra* note 22, at 445-46) seems suggestive:

"Certes, le temps n'est plus où le droit international était conçu comme une tentative de stabiliser l'état des rapports interétatiques à un moment donné, en cristallisant définitivement un accord de volontés, provisoire par

2.   The majority opinion, in addition to the evolutionary approach mentioned above, resorted to firstly, a positive presumption that the silence of a treaty does not exclude an application of a right of general international law, and secondly, various methods of interpretation, as occasion demands, as is shown by an example of a wide interpretation based upon the Charter text of the Security Council power to make binding decisions. Both of these points were criticized by Judge Fitzmaurice who placed greater weight on the State sovereignty. The first point was referred to in the reasoning of Judge Fitzmaurice. As to the second point, he stated as follows:

"I am unable to agree with the extremely wide interpretation which the Opinion of the Court places on [Article 24].... [T]he second paragraph of Article 24 states in terms that the *specific* powers granted to the Security Council for these purposes are laid down in the indicated Chapters (VI, VII, VIII and XII). According to normal canons of interpretation this means that so far as *peace-keeping* is concerned, they are not to be found anywhere else, and are exercisable only as those Chapters allow. It is therefore to them that recourse must be had in order to ascertain what the *specific* peace-keeping powers of the Security Council are, *including the power to bind*. If this is done, it will be found that only when the Council is acting under Chapter VII, or possibly in certain cases under Chapter VIII, will its resolutions be binding on member States. In other cases their effect would be recommendatory or hortatory only."[189] [Italics original]

Thus, both of the majority opinion and Judge Fitzmaurice resorted to the textual approach in their respective way. This indicates that the difference of value judgments underlying their

---

essence, dans la forme immuable d'une convention ... [I]l n'en demeure pas moins que le juge sortirait incontestablement de sa fonction judiciaire s'il se croyait autorisé, sous couvert d'adaptation du droit aux nécessités évolutives du fonctionnement de l'organisation, à interpréter les conventions en tenant compte exclusivement des 'exigences de la vie contemporaine et non des intentions de ceux qui les ont rédigées'. C'est pourquoi il semble largement excessif d'affirmer que le dynamisme intrinsèque des traités constitutifs d'organisations internationales a provoqué, dans la jurisprudence internationale, l'abandon d'une doctrine traditionnelle, statique et rigide, fondée sur la recherche des intentions initiales des parties, au profit d'une méthode nouvelle, dynamique et évolutive, voire d'un 'nouveau principe général du droit international' selon lequel les conventions constitutionnelles doivent s'interpréter exclusivement 'en regardant en avant'. S'il est vrai en effet que le juge international s'est donné les moyens d'une interprétation donnant effet à la volonté des parties, un examen attentif de la jurisprudence montre à l'évidence que cette attitude est loin d'être générale et absolue."

In this way, Simon tried to understand the second point mentioned in the text within the framework of the first point when he said (*id.* at 449-50): "seules les notions 'évolutives par définition', conçues comme telles par les parties dès la conclusion de la convention, devaient être interprétées en tenant compte des transformations de leur environnement juridique et en adaptant leur signification aux nouvelles données du 'corpus juris gentium'." This understanding is logical and persuasive although it seems incompatible with "tout instrument international" in the French text of the majority opinion.

[189] *Namibia* case, *supra* note 172, at 293.

approaches played a decisive role.[190]

3.   The judicial philosophy of Judge Fitzmaurice who appended a dissenting opinion in the present advisory opinion and also played a leading role in the 1966 judgment was concisely summarized by Merrills as follows:

"Far from conceiving them as 'manifestations of the organized world community' or other noble abstraction, Fitzmaurice ... has regarded international organizations as fundamentally contractual entities possessed of few powers beyond those specifically conferred by their constituent instruments. Hence the narrow approach to implied powers in the *Namibia* opinion, the cautious attitude towards the financial powers of the General Assembly in the *Expenses* case, and the emphasis upon consent as the key to the question of succession in the *South West Africa* cases. In these opinions Fitzmaurice did not, of course, deny the political importance of the institutions in question, nor the legal significance of their activities. He was, however, concerned to maintain the principle that their powers were limited by international law and to construe those limitations strictly....

... Fitzmaurice's approach to interpretation was strict because his conception of international law is fundamentally conservative. The *Namibia* and *South West Africa* cases, both of which arose out of an extreme tension between the political ideas of the present and those of the past, highlighted this."[191]

Such an approach of Judge Fitzmaurice is not immune from criticism. Zacklin, for example, stated as follows:

"[I]t is possible to admire the rigour of his legal reasoning and the very high standards of positivist interpretation he so forcefully projects without, however, being fully convinced. It is ... not merely a rigid approach to interprertation and the judicial function; it is a static approach. It is an approach which in order to maintain its own internal logic consigns international law and international institutions to a permanent state of ineffectiveness."[192]

4.   Finally, it would be useful to introduce briefly the view of Judge de Castro who positively admitted the specific character of constituent instruments. According to Judge de Castro, a distinction should first of all be made between the various types of legal texts: (a) treaties dominated by bargaining, each party seeking its own advantage, to obtain the maximum and give the minimum; (b) agreements by which an organization grants certain powers or privileges to a State, which the latter accepts; (c) treaties by which an international organization is set up, and the resolutions of such an organization.[193] In particular, he elaborated on constituent instruments

---

[190] This is a controversial point. *See, e.g.*, Higgins, 'The Advisory Opinion on Namibia: Which UN Resolutions Are Binding under Article 25 of the Charter ?', 21 *Int'l & Comp. L. Q.* 270, 286 (1972); Dugard, 'Namibia (South West Africa): The Court's Opinion, South Africa's Response, and Prospects for the Future', *supra* note 168, at 29-32.

[191] Merrills, 'Sir Gerald Fitzmaurice's Contribution to the Jurisprudence of the International Court of Justice', 48 *Brit. Y. B. Int'l L.* 183, 238-39 (1976-77).

[192] Zacklin, *supra* note 100, at 305.

[193] *Namibia* case, *supra* note 172, at 305.

as follows:

"3.   Multilateral treaties, conventions establishing an international organization and above all the Charter, are subject to particular rules of interpretation.

The Charter would appear not to fall within the framework of the Convention on the Law of Treaties. To interpret it, one should not apply by analogy the rules of municipal law on contracts, but rather rules for the interpretation of laws and statutes.

It should not be forgotten that the General Assembly and Security Council have the responsibility of promoting the purposes laid down in the Charter. *They cannot remain bound by the possible intentions of the draftsmen, not only because it is difficult to know what those intentions were* (while the intentions of those who speak are known, the intentions of those who give their vote in silence are not), *but also because interpretation necessarily undergoes a process of development, and, as in municipal law, must adapt itself to the circumstance of the time and to the requirements, so far as they are foreseeable, of the future. The text breaks away from its authors and lives a life of its own.*"[194] [Italics ours]

Section 4 Questions Relating to Specialized Agencies

1. Constitution of the Maritime Safety Committee
of the Inter-Governmental Maritime Consultative Organization [1960][195]

In 1959, the Assembly elected eight Members (the largest ship-owning nations) of the Maritime Safety Committee in accordance with Article 28 (a), but did not elect Liberia and Panama that appeared, respectively, as the third and eighth largest in Lloyd's Register of Shipping Statistical Tables 1958 because, presumably, of the flag of convenience. Consequently, the Assembly decided to submit to the ICJ a request for an advisory opinion on the following question: "Is the Maritime Safety Committee of the Inter-Governmental Maritime Consultative Organization, which was elected on 15 January 1959, constituted in accordance with the Convention for the Establishment of the Organization?". The Court reached a negative conclusion by 9[196] votes to 5[197]. President Klaestad and Judge Moreno Quintana appended their dissenting

---

[194] *Id.* at 184.

[195] For the relevant bibliography on the present advisory opinion, *see* Colliard, 'Avis Consultatif relatif à la composition du Comité de Sécurité maritime de l'Orgnisation intergouvernementale consulatative de la Navigation maritime du 8 juin 1960', 6 *A. F. D. I.* 338 (1960); Simmonds, 'The Constitution of the Maritime Safety Committee of IMCO', 12 *Int'l & Comp. L. Q.* 56 (1963); 'The IMCO Opinion: A Study in Treaty Interpretation', *Duke L. J.* 288 (1961); H. Meyers, *The Nationality of Ships* 227-39 (1967).

[196] The nine judges were among the following twelve: Zafrulla Khan (Vice-President), Basdevant, Hackworth, Winiarski, Badawi, Armand-Ugon, Kojevnikov, Córdova, Wellington Koo, Spiropoulos, Sir Percy Spender and Alfaro.

[197] The five judges were Klaestad (President), Moreno Quintana and three judges among the twelve listed above.

opinions.

(1) The Reasoning of the Majority Opinion

1.   The majority opinion could be considered, for convenience, to consist of three parts: (1) summary of three contentions, (2) consideration of "a discretionary power" vested in the Assembly relating to the first and second contention, by reference to (a)the text and (b) its *travaux préparatoires,* (3) consideration of "the largest ship-owning nations" relating to the third contention.

2.   The majority opinion, at the outset, summarized a series of contentions claiming that the Assembly was vested with a discretionary power in electing the Members of the Committee as follows:

"It has been contended before the Court that the Assembly was entitled to refuse to elect Liberia and Panama, by virtue of a discretion claimed to be vested in it under Article 28 (a). The substance of the argument is as follows: The Assembly is vested with a discretionary power to determine which Members of the Organization have 'an important interest in maritime safety' and consequently in discharging its duty to elect the eight largest ship-owning nations, it is empowered to exclude as unqualified for election those nations that in its judgment do not have such an interest. Furthermore, it was submitted that this discretionary power extended also to the determination of which nations were or were not 'the largest ship-owning nations'.

In the first place, it was sought to find in the expression 'elected', which applies to all Members of the Committee, a notion of choice which was said to imply an individual judgment on each member to be elected and a free appraisal as to the qualifications of that member....

In the second place it is contended that 'having an important interest in maritime safety' is a dominant condition in the qualification for membership on the Committee and being one of the 'eight largest ship-owning nations' is a subordinate condition....

It is further claimed that the words 'ship-owning nations' have a meaning which embraces consideration of many factors, and that the Assembly was, in the exercise of its discretion, entitled to take those factors into account in the election of the Committee."[198]

3.   The majority opinion, after summarizing the three contentions, proceeded to the consideration of the basic issue common to the first and second contentions: whether the Assembly was vested with a discretionary power in discharging its duty to elect the eight largest ship-owning nations. It set its approach to the interpretation of Article 28 (a) of the Convention for the Establishment of the Organization as follows:

"The words of Article 28 (a) must be read in their *natural and ordinary meaning*, in the sense which they would normally have in their context. *It is only if, when this is done,*

---

[198]   Advisory Opinion on Constitution on the Maritime Safety Committee of the Inter-Governmental Maritime Consultative Organization, [1960] I. C. J. 158-59.

119

the words of the Article are ambiguous in any way that resort need be had to other methods of construction. (Competence of the General Assembly for the Admission of a State to the United Nations, I. C. J. Reports 1950, p. 8.)"[199] [Italics ours]

4.   Following the above quotation, the majority opinion developed its reasoning based upon the above approach, and reached a negative conclusion as to the discretionary power. This part would be the core of the present advisory opinion.

"From the terms of Article 28 (a) it is clear that the draftsmen deliberately contemplated that *the preponderant control of the Committee was in all circumstances to be vested in 'the largest ship-owning nations'....* The language employed --- 'of which not less than eight shall be the largest ship-owning nations' --- in *its natural and ordinary meaning conveys this intent of the draftsmen.*

The words 'having an important interest in maritime safety' clearly express a qualification for membership on the Committee which is required of each group referred to in Article 28 (a). But, in the context of the whole provision, possession of this interest is implied in relation to the eight largest ship-owning nations as a consequence of the language employed....

This interpretation accords with the structure of the Article....

The argument based on discretion would permit the Assembly, in use only of its discretion, to decide through its vote which nations have or do not have an important interest in maritime safety and to deny membership on the Committee to any State regardless of the size of its tonnage or any other qualification. *The effect of such an interpretation would be to render superfluous the greater part of Article 28 (a)* and to erect the discretion of the Assembly as the supreme rule for the constitution of the Maritime Safety Committee. This would in the opinion of the Court be *incompatible with the principle underlying the Article.*

The underlying principle of Article 28 (a) is that the largest ship-owning nations shall be in predominance on the Committee. No interpretation of the Article which is not consonant with this principle is admissible."[200] [Italics ours]

5.   While the majority opinion reached the above conclusion, it also considered the *travaux préparatoires* without indicating the reason for it. It devoted to its consideration four pages out

---

[199]   *Id.* at 159-60. When the majority opinion summarized the first contention, it added the following contextual comment (*id.* at 158):

"The meaning of the word 'elected' in the Article cannot be determined in isolation by recourse to its usual or common meaning and attaching that meaning to the word where used in the Article. The word obtains its meaning from the context in which it is used. If the context requires a meaning which connotes a wide choice, it must be construed accordingly, just as it must be given a restrictive meaning if the context in which it is used so requires."

[200]   *Id.* at 160-61.

of fourteen corresponding to the substantive part of its reasoning and stated at its conclusion as follows: under the first three drafts of Article 28, the intention that it should be obligatory upon the Assembly to appoint to the Committee a predominating number of the largest ship-owning nations remained constant; the words of Article 28 have a mandatory and imperative sense and precisely carry out the intention of the framers of the Convention.[201]

6.   Finally, the majority opinion considered *the meaning of "the largest ship-owning nations"* relating to the third contention. At the outset, the majority opinion introduced the opinions of the Netherlands and the United Kingdom summarized above as the third contention, and pointed out as follows:

> "[Under such an interpretation,] the mandatory words 'not less than eight shall be the largest ship-owning nations' would be left without significance. To give to the Article such a construction would mean that the structure built into the Article to ensure the predominance on the Committee of 'the' largest ship-owning nations in the ratio of at least eight to six would be undermined and would collapse. The Court is unable to accept an interpretation which would have such a result."[202]

The majority opinion continued. In order to determine which nations were the largest ship-owning nations, it was apparent that some basis of measurement must be applied. There appeared to be but two meanings which could demand serious consideration: (1) the tonnage beneficially owned by the nationals of a State and (2) the registered tonnage of a flag State regardless of its private or State ownership. The majority opinion adopted the second criterion by relying upon, firstly, the actual practice followed in the IMCO Convention and, secondly, international practice and maritime usage. Firstly, by stating "[a]n examination of certain Articles of the Convention and the actual practice which was followed in giving effect to them throws some light on the Court's consideration of the question"[203], it considered Article 60 providing for entry into force of the Convention and Article 17 (c) providing for election of two members. Secondly, by stating "the test of registered tonnage is that which is most consonant with international practice and with maritime usage"[204], it referred to such conventions as the Load Line Convention of 1930.

7.   While the majority opinion rejected the three contentions, it also attempted some justification of the conclusion it reached. By relying upon such considerations as harmony with the purposes of the Convention and effective performance of IMCO's duty, it stated as follows:

> "The interpretation the Court gives to Article 28 (a) is consistent with the general purpose of the Convention and the special functions of the Maritime Safety Committee. The Organization established by the Convention is a consultative one only, and the Maritime Safety Committee is the body which has the duty to consider matters within the

---

[201] *Id.* at 164-65.

[202] *Id.* at 166.

[203] *Id.* at 167.

[204] *Id.* at 169.

scope of the Organization and of recommending through the Council and the Assembly to Member States, proposals for maritime regulation. In order effectively to carry out these recommendations and to promote maritime safety in its numerous and varied aspects, the co-operation of those States who exercise jurisdiction over a large portion of the world's existing tonnage is essential. The Court cannot subscribe to an interpretation of 'largest ship-owning nations' in Article 28 (a) which is out of harmony with the purposes of the Convention and which would empower the Assembly to refuse Membership of the Maritime Safety Committee to a State, regardless of the fact that it ranks among the first eight in terms of registered tonnage."[205]

(2) The Reasoning of the Dissenting Opinions

While President Klaestad and Judge Moreno Quintana appended their dissenting opinions, they do not seem to go beyond the summary of the three contentions by the majority opinion. Suffice it to draw attention to the following two points.

Firstly, according to President Klaestad, the interpretation that, of the Members which the Assembly had found to have "an important interest in maritime safety" (the first condition), not less than eight should be "the largest ship-owning nations" (the second condition), would not render superfluous the second condition. The interpretation of the majority opinion, however, rendered superfluous the first condition as far as the eight largest ship-owning nations. This would not be in accordance with the usual canons of interpretation.[206]

Secondly, Judge Moreno Quintana criticized conferring upon the gross tonnage figures listed in *Lloyd's Register of Shipping* a determining function, and stated: "Had such been the intention of the drafters of the Convention, they would not, in order to achieve this purpose, have selected the procedure of election, but that of *ex officio* nomination."[207]

(3) Some Comments

1. The present advisory opinion resorted to various methods of interpretation. A study[208] which anayzed this opinion in the light of treaty interpretation pointed out that it resorted to six methods of interpretation: (1) natural and ordinary meaning; (2) reading the treaty as a whole; (3) preparatory documents; (4) apparent purpose of the treaty; (5) subsequent practice; and (6) contemporareous usage. What is interesting for us in the present context is the following opinion stated at the conclusion of this study:

"That the Court has utilized principles of interpretation which are severally characteristic of the approach of the intentionist, the teleologist, and the textualist does not mean that it has failed to develop a consistent theory of interpretation. The relationship which the

---

[205] *Id.* at 170-71.

[206] *Id.* at 175.

[207] *Id.* at 177.

[208] A Study in Treaty Interpretation, *supra* note 195.

Court has itself assigned to these principles indicates that *it puts its first reliance on the textualist principle of ordinary and natural meaning* and that *it resorts to other principles, of whatever theoretical allegiance, only to confirm its textual analysis or to resolve an ambiguity in the text itself.*"[209] [Italics ours]

2.   As to the conclusion of the majority opinion, there exist different opinions as is shown by the voting confrontation of 9 votes to 5. For example, Simmonds, in the light of established canons of treaty interpretation, criticized as follows: Does the application of the principles of *actuality*, and of *natural and ordinary meaning* lead to the substitution of the word "determine" for the word "elect"? Does not the principle of *integration* lead also to the conclusion that interest in maritime safety is an essential qualification of all candidates? It does not appear from the *travaux préparatoires* that that interest was intended to be regarded as axiomatic; it is only by the attribution to the IMCO Assembly of a discretionary power that one can arrive at a "reason and meaning" in all parts of the disputed text as the principle of *effectiveness* would require. "In sum, the opinion may be regarded as disappointing in its application of the rules of treaty interpretation and unhelpful in relation to the purposes and functions of the Inter-Governmental Maritime Consultative Organisation."[210]

It is clear that at the basis of these criticisms lay the problem of "flags of convenience" and the consideration of a genuine link between the owner of a ship and the flag it flies.[211] These questions were, however, not the issue before the Court.[212] The Court was requested to judge the validity of the election in the light of the terms of the constituent instrument of IMCO. From this viewpoint, it could be reasonably pointed out[213] that the attempt to exclude Liberia and Panama by virtue of a criterion of "genuine link" would be an argument *de lege ferenda* and that, unless the constituent instrument would not be amended to that effect, the majority opinion would be correct.

In fact, Article 28 was amended in 1965 (entered into force in 1966) and became consonant with the contentions and the dissenting opinions that the majority opinion rejected: "The Maritime Safety Committee shall consist of sixteen Members elected by the Assembly from Members, Governments of those States having an important interest in maritime safety of

---

[209] *Id.* at 301.

[210] Simmonds, *supra* note 195, at 85-86. *See also* Colliard, *supra* note 194, at 354-55.

[211] This point was clear from the written statements of governments, and Judge Moreno Quintana specifically took up this point. IMCO Case, *supra* note 198, at 178.

[212] The majority opinion lightly dismissed this contention as follows (*id.* at 171):

"The Court having reached the conclusion that the determination of the largest ship-owning nations depends solely upon the tonnage registered in the countries in question, any further examination of the contention based on a genuine link is irrelevant for the purpose of answering the question which has been submitted to the Court for an advisory opinion."

[213] *Kihon Hanrei Sôsho Kokusaiho (Basic Cases on International Law)* 99 (Miyazaki ed. 1981).

which: (a) Eight Members shall be elected from among the ten largest shipowing States.... "[214] This provision was further amended in 1974 (entered into force in 1978) and stipulates as follows: "The Maritime Safety Committee shall consist of all Members."

2. Appeal relating to the Jurisdiction of the ICAO Council [1972][215]

In 1971, India instituted, by invoking Article 84 of the Convention on International Civil Aviation, Article II of the International Air Services Transit Agreement and Articles 36 and 37 of the Statute of the ICJ, an appeal from the decisions rendered by the Council of the International Civil Aviation Organization (ICAO) on the Preliminary Objections raised by India in respect of an Application and a Complaint brought before the Council by Pakistan. Consequently, the Court must deal with not the substance of the dispute as placed before the Council, but the purely jurisdictional issue, namely the competence of the Council to hear and determine the case submitted by Pakistan. India demanded that the Court declare that the Council has no jurisdiction to handle the matters presented by Pakistan in its Application and Complaint. Pakistan demanded that the Court reject the Appeal of India and confirm the decisions of the Council. While the judgment consisted of two parts ((1) jurisdiction of the Court to entertain the appeal, and (2) jurisdiction of the Council of ICAO to entertain the merits of the case), the Court, by thirteen votes[216] to three[217], (1) rejected Pakistan's objections and found its jurisdiction, and, by fourteen votes to two[218], (2) held the Council to be competent to entertain the Application and Complaint and rejected India's appeal. President Sir Muhammad Zafrulla Khan and Judge Lachs made declarations; Judges Petrén, Onyeama, Dillard, de Castro and Jiménez de Aréchaga appended separate opinions; Judge Morozov and Judge *ad hoc* Nagendra Singh appended dissenting opinions.

(1) The Reasoning of the Majority Opinion

I Jurisdiction of the Court to Entertain the Appeal

1.	The majority opinion, in the former part of the judgment, dealt with certain objections,

---

[214]	Kano, 'Revision of the IMCO Convention and Flags of Convenience [in Japanese]', 28(4) *Kobe L. J.* 369, 396-437 (1979).

[215]	For the relevant bibliography on the present judgment, *see, e.g.,* FitzGerald, 'The Judgement of the International Court of Justice in the Appeal Relating to the Jurisdiction of the ICAO Council', 12 *Canadian Y. B. Int'l L.* 153 (1974); Huntzinger, 'L'affair de l'appel concernant la compétence de Conseil du l'O. A. C. I. devant la Cour international de Justice (arrét du aout 1972)', 78 *R. G. D. I. P.* 975 (1974); Manin, 'Appel concernant la compétence du Conceil de l'O. A. C. I. ', 19 *A. F. D. I.* 290 (1973).

[216]	The thirteen judges were Ammoun (Vice-President, Acting President), Sir Gerald Fitzmaurice, Padilla Nervo, Forster, Gros, Bengzon, Lachs, Dillard, Ignacio-Pinto, de Castro, Morozov, Jiménez de Aréchaga and Nagendra Singh (Judge *ad hoc*).

[217]	The three judges were Sir Muhammad Zafrulla Khan (President), Petrén and Onyeama.

[218]	The two judges were Morozov and Nagendra Singh.

which had been advanced by Pakistan, to its own jurisdiction to entertain India's appeal. It summarized Pakistan's objections, added some comments and examined them individually. These objections related to the following three issues.

Firstly, it was contended that India was precluded from affirming the competence of the Court because she herself maintained (on the merits of the dispute) that the Treaties were not in force between the Parties, and that India's claim, if correct, would entail that their jurisdictional clauses were inapplicable and that the conditions of Article 36 (1) ("treaties and conventions in force") would not be fulfilled.

Secondly, it was contended that, on their correct interpretation, these Treaties only provided for an appeal to the Court against a final decision of the Council on the merits of any dispute referred to it, and not against decisions of an interim or preliminary nature such as were involved here.

Thirdly, the contention related to a special jurisdictional issue not on Pakistan's Application to the Council, but on her Complaint ostensibly made under and by virtue of Section 1 of Article II of the Transit Agreement.

2.   The majority opinion rejected Pakistan's objections and found that it was invested with jurisdiction under those jurisdictional clauses. In the context of our study, it is important to draw attention to the following *general observation* the majority opinion added to its reasoning:

"26.   Before leaving this part of the case, and since this is the first time any matter has come to it on appeal, the Court thinks it useful to make a few observations of a general character on the subject. The case is presented to the Court in the guise of an ordinary dispute between States (and such a dispute underlied it). Yet in the proceedings before the Court, it is the act of a third entity --- the Council of ICAO --- which one of the Parties is impugning and the other defending. In that aspect of the matter, *the appeal to the Court contemplated by the Chicago Convention and the Transit Agreement must be regarded as an element of the general régime established in respect of ICAO.* In thus providing for judicial recourse by way of appeal to the Court against decisions of the Council concerning interpretation and application --- a type of recourse already figuring in earlier conventions in the sphere of communications --- the Chicago Treaties gave member States, and through them the Council, the possibility of ensuring a certain measure of supervision by the Court over those decisions, To this extent, *these Treaties enlist the support of the Court for the good functioning of the Organization*, and therefore the first reassurance for the Council lies in the knowledge that means exist for determining whether a decision as to its own competence is in conformity or not with the provisions of the treaties governing its action. *If nothing in the text requires a different conclusion, an appeal against a decision of the Council as to its own jurisdicition must therefore be receivable since, from the standpoint of the supervision by the Court of the validity of the Council's acts, there is no ground for distinguishing between supervision as to ju-*

risdiction, and supervision as to merits."[219] [Italics ours]

II *Jurisdiction of the Council of ICAO to Entertain the Merits of the Case*

1.   The latter part of the judgment consisted of the following three parts: (1) clarification of the question and consideration of the negative aspects of the case, that is, the reasons why the various contentions advanced did not have any real bearing on the question of the competence of the Council; (2) consideration of the positive aspects of the case, from which it would appear not only that Pakistan's claim disclosed the existence of a "disagreement ... relating to the interpretation or application" of the Treaties, but also that India's defences equally involved questions of their interpretation or application; and (3) procedural irregularities in the Council's decision.

2.   The majority opinion set its starting point as follows:

"The question is whether the Council is competent to go into and give a final decision on the merits of the dispute in respect of which, at the instance of Pakistan, and subject to the present appeal, it has assumed jurisdiction. The answer to this question clearly depends on whether Pakistan's case, considered in the light of India's objections to it, discloses the existence of a dispute of such a character as to amount to a 'disagreement ... relating to the interpretation or application' of the Chicago Convention or of the related Transit Agreement. If so, then prima facie the Council is competent."[220]

The majority opinion specifically considered each of India's and Pakistan's contentions and reached an affirmative conclusion on both of the negative and the positive aspects of the case.

3.   Finally, the majority opinion dealt with the problem of *procedural irregularities of the Council's decision*. India contended that the Coucil's decision was vitiated by various procedural irregularities, and that the Court should declare the decision null and void, and send the case back to the Council for re-decision.

The majority opinion rejected this contention by stating as follows:

"45.   The Court however does not deem it necessary or even appropriate to go into this matter, particularly as the alleged irregularities do not prejudice in any fundamental way the requirements of a just procedure. The Court's task in the present proceedings is to give a ruling as to whether the Council has jurisdiction in the case. This is an objective question of law, the answer to which cannot depend on what occurred before the Council. Since the Court holds that the Council did and does have jurisdiction, then, if there were in fact procedural irregularities, the position would be that the Council would have reached the right conclusion in the wrong way. Nevertheless it would have reached the right conclusion. If, on the other hand, the Court had held that there was and is no jurisdiction, then, even in the absence of any irregularities, the Council's decision to as-

---

[219] Appeal Relating to the Jurisdiction of the ICAO Council (India v. Pakistan), [1972] I. C. J. 60-61.

[220] *Id.* at 61.

sume it would have stood reversed."[221]

(2) The Reasoning of the Separate and the Dissenting Opinions

I Jurisdiction of the Court --- Interpretation of Article 84 of the Chicago Convention

The jurisdiction of the Court (former part of the judgment) was approved by thirteen votes to three, and the main reasons for the three dissenting judges to disagree with the majority opinion seem to come from different interpretations of Article 84 of the Chicago Convention. Since the grounds for adopting these different interpretations were persuasively criticized by the majority opinion, it would not be necessary in the context of our study to examine them further.

On the other hand, there are some points to be noted in the separate opinions. Judge Lachs, for example, stated as follows: Great caution and restraint have been exercised by the Court and its predecessor when ascertaining their own jurisdiction. This is not to impose more onerous obligations on States than those they have expressly assumed. However, in regard to appeals from other fora, the same consideration works to the contrary. To apply a restrictive interpretation of rights of appeal --- and thus of the powers of the "court of appeal" --- would obviously entail an extensive interpretation of the jurisdictional powers of the "court of first instance", which would in fact imply more onerous obligations on the States concerned. To restrict the rights of States to seek relief from what they deem to be wrongful decisions would to some extent, at least, defeat the very object of the institution of appeals.[222]

Judge de Castro, furthermore, pointed out the necessity of judicial supervision for international organizations: For international organizations, it is necessary that there should be a supervisory body, to exercise supervision over complicated legal decisions, and over the interpretation and application of their constitutional and internal rules. It is indeed a fact that the administrative and technical nature of the ICAO Council makes it a practical necessity that there should be the widest possibility of appeal to a judicial body such as the Court.[223]

II Jurisdiction of the Council of ICAO --- Problems of Procedural Irregularities
of the Council's Decision

The jurisdiction of the ICAO Council (the latter part of the judgment) was approved by fourteen votes to two, and the reasons for the two judges to disagree with the majority opinion related to the procedural irregularities in the Council's decision.

While Judges Dillard and Aréchaga supported the majority opinion by specifically considering the irregularities and concluding that, in the present case, the alleged procedural deficiencies had not enough importance to justify the finding of nullity[224], there are also some

---

[221] *Id.* at 69-70.

[222] *Id.* at 73-74.

[223] *Id.* at 123.

[224] *Id.* at 98-101, 154-55.

points to be noted. Judge Lachs, for example, stated as follows: In general, not all departures from established rules affect the validity of decisions, but there are some which may prejudice the rights and interests of the parties. It is therefore reasonable, if one of the parties concerned should submit before this Court that procedural irregularities occurred, that these submissions should attract the Court's attention. To pronounce upon any formal deficiencies the Court may find in the decision-making of the Council, or to draw that body's attention to them, would surely come within that "supervision by the Court over those decisions" referred to in the Judgment.[225]

In the same way, Judge Aréchaga stated as follows: The right of appeal granted by Article 84 comprises not only the right to obtain a pronouncement from the Court on whether the decision of first instance is correct from the point of view of substantive law but also on whether that decision was validly adopted in accordance with the essential principles of procedure which must govern the quasi-judicial function entrusted to the organ of first instance. This is further supported by the general observation in the Judgement.[226]

The dissenting judges severely criticized this point. Judge Morozov stated as follows: The majority opinion almost stated that "the end justifies the means". The right judicial decision can never be reached by the wrong way. It is no possible to make such a distinction between the conclusion reached, and the way in which it is reached and the form in which it is embodied.[227] Judge Nagendra Singh, furthermore, developed an elaborate criticism. He examined specific procedural issues and concluded that the decision of the Council must be held to be null and void and that the Court would have to send the case back to the Council.[228]

(3) Some Comments

1. While there might be some difference of opinion on specific point of issue, the conclusion of the majority opinion as a whole seems to be sufficiently persuasive as is indicated by the result of thirteen votes to three or fourteen votes to two. We will make some observations in the light of the relation between an international organization and its constituent instrument.

2. As was pointed out in the general observations of the majority opinion, what was in question in the present case was the act of a third entity (the Council of ICAO) although the case was present in the guise of an ordinary dispute between States. While the jurisdiction of the Court is based upon the consent of the parties in the ordinary dispute between States, it was, in the present case, based upon the jurisdictional clauses of the Chicago Convention and the Transit Agreement, the former of which was the constituent instrument of ICAO. Manin, in this connection, considered that this difference in the jurisdictional basis of the Court had a determining importance in the juridical reasoning the Court followed. She pointed out that the

---

[225] *Id.* at 75.

[226] *Id.* at 153-54.

[227] *Id.* at 159.

[228] *Id.* at 164-79.

Court put greater weight upon the aspect of "control of legality" to the detriment of the aspect of "ordinary inter-State dispute" which the litigation equally constituted.[229] It is certainly true that *such considerations as "the support of the Court for the good functioning of the Organization" or "the supervision by the Court of the validity of the Council's acts" underlay the reasoning of the majority opinion.* To this extent, we could consider that it was the teleological reasoning.[230]

3.   The majority opinion were frequently criticized on the point that it did not examine the procedural question of the Council's decision. This lack of examination certainly left some room for criticism that it was not consonant with the considerations that the validity of the Council's acts should be supervised by the Court in the light of the good functioning of the Organization as was indicated in the general observations.[231] FitzGerald, who once worked as principal legal officer in the ICAO, pointed out that the Council was not an appropriate organ, by its very structure, to carry out judicial functions, and that it needed "guidance" given by a supervisory body like the ICJ in appeal proceedings.[232]

4.   Last but not least, we will note the reference to the characteristics of the constituent instrument made by Judge de Castro. In considering the argument of India to the effect that the Convention and Agreement were terminated or suspended *vis-à-vis* Pakistan because of their material breaches (Article 60 of the Vienna Convention on the Law of Treaties), Judge de Castro pointed out that the differences between bilateral and multilateral treaties, and those which give rise to an international organization, must be taken into account. He elaborated on this problem as follows:

> "In any treaty creating an organization a distinction is to be drawn between: (1) the constituent instrument of the organization, which is subject to the *lex generalis* on the coming to birth of treaties, and (2) the constitution which sets up the *lex specialis* or rules to govern the life and functioning of the organization. It is this special aspect which is responsible for the classification of this type of treaty by writers among 'treaty-laws' or 'Vereinbarungen'....
>
> Whatever the nature of its legal personality may be, each organization has a constitution which provides it with a general rule to which all its members are subject. Their rights and obligations towards each other flow from this constitution. It is the fact that the organization is a legal person which prevents the legal relationships between its members being considered as governed by a series of independent bilateral treaties. The life of the organization is not governed disjunctively by an accumulation of bilateral treaties. Members of the organization are linked together by the constitution, and their relationships are governed by the constitution. Such relationships are those resulting from the

---

[229] Manin, *supra* note 215, at 300.

[230] *Id.* at 301.

[231] *Id.* at 315.

[232] FitzGerald, *supra* note 215, at 168-72, 185.

status of member of the organization, and not the status of a party to bilateral treaties. This is of the very essence of organizations; it is required by the common interest, and is a necessity for their functioning and effectiveness.

The State which is in breach of those of its obligations or duties which derive from this constitution, towards another member State of the organization, is not in breach of a single bilateral treaty between them, it is in breach of the constitution of the organization. The effects of such a breach are governed by that constitution. It is only in a supplementary way that the general rules of international law, those enshrined in the Vienna Convention, may be applied."[233] [Italics mostly ours]

Therefore, Judge de Castro pointed out, in considering the India's argument, one must take into account the constitutional significance of the Convention and the Transit Agreement. The ICAO has its own legal personality, its own aims and objects, and the system for settlement of disputes in order to facilitate the achievement of the objects, principles, and functioning of the Organization. The Convention has two groups of provisions, the first group of provisions laying down the principle of non-discrimination between member States, the second group governing the way in which States' obligations come to an end. From these considerations, Judge de Castro drew the following conclusions:[234]

(1) Treaties creating organizations are subject to special rules, and not to the rule laid down in Article 60 of the Vienna Convention.

(2) The rules of the Chicago Convention do not recognize the possibility of a State declaring the Convention at an end vis-à-vis one other State.

(3) The special rules of the Convention and the Transit Agreement exclude any possibility of applying the rule laid down in Article 60 of the Vienna Convention.

(4) The interpretation of Article 84 of the Convention, and Article II of the Transit Agreement, advanced by India, is contrary not only to the letter and to the purpose of those Articles, but also to the system of ICAO as an international organization.

3   Interpretation of the Agreement of 25 March 1951 between the WHO and Egypt [1980][235]

Agreement was reached between the WHO and Egyt in 1949 that the operation of the existing long-established Alexandria Sanitary Bureau should be taken over by the new Organization (the WHO). While negotiations for the conclusion of a host agreement for the Regional

---

[233] *ICAO* case, *supra* note 219, at 129-30.

[234] *Id.* at 132.

[235] For the relevant bibliography on the present advisory opinion, *see, e.g.,* Simon,' L'interprétation de l'accord du 25 mars 1951 entre l'O. M. S. et l'Égypte', 85 *R. G. D. I. P.* 793 (1981); Combacau, 'La question du transfert du Bureau régional de l'O. M. S. devant la Cour international de Justice', 26 *A. F. D. I.* 225 (1980).

Office had been begun at least five months before the WHO's Regional Office commenced operating at the seat of the former Sanitary Bureau on 1 July 1949, they made slow progress; it was on 25 March 1951 that the Agreement was signed and it ultimately entered into force on 8 August of that year. That agreement, in the words of its preamble, was concluded for the purpose of determining the privileges, immunities and facilities to be granted by Egypt to the WHO, and of regulating other related matters. Because of the tense political situation in the Middle East, Sub-Committee A of the Regional Committee for the Eastern Mediterranean decided to recommend the transfer of the Regional Office to a different country. The WHO, taking note of the differing views on the question of whether the WHO may transfer the Regional Office without regard to the Provisions of Section 37 --- concerning the negotiations for modifications of the Agreement and the notice for its denounciation --- of the Agreement, decided to submit to the ICJ for its Advisory Opinion the question of applicability of Section 37 of the Agreement to the present case. The Court, by twelve votes[236] to one[237], indicated the legal principles and rules, and the mutual obligations which they imply, regarding consultation, negotiation and notice, applicable as between the WHO and Egypt.

(1) The Reasoning of the Majority Opinion

1.   The majority opinion began by setting out the pertinent elements of fact and of law which constituted the context of the question, and then proceeded to the consideration of the meaning and implications of the question. Having indicated various points of issue that the differing views in the World Health Assembly concerned, the majority opinion concluded that "the true legal question" under consideration in the Assembly was: "What are the legal principles and rules applicable to the question under what conditions and in accordance with what modalities a transfer of the Regional Office from Egypt may be effected?".

2.   The majority opinion, after summarizing the two opposing views[238] on the question and

---

[236]   The twelve judges were Sir Humphrey Waldock (President), Elias (Vice-President), Forster, Gros, Lachs, Nagendra Singh, Ruda, Mosler, Oda, Ago, El-Erian and Sette-Camara.

[237]   The judge was Morozov.

[238]   Those judges supporting the non-applicability of Section 37 of the Agreement were Lachs, Ruda, Oda, Sette-Camara and Morozov. This view was summarized as follows (Advisory Opinion on Interpretation of the Agreement of 25 March 1951 between the WHO and Egypt, [1980] I. C. J. 90):

"[This] view ... has been that the establishment of the Regional Office in Alexandria took place on 1 July 1949, pursuant to an agreement resulting either from Egypt's offer to transfer the operation of the Alexandria Bureau to the WHO and the latter's acceptance of that offer, or from Egypt's acceptance of a unilateral act of the competent organs of the WHO determining the site of the Regional Office. Proponents of this view maintain that the 1951 Agreement was a separate transaction concluded after the establishment of the Regional Office in Egypt had been completed and the terms of which only provide for the immunities, privileges and facilities of the Regional Office."

On the other hand, those judges supporting the applicability of Section 37 were Gros, Mosler, Ago and El-Erian. This view was summarized as follows (id. at 90-91):

"Proponents of the opposing view say that the establishment of the Regional Office and the integration of the Alexandria Bureau with the WHO were not completed in 1949; they were accomplished by a series of acts in a composite process, the final and definitive step in which was the conclusion of the 1951 host agreement.

their underlying interpretations, set its own approach as follows:

"Whatever view may be held on the question whether the establishment and location of the Regional Office in Alexandria are embraced within the provisions of the 1951 Agreement, and whatever view may be held on the question whether the provisions of Section 37 are applicable to the case of a transfer of the Office from Egypt, the fact remains that certain legal principles and rules are applicable in the case of such a transfer. These legal principles and rules the Court must, therefore, now examine."[239]

This was the key paragraph determining the basic direction of this advisory opinion. In fact, the majority opinion, based upon this approach, developed its reasoning as follows:

"43.   By the mutual understandings reached between Egypt and the Organization from 1949 to 1951 with respect to the Regional Office of the Organization in Egypt, whether they are regarded as distinct agreements or as separate parts of one transaction, *a contractual legal régime was created between Egypt and the Organization which remains the basis of their legal relations today.* Moreover, ... *[t]he very fact of Egypt's membership of the Organization entails certain mutual obligations of co-operation and good faith incumbent upon Egypt and upon the Organization.* Egypt offered to become host to the Regional Office in Alexandria and the Organization accepted that offer; Egypt agreed to provide the privileges, immunities and facilities necessary for the independence and effectiveness of the Office. As a result *the legal relationship between Egypt and the Organization became, and now is, that of a host State and an international organization, the very essence of which is a body of mutual obligations of co-operation and good faith....*

... In short, the situation in the event of a transfer of the Regional Office from Egypt is one which, by its very nature, demands *consultation, negotiation and co-operation between the Organization and Egypt.*"[240] [Italics ours]

3.   Next, the majority opinion classified a considerable number of host agreements of different kinds, and indicated the significance that they had in the present connection despite their variety and imperfections, as follows:

"In the first place, they confirm the recognition by international organizations and host States of the existence of mutual obligations incumbent upon them to resolve the problems attendant upon a revision, termination or denunciation of a host agreement. But they do more, since they must be presumed to reflect the views of organizations and host States as to the implications of those obligations in the contexts in which the provi-

---

To holders of this view, the act of transferring the operation of the Alexandria Bureau to the WHO in 1949 and the host agreement of 1951 are closely related parts of a single transaction whereby it was agreed to establish the Regional Office at Alexandria."

[239] *Id.* at 92.

[240] *Id.* at 92-94.

sions are intended to apply. In the view of the Court, therefore, they provide certain general indications of what the mutual obligations of organizations and host States to co-operate in good faith may involve in situations such as the one with which the Court is here concerned."[241]

The majority opinion continued as follows:

"47. A further general indication as to what those obligations may entail is to be found in the second paragraph of Article 56 of the Vienna Convention on the Law of Treaties and the corresponding provision in the International Law Commission's draft articles on treaties between States and international organizations or between international organizations. Those provisions, as has been mentioned earlier, specifically provide that, when a right of denunciation is implied in a treaty by reason of its nature, *the exercise of that right is conditional upon notice, and that of not less than twelve months*. Clearly, these provisions also are based on *an obligation to act in good faith and have reasonable regard to the interests of the other party to the treaty.*"[242] [Italics ours]

4.   Finally, the majority opinion, based upon the above reasoning, indicated the content of the above-mentioned "mutual obligations" in the following way: (1) both parties must consult together in good faith as to the question; (2) in the event of the transfer being finally decided, both parties must consult and negotiate to effect the transfer in an orderly manner and with a minimum of prejudice to both parties; and (3) the party which wishes to effect the transfer must give a reasonable period of notice to the other party to effect an orderly and equitable transfer. What is reasonble and equitable in the application of the general legal principles and rules to any given case must depend on its particular circumstances. Moreover:

"[T]he paramount consideration both for the Organization and the host State in every case must be *their clear obligation to co-operate in good faith to promote the objectives and purposes of the Organization as expressed in its Constitution*; and this too means that they must in consultation determine a reasonable period of time to enable them to achieve an orderly transfer of the Office from the territory of the host State."[243] [Italics ours]

(2) Some Comments

1.   What is clear from the reasoning of the majority opinion is the importance of the key paragraph which was to determine the basic direction of the majority opinion. In other words, since there was a fundamental confrontation between the judges as to the "applicability of Section 37 of the 1951 Agreement to the present transfer", it was difficult to form a large majority among the judges; the majority opinion virtually avoided this question of the applicability of

---

[241] *Id.* at 94.

[242] *Id.* at 94-95.

[243] *Id.* at 96.

Section 37 by setting "the true legal question" and by contending that the general legal framework in which the true legal issues before the Court have to be resolved would in some measure be distorted. *The majority opinion attempted to demonstrate that certain legal principles and rules are applicable in the present case irrespective of the question of Section 37.*

This approach was described as "le fruit d'un compromis".[244] The majority opinion deduced a common point of "reasonable protection of the interests of both parties" based upon the considerations of good faith and equity from two fundamentally opposing views as to the question of Section 37. While the majority opinion made this deduction as an "interpretation" of the question, this would be rather pointed out as a "substitution"[245] or as a "reconstruction".[246] It would be for that reason that Judge Morozov described it as a "legal miracle", qualified it as "an attempt to give a legal appearance to an artificial basis"[247] and contended that one could not find in the Advisory Opinion a positive answer to the question.

On the other hand, this approach was actively supported by some judges. Judge El-Erian, for example, stated that the power of the Court to interpret a question was inherent in the quality of the Court as a judicial organ and that it was consonant with the principle of effective interpretation inherent in the purpose and raison d'être of the advisory jurisdiction of the Court.[248] Similarly, Judge Mosler stated that the method of reasoning followed by the majority opinion was justified in the present case by the duty incumbent upon the Court as a judicial institution to define the legal position as precisely as possible.[249] Judge Sette-Camara stated that the broad consideration of all the pertinent legal issues involved was consistent with the jurisprudence of the Court.[250]

2.   As to the confrontation among judges over the interpretation of Section 37, two points should be noted in the context of our study.

In the first place, *the textual interpretation of Section 37 could reasonably be considered to support the view that it was not applicable.* In fact, as far as the textual interpretation of Section 37 was concerned, non-applicability of Section 37 was not only strongly claimed by those judges supporting the view that it is not applicable, but also acknowledged by Judge Mosler supporting the view that it is applicable.

For example, Judge Sette-Camara considered that Article 31 of the Vienna Convention on the Law of Treaties embodied the rules of general international law on the interpretation of treaties, and interpreted Section 37 in good faith in accordance with the ordinary meaning of its

---

[244] Simon, *supra* note 235, at 829.

[245] *Id.* at 826.

[246] Combacau, *supra* note 235, at 247.

[247] *WHO* case, *supra* note 238, at 193.

[248] *Id.* at 166-67.

[249] *Id.* at 125.

[250] *Id.* at 179.

terms and in the light of the object and purpose of the treaty, taking into consideration the context of the treaty and, furthermore, having recourse to supplementary means of interpretation (Article 32), and concluded that removal of the Office would fall outside the scope of Section 37.[251] Similarly, Judge Lachs referred to "an undeniable conclusion resulting from *the ordinary meaning of the words, their context and the text as a whole*".[252] [Italics ours]

Furthermore, Judge Mosler supporting view that it is applicable stated as follows: If the term "revision" be understood in accordance with the ordinary meaning to be given to it, it suggests the idea of introducing partial changes rather than the complete and total cessation; since to cease to apply the Agreement cannot be construed as a revision, Section 37 is not applicable in the present case.[253]

3.   In the second place, those judges supporting the view that Section 37 is applicable could be considered to rely upon *the teleological reasoning*. The fundamental judgments and considerations upon which those judges were based was aptly explained by Judge El-Erian as follows:

> "Section 37 of the 1951 Agreement ... provides for guarantees to guard against abrupt denunciation or disruptive termination of the Agreement.... It also requires two years' notice for denunciation of the Agreement ... [These] manifest the intention of the parties to ensure the security and stability of a regional office ...
>
> It has been argued in some of the statements submitted to the Court that Section 37 is not a denunciation but a revision clause.... I have not found the arguments in support of such a restrictive interpretation of Section 37 to be warranted or well conceived. Both the legslative history and the general law of international organizations lead me to opt for *the effective interpretation of Section 37....*
>
> The transfer of the seat of the Regional Office at Alexandria would connote revision of the 1951 host agreement inasmuch as it would deprive it of its subject-matter at a stroke. *To argue that the safeguards provided for in Section 37 do not apply to the transfer of the seat would imply conceding to one party to the Agreement the power to circumvent these guarantees by resorting to a technicality which would allow it to frustrate the very object of the instrument without complying with the procedure prescribed for denunciation consequent upon a request for revision of one or more provisions of the Agreement."*[254] [Italics ours]

Similar considerations were advanced by Judge Ago from the viewpoint of a precise and complete definition of the very concept of the "establishment" of an international organization in the territory of a host State. Because an international organization is, unlike a State, a sub-

---

[251] *Id.* at 184-86.

[252] *Id.* at 110.

[253] *Id.* at 128.

[254] *Id.* at 174-75.

ject of law which lacks all territorial basis, stated Judge Ago, its "establishment" in the territory of a given State is a *conditio sine qua non* of its actually functioning as an organization, carrying on its activities and fulfilling its object and purpose. This term of "establishment" is a "legal" concept and involves not only a physical installation but also indispensable elements of a legal nature; these include, in particular, the determination of the legal status which the organization is to enjoy in the territory of the host State. *For the purpose of defining the concept of establishment, it makes no real difference whether its various component elements all materialize at the same time or appear separately in a gradual process.* This latter case is the present one.[255] Judge Mosler, also considering that the establishment of the seat of the regional organization could not be dissociated from the agreement regulating its legal status, concluded that *the negotiations between the WHO and Egypt must be regarded as a continuing process leading first of all to the transfer of the Bureau to the WHO as from 1949 and concluding with the entry into force of the Agreement of 1951, and that Section 37 is applicable to any transfer of the Office.*[256]

On the other hand, while those judges supporting the view that Section 37 is not applicable did admit that the determination of the legal status of an organization was important for its establishment, *they denied the applicability of Section 37 based upon, among others, the interpretation of provisions of the Agreement.* Judge Oda, for example, examined the relation between the 1951 WHO/Egypt Agreement, on the one hand, and, on the other hand, the establishment and location of the Regional Office in Alexandria in the light of the negotiating history, and concluded as follows:

"It is certainly true that the WHO/Egypt Agreement would not have been concluded if the office had not been located in Alexandria. This, however, is very far from justifying an assertion that an agreement for the establishment or location of the Regional Office in Alexandria is contained in the said Agreement. If, in fact, no such agreement is contained in the instrument, it is a matter of course that the negotiation and notice provisions of its Section 37 do not govern the transfer of the Regional Office."[257]

3.   The majority opinion gave some comments as to the power of an international organization.   Reference was made to the concept of "[la] vononté souveraine [de l'Assemblée mondiale de la Santé]".[258]   Yasseen, representing the United Arab Emirates, stated as follows:

"Ce principe [que l'organisation garde toute liberté de transférer son siège ou son bureau régional à moins qu'il n'en soit convenu autrement] se présume, car il se justifie, étant nécessaire au bon fonctionnement des organisations internationales, il peut à ce titre re-

---

[255] *Id.* at 155-57.

[256] *Id.* at 127.

[257] *Id.* at 149.

[258] Exposé écrit du Gouvernement de la République Arabe Syrienne, Advisory Opinion on Interpretation of the Agreement of 25 March 1951 between the WHO and Egypt, I. C. J. Pleadings 208, 210 (1981).

fléter raisonnablement l'intention commune des parties. Comme il n'est pas possible de présumer des restrictions à la souveraineté de l'État, il n'est pas possible de présumer des restrictions à la compétence constitutionnelle de l'organisation internationale."[259]

To these contentions, the majority opinion gave a well-balanced judgment and stated as follows:

"The Court notes that in the World Health Assembly and in some of the written and oral statements before the Court there seems to have been a disposition to regard international organizations as possessing some form of absolute power to determine and, if need be, change the location of the sites of their headquarters and regional offices. But States for their part possess a sovereign power of decision with respect to their acceptance of the headquarters or a regional office of an organization within their territories; and an organization's power of decision is no more absolute in this respect than is that of a State. As was pointed out by the Court in one of its early Advisory Opinions, there is nothing in the character of international organizations to justify their being considered as some form of 'super-State' (*Reparation for Injuries Suffered in the Service of the United Nations, Advisory Opinion, I. C. J. Reports 1949*, p. 179). International organizations are subjects of international law and, as such, are bound by any obligations incumbent upon them under general rules of international law, under their constitutions or under international agreements to which they are parties."[260]

This judgment seems to have been shared among the judges of the majority opinion.[261]

Section 5 Questions Relating to Judgments
of the Administrative Tribunals

All three cases dealt with in the present section consist of two parts: (1) whether the Court should comply with the request for an advisory opinion, and (2) the answer to this question. The second part, however, relates, among others to the issues concerning the contracts between individual staff members and their respective organizations rather than the functions and powers of the organizations *vis-à-vis* the Member States. For this reason, we will deal with only the first part here.

---

[259] Exposé oral de M. Yasseen, *id.* at 217, 218. "This principle [that the organization retains all the liberty to transfer its seat and its regional bureau unless it is otherwise agreed] is presumed, because it is justified, being necessary for the good functioning of the international organizations, it could on this ground reasonably reflect the common intention of the parties. Since it is not possible to presume restrictions to the sovereignty of the State, it is not possible to presume restrictions to the constitutional competence of the international organization." [Our translation]

[260] *WHO* case, *supra* note 238, at 89-90.

[261] *See, id.* at 103-05 (J. Gros), 127 (J. Mosler), 155-57 (J. Ago), 168-70 (J. El-Erian). *But see, id.* at 190 (J. Morozov).

1. Judgments of the Adminstrative Tribunal of the International Labour Organisation upon Complaints Made against the United Nations Educational, Scientific and Cultural Organization [1956] [262]

Duberg, whose renewal of appointment was refused by the Director-General of the United Nations Educational, Scientific and Cultural Organization (UNESCO), submitted an appeal to the Appeals Board, which, by a majority, expressed the opinion supporting his claim. Then, Duberg brought his complaint before the Administrative Tribunal, which also gave a decision supporting his claim. The Executive Board of the UNESCO, acting within the framework of Article XII of the Statute of the Administrative Tribunal of the International Labour Organisation, decided to challenge the decision rendered by the Tribunal, and requested the ICJ an advisory opinion on this question. The Court, by nine votes[263] to four[264], decided to comply with the request for an advisory opinion.

(1) The Reasoning of the Majority Opinion

While the majority opinion recognized that the question was a legal one arising within the scope of the activities of the UNESCO, its subsequent reasoning related to the following two issues.

The first issue was the relation between the *advisory* opinion and the opinion becoming *binding*. The majority opinion stated on this point as follows:

"Under Article XII of the Statute of the Administrative Tribunal, the Opinion thus requested will be 'binding'. Such effect of the Opinion goes beyond the scope attributed by the Charter and by the Statute of the Court to an Advisory Opinion. However, the provision in question is nothing but a rule of conduct for the Executive Board, a rule determining the action to be taken by it on the Opinion of the Court. It in no wise affects the way in which the Court functions; that continues to be determined by its Statute and its Rules. Nor does it affect the reasoning by which the Court forms its Opinion or the content of the Opinion itself. Accordingly, the fact that the Opinion of the Court is accepted as binding provides no reason why the Request for an Opinion should not be complied with."[265]

The second issue was *the compatibility of the special feature of the expedient procedure adopted by the UNESCO and the judicial character of the Court.* According to generally accepted

---

[262] For the relevant bibliography on the present advisory opinion, *see, e.g.,* Hardy, 'Jurisdiction of the Administrative Tribunal of the I. L. O., The Advisory Opinion of the International Court of Justice of October 23, 1956', 6 *Int'l & Comp. L. Q.* 338 (1957); De Lacharrière, 'Cour international de Justice --- Jugement du Tribunal administratif de l'O. I. T. sur requêtes contre l'U. N. E. S. C. O., Avis consultatif du 23 octobre 1956', 2 *A. F. D. I.* 383 (1956); M. B. Akehurst, *The Law Governing Employment in International Organizations* (1967).

[263] The nine judges were Hackworth (President), Badawi (Vice-President), Basdevant, Zoričić, Read, Armand-Ugon, Kojevnikov, Sir Hersch Lauterpacht and Moreno Quintana.

[264] The four judges were Winiarski, Klaestad, Sir Muhammad Zafrulla Khan and Córdova.

[265] Advisory Opinion on Judgments of the Administrative Tribunal of the International Labour Organisation upon Complaints Made against the United Nations Educational, Scientific and Cultural Organization, [1956] I. C. J. 84.

practice, legal remedies against a judgment are equally open to either party, and each possesses equal rights for the submission of its case to the tribunal called upon to examine the matter (*equality of parties to judicial proceedings*: Article 35, paragraph 2, of the Statute of the Court). In this connection, two kinds of inequality exist in this procedure.

In the first place, *Article XII of the Statute of the Administrative Tribunal confers on the Executive Board alone an exclusive right to challenge judgments of the Tribunal and apply to the Court, not on Officials.* This inequality was dealt with as follows:

"However, the inequality thus stated does not in fact constitute an inequality before the Court. It is antecedent to the examination of the question by the Court. It does not affect the manner in which the Court undertakes that examination. Also, in the *present* case, that absence of equality between the parties to the Judgments is somewhat nominal since the officials were successful in the proceedings before the Administrative Tribunal and there was accordingly no question of any complaint on their part. This being so, it is not necessary for the Court to express an opinion upon the legal merits of Article XII of the Statute of the Administrative Tribunal. The Court must confine itself to the facts of the present case. In this respect, it is enough for it to state that the circumstance that only the Executive Board was entitled to institute the present proceedings does not constitute a reason for not complying with the Request for an Advisory Opinion."[266] [Italics ours]

In the second place, because the advisory opinion will affect the right of the officials to the benefit of the Judgments of the Tribunal and the obligation of the UNESCO to comply with them, *the judicial character of the Court requires that both sides directly affected by these proceedings should be in a position to submit their views and their arguments to the Court. The Statute and the Rules of the Court, however, do not admit the necessary facilities on the part of the Officials.* This inequality was dealt with as follows:

"It was with that difficulty that the Court was confronted. The difficulty was met, on the one hand, by the procedure under which the observations of the officials were made available to the Court through the intermediary of Unesco and, on the other hand, by dispensing with oral proceedings. The Court is not bound for the future by any consent which it gave or decisions which it made with regard to the procedure thus adopted. In the present case, the procedure which has been adopted has not given rise to any objection on the part of those concerned. It has been consented to by counsel for the officials in whose favour the Judgments were given. The principle of equality of the parties follows from the requirements of good administration of justice. These requirements have not been impaired in the *present* case by the circumstance that the written statement on behalf of the officials was submitted through Unesco. Finally, although no oral proceedings were held, the Court is satisfied that adequate information has been made available to it. In view of this *there*

---

[266] *Id.* at 85-86.

would appear to be no compelling reason why the Court should not lend its assistance in the solution of a problem confronting a specialized agency of the United Nations authorized to ask for an Advisory Opinion of the Court. Notwithstanding the permissive character of Article 65 of the Statute in the matter of advisory opinions, only compelling reasons could cause the Court to adopt in this matter a negative attitude which would imperil the working of the régime established by the Statute of the Administrative Tribunal for the judicial protection of officials. *Any seeming or nominal absence of equality ought not to be allowed to obscure or to defeat that primary object.*[267] [Italics ours]

(2) The Reasoning of the Dissenting Opinions

The views in the dissenting opinions were common and could be summarized as follows:[268]

(a)   A proposal to give the Court a competence to examine an appeal from the Administrative Tribunal was defeated at the San Francisco Conference, and such an appeal was not contemplated by the Statute of the Court both in terms of the party and of the applicable law.

(b)   While the expedient procedure of the UNESCO was not enough to ensure the necessary equality of status, in fact and in law, between the Organization and the individuals concerned, oral proceedings were necessary for clarification of the issue before the Court.

(c)   The individuals were not accorded the right to challenge the validity of the decisions of the Administrative Tribunal by requesting the Court for an advisory opinion, and the provisions of Article XII thus established a manifest inequality between the parties.

(d)   It was open to any of the States or international organizations entitled to appear before the Court, under Article 66 (2) of the Statute, to request the Court for an oral hearing. This could mean that a single State or international organization could exercise a veto upon the Court's authority to deliver an opinion, and that the Court would have been confronted with a dilemma.

(3) Some Comments

In the context of our study, we would like to draw attention to the point that *the majority opinion endeavored to find the* de facto *equality of the parties in the expedient procedure despite the existence of some reasons for reasonably refusing to give an opinion in the present case.* In this connection, it is to the point that Elihu Lauterpacht stated as follows:

"The issue here considered by the Court was not, of course, strictly one of the determination of the powers of an organization. Nevertheless, the problem was an analogous one, in that the Court was faced by a question of the scope of its competence to be decided by reference to instruments (the Statutes of the ILO Administrative Tribunal and of the International Court of Justice itself) creating powers which would not otherwise have existed. And the point that matters ... is that *the Court chose to adopt an interpretation*

---

[267] *Id.* at 86.

[268] *See id.* at 104-08 (Winiarski), 109-13 (Klaestad), 114-15 (Khan) and 155-68 (Córdova).

conferring upon itself greater scope of action, on the basis that this was necessary for the full achievement of the objectives of the régime governing the relationships between international organizations and their staffs."[269] [Italics ours]

Here we could conclude that consideration of the objects of the organization played an important role for the benefit of the general interests of international organizations.

2 Application for Review of Judgement No. 158 of the United Nations Administrative Tribunal [1973][270]

Mr. Mohamed Fasla, a former staff member, filed an application with the United Nations Administrative Tribunal for the extension of his contract of employment. The Tribunal gave a judgement in 1972, but Mr. Fasla raised objections to the decision and asked the Committee on Applications for Review of Administrative Tribunal Judgements to request an advisory opinion of the ICJ. The Committee decided that there was a substantial basis for the application made for review of Judgement No. 158, and accordingly decided to request an advisory opinion of the Court. The Court, by ten votes[271] to three,[272] decided to comply with the request for an advisory opinion.

(1) The Reasoning of the Majority Opinion

1.   The majority opinion, after quoting the whole provisions of Article 11 which provided for the possibility of challenging judgements of the Tribunal before the Court through the machinery of a request for an advisory opinion, referred to the fact that a number of delegations questioned the legality or the propriety of various aspects of this procedure. It stated that since this was the first occasion to consider a request for an opinion made under this procedure, it would examine the two questions as to the competence of the Court to give the opinion and as to the propriety of its doing so.

2.   As to *the Court's competence to give the opinion.*

In the first place, it was contended that the contentious jurisdiction of the Court was limited by Article 34 of its Statute to disputes between States, and that the advisory jurisdiction could not be used for the judicial review of contentious proceedings to which individuals were parties.

The majority opinion, by relying upon the Opinion concerning *Judgments of the Administrative Tribunal of the ILO upon Complaints Made against Unesco*, stated that,

---

[269]   Lauterpacht, *supra* note 69, at 421.

[270]   For the relevant bibliography on the present advisory opinion, *see, e.g.*, Ruzié, 'L'avis consultatif de la Cour internationale de Justice du 12 juillet 1973 dans l'affaire de la demande de réformation du jugement n° 158 du tribunal administratif des Nations Unies', 19 *A. F. D. I.* 320 (1973).

[271]   The ten judges were Lachs (President), Ammoun, Forster, Bengzon, Dillard, de Castro, Jiménez de Aréchaga, Sir Humphrey Waldock, Nagendra Singh and Ruda.

[272]   The three judges were Gros, Onyeama and Morozov.

irrespective of the existence of a dispute in the background, the Court's task was to answer the question put to it with regard to a judgment. It rejected this contention by concluding that the mere fact that it was not the rights of States which were in issue in the proceedings could not suffice to deprive the Court of a competence expressly conferred on it by its Statute.

In the second place, it was questioned whether the requesting body itself was a body duly authorized under the Charter to initiate advisory proceedings before the Court. Firstly, it was contended that the Committee was not such a body as could be considered one of the 'organs of the United Nations' entitled to request advisory opinions under Article 96 of the Charter. The majority opinion rejected this contention by stating as follows:

"16. Article 7 of the Charter, under the heading 'Organs', after naming the six principal organs of the United Nations in paragraph 1, provides in the most general terms in paragraph 2: 'Such subsidiary organs as may be found necessary may be established in accordance with the present Charter.' Article 22 then expressly empowers the General Assembly to 'establish such subsidiary organs as it deems necessary for the performance of its functions'. *The object of both those Articles is to enable the United Nations to accomplish its purposes and to function effectively. Accordingly, to place a restrictive interpretation on the power of the General Assembly to establish subsidiary organs would run contrary to the clear intention of the Charter.* Article 22, indeed, specifically leaves it to the General Assembly to appreciate the need for any particular organ, and the sole restriction placed by that Article on the General Assembly's power to establish subsidiary organs is that they should be 'necessary for the performance of its functions'.

17. In its Opinion on the *Effect of Awards of Compensation Made by the United Nations Administrative Tribunal,* it is true, the Court expressly held that the Charter 'does not confer judicial functions on the General Assembly' and that, when it established the Administrative Tribunal, it 'was not delegating the performance of its own function' (*I. C. J. Reports 1954,* at p. 61). At the same time, however, the Court pointed out that under Article 101, paragraph 1, of the Charter the General Assembly is given power to regulate staff relations, and it held that this power included 'the power to establish a tribunal to do justice between the Organization and the staff members' (*ibid.,* at p. 58). From the above reasoning it necessarily follows that the General Assembly's power to regulate staff relations also comprises the power to create an organ designed to provide machinery for initiating the review by the Court of judgments of such a tribunal."[273] [Italics ours]

In the third place, it was also contended that, while Article 96 (2) of the Charter empowered the General Assembly to authorize organs of the United Nations to "request advisory opinions of the Court on legal questions arising within the scope of their activites", the Committee had no other activity than to request advisory opinion, and that the 'legal question' in regard to which Article

---

[273] Advisory Opinion on Application for Review of Judgement No. 158 of the United Nations Administrative Tribunal, [1973] I. C. J. 172-73.

11 authorized it to request an opinion arose not within the scope of 'its activities' but of those of another organ, the Administrative Tribunal.

The majority opinion confirmed that the functions entrusted to the Committee by Article 11 were to receive applications, to decide whether or not there was a substantial basis for the application and, if it so decided, to request an advisory opinion. It then rejected this contention by stating as follows:

"The scope of the activities of the Committee which result from these functions is, admittedly, a narrow one. But the Committee's activities under Article 11 have to be viewed in the larger context of the General Assembly's function in the regulation of staff relations of which they form a part. This is not a delegation by the General Assembly of its own power to request an advisory opinion; it is the creation of a subsidiary organ having a particular task and invested it with the power to request advisory opinions in the performance of that task....

21.   In fact, the primary functions of the Committee is not the requesting of advisory opinions, but the examination of objections to judgements in order to decide in each case whether there is a substantial basis for the appliation so as to call for a request for an advisory opinion.... They are therefore questions which, in the view of the Court, arise within the scope of the Committee's own activities; for they arise not out of the judgements of the Administrative Tribunal but out of objections to those judgements raised before the Committee itself."[274]

3.   As to *the propriety of the Court to give the opinion*. This question of propriety related to the Court's judicial character and the compatibility with its judicial character.

In the first place, it was contended that, while Article 11 inserted a political organ into the judicial process for settling disputes between staff members and the Organization, it was incompatible with the nature of the judicial process that a political organ should be involved in the judicial review of its judgements. The majority opinion rejected this contention by stating, among others, that, while there was no necessary incompatibility between the exercise of these functions by a political body and the requirements of the judicial process inasmuch as these functions merely furnished a political link between two judicial procedures, the compatibility or otherwise of any given system of review with the requirements of the judicial process depended on the circumstances and conditions of each particular system, that, in the present instance, the Rules which the Committee adopted took acount of the quasi-judicial character of its functions, and that while it might be desirable for the applicant to receive some indication of the grounds for the Committee's decision in those cases in which the application was rejected, the fact that the Committee's reports were confined to a bare statement of the decision reached did not deprive the review proceedings as a whole of their judicial character, nor constituted a valid reason for the Court's declining to answer the present request.

---

[274] *Id.* at 174.

In the second place, it was contended that the member State would not be a party to the proceedings before the Administrative Tribunal, and that to allow it to initiate proceedings for the review of the judgement would be contrary to the general principles governing judicial review. The majority opinion rejected this contention by stating that this contention was without relevance in the *present* proceedings in which the request for an opinion resulted from an application to the Committee by a staff member.

In the third place, as to the inherent inequality under the Statute of the Court between the staff member, on the one hand, and the Secretary-General and member States, on the other, the majority opinion, recalling the Opinion concerning *Judgments of the Administrative Tribunal of the ILO upon Complaints Made against Unesco*, maintained the view that it was capable of being cured by the adoption of appropriate procedures which would ensure actual equality in the particular proceedings.

In the fourth place, although the questions submitted to the Court related to a contentious case between a staff member and the Secretary-General, the majority opinion pointed out that the proceedings before the Court were still advisory proceedings, in which the task of the Court was not to retry the case but to reply to the questions put to it, and that it was satisfied that the requirements that the interested parties should have a fair and equal opportunity to present their views to the Court and that the Court should have adequate information were met in the *present* proceedings.

In the fifth place, as to the fact that the opinion was to have a conclusive effect with respect to the matters in litigation in that case, the majority opinion, again referring to the above 1956 UNESCO Opinion, stated that such an effect would result not from the advisory opinion itself but from a provision of an autonomous instrument having the force of law for the parties, and that it would not furnish no reason for refusing to comply with the request for an opinion in the present instance.

In the light of what was said above, the majority opinion concluded that it did not appear that there was any compelling reason, both as to the Court's competence and the propriety of the procedure, why it should decline to reply to the request in the present instance.

(2) The Reasoning of the Separate and the Dissenting Opinions

There was no specific view to introduce here in the present context of our study. Some important points indicated in the separate and the dissenting opinions were considered in the majority opinion, and suffice it to refer to them in the next comments.

(3) Some Comments

1.	In the first place, the legality of the review procedure was questioned. The majority opinion relied upon the reasoning of implied powers in the *Effect of Awards* Case, and concluded that the General Assembly's power to regulate staff relations also comprised the power to create an organ designed to provide machinery for initiating the review. Similarly it concluded that the primary function of the Committee was to examine and decide whether there was a substantial basis for the application, and that the questions arose within the scope of the Committee's own activites.

All three dissenting judges based their opinions partly upon the legal nature of the Committee. Judge Onyeama, for example, while admitting that the establishment of the Committee was a valid exercise of the General Assembly's power to regulate staff relations, considered that the Committee had an extremely narrow compass of activities, and that the four grounds on which it was "authorized" to request an advisory opinion from the Court could not possibly arise within the scope of its own activities.[275] Judge Gros stated that the Committee was not an organ in the proper, institutional sense, but merely a kind of occasional panel meeting at irregular intervals, and that, the activity of the Committee being to transmit to the Court --- or not --- an application for review, the legal questions transmitted were quite unconnected with the activity of the Committee.[276]

Consequently, we could conclude that, *in the light of the views of the dissenting judges, the majority opinion resorted to the teleological reasoning both as to the General Assembly's power and the activitiy of the Committee so as to enable the Organization to effectively perform its objectives.*

2.   In the second place, the legal nature of the Committee was also questioned in the light of the compatibility with the judicial requirements. The majority opinion, basically relying upon the 1956 UNESCO Opinion, concluded that any inequality inherent in the institution was capable of being cured by the adoption of appropriate procedures ensuring actual equality in the particular proceedings. *A series of reasonings of the majority opinion on this point appear to be directed by a strong teleological orientation that the review procedure should be enabled to function unless it fundamentally collides with the judicial requirements.* In fact, Judge Aréchaga pointed out as follows: The essential feature of the system of judicial review is that a judgment the validity of which has been challenged may only be treated as invalid by the United Nations if the Court has found that the challenge is well founded; the fact that an organ such as this Committee is called upon to screen the application and seise the Court cannot be considered to be such a serious defect as to counteract the progressive step taken, and still less to justify the adoption by the Court of a negative position which would frustrate the purpose of the system of judicial review established in 1955.[277] The teleological orientation of the majority opinion would be put in relief by the following position of Judge Gros: Judge Gros, while standing on the same starting point that "each case should be considered on its merits", reached a negative conclusion in the present case in the light of "the requirements of good administration of Justice"; he further criticized the discretionary and secretive operation of the political Committee by stating that the seisin of the Court could not be left to chance, "a lottery".[278]

---

[275] *Id.* at 227-29.

[276] *Id.* at 259. *See also id.* at 298 (Morozov). Rosenne is also negative on the question whether the matters on which the Committee may request advisory opinions are "legal questions arising within the scope of" the Committee's activities. Sh. Rosenne, *The Law and Practice of the International Court* 690 (2nd rev. ed. 1985).

[277] *Id.* at 243-44.

3 Application for Review of Judgement No. 273 of the United Nations Administrative Tribunal [1982][279]

Mr. Mortished filed an application, in October 1980, with the United Nations Administrative Tribunal, which recognized his claim. The United States of America, in June 1981, addressed a letter to the Acting Legal Counsel of the United Nations by way of application to the Committee on Application for Review of Administrative Tribunal Judgements, under Article 11 (1) of the Statute of the Tribunal, asking the Committee to request an advisory opinion of the Court. The Committee decided that there was a substantial basis for the application and decided to request an advisory opinion of the Court. The Court, by nine votes[280] to six,[281] decided to comply with the request for an advisory opinion.

(1) The Reasoning of the Majority Opinion

1. The majority opinion, just like in the 1973 Opinion, considered whether it was competent to comply with the request for an advisory opinion, and whether it should exercise its discretion to do so.

As to *the Court's competence*, the majority opinion, while referring to the necessity of considering the review procedure in the light of the compatibility, firstly with the judicial requirements of the Court, and secondly with Article 96 of the Charter, concluded that "[t]he special features of the proceedings leading up to the present request for advisory opinion afford the Court no grounds for departing from its previous position on the point under consideration".

2. As to *whether it should give the advisory opinion*, the majority opinion started the same examination as in the 1973 Opinion.

At the beginning, the majority opinion took the same position as in the 1973 Opinion by quoting that "the compatibility or otherwise of any given system of review with the requirements of the judicial process depends on the circumstances and conditions of each particular system". In that connection, it was contended that the part played by a member State in submitting an application for review was tantamount to intervention in the review process by an entity which was not a party to the original proceedings, and that it was contrary to fundamental principles of the

---

[278] *Id.* at 253-56, 263.

[279] For the relevant bibliography on the present opinion, *see, e.g.,* Tavernier, 'L'avis consultatif de la Cour international de Justice du 20 juillet 1982 dans l'affaire de la demande de réformation du jugement n° 273 du Tribunal administratif des Nations Unies (affaire Mortished)', 28 *A. F. D. I.* 392 (1982); Ruzié, 'L'avis consultatif de la Cour international de Justice du 20 juillet 1982 dans l'affaire de la demande de réformation du jugement n° 273 du Tribunal administratif des Nations Unies', 100 *Journal du Doit International* 76 (1983).

[280] The nine judges were Elias (President), Sette-Camara (Vice-President), Nagendra Singh, Mosler, Ago, Schwebel, Sir Robert Jennings, de Lacharrière and Mbaye.

[281] The six judges were Lachs, Morozov, Ruda, Oda, El-Khani and Bedjaoui.

judicial process. The majority opinion observed, firstly that a member State may well have a legal interest in giving rise to a review of the Judgement, and secondly that once the Committee decided that there was a substantial basis for the application, the request for advisory opinion came from the Committee and not from the member State.

Next, it was contended, concerning the scope of the advisory opinion, that the fact that the Court's opinion was to have a conclusive effect with respect to the matters in litigation afforded a ground for objecting to the exercise of the Court's advisory jurisdiction on the one hand, and, on the other hand, that if the Court declined to give an opinion, that would put in question the status of Judgement No. 273 of the Administrative Tribunal. The majority opinion, relying upon the 1973 Opinion or the 1956 Opinion, pointed out that these contentions did not furnish any reason "for refusing to comply with the request for an opinion", nor did it "affect the reasoning by which the Court forms its Opinion or the content of the Opinion itself".

It was also contended that the initiative taken by a member State to seise the Committee impinged upon the authority of the Secretary-General under Article 97 of the Charter as Chief Administrative Officer of the Organization, and conflicted with Article 100 regarding the "exclusively international character" of the Secretariat. The majority opinion recognized that an application would lead to delay in the judgement of the Tribunal becoming final, but pointed out that this was no more than the normal effect of the operation of a review procedure.

Finally, the principle of equality of the parties was dealt with. The majority opinion recalled the 1956 and 1973 Opinions in which the Court took the position that what was essential was that actual equality should be ensured by practical measures and that any seeming or nominal absence of equality should not prevent it from giving effect to a request for advisory opinion. As in those cases, the majority opinion stated that it "is satisfied that these requirements have been met in the present proceedings".

3.   However, the majority opinion observed, the problem was not merely that of equality before the Court. Comparison of the review procedure with the requirements governing the judicial process and the principle of equality of the parties must also be made with regard to that stage of the review procedure which involved the intervention of the Committee. In the review procedure, one of the parties --- the United Nations --- has the right to decide the fate of the application for review made by the other party, staff member, through the will of a political organ; furthermore, when a member State of the Committee is the applicant State, the government in question can itself present its application, take an active part in the discussion thereof, and even take part in the vote at the close of the discussion. Whether this inequality on the theoretical level also existed on the practical level was examined next.

At the outset, the irregularity in the composition of the Administrative Tribunal was pointed out: while the Tribunal was to be composed of three members in accordance with its Statute, four members sat in the case. The majority opinion also observed that the Tribunal sat in the past on many occasions with more than three members present, without any explanation, and that this matter of composition did not appear on its face to disclose any failure of justice.

Next, however, a number of notable irregularities attending the proceedings of the

Committee were pointed out.

In the first place, a member of the Committee, Sierra Leone, was replace by an unqualified State, Canada, which, furthermore, became Chairman of the Committee.

In the second place, the application of the United States was wrongly addressed, and was formally defective in not complying fully with the requirement of the Committee's Provisional Rules of Procedure. As a consequence, Mr. Mortished was unable to comment on the two specific grounds eventually selected by the Committee. The majority opinion considered that such action exacerbated on the practical level the inequality already established on the theoretical level.

In the third place, the refusal of the Committee to grant the request of counsel for Mr. Mortished to be given the opportunity to participate in the proceedings of the Committee at which the United States application was considered, was, from the point of view of the Committee's quasi-judicial functions, a startling irregularity. The majority opinion pointed out that the Committee was under a duty in the circumstances of this case to take such steps as to make the United States representative refrain from participating in the discussion and in the votes to mitigate the basic inequality on the theoretical level between the applicant State and the staff member.

4.   Despite these irregularities, and despite also the failure of the Committee to show the concern for equality appropriate to a body discharging quasi-judicial functions, the majority opinion felt called upon to accept the task of assisting the United Nations Organization. It is the reasons explained below that are important in the present context.

"Of course the irregularities which feature throughout the proceedings in the present case could well be regarded as constituting 'compelling reasons' for a refusal by the Court to entertain the request. *The stability and efficiency of the international organizations, of which the United Nations is the supreme example, are however of such paramount importance to world order, that the Court should not fail to assist a subsidiary body of the United Nations General Assembly in putting its operation upon a firm and secure foundation.* While it would have been a compelling reason, making it inappropriate for the Court to entertain a request, that its judicial role would be endangered or discredited, that is not so in the present case, and the Court thus does not find that considerations of judicial restraint should prevent it from rendering the advisory opinion requested. In the present case such a refusal would leave in suspense a very serious allegation against the Administrative Tribunal, that it had in effect challenged the authority of the General Assembly. While there can be no question ... of any restriction on the Court's discretion, *the Court will not refuse 'its participation in the activities of the Organization',* so that the important legal principles involved may be disposed of, whilst at the same time the Court must point out the various irregularities. It is not by appearing to shy away from the latter that the Court can discharge its true judicial functions."[282] [Italics ours]

---

[282] Advisory Opinion on Application for Review of Judgement No. 273 of the United Nations Administrative Tribunal, [1982] I. C. J. 347-48.

(2) The Reasoning of the Separate and the Dissenting Opinions

There was no specific view to introduce here in the present context of our study. Some important points indicated in the separate and the dissenting opinions were considered in the majority opinion, and suffice it to refer to them in the following comments.

(3) Some Comments

In the present context of our study, attention must be drawn to the reasons for which the majority opinion decided that, despite the existence of a number of notable irregularities which could well be regarded as constituting "compelling reasons" for a refusal to give the advisory opinion, they should not refuse to give it. Here we clearly find *a strong teleological orientation that the Court should not fail to assist for "[t]he stability and efficiency of the international organizations, of which the United Nations is the supreme example"*. As was shown by the division of nine votes to six, and as was recognized by the majority opinion itself, there existed strong grounds on the part of the claim that the Court should refuse to give the advisory opinion. The fact that the majority opinion decided not to refuse the request even in these circumstances seems to us to demonstrate *how strong the teleological orientation for the stability and efficiency of the international organizations are among the judges in the Court.*

This conclusion would be supported by the following critical statement of Judge Ruda:

"The Court bases its main reason for delivering the opinion on the need 'to assist a subsidiary body of the United Nations General Assembly in putting its operation upon a firm and secure foundation'. I have no doubt that this is a very important value that the Court ought to preserve.... [However, the limits beyond which the assistance should not be given] arise from the fact that the Court, even when exercising its advisory competence, remains a tribunal and, as such, is primarily bound to safeguard *the requirements of a judicial process*, in every stage of this review process. This is, for me, the paramount consideration to be taken into account, *the very nature of the functions of the Court cannot be sacrificed because of the need of assistance to a United Nations organ.* Since the delivery of the opinion is within its discretionary power, *the Court has to choose, in the present case, which is more important, the assistance to another organ of the United Nations or the safeguarding of the requirements of the judicial character of the review procedure.* I believe ... that the Court should refuse to give this Advisory Opinion."[283] [Italics ours]

Section 6   Conclusion

1.   **Introduction**: What conclusions can be reached from the analyses of the sixteen cases developed in the present chapter? Generally, we could consider that the jurisprudence of the Court

---

[283] *Id.* at 377-78.

has not reached the level, both in terms of quantity and quality, which would permit a construction of any systematic doctrine of constitutional interpretation. It is true that we found in our comments that each case had relatively rich implications; consequently, one would be tempted to construct a systematic theory by using only those parts in those cases which are favorable to one's theory. This must be avoided. We should restrain ourselves to construct a moderate but solid doctrine rather than a fragile house of cards.

It could be concluded, however, that the examination of the relevant judgments and advisory opinions of the Court indicates *certain fundamental features*, if not a systematic theory. Some of them will be concisely pointed out below. In this connection, it would be useful to illustrate the patterns of confrontation among judges of each case in the following manner. [⇒ Chart I]

Chart I   An Overview of the Jurisprudence

Condition of Admissions case (1948)
《Majority Opinion》　　　〔Majority of 9:6〕　　《Dissenting Opinions》
　(Textual App.)　　　　　　　　　　　　　　　("Intentions of the Parties" App.)
　Hackworth, de Visscher, et al.　　　　　　　McNair, Read, Winiarski, et al.

Competence of the General Assembly case (1950)
《Majority Opinion》　　　〔Majority of 12:2〕　《Dissenting Opinions》
　(Textual App.)　　　　　　　　　　　　　　　(Teleological App.)
Hackworth, McNair, Read, Winiarski, et al.　　Alvarez, Azevedo

Reparation case (1949)
《Majority Opinion》　　　〔Majority of 11:4〕　《Dissenting Opinions》
　(Teleological App.)　　　　　　　　　　　　　(Textual App.)
de Visscher, McNair, Read, et al.　　Hackworth, Krylov, Badawi Pacha,et al.

Effect of Awards case (1954)
《Majority Opinion》　　　〔Majority of 9:3〕　　《Dissenting Opinions》
(Textual & Teleological App.)　　　　　　　　　(Textual App.)
McNair, Read, Winiarski, et al.　　　　　　　Hackworth, et al.

Certain Expenses case (1962)
《Majority Opinion》　　　〔Majority of 9:5〕　《Dissenting Opinions》
Tanaka, Jessup, Spender, Morelli, Fitzmaurice, et al.　Winiarski, Koretsky, Basdevant, et al.
(1) **Teleological Interpretation of the Charter**
(Affirmative) Majority Opinion, Spender　　　(Negative) Winiarski

(2) Significance of the Practice of Organs of the United Nations

(Affirmative) Majority Opinion   (Negative) Spender

(3) Who has the Power to Authoritatively Interpret the Charter

(a) Final Interpretation by the General Assembly: Spender, Morelli

(b) Presumption of Constitutionality: Majority Opinion, Fitzmaurice

(c) Member States: Winiarski

International Status of South-West Africa case (1950)

(1) Competence of Supervision by the United Nations

《Majority Opinion》   〔Majority of 12:2〕   《Dissenting Opinions》

(Teleological App.)   (Textual App.)

de Visscher, Hackworth, et al.   McNair, Read

(2) Obligation to Take Part in Negotiations

《Majority Opinion》   〔Majority of 8:6〕   《Dissenting Opinions》

(Textual App.)   (Teleological App.)

Hackworth, McNair, Read, Winiarski, et al.   de Visscher, Krylov, Guerrero, Badawi Pacha,et al.

Voting Procedure case (1955)

《Majority Opinion》   〔Unanimous〕   《Separate Opinions》

(Textual App.)

Hackworth, Read, Winiarski, et al.   Lauterpacht, Klaestad, Basdevant

Admissibility of Hearings case (1956)

《Majority Opinion》   〔Majority of 8:4〕   《Dissenting Opinions》

(Teleological App.)   Basdevant, Badawi, et al.

Hackworth, Read, Klaestad,et al.   《Separate Opinion》

                                                              Lauterpacht

South West Africa cases (1962 & 1966)

(1) 1962

《Majority Opinion》   〔Majority of 8:7〕   《Joint Dissenting Opinion》

(Teleological App.)   Spender & Fitzmaurice

Jessup, Badawi, Koretsky, Wellington Koo,   《Dissenting Opinions》

Alfaro, Moreno Quintana, et al.   Winiarski, Morelli, et al.

(2) 1966

《Majority Opinion》   〔Majority of 8:7〕   《Dissenting Opinions》

(Textual App.)   (Teleological App.)

Spender, Morelli, Fitzmaurice   Jessup, Tanaka, Koretsky, Nervo

Gros, Winiarski, et al.   Wellington Koo, et al.

Namibia case (1971)

(1) Illegality = Obligation to Put an End

⟨Majority Opinion⟩　　　〔Majority of 13:2〕　　　⟨Dissenting Opinions⟩
(Teleological App.)　　　　　　　　　　　　　　　(Textual App.)
Khan, Dillard, Lachs, Aréchaga, et al.　　　　　　Fitzmaurice, Gros

(2) Obligations for Member States and Non-Member States

⟨Majority Opinion⟩　　　〔Majority of 11:4〕　　　⟨Dissenting Opinions⟩
same as above　　　　　　　　　　　　　　additionally Petrén, Onyeama

IMCO case (1960)

⟨Majority Opinion⟩　　　〔Majority of 9:5〕　　　⟨Dissenting Opinions⟩
(Textual App.)　　　　　　　　　　　　　Klaestad, Moreno Quintana

ICAO case (1972)

(1) Jurisdiction of the ICJ

⟨Majority Opinion⟩　　　〔Majority of 13:3〕　　　⟨Dissenting Opinions⟩
Fitzmaurice, Lachs, Aréchaga, de Castro, et al.　　Khan, Petrén, Onyeama

(2) Jurisdiction of the Council of ICAO

⟨Majority Opinion⟩　　　〔Majority of 14:2〕　　　⟨Dissenting Opinions⟩
same as above　　　　　　　　　　　　　　Morozov, Singh

WHO case (1980)

⟨Majority Opinion⟩　　　〔Majority of 12:1〕　　　⟨Dissenting Opinion⟩
Waldock, Elias, et al.　　　　　　　　　　　Morozov

Applicability of Article 37

(Applicable = Teleological App.)　　　　　　(Not Applicable = Textual App.)
Gros, Mosler, Ago, El-Erian　　　　Lachs, Ruda, Oda, Sette-Camara, Morozov

ILOAT case (1956)

⟨Majority Opinion⟩　　　〔Majority of 9:4〕　　　⟨Dissenting Opinions⟩
Hackworth, Badawi, Read, Basdevant　　　　Winiarski, Klaestad, Khan, Córdova
Lauterpacht, et al.

UNAT No. 158 case (1973)

⟨Majority Opinion⟩　　　〔Majority of 10:3〕　　　⟨Dissenting Opinions⟩
Lachs, Ammoun, Dillard, Aréchaga　　　　Gros, Onyeama, Morozov
Waldock, Singh, et al.

UNAT No. 273 case (1982)

⟨Majority Opinion⟩　　　〔Majority of 9:6〕　　　⟨Dissenting Opinions⟩

Elias, Singh, Ago, Mosler
Schwebel, Jennings, et al.

Lachs, Ruda, Morozov, Bedjaoui
Oda, El-Khani

? **The primary importance of the treaty (constituent instrument) text**: If the treaty text is sufficiently clear at all, then, in most cases, it would not cause a controversy or a dispute among States.

Even if a dispute has arisen, the Court would only apply a textual approach. In the *Competence of the General Assembly* case (1950), for example, because of the clarity of the relevant text (Article 4, Paragraph 2 of the Charter), the Court applied the textual approach quasi-unanimously except two judges who developed arguments *de lege ferenda*. It was all the more impressive because the six judges who, in the *Conditions of Admission* case (1948), dissented and criticized the textual approach of the majority, joined the textual approach of the majority in the present case. Thus, *when the treaty text is sufficiently clear on an inter-subjective basis, respect of the treaty text would become a dominant factor irrespective of whether the consequence of the textual approach would promote the efficient functioning and the effective activities of international organizations.*[284]   As the Court pointed out in the *Certain Expenses* case, "it has followed the principles and rules applicable in general to the interpretation of treaties".

---

[284]   Rosenne takes a similar position in this regard. According to Rosenne, examination of the major cases of interpretation of the constituent instrument in the International Court since 1945 shows that *two broad categories of interpretative problems* have been encountered, namely those which did not, and which did turn upon the issue of the attribution of competences, whether between the individual States and the organization, or as between organs of the organization. In the first type of case, relating to subjective rights of States, the issue with which the Court is seen to have been confronted was one which, in the final analysis, related to the subsumed treaty element of the constituent instrument and turned on the Court's interpretation of the intentions of the negotiating States. Here the Court has proceeded in a fairly conservative manner and based itself on the ascertainable or presumed intentions of those States as expressed in the text or derived from it. In the second class of case, the Court has completely passed over any subsumed treaty element (and therefore disregarded as irrelevant the intentions of the parties to that treaty, assuming those intentions to be ascertainable), and has proceeded directly to an interpretation of the constituent instrument as it stands at the time of the interpretation. What is important here is that, before doing this, *a preliminary question is set whether an answer is provided directly by the constituent instrument itself, that instrument being 'interpreted' by application of the usual exegetical techniques if necessary. If this preliminary question is answered in the affirmative, the substantive conclusion will follow logically and that is the end of the matter.* But if the answer is in the negative, resort is legitimately had to all the resources of the interpretative --- and not merely exegetical --- techniques. Rosenne pointed out three major characteristic elements in this connection: *(1) lack of interest in the intentions of the original members with corresponding disinterest in the travaux préparatoires; (2) analysis of the function of the provision in question in the context of the constituent instrument as a whole, with particular stress on the relations between the different organs of the organization according to the constituent instrument, and on the practice of those different organs; (3) a powerful --- yet politically highly controversial --- teleological approach which reflects more the 'ought' than the 'is' of the constituent instrument.* He seems critical on this last point when he says that, unless (as in the *Reparation* case) it is backed by a unanimous or virtually unanimous Court, this last factor is the most controversial and, as experience has shown, the most unproductive in the political sense and the most prejudicial to the authority of the Court. Rosenne, *supra* note 1 in Chap. 1, at 234-7.

This conclusion would be supported by the textual approach of the majority opinion in the *Conditions of Admission* case and the textual approach of the majority opinion in the *IMCO* case.[285]

3.   **The guiding principle and the various concrete methods of interpretation**: *The guiding principle*, under the reservation of the primary importance of the treaty text mentioned above, *is to promote the effectiveness of international organizations*. The Court reasoned in that way with respect to the following issues among others: (1) the capacity to exercise a measure of functional protection of its agents in the *Reparation* case (1949); (2) the power to establish a judicial tribunal competent to render judgments binding on the United Nations in the *Effect of Awards* case (1954); (3) the budgetary authority of the General Assembly with respect to the deployment of the peace-keeping operations in the *Certain Expenses* case (1962); (4) the competence of the General Assembly to exercise the supervisory functions with regard to mandated territories in the *Status of South-West Africa* cases (1950, 1955, 1956); (5) the support of the Court for the good functioning of the ICAO in the *ICAO* case (1972); (6) the obligation for the WHO and the host State to co-operate in good faith to promote the objectives and purposes of the WHO in the *WHO* case (1980); and (7) the task of assisting international organizations for their stability and efficiency in the *Review of Judgment (No. 273)* case (1982).

On the other hand, *the variety of interpretation methods used in concrete cases* must be pointed out. The Court, under the guiding principle of promoting the effectiveness of international organizations, applied either *the teleological approach* or *the textual approach* whenever the occasion requires. It, for example, relied on the textual in the *Conditions of Admission* case (1948), but on the teleological in the *Reparation* case (1949); in the *Effect of Awards* case (1954), on the textual for finding the judicial nature of the Administrative Tribunal, but on the teleological for the compentence of the General Assembly to establish it; in the *Status of South-West Africa* cases, on the teleological for the competence to exercise the supervisory functions (1950), but on the textual in the *Voting Procedure* case (1955) and on the teleological in the *Admissibility of Hearings* case (1956); partly on the textual in the *South-West Africa* cases (1962), but on the teleological in the *Namibia* case (1971).

It is, therefore, wrong to connect the constituent instruments of international organizations

---

[285]   Another quite interesting case is the confrontation over the existence of the obligation to take part in negotiations with a view to concluding an agreement in the *Status of South-Africa* case (1950). In his dissenting opinion, de Visscher, although he conceded that the relevant Charter provisions do not impose the Union of South Africa a legal obligation to conclude an agreement, did recognize the existence of the obligation mentioned above. By referring to the interpretation of the text of a treaty of a constitutional character like the United Nations Charter, he contended as follows (Advisory Opinion on International Status of South-West Africa, [1950] I. C. J. 189):

"[O]ne must bear in mind that in the interpretation of a great international constitutional instrument, like the United Nations Charter, the individualistic concepts which are generally adequate in the interpretaion of ordinary treaties, do not suffice."

The majority opinion responded by applying a textual approach (*id.* at 139-40) It must be noted that *the Court refrained from stepping out of the textual approach by a slight majority of eight votes to six.*

with the teleological approach of interpretaion in a simplified manner. It is noted here that the textual approach could lead to the promotion of the effectiveness of international organizations as it depends on the content of the text itself.

4.   **The existence of a confrontation with respect to the interpretative framework of constituent instruments.** It can be concluded that the same confrontation with that among the principal doctrines mentioned earlier (Chapter Two, Section 2) appeared among the judges in the Court. On the one hand, those judges who belong to the liberal position free from the law of treaties have been few (such as Alvarez and Azevedo) and had little effect upon the jurisprudence. On the other hand, *the confrontation between the strict framework of the law of treaties and the functional framework based upon the law of treaties has appeared in most of the issues presented to the Court.* Some typical examples are given as follows: (1) the majority opinion against the dissenting opinions (such as Hackworth) in the *Reparation* case (1949); (2) the majority opinion against the dissenting opinions (such as Hackworth) in the *Effect of Awards* case (1954); (3) the majority opinon against the separate opinions (McNair and Read) with respect to the competence of the General Assembly to exercise the supervisory functions in the *Status of South-West Africa* case (1950); (4) the majority opinion against the dissenting opinions (such as de Visscher) in the same case; (5) the majority opinion against the dissenting opinions (such as Fitzmaurice) in the *Namibia* case (1971); and (6) those claiming the application of, and those claiming the non-application of, Article 37 in the *WHO* case (1980).

The fact that these and other similar confrontations have appeared with regard to the interpretative framework of constituent instruments in the Court, and that the functional framework has been applied by the majority in most cases, clearly demonstrates the following point; in those cases, *the question was whether to apply such "interpretations" of the relevant provision(s) which were nothing but the modification of their texts in the light of the textual interpretative framework in the law of treaties*; and the victory of the functional framework indicates that *the interpretation of constituent instruments has begun to be governed by the interpretative framework which allows such degree of teleological reasoning as to deviate from that of ordinary treaties.*[286]

---

[286] In the opinion of Gross, the Court has the duality of the function: *the advisory or United Nations function corresponding to its role of a principal organ,* and *the contentious function corresponding to its role of organ of international law,* to which also corresponds the duality of the approach shown by the Court's behaviour in the application of international law. In the latter capacity the Court seems to have accepted and even fortified the consensual nature of customary international law and, following the positivist theory, applied international law as it found it. In the former capacity the Court, particularly when applying and interpreting the Charter or instruments closely related to the United Nations such as the Mandate for South West Africa, the Court appears to have adopted *a dynamic or progressive, if not a frankly teleological, approach.* This statement seems to correspond to the distinction between the textual interpretative framework of ordinary treaties and the functional interpretative framework of constituent instruments as the constitutions of international organizations developed in the present article. The point in his statement, however, seems to be to indicate that most of the judgments based on positive international law have been respected and accepted, and that many of the advisory opinions where the Court has displayed judicial boldness amounting to judicial legislation have been

5.   Finally, we would draw attention to **some other points of issue** with regard to the interpretative framework proper to the constituent instruments of international organizations.

The first is **the relevance of the organic factor**. Simon, in the book referred to in Chapter One, Section 2, concluded that the decisive criterion in the choice of interpretation methods is not an 'organic' criterion opposing the conventions creating an international organization to the so-called ordinary treaties, but a complex criterion of the degree of integration of the conventional system in question. He elaborated on this point as follows.

"S'il est vrai que la création d'une institution internationale s'accompagne parfois de la 'fondation' d'une structure organique qui constitue le moyen choisi par les auteurs du traité pour mettre en oeuvre les objectifs communs, la composante organique est loin d'être un attribut essentiel des institutions juridiques, qui s'analysent comme des ensembles de dispositions normatives interdépendantes, affectées à la réalisation d'une fin : tel est bien le sens orginel de la notion d'institution ... avant d'être pratiquement confondue par la suite avec le concept d'organisation proprement dite. Or l'idée d'institution, ou pour employer un vocabulaire plus moderne, de 'système' juridique autonome, apparaît comme un instrument fondamental pour préciser les critères qui dirigent la méthode du juge dans l'interprétation des conventions....

Mais les traités constitutifs d'organisations internationales ne sont pas les seules conventions susceptibles de donner naissance à un système juridique doté d'une relative autonomie et d'une structure spécifique : toute convention affectant un ensemble de moyens organisés à la réalisation d'un objectif commun, c'est à dire toute convention créant une 'institution' au sens défini précédemment, engendre un ordre juridique propre destiné à mettre en forme juridique la coordination des instruments normatifs permettant la poursuite des finalités collectives."[287]

---

remarkably less successful. In other words, *the application of the principle of effectiveness in legal interpretation leads to the paradoxical consequence of the ineffectiveness in the actual political settlement of disputes.* Therefore, Gross emphasizes the importance of State parties' consent in the current decentralized international society, and is critical on the teleological tendency in the reasoning of the Court. Gross, 'The International Court of Justice and the United Nations', 120 *Recueil des cours* 313, 320-2, 370-1, 413 (1967), *reprinted in* L. Gross, *Essays on International Law and Organization* 845 (1984). The fact that advisory opinions based upon the teleological approach tend to lack political effectiveness certainly warns us against a hasty conclusion in appreciating to what extent the functional framework of constituent instruments distinguished from the textual framework of ordinary treaties has been accepted by States as *lex lata*.

[287] D. Simon, *L'interprétation judiciaire des traités d'organisations internationales* 486-8 (1981). "Even if it is true that the creation of an international institution has sometimes the 'foundation' of an organic structure that constitutes the means chosen by the authors of the treaty to implement the common objectives, the organic component is far from an essential attribute of the juridical institutions, which are analyzed as the wholes of interdependent normative dispositions assigned to the realization of an end: such is really the original meaning of the notion of institution ... before being merged later on in practice with the concept of organization in its proper sense. Now the idea of institution, or if we use a more modern vocabulary, of autonomous juridical 'system', appears as a fundamental instrument to specify the criteria that direct the method of the judge in the interpretation of the conventions... But the constitutive treaties of international organizations are not the only conventions capable of giving birth to a juridical system endowed with a relative autonomy

Simon's contention based upon the traditional theory of institution seems to have certain persuasiveness. It would be true that the constituent instrument creating an organization is at the higher level in terms of integration of the conventional system among various 'institutions', and that this leads to the interpretations most favorable to the enlargement of the competences of the international organizations in many cases by reference to teleological methods of interpretation.

We would note, however, that, on the one hand, Simon's contention seems to correspond to the teleological aspect of our doctrine of the interpretative framework of constituent instruments as the constitutions of international organizations. To this extent, it would be supported by the jurisprudence of the Court as concluded above. In this sense, the theory of institution is worth examining (Chapter Five, Section 3, (3)).

On the other hand, we consider that the relevancy of the organic factor cannot be denied.[288] While the constituent instrument is the legal basis for establishing an organization independent of individual member States, various organs of the organization will inevitably interpret the relevant provisions of the constituent instrument in their daily process of operation and accumulate their practices. It would be quite reasonable to assume that a consistent practice by these organs developed in the light of ensuring the effectiveness of the organization could have some impact on the interpretation of the constituent instrument (Chapter Five, Sectin 2). In fact, the Court made frequent reference to the practice of organs of the United Nations in the *Certain Expenses* case despite severe criticisms by, *inter alia*, Judge Spender.

6.   The second is **the problem of inter-temporal law**. At the core of the confrontation between the majority opinion and Judge Fitzmaurice in the Namibia case, there was clearly the problem of the applicability of inter-temporal law to Article 22 of the Covenant of the League of Nations and the mandate. Judge Fitzmaurice denied it by relying on their conventional (contractual) aspect and aimed at seeking the intentions of the parties at the time when the treaty was concluded, while the majority opinion approved it by relying on their institutional aspect and stated that the concepts embodied in Article 22 and the Mandate were by definition evolutionary. This question of the applicability of inter-temporal law to the constituent instruments of international organizations must be examined (Chapter Five, Section 3, (4)).

7.   The third is **the distinction between the internal and the external functions of international organizations**. What significance would it have for the scope of applicability of the doctrine of implied powers and for the guiding principle in the interpretation of constituent instruments whether the competence or the action in question relates to the internal or the external functions of the organization concerned?

Some scholars contend affirmatively. Judge Fitzmaurice, for example, expressed his

---

and a specific structure: any convention assigning a whole of organized means to the realization of a common objective, in another words, any convention creating an 'institution' in the previously defined meaning, produces a proper juridical order intended to put in a juridical form the coordination of the normative instruments permitting the pursuit of the collective finalities." [Our translation]

[288] Simon's analysis on the role of the practice of organs is less persuasive than other parts. *Id*. at 378-91, 444-50.

restrictive understanding of the doctrine of implied powers in his dissenting opinion in the *Namibia* case by stating that the Assembly had no implied powers except those purely domestic, internal, and procedural executive powers without which such a body could not function.[289] Morawiecki explained the grounds for this distinction as follows.

"In relation to the sphere of the organization's internal functioning it is to be assumed that the ensurance of indispensable conditions of its mere existence and the realization of its decision making processes ... constitutes the indispensable *minimum* of obligations of States, which logically follow from their assuming the roles of members of the organization and by the mere fact of participating in it. This presupposition is necessary for the organization itself. At the same time, the presupposition can be accepted by Member-States, because the scope and dimensions of resulting obligations and burdens are relatively limited and foreseeable and can be calculated at the time when a decision on the acceptance of the role of a member of the organization is made....

The situation is different in relation to the [external sphere of functioning].... A high degree of incertitude as to the possible range and consequences of its decision [exists].... The possibility of politically biased orientation of these decisions involves a significant risk for the interests of Member-States.... It involves a serious risk as well for the organization itself which faces the danger of desintegration as the result of withdrawal of States deeply dissatisfied with the activity of the organization when it exceeds tolerable limits of deviation from an equilibrium when it should be of some benefit for all its members.

In order to maintain this risk within acceptable boundaries States joining an international organization rather cannot be expected to agree to grant it larger implied powers and an inherent capacity to act in its external sphere of functioning."[290]

This distinction is quite logical, and persuasive to that extent. Problems, however, seem to remain. In the first place, the criteria by which to distinguish the internal and the external functions would, although apparently clear, prove not so clear when we begin to examine concrete cases. Could we consider that all of the following cases, for example, constitute the internal functions: (1) the capacity to exercise a measure of functional protection of its agents in the *Reparation* case (1949); (2) the power to establish a judicial tribunal competent to render judgments binding on the United Nations in the *Effect of Awards* case (1954); (3) the budgetary authority of the General Assembly with respect to the deployment of the peace-keeping operations in the *Certain Expenses* case (1962); and (4) the competence of the General Assembly to exercise

---

[289] Judge Fitzmaurice applied the same reasoning to the financial obligation for Member States of the United Nations and concluded that even in the absence of Article 17, paragraph 2, a general obligation for Member States collectively to finance the Organization would have to be read into the Charter to the extent necessary to make the Organization workable. *Certain Expenses* case, *supra* note 77, at 208.

[290] Morawiecki, 'Legal Regime of the International Organization', 15 *Polish Y. B. Int'l L.* 71, 76-8 (1986). *See also* Skubiszewski, 'Implied Powers of International Organizations', in *International Law at a Time of Perplexity, Essays in Honour of Shabtai Rosenne* 855, 859 (Y. Dinstein & M. Tabory eds. 1989).

the supervisory functions with regard to mandated territories in the *Status of South-West Africa* cases (1950, 1955, 1956)?

In the second place, this distinction is not necessarily supported by the analysis of the jurisprudence of the Court. In fact in all of the above cases among others, the majority opinion made use of a wide concept of implied powers or a teleological reasoning. It is furthermore demonstrated by the fact that the above contention of Judge Fitzmaurice was in his dissenting opinion *vis-à-vis* the overwhelming majority opinion by thirteen out of fifteen judges in the *Namibia* case.

Consequently, we would be safer to conclude that the distinction between the internal and the external functions of an international organization in relation to the applicability of the doctrine of implied powers or the teleological reasoning could provide a *prima facie* or presumptive, but not a conclusive or definitive criterion.

8.   The fourth is **who has the power to authoritatively interpret the constituent instrument of an international organization**. In the *Certain Expenses* case, there was a difference of opinion among judges with regard to the question of who has the power to authoritatively --- in the sense of legally binding all the organs and all the Member States --- interpret the Charter. Since who is to interpret a constituent instrument and how it is to be done are inherently related in the actual process of interpretation, this is an important problem which demands an elaborate and concrete examination (Chapter Four; Chapter Five, Section 2, (2)).

9.   The fifth is **the lack of consistency in the reasoning of some judges**. The above chart indicating the confrontations and judges in the jurisprudence of the Court reveals inconsistency in the reasoning on the part of some judges at least in the context of our study. For example, Judge Hackworth dissented by relying on the textual approach in the *Reparation* case (1949) and the *Effect of Awards* case (1954), but later joined the majority opinion that relied on the teleological approach in connection with the competence of the General Assembly to exercise the supervisory functions with regard to mandated territories in the *International Status of South-West Africa* cases (1950). Judges McNair and Read, to the contrary, contributed to the majority opinion in the former two cases that relied on the teleological approach, but relied on the textual approach and went against the majority opinion in the latter case. While Judge Spender developed a teleological approach in his separate opinion in the *Certain Expenses* case (1962), he took a conservative position in the *South West Africa* cases (1962, 1966). While Judge Fitzmaurice joined the teleological majority opinion in the *Certain Expenses* case (1962), he appended a long dissenting opinion that relied on the textual approach in the *Namibia* case.

Reasons for these inconsistencies[291] might be found in various individual factors in each case, or more subtly in relatively different degrees of teleological reasoning in the cases which we categorized, for analytical convenience, as the "teleological approach" in contrast with the "textual

---

[291] *See also* Gross, *supra* note 286, at 322.

approach", or the different concepts of international law and organization of each judge. It is not clear what influences these apparent inconsistencies might have on our conclusions reached above with regard to the interpretative framework of the constituent instruments of international organizations.

Chapter Four

Interpretative Procedures
of
Constituent Instruments

Organs of International Organizations
as
Principal Interpreters of Constituent Instruments

Section 1   The Method of Analysis

The norm system that presents itself as a legal order, says Kelsen, has essentially a dynamic character. A legal norm is not valid because it has a certain content, that is, because its content is logically deducible from a presupposed basic norm, but because it is created in a certain way --- ultimately in a way determined by a presupposed basic norm.[1] If so, problems of *who is to interpret and apply a norm and how it is to be done are inevitably combined in the substantive problem of determining the content of the norm concerned.* The interpretation of law always leaves some room for discretion and involves *a value judgment of the interpreter* in selecting one of several possible meanings within the frame set by the norm concerned.[2] Equally in the interpretation of treaty, who is to interprete it is an important factor in determining the meaning of a treaty provision.

The effects of treaty interpretation could be arranged, from the viewpoint of interpreters, in the following way. Treaties are generally interpreted and applied by the States parties themselves. As a result of sovereign equality, a unilateral interpretation by a State party will not bind the other States parties. It is of course possible that a State party might be bound in future by estoppel or otherwise based upon its unilateral interpretation. At any rate, unilateral interpretations could lead to a confrontation of interpretations or a dispute among States. It is only when an agreement exists in advance or later among the States concerned that a single meaning is legally established by the interpretation of an international tribunal.

Authentic interpretation will come into existence when a unilateral interpretation is accepted by the other States parties or when all the States parties adopt a common interpretation. Authentic interpretation signifies the existence of an agreement among the States parties, and, based upon the principle of *ejus est interpretari cujus est condore*, the distinction between interpretation and modification tends to be blurred.

In the case of constituent instruments, *the organs of international organizations* will also interpret and apply those provisions related to their activities as an indispensable process of their operation. In these circumstances, it is necessary to analyze *the legal effects attributed to these interpretations by the organs* and *the institutional mechanism through which different and conflicting interpretations are to be unified.* These cannot be analyzed in abstract, but only upon an examination of the relevant provisions of various constituent instruments and the actual operation of such provisions.

---

[1]   H. Kelsen, *Pure Theory of Law* 198 (2nd ed. M. Knight trans. 1967).

[2]   *See* the statement of the ILC cited in footnote 63 in Chap. 2.

Section 2   The United Nations[3]

(1) *Travaux Préparatoires* of the San Francisco Conference

1.   There is no provision concerning interpretation in the Charter of the United Nations. We only have, as indicating the conclusion of discussions in the San Francisco Conference, the following final report[4] of Committee IV/2 (Legal Problems) of the Conference:

"*In the course of the operations from day to day of the various organs of the Organization, it is inevitable that each organ will interpret such parts of the Charter as are applicable to its particular functions.* This process is inherent in the functioning of any body which operates under an instrument defining its functions and powers. It will be manifested in the functioning of such a body as the General Assembly, the Security Council, or the International Court of Justice. *Accordingly, it is not necessary to include in the Charter a provision either authorizing the normal operation of this principle.*

Difficulties may conceivably arise in the event that there should be a difference of opinion among the organs of the Organization concerning the correct interpretation of a provision of the Charter. Thus, two organs may conceivably hold and may express or even act upon different views.   Under unitary forms of national government the final determination of such a question may be vested in the highest court or in some other national authority. However, *the nature of the Organization and of its operation would not seem to be such as to invite the inclusion in the Charter of any provision of this nature.* If two Member States are at variance concerning the correct interpretation of the Charter, they are of course free to submit the dispute to the International Court of Justice as in the case of any other treaty. Similarly, it would always be open to the General Assembly or to the Security Council, in appropriate circumstances, to ask the International Court of Justice for an advisory opinion concerning the meaning of a provision of the Charter. Should the General Assembly or the Security Council prefer another course, an *ad hoc* committee of jurists might be set up to examine the question and report its views, or recourse might be had to a joint conference. In brief, *the Members or the organs of the Organization might have recourse to various expedients in order to obtain an appropriate interpretation.* It would appear neither necessary nor desirable to list or to describe in the Charter the various

---

[3] As to the interpretation of the Charter of the United Nations, *see, e.g.,* Pollux, 'The Interpretation of the Charter', 23 *Brit. Y. B. Int'l L.* 54 (1946); L. Kopelmanas, *L'organisation des Nations Unies* 253-78 (1947); Vallat, 'The Competence of the United Nations General Assembly', 97 *Recueil des cours* 203, 207-13 (1959); D. Ninčić, *The Problem of Sovereignty in the Charter and in the Practice of the United Nations* 322-26 (1970); Conforti, 'Le rôle de l'accord dans le système des Nations Unies', 142 *Recueil des cours* 203 (1974); D. Ciobanu, *Preliminary Objections Related to the Jurisdiction of the United Nations Political Organs* 153-79 (1975).

[4] As to the legal value of this report itself, we could say that, since it was unanimously adopted by the Conference, it possesses much probative value indicating the framers' intention. *See* on this point Pollux, *supra* note 3, at 73-74; Kopelmanas, *supra* note 3, at 303; Ciobanu, *supra* note 3, at 154-55.

possible expedients.

It is to be understood, of course, that *if an interpretation made by any organ of the Organization or by a committee of jurists is not generally acceptable it will be without binding force.* In such circumstances, or in cases where it is desired to establish an *authoritative interpretation as a precedent for the future*, it may be necessary to embody the interpretation in *an amendment to the Charter.* This may always be accomplished by recourse to the procedure provided for amendment."[5] [Italics ours]

2. What could be pointed out from the above report and other related materials?

In the first place, *the possibility was clearly rejected that an organ (e.g., the ICJ or the General Assembly) of the United Nations be given the power to authoritatively interpret the whole Charter, its interpretation binding all the other organs and all the Member States of the United Nations.* This is demonstrated by the fact that both of the Belgian proposal[6] to refer to the ICJ for binding interpretation disagreements as to the meaning of the Charter provisions and the proposal by the same government[7] that the General Assembly should have sovereign competence to interpret the provisions of the Charter were rejected at the Conference. It would have been felt that a system providing for the authentic interpretation of the Charter was incompatible with the basic character of the Organization as a community of sovereign States.[8] There exists a strong opposition on the part of States to the possibility that new obligations be imposed upon them without their consent.

3. In the second place, by focusing on the expression "generally acceptable" in the report, it was advocated that a break-through from the traditional rule of unanimity in the interpretation of general multilateral treaties was introduced by the drafters of the Charter by substituting the requirement of general acceptability for the unanimity rule as a device for avoiding the inconveniences raised by that rule.[9] As to the scope of accepting States necessary to be "generally acceptable", however, there are various opinions and no sufficient consensus.[10]

---

[5] Report of the Rapporteur of Committee IV/2, as Approved by the Committee, Doc. 933 IV/2/42 (2), 13 U. N. C. I. O. Docs. 645 (1945).

[6] Doc. 843, IV/2/37, 13 U. N. C. I. O. Docs. 645 (1945).

[7] Doc. 2, G/7 (K) (I), 3 U. N. C. I. O. Docs. 339 (1945).

[8] Ninčić, *supra* note 3, at 324-25.

[9] *See, e.g.,* Ciobanu, *supra* note 3, at 170.

[10] Goodrich, 'The Changing United Nations', in *Transnational Law in a Changing Society, Essays in Honor of Philip C. Jessup* 259, 262-63 (1972). For example, Tunkin once thought it to be unanimous. Tunkin, 'The Legal Nature of the United Nations', 119 *Recueil des cours* 1, 35-36 (1966); *but see* ditto, 'International Law in the International System', 147 *Recueil des cours* 1, 150-51 (1975). Castañeda, while conceding that politically the necessary majority must clearly include all the significant members in a given case, stated that "it probably means, from a strictly technical point of view, acceptable to the majority of the members of the organ in question, in accordance with the voting majority applicable to that organ and to the nature of the matter being treated". J. Castañeda, *Legal Effects of United Nations Resolutions* 123, 218 (1969). Schachter stated that it meant "an interpretation of the Charter adopted by all the Members (or even 'by the overwhelming majority' except for some abstentions) in the General Assembly". Schachter, 'The

165

It is suggestive in this connection that the Permanent Court of International Justice, in the Case of *Delimitation of the Polish-Czechoslvakian Frontier*, stated as follows:

"It is an extablished principle that the right of giving an authoritative interpretation of a legal rule belongs solely to the person or body who has power to modify or suppress it."[11]

Taking into account the reference made to an amendment to the Charter, it seems possible to rely upon the above principle mentioned by the Court in the following manner: Articles 108 and 109 of the Charter provide that amendments to the Charter shall take effect when ratified by two thirds of the Member States, including all the permanent members of the Security Council; consequently, *according to the logic mentioned by the Court, two thirds of the Member States, including all the permanent members of the Security Council, would, by acting as a whole, possess the power to authoritatively interpret the Charter, and their ratification would fulfill the requirement of general acceptability.*[12] [13]

4.   In the third place, three procedures were pointed out in the report as useful for unifying different interpretations of the Charter. (1) Two Member States at variance concerning the correct interpretation of the Charter could submit the dispute to the ICJ. (2) The General Assembly or the Security Council could ask the ICJ for an advisory opinion concerning the meaning of a provision of the Charter. (3) An *ad hoc* committee of jurists could be set up to examine the question and report its views, or recourse could be had to a joint conference. It must be examined whether these procedures could really be effective in unifying different interpretations of the Charter.

As to the first procedure, reference must be made as its limit to Article 59 of the ICJ Statute, which provides that the decision of the Court has "no binding force except between the parties and in respect of that particular case". Furthermore, only States may be parties in cases before the Court (Article 34 (1) of the Statute). It is of course to be noted that whenever the construction of a convention to which States other than those concerned in the case are parties is in question, every such State has the right to intervene in the proceedings, provided that, if it uses this right, the construction given by the judgment will be equally binding upon it (Article 63). Be that as it may, if a judicial interpretation of the Charter differs from that given it by the political organs such as the General Assembly or the Security Council of the United Nations, such States will find

---

Relation of Law, Politics and Action in the United Nations', 109 *Recueil des cours* 165, 186 (1963). Goodrich, while supporting the view of Schachter, pointed out that "[i]t still leaves open the question of what constitutes an overwhelming majority and how many abstentions are permitted". Goodrich, *id.* at 263.

[11]   Delimitation of the Polish-Czechoslovakian Frontier, [1923] P. C. I. J., Ser. B, No. 8, at 37.

[12]   *See, e.g.,* Gross, 'The International Court of Justice and the United Nations', 120 *Recueil des cours* 313, 428 (1967), *reprinted in* L. Gross, 2 *Essays on International Law and Organization* 845, 923 (1984); Akehurst, 'The Hierarchy of the Sources of International Law', 47 *Brit. Y. B. Int'l L.* 273, 278 (1974-1975); Sloan, 'General Assembly Resolutions Revisited (Forty Years Later)', 58 *Brit. Y. B. Int'l L.* 39, 59 (1987).

[13]   This approach, however, seems to leave unsolved a question: what is the siginificance of the existence in the Charter of express amendment provisions? Taking into account conflicting doctrines and unestablished State practice on this point, there might be some room even for the contention that unless the decisions are made without objections it cannot be confidently affirmed that they are in accordance with the Charter. Ciobanu, *supra* note 3, at 172.

themselves in the delicate position of either observing the judgment of the Court (and risking the condemnation by the political organs), or observing the resolution of the political organs (and breaching the obligation it has assumed under the Statute).[14] This procedure has never been used.

As to the second, it has certainly been used. However, the legal effect of an advisory opinion is only of an advisory, recommendatory character and, as such, has no binding force. Furthermore, even if the political organ concerned accepts the advisory opinion given by the Court, the resolution accepting the opinion will not bind the Member States (unless there exists an express provision to that effect and, in the case of the Charter, no such provision exists).

As to the third, the situation is the same as the second case. The political organs are free to have or not to have recourse to these procedures, retain the liberty to appraise the legal opinion of such a committee even if one is used, and, furthermore, cannot bind the Member States by their resolution accepting the legal opinion concerned. (The General Assembly has rather preferred to turn to its own Sixth Committee (Legal Questions). However, since this committee is a political one composed of government representatives, it is assumed that political considerations would prevail over legal considerations for these representatives.)

For these reasons, we must conclude that the three procedures pointed out in the Report are not effective in unifying different interpretations of the Charter. This is why *the question of interpretation of the Charter was considered to be left unsolved at the San Francisco Conference.*[15]

(2) Discussions in the International Court of Justice

1.   We have pointed out, in Chapter Three of our present study analyzing the jurisprudence of the Court, that there was a question of who has the power to interpret authoritatively the Charter of the United Nations. We will now consider the views of some judges on this point.

2.   The majority opinion, as was previously indicated, took the position that the resolutions clearly for the fulfillment of one of the stated purposes of the United Nations are presumed to be valid and constitutional. In fact, it stated as follows:

"[W]hen the Organization takes action which warrants the assertion that it was appropriate for the fulfilment of one of the stated purposes of the United Nations, the presumption is that such action is not *ultra vires* the Organization."[16]

Judge Fitzmaurice elaborated on this point as follows:

"[W]hen, on the basis of an item which has been regularly placed on the agenda, and has gone through the normal procedural stages, the Assembly, after due discussion, adopts by the necessary two-thirds majority, a resolution authorizing or apportioning certain expenditures incurred, or to be incurred, in the apparent furtherance of the purposes of the Organization, there must arise at the least a strong *prima facie* presumption that these

---

[14] *Id.* at 157-59.

[15] Pollux, *supra* note 3, at 56; Ciobanu, *supra* note 3, at 154.

[16] Advisory Opinion on Certain Expenses on the United Nations (Article 17, Paragraph 2, of the Charter), [1962] I. C. J. 168.

expenditures are valid and proper ones. Unless that is so, a potentially unworkable situation exists; but clearly it must be so, and in consequence, an apportionment by the Assembly has, initially at least, the effect that Member States become obliged to pay their apportioned shares. This is because, if such a presumption arises, it must in principle continue to exist unless and until it is rebutted and the contrary position is established, by whatever means it may be practicable to have recourse to ... Only if the invalidity of the expenditure was apparent on the face of the matter, or too manifest to be open to reasonable doubt, would such a *prima facie* presumption not arise."[17]

3. A view that the interpretation by the General Assembly (at least of Article 17) was final and binding was presented. According to Judge Morelli, in the case of acts of international organizations, and in particular the acts of the United Nations, there is nothing comparable to the remedies existing in domestic law in connection with administrative acts; consequently, there is no possibility of applying the concept of voidability to the acts of the United Nations; in other words, there are only two alternatives for the acts of the Organizations: either the act is fully valid, or it is an absolute nullity, because absolute nullity is the only form in which invalidity of an act of the Organization can occur; the certainty of the legal situations arising from the acts of the Organization requires that it is only in especially serious cases that an act of the Organization could be regarded as invalid, and the violations of the rules governing competence by an organ of the United Nations, Judge Morelli considered, cannot entail the effect of the absolute nullity of the act. In this context, Judge Morelli stated as follows:

"This means that the failure of the act to conform to the rules concerning competence has no influence on the validity of the act, which amounts to saying that each organ of the United Nations is the judge of its own competence....

In my view it is not possible to suppose that the Charter leaves it open to any State Member to claim at any time that an Assembly resolution authorizing a particular expense has never had any legal effect whatever, on the ground that the resolution is based on a wrong interpretation of the Charter or an incorrect ascertainment of situations of fact or of law. It must on the contrary be supposed that the Charter confers finality on the Assembly's resolution irrespective of the reasons, whether they are correct or not, on which the resolution is based; and this must be so even in a field in which the resolution is based; and this must be so even in a field in which the Assembly does not have true discretionary power."[18]

---

[17] *Id.* at 204. Conforti criticized that it was not clear upon which provisions of the Charter or other facts of the legal order the view of Fitzmaurice was based. Conforti, *supra* note 3, at 231-32.

[18] *Id.* at 223-24. Against this view, Fitzmaurice argued as follows (*id.* at 203):
"[The view that the mere fact that certain expenditures had been actually apportioned by the Assembly, was conclusive as to their validity] amounts to saying that even if, on an objective and impartial assessment, given expenditures had in fact been invalidly and improperly incurred or authorized, they would nevertheless stand automatically validated by the act of the Assembly in either apportioning them among Member States or, in the event of a challenge, subsequently resolving that the apportionment was good.

The view of Judge Spender was categorical. While limited to a decision by the General Assembly whether a certain expenditure constitutes the expenses of Article 17 (2), Judge Spender stated as follows:

"Once the General Assembly has passed upon what are the expenses of the Organization, and it is apparent that the expenditure incurred and to be incurred on behalf of the Organization is in furtherance of its purposes, their character as such and any apportionment thereof made by the General Assembly under Article 17 (2) of the Charter cannot legally be challenged by any Member State. Its decision may not be impugned and becomes binding upon each Member State. It would be anarchic of any interpretation of the Charter were each Member State its own interpreter of whether this or that particular expense was an expense of the Organization, within the meaning of Article 17 (2), and could, by its own interpretation, be free to refuse to comply with the decision of the General Assembly."[19]

4.   The importance of the report mentioned above of the San Francisco Conference was pointed out by Judge Winiarski as follows:

"[I]t has also been said that the Assembly, which is a political organ, interprets the Charter by applying it and that its interpretation is final. This is true to a certain extent and particularly where its interpretation has been generally accepted by Member States. This question was very thoroughly considered at the San Francisco Conference and the results of the deliberations were formulated in the report of the Special Subcommittee of Committee IV/2 which concludes thus:

'It is to be understood, of course, that if an interpretation made by any organ of the Organization or by a committee of jurists is not generally acceptable it will be without binding force.'

And the report continues:

'In such circumstances, or in cases where it is desired to establish an authoritative interpretation as a precedent for the future, it may be necessary to embody the interpretation in an amendment to the Chareter. This may always be accomplished by recourse to the procedure provided for amendment.'

This decision was adopted --- unopposed --- on 22 June 1945; the rule would seem still to hold good."[20]

As was explained above, we must acknowledge that the question of interpretation of the Charter was left unresolved at the San Francisco Conference as far as we rely on its *travaux*

        This is a view which I am unable to accept. It is too extreme.... [I]f the Assembly had the power automatically to validate any expenditure ... this would mean that, merely by deciding to spend money, the Assembly could, in practice, do almost anything, even wholly outside its functions, or maybe those of the Organization as a whole."

[19] *Id.* at 183.

[20] *Id.* at 229.

préparatoires. As a result of taking this position, Judge Winiarski admitted a right of a Member State to refuse a resolution of the General Assembly by saying that the reasoning that the nullity of a legal instrument could be relied upon only when there had been a finding of nullity by a competent tribunal must be regarded as echoing the position in municipal or State law, in the international legal system. He elaborated on this point as follows:

"In the international legal system, however, there is, in the absence of agreement to the contrary, no tribunal competent to make a finding of nullity. *It is the State which regards itself as the injured party which itself rejects a legal instrument vitiated, in its opinion, by such defects as to render it a nullity. Such a decision is obviously a grave one and one to which resort can be had only in exceptional cases, but one which is nevertheless sometimes inevitable and which is recognized as such by general international law.*

A refusal to pay, as in the case before the Court, may be regarded by a Member State, loyal and indeed devoted to the Organization, as the only means of protesting against a resolution of the majority which, in its opinion, disregards the true meaning of the Charter and adopts in connection with it a decision which is legally invalid; in such a case it constitutes a grave symptom indicative of serious disagreement as to the interpretation of the Charter. As this Court has on one occasion said, the United Nations is not a super-State, and paragraph 1 of Article 2 of the Charter states that 'The Organization is based on the principle of the sovereign equality of all its Members'."[21] [Italics ours]

5.   We could conclude that while the majority opinion and Judge Fitzmaurice contented themselves with stating that a resolution of the General Assembly properly adopted in accordance with its rules of procedure must be presumed to be valid, Judges Morelli and Spender went as far as admitting a final and binding effect to it. While the position of Judge Winiarski does not necessarily seem to be incompatible with that of the majority opinion and Judge Fitzmaurice, it is incompatible with the position of Judges Morelli and Spender.

(3) Differences in the Doctrine

1.   As to the question of interpretation of the Charter, differences of opinion also exist among the doctrines just like among the judges. Let us look at some of the useful views of scholars.

2.   Pollux, in analyzing the main problems of the Charter interpretation in an excellent manner in 1946, admitted that a State possesses the right to interpret the Charter by saying as follows:

"*The easiest, the most primitive, and the most unsatisfactory solution is to say that each individual Member has the right to decide for itself how to interpret the Charter.* This might be considered to follow naturally from *the sovereignty of the states.* No state is obliged to accept any jurisdiction without previous consent. A state might consequently say that it and no one else had the power of deciding.... [But the Charter has to be interpreted in accordance with the canons of good faith, and Member States are not left

---

[21] *Id.* at 232.

170

entirely free to adopt their own individual interpretations.]

On the other hand, it must be admitted that it may at times be extremely difficult for a Member of the United Nations to follow any course other than that of deciding for itself what is the right interpretation of the Charter. *No state can reasonably be expected meekly to accept an interpretation of the Charter which it considers completely wrong, however large the majority in favour of such an interpretation may be.*"[22] [Italics ours]

3.   The right of a State to interpret international law in general and the law of the United Nations in particular has been widely admitted by scholars.[23] It was Ciobanu who exhaustively examined this question of interpretation of the Charter and, relying on an extensive body of literature, gave to such a right of a State the symbolic name of "right of last resort".[24] Ciobanu stated as follows:

"[T]he States possess, under the law of the United Nations as it stands at present, the so-called 'right of last resort'. In exercising such a right, ... a State itself corrects any defects which it may have found in the application by the relevant organ of the provisions pertaining to its competence or in the substance of the decision. Obviously, there are no pre-established means, procedures and conditions for the exercise by States of the right of last resort except its conformity with the rules of general international law and (in the large majority of cases) the obligations undertaken under the Charter."[25]

---

[22] Pollux, *supra* note 3, at 56-57.

[23] Tammes, for example, stated as follows ('Decisions of International Organs as a Source of International Law', 94 *Recueil des cours* 261, 338-39 (1958)):

"What cannot be easily accepted is the assumption that the Member-government would find that it had lost its own right of interpreting existing international law (general, conventional, constitutional, or decisional), as soon as an organ had adopted a recommendation involving that organ's interpretation of the relevant law as applicable to a concrete question or situation.... In the absence of any instance of review ... the assumption just referred to would imply that international organs would be invested with uncontrolled law-making powers exercised by way of interpretative opinions."

See also Report of Special Committee on Reference to the International Court of Justice of Questions of United Nations Competence, 44 *Proc. Am. Soc'y Int'l L.* 256, 267 (1950); Waldock, 'General Course on Public International Law', 106 *Recueil des cours* 1, 108 (1962).

[24] This expression was already used by Fitzmaurice in his separate opinion in the *Certain Expenses* case. Fitzmaurice, after referring to a last resort right retained by Member States not to pay, stated as follows (*Certain Expenses* case, *supra* note 15, at 204):

"The problem is to determine what that right consists of and, more particularly, in what conditions it can be exercised.... [I]t can only be a right of last resort, for an unlimited right on the part of Member States to withhold contributions at will, on the basis of a mere claim that in their view the expenditures concerned had been improperly incurred, not only could speedily cause serious disruption, but would also give those Member States which, on the basis of the normal scales of apportionment, are major contributors, a degree of control and veto over the affairs of the United Nations ..."

The idea of this right of last resort was recognized by Fitzmaurice in his Fourth Report on the Law of Treaties. Fitzmaurice, Fourth Report on the Law of Treaties [1959] 2 Y. B. Int'l L. Comm'n 37, 50-51, U. N. Doc. A/CN. 4/120. *See also* Ciobanu, *supra* note 3, at 174, n. 61.

[25] Ciobanu, *supra* note 3, at 174-75.

4.   There certainly exists some criticism on this right of last resort.[26] Osieke, for example, stated as follows:

> "Because of the divergencies of opinion that still exist on the matter, it is clear that the right of member states to reject decisions of international organizations that they consider to be *ultra vires*, or indeed the right of autointerpretation, cannot be regarded as a generally accepted principle of international law or of the law and practice of international organizations, there in no doubt that in the course of the proceedings of international organizations, member states are continuously interpreting the constitutions of these bodies to determine the basis of the proposed acts or decisions and the nature and extent of their obligations, and to contest any proposals that appear to them to be incompatible with the express provisions of the constitutions. But to arrogate to the member states a general right to reject a properly adopted decision on the basis of a unilateral determination that it is *ultra vires* would be tantamount to making the members judges in their own cases --- a situation that would be similar to the much criticized principle of *compétence de la compétence* of international organizations."[27]

Osieke, however, admitted that international organizations possess the *competence to determine* the claims that arise while also admitting that member states had an inherent *right to challenge* the legal validity of acts and decisions. Osieke stated as follows:

> "The main justification for the attribution of competence to international organizations to determine claims against their jurisdiction, or the legal validity of their acts and decisions, is the absence of review bodies with original or appellate jurisdiction to deal with these cases. To deny international organizations competence in these circumstances would create a lacuna; and it could seriously impede the effective attainment of their objects and purposes because all that a member state would have to do to create an impasse or prevent the adoption of a decision is to challenge the competence of the organ or the organization, or indeed the legal validity of the decision.
>
> It appears, *therefore*, that the determination of jurisdictional claims by international organizations, though perhaps not as satisfactory as a judicial determination, is necessary

---

[26] Wright, for example, stated as follows ('The Strengthening of International Law', 98 *Recueil des cours* 1, 125 (1959)):
  " [T]he suggestion occasionally made, that the States themselves should interpret the Charter, would tend toward nullification and a hopeless incapacity of the United Nations to function. The society as a whole must be able to interpret the law which is binding upon the parties, if law is to prevail in the society."

[27] Osieke, 'The Legal Validity of Ultra Vires Decisions of International Organizations', 77 *Am. J. Int'l L.* 239, 255 (1983). *See also* ditto, '"Ultra-Vires" Acts in International Organizations --- The Experience of the International Labour Organization', 48 *Brit. Y. B. Int'l L.* 259 (1976-77); ditto, 'The Exercise of the Judicial Function with Respect to the International Labour Organization', 47 *Brit. Y. B. Int'l L.* 315 (1974-75); ditto, 'Unconstitutional Acts in International Organizations: The Law and Practice of the International Civil Aviation Organization (ICAO)', 28 *Int'l & Comp. L. Q.* 1 (1979); ditto, 'Admission to Membership in International Organizations: The Case of Namibia', 51 *Brit. Y. B. Int'l L.* 189 (1980).

at the present time."[28] [Italics ours]

5.   Facing such arguments, what position should we take? Minagawa, relying on the opinion of Sperduti in connection with the question of Article 2, paragraph 7 (domestic jurisdiction) of the Charter, made a following suggestive statement.

> "Presumably, the confusing discussion may be due to the mal-position of the question. In legal litigation, if any objection to the jurisdiction of the Court is raised by a party, the proceedings on the merits are suspended until the Court shall give its decision on the jurisdictional question. Political litigation is 'unschematic,' and nothing is contemplated in Article 2 (7) to institute the comparable preliminary stage of the proceedings before the judicial organ."[29]

From this position, Minagawa deduced three consequences. Firstly, it should be inferred that applicability of Article 2 (7) in a concrete case is not subject to a previous and binding decision of a preliminary character before proceeding to the discussion and examination on the merits of the question. Secondly, a State may raise an objection to the question being placed on the agenda, claiming that the matter is essentially within its domestice jurisdiction; but the State is not in a position to impose its self-judgement on the organ or its Members; even granting that the power of auto-interpretation exists for an individual State, it implies at most that the State is not bound to accept the view contrary to its own interpretation. Thirdly, when a difference is revealed to subsist concerning the question of jurisdiction within the organ, it is the organ itself which must proceed to voting in order to form a collective judgement on that issue; the result of voting, however, does not amount to a decision on a statutory basis binding the interested State or the dissenting Members, although both sides ought to act in good faith.

The legal situation relating to Article 2 (7) of the Charter would, it is submitted, apply, in principle, to all the other provisions of the Charter.

6.   Differences of opinion relating to the right of last resort, it is submitted, derive from, at least partly, ambiguous usages of such terms as "right" and "decision". The legal situation relating to "interpretation" under general international law was correctly analyzed by Gross. Gross wrote in 1953 as follows:

> "The technical organizational insufficiency of international law may, and in fact does, make it difficult to determine whether a state acts in accordance with, or contrary to, international law. *It is one thing to admit the insufficiency and, I submit, quite another thing to exploit its existence to the point of contending that every state has a right of autodecision and autoenforcement.* It is generally recognized that the root of the unsatisfactory situation in international law and relations is the absence of an authority generally competent to declare what the law is at any given time, how it applies to a given situation or dispute, and what

---

[28] *Id.* at 255.

[29] Minagawa, 'The Principle of Domestic Jurisdiction and the International Court of Justice', 8 *Hitotsubashi J. L. & Pol.* 9, 12 (1979).

the appropriate sanction may be. *In the absence of such an authority, and failing agreement between the states at variance on these points, each state has a right to interpret the law, the right of autointerpretation, as it might be called. This interpretation, however, is not a 'decision' and is neither final nor binding upon the other parties.* In consequence of the technical insufficiency prevailing in general international law, we may never know, or, in some cases, we may not know for a time, which autointerpretation was correct. A controversy, in other words, may remain unsettled forever or for a long time. This is, for better or worse, the situation resulting from the organizational insufficiency of international law."[30] [Italics ours]

If this legal situation under general international law also applies to the Charter of the United Nations, the legal situation of interpretation of the Charter would be as follows: *Both the United Nations as well as the Member concerned are legally entitled to interpret the relevant provision of the Charter but neither is legally empowered to decide its interpretation with binding effect for the other; the interpretation of the United Nations organs cannot legally oust the interpretation of the Member and the Member's interpretation cannot legally oust that of the United Nations organs.*[31] It is a matter of definition whether we should call such an "autointerpretation" a right. What is important is that neither the interpretation by the United Nations nor that of the Member concerned is *legally* binding upon the other party.

7.   The question, in the final analysis, comes down to whether the legal situation under general international law still applies to the Charter of the United Nations or a different legal situation has come into existence in the realm of the United Nations. *As a matter of strict law*, we should take the former position that the legal situation under general international law still applies to the Charter of the United Nations.

This position could be based upon the following three grounds.[32] Firstly, the above-mentioned report of the San Francisco Conference did not bestow the authoritative power --- in the sense of binding all the other parties --- of interpreting the Charter upon any organ or any Member State of the United Nations. Secondly, the Charter itself does not include any express provision relating to its interpretation, thus not bestowing such an authoritative power of interpreting the Charter upon any organ or any Member State of the United Nations. Thirdly, the practice of the United Nations supports this position: while the organs appear to have exercised their power of decision by rejecting the objections of Member States, the objecting States usually if not always protested against the decision and opposed to it in various possible measures; in these circumstances, it is

---

[30] Gross, 'States as Organs of International Law and the Problem of Autointerpretation', in *Law and Politics in the World Community: Essays on Hans Kelsen's Pure Theory and Related Problems in International Law* 59, 76-77 (G. A. Lipsky ed. 1953), *reprinted in* L. Gross, 1 *Essays on International Law and Organization* 367, 386 (1984).

[31] Gross, 'Domestic Jurisdiction, Enforcement Measures and the Congo', *Australian Y. B. Int'l L.* 137, 141-45 (1965), *reprinted in* L. Gross, 2 *Essays on International Law and Organization* 1173, 1177-80 (1984).

[32] Conforti, *supra* note 3, at 226-30.

impossible to consider that a customary rule of international law to the effect that such an authoritative power of interpreting the Charter is bestowed on the organs of the United Nations has come into existence.

(4) Toward Uniformity and Stability in Charter Interpretations

(1) The Ambiguous Importance of Consent

1.   As a result of the authoritative power of interpreting the Charter not being bestowed upon any organ or any Member State of the United Nations, the legal question of Charter interpretations is to be analyzed on the level of general international law. Thus, for example, Conforti explained as follows:

"Quels sont donc, dans le système des Nations Unies, les mécanismes juridiques dont on peut se servir et dont on se sert pour résoudre les contestations, pour rendre définitives et incontestables les résolutions des organes, en bref pour permettre à ces résolutions de produire leurs effets? Nous estimons que ces mécanismes sont encore aujourd'hui les mécanismes propres au droit international classique, c'est-à-dire *l'accord* et d'autres types juridiques similaires, tels que *l'acceptation tacite (acquiescement)*; nous estimons que, à défaut d'accord ou d'acquiescement de la part d'un Etat, la résolution ne produit pas d'effets pour celui-ci; *nous estimons enfin que le mécanisme de l'accord est à même d'augmenter plutôt que de réduire la force juridique des résolutions de l'ONU.*"[33] [Italics ours]

2.   This statement could be, to some extent, supported by several events in the past fifty years of the United Nations' history. Firstly, a confrontation based upon the conditions of admission in Article 4 (2) of the Charter was resolved not by its judicial interpretation indicated in the advisory opinion of the Court, but by the change of political circumstances enabling the confronting States to reach a political compromise. Secondly, a confrontation based upon the "expenses of the Organization" in Article 17 (2) of the Charter was not resolved by the advisory opinion of the Court; the question of whether to apply Article 19, which also arose from this confrontation, was resolved by the political compromise reached in the Special Committee on Peace-keeping Operations. These examples certainly demonstrate the importance of consent and acquiescence[34]

---

[33] Conforti, *supra* note 3, at 222.

"What are then, in the United Nations system, the legal mechanisms which one can use and which one uses for resolving the disputes, for making definitive and incontestable the resolutions of the organs, in brief for permitting these resolutions to produce their effects? We estimate that these mechanisms are still now the mechanisms proper to the classic international law, that is to say, consent and other similar legal types, such as *tacit acceptance (acquiescence)*; We estimate that, in the absence of consent or acquiescence on the part of a State, the resolution does not produce any effect for that State; *we estimate finally that the mechanism of consent is able to increase rather than decrease the legal force of the resolutions of the U. N.*"[Our translation]

[34] Acquiescence is generally used to describe the inaction of a state which is faced with a situation constituting a threat to or infringement of its rights, and takes the form of silence or absence of protest in circumstances which generally call for a positive reaction signifying an objection. The function of acquiescence could be equated with that of consent, and it serves as a form of recognition of legality and condonation of illegality. MacGibbon, 'The Scope of Acquiescence in International Law', 31 *Brit. Y. B. Int'l L.* 143, 143-47 (1954).

on the part of the States concerned for effectiveness of the operations and activities of the United Nations.

3.   The above statement, however, must be modified by several conditions.   Firstly, the effectiveness of a resolution depends upon the purpose and nature of the resolution.   As far as the resolution aims at the change of behavior by a target State, the consent of that State would be indispensable.   There are, however, many other resolutions recommending various kinds of activities on the part of the United Nations (for example, to take up certain problems on the agenda and consider them, and, furthermore, criticize relevant States; to establish some auxiliary organs for certain purposes and authorize them to pursue certain activities; to decide to impose some unfavorable treatments upon certain States within the activities of the United Nations), or on the part of the other Member States (for example, to impose certain sanctions upon the target State).   These many resolutions do not, for their effectiveness, depend upon the consent of the

---

It is this acquiescence that would play greater role in disolving differences of opinion among States which do not develop into outright conflicts. Elihu Lauterpacht aptly pointed out as follows ('The Legal Effect of Illegal Acts of International Organizations', in *Cambridge Essays in International Law: Essays in Honour of Lord McNair* 88, 117-18 (1965)):

> "As a matter of practice, perhaps the most important factor leading to the satisfaction of the demands of legal principle, as well as of the requirements of the efficient functioning of the organisation, is the operation of the concept of acquiescence. This is particularly true in organisations where there is no procedure for judicial review."

States whose objections were rejected would protest against the resolution in various ways.   A protest in the most radical form is a withdrawal as a measure of last resort. *What is then the relation between non-withdrawal and acquiescence?* Judge Spender stated, in the *Certain Expenses* case, as follows (*Certain Expenses* case, *supra* note 15, at 196):

> "It is no answer to say that the protesting minority has the choice of remaining in or withdrawing from the Organization and that if it chooses to remain or because it pays its contributions according to apportionment under Article 17 (2) the Members in the minority 'acquiesce' in the practice or must be deemed to have done so. They are bound to pay these contributions and the minority has a right to remain in the Organization and at the same time to assert what it claims to be any infringement of its rights under the Charter or any illegal use of power by any organ of the United Nations."

On the other hand, Lauterpacht took an opposite view.   While conceding that the legal construction to be placed upon the fact of non-withdrawal in such circumstances that States concerned use a variey of devices to protest against the measures of organizations which, in their view, are illegal cannot be stated with certainty, Lauterpacht expressed the following view (Elihu Lauterpacht, *id.* at 119):

> "There would be a strong case for saying that, despite the fact that a protest was recorded, the state in question must be regarded as having considered that the balance of convenience was in favour of remaining within the organisation and on that basis must be deemed to have decided to accept the validity of what was done. If some formal action of acquiescence must be sought, it may well be found in the fact that in each instance the state concerned has contributed its share of the budget of the organisation --- a budget which was normally drawn up in terms such as to cover every act of the organisation."

The legal significance of non-withdrawal is not established.   In this connection, as to withholding of contributions, Zoller stated as follows ('The "Corporate Will" of the United Nations and Rights of the Minority', 81 *Am J. Int'l L.* 610, 634 (1987)):

> "[I]t is just as wrong to believe that the minority must always yield to the 'corporate will' of the Organization as determined by the majority as to believe that the minority may freely impose its own interests through financial blackmail. The power to withhold is not a freedom, but an inherent right of members to remind the Organization, if need be, of certain obligations."

176

target State, but will be unilaterally implemented by the United Nations or the other Member States.[35]

Secondly, the effectiveness of a resolution also has a close relationship with the graveness of the problem treated in the resolution and the political power of the target State. The more grave the problem is and the more powerful the target State is, the more difficult it would be for the resolution to be implemented by the United Nations and the other Member States because of the politically destructive influences it might cause (as was indicated by the second example given in the above sub-section).

(2) Failed Attempts to Establish a Judicial Control

1.   It is unquestionable, in the long perspective, that the respect of the Charter and other relevant rules by the United Nations is indispensable for its effective operation. In the light of the horizontal structure of the international society upon which the United Nations was created and still based, the Charter of the United Nations as an agreement among the Member States should be faithfully observed. Consequently, it has been constantly contended that any objections to the legality of resolutions or activities of the United Nations should, in principle, be judged objectively by an independent tribunal. It will be useful to look at briefly some of the main attempts in this direction.[36]

2.   In 1949, the American Society of International Law established a committee to study the attitude and action of the United Nations in cases wherein one or more Member States, challenging its competence under the Charter, suggested that the question be submitted to the Court. The report of the committee submitted in 1950 contained the following conclusions: if an organ disagrees with a Member State(s) on the question of its competence to deal with a matter at issue, it shall consider the advisability of referring the question to the Court for an advisory opinion; it may make a reference to the Court conditional on a declaration by the State(s) challenging its competence that it (they) will accept the opinion as decisive; the organ may either decide itself the question of competence, or refer it to a special committee of jurists appointed by it, if the challenging state refuses to make such a declaration.[37]

3.   When the Grotius Society dealt with the problem of redress against the decisions of international organizatins in 1950, the Rapporteur, Gros, expressed a positive opinion on the possibility of having the decision of the international organisation carried directly before a jurisdictional body by a State demanding its annulment; he stated that the establishment of appeals would encourage States to adhere to those international organizations since they would then be in a position to protect their own interests by applying for the annulment by an impartial jurisdiction of any decision which were proved to have been rendered by an "excess of power" or jurisdiction. Against such an opinion, some prudent opinions were also expressed for various

---

[35] *See*, for these and other examples, B. Sloan, *United Nations General Assembly Resolutions in Our Changing World* (1991).

[36] Ciobanu, *supra* note 3, at 193-201.

[37] Report of Special Committee on Reference to the International Court of Questions of United Nations Competence, 44 *Proc. Am. Soc'y Int'l L.* 256-69. The members were Louis B. Sohn (Chairman), Joseph P. Chamberlain and Lester H. Woolsey.

reasons.[38]

4.   The "Institut de Droit International" dealt with the problem of judicial redress against the decisions of international organs since 1952 with Wengler as Rapporteur. The report of Wengler was an excellent one dealing with the merits and demerits of judicial redress and was supported by most members, though some negative opinions were also expressed regarding the possible development of activities by international organizations. The Institut adopted a resolution in 1957 by a vote of 39 to 0 with 2 abstentions. It stated, among other things, that the possibilities of establishing judicial redress against the decisions of international organs would depend essentially on the nature, structure and powers of the organs under consideration, and that, in consequence, the establishment of this control, its means and its effects would not appear realizable, in the present state of affairs, except through the conclusion of treaties or other instruments particularly suited to each organ or organization.[39]

5.   The International Law Association adopted a resolution relating to the problem of review of the Charter of the United Nations in 1957 with Schwarzenberger as Rapporteur. In this resolution, it was stated, among other things, that "Article 96 of the Charter should be amended so as to impose upon the organs of the United Nations the obligation to request from the International Court of Justice an advisory opinion concerning any situation in which the claim is made by a member that the organ had exceeded its jurisdiction under the Charter".[40]

6.   From the above brief overview, the following points could be made. Firstly, it was commonly recognized that the institutional assurance for a uniform Charter interpretation, especially a judicial guarantee for it in the form of redress against the decisions of international organizations in the light of protecting the rights of Member States, was necessary. Secondly, such a guarantee was considered to be possible only by a legislative measure of the Charter amendment or the conclusion of a treaty to that effect, and not by a request of an advisory opinion to the Court. Thirdly, the possibility for such a legislative measure is quite small; in fact, all of the above suggestions were made in 1950s. Ciobanu, upon these experiences, concluded as follows:

> "[I]t appears that the incorporation of some sort of judicial redress in the law of the United Nations requires a major political decision by member States of the Organization. There is no indication that, for the time being, they are ready and willing to make such a decision."[41]

(3) Non-Use of the Advisory Competence of the Court and its Impact
**   upon Charter Interpretations**

1.   While the report of the San Francisco Conference suggested an advisory opinion as a means

---

[38] Gros, 'The Problem of Redress against the Decisions of International Organizations', 36 *Transactions of the Grotius Soc'y Int'l L.* 30-48 (1950).

[39] Wengler, 'Recours judiciaire à instituer contre les décisions d'organes internationaux', 44-I *Annuaire de l'Institut de Droit International* 224-360 (1952). *See also* 45-I *id.* at 265-309 (1954); 47-I *id.* at 5-33 (1957); 47-II *id.* at 274-327, 488-91 (1957).

[40] Schwarzenberger, 'Review of the Charter of the United Nations', 47 *Int'l L. A.* viii-ix (1957).

[41] Ciobanu, *supra* note 3, at 200. *See also* Gros, 'Concerning the Advisory Role of the International Court of Justice', in *Transnational Law* (*supra* note 10) 313, 324 (1972).

of assuring the uniformity of Charter interpretations, this measure was never used sufficiently. The General Assembly of the United Nations considered the item "Need for greater use by the United Nations and its organs of the International Court of Justice in connexion not only with disputes of a legal character, but also with legal aspects of disputes and situations" in 1947, and it adopted, by a vote of 45 to 6 with 3 abstentions, Resolution 171 titled "Need for greater use by the United Nations and its organs of the International Court of Justice", which included the following recommendation:

> "The General Assembly, ... [c]onsidering that it is of paramount importance that the interpretation of the Charter of the United Nations and the constitutions of the specialized agencies should be based on recognized principles of international law; ... [r]ecommends that organs of the United Nations and the specialized agencies should, from time to time, review the difficult and important points of law within the jurisdiction of the International Court of Justice which have arisen in the course of their activities and involve questions of principle which it is desirable to have settled, including points of law relating to the interpretation of the Charter of the United Nations or the constitutions of the specialized agencies, and if duly authorized according to Article 96, paragraph 2, of the Charter, should refer them to the International Court of Justice for an advisory opinion."[42]

The impact of this resolution was small. In fact, there were only thirteen requests for advisory opinions from organs of the United Nations and specialized agencies during the twenty-four years between 1947 and 1970.

2. The General Assembly considered an item entitled "Review of the Role of the International Court of Justice" since 1970 and adopted Resolution 3232 (XXIX) by consensus in 1974. This resolution contained a recommendation similar to that quoted above in Resolution 171, but it simply recommended that United Nations organs and the specialized agencies should study the advisability of referring legal questions to the Court for an advisory opinion.[43] At any rate, this resolution did not have much impact either. There were only three requests for advisory opinions during the ten years between 1971 and 1980.

3. Comparison with the figures of the Permanent Court of International Justice will clearly demonstrate the negative attitude of United Nations organs and specialized agencies for utilizing the Court.[44] The Permanent Court gave twenty-seven advisory opinions during the seventeen years between 1922 and 1939. The International Court of Justice, on the other hand, gave only twenty-one advisory opinions during the forty-nine years between 1946 and 1994. Furthermore, while, in the League period, only the Assembly and the Council were entitled to request advisory opinions, the number of organs of the United Nations entitled to make requests increased to six and the number of agencies so entitled increased to sixteen by 1987.

---

[42] 1947-1948 *I. C. J. Y. B.* 15-20 (1948).

[43] 1974-1975 *I. C. J. Y. B.* 124-27 (1975).

[44] Gross, 'Underutilization of the International Court of Justice', 27 *Harvard Int'l L. J.* 571, 577 (1986); Rosenne, 'On the Non-Use of the Advisory Competence of the International Court of Justice', 39 *Brit. Y. B. Int'l L.* 1, 21 (1963).

4.   The negative attitude of United Nations organs and specialized agencies for utilizing the Court is also demonstrated by the fact that the General Assembly and the Security Council, among others, have, on various occasions, considered and rejected proposals and suggestions aimed at putting a request to the Court.[45] It could be concluded that the majority States in the political organs did not like their autointerpretation to be restricted by a judicial interpretation of the Court. The fact that most of the advisory opinions given by the Court supported the position of the majority States implies that the majority States had taken advantage of the system of advisory opinions only to strengthen and justify their political position. On the other hand, when we take into consideration the fact that many of the advisory opinions, while accepted by the requesting organ itself, were not necessarily accepted by the States concerned and did not solve the original cause of conflict, we could also conclude that the minority States did not want their autointerpretation to be restricted by the judicial interpretation of the Court either. Consequently, the problem seems to come back to the negative attitude prevalent among States against the judicial means of dispute resolution, at least in the field of the operations and activities of international organizations.

5.   When we come back to the context of our study with the above analysis in mind, we could conclude as follows. The negative attitude toward the judicial control of the operations and activities of international organizations will, as a matter of fact, increase the influence of the political organs dominated by the majority States as a result of majority voting system. The interpretations and applications of the Charter in the operations and activities of the United Nations are, in most cases, made by their political organs, and not by the Court, not by any individual State, not even by minority States.

It is certainly true that consent and acquiescence by States are quite important to the United Nations in operating in a horizontal and decentralized international society. This is partially proved by the fact that the system of consensus is increasingly used in the voting system of many organs of the United Nations and specialized agencies.

When we consider the interpretations and applications of the Charter in the operations and activities of the United Nations as a whole, however, the dominant position of (the majority States of) the political organs *vis-à-vis* any individual Member State is quite clear. All of the subsidiary organs and committees of, for example, the General Assembly and the Security Council are administered and operated in accordance with the interpretations and decisions of the General Assembly and the Security Council. In spite of the existence of any individual objecting Member State, the interpretations and decisions in the daily operations and activities of such political organs are accumulating and becoming customarily established in the United Nations if not undoubtedly established in the sense of customary international law. There is practically no means to be taken by minority Member States other than protesting against the adoption of a resolution or withholding such part of their contributions to the United Nations as corresponding to those

---

[45] Rosenne, *supra* note 43, at 9-14; Weissberg, 'The Role of the International Court of Justice in the United Nations System: the First Quarter Century', in *The Future of the International Court of Justice* 131, 151-56 (L. Gross ed. 1976).

activities to which they objected. Under these circumstances, any objective analysis of the meaning and interpretation of provisions of the Charter must take into consideration the practice (interpretations and applications of the Charter) of the political organs of the United Nations. The practice of these organs plays an important part in the actual operation and development of the Charter as law governing the operations and activities of the organs of the United Nations.

Section 3 Specialized Universal International Organizations[46] (Except Economic International Organizations)

(1) Preliminary Analysis

We will deal, in the present section, with eleven international organizations (the ILO, FAO, UNESCO, WHO, ICAO, UPU, ITU, WMO, IMO, WIPO and IAEA). These include ten specialized agencies (excluding six economic specialized agencies out of a total sixteen), and the IAEA being "under the aegis of the UN".

All of the constituent instruments of these eleven specialized international organizations, except that of the WIPO, include provisions related to "interpretation" or "settlement of disputes".[47]

---

[46] For the relevant bibliography of the present section, *see, e.g.*, Colliard, 'Le règlement des différends dans les organisations intergouvernementales de caractère non politique', in *Hommage d'une génération de juristes au Président Basdevant* 152 (1960); Bindschedler, 'Le règlement des différends relatifs au statut d'un organisme international', 124 *Recueil des cours* 453 (1968); Audéoud, 'La Cour internationale de Justice et le règlement des différends au sein des organisations internationales', 18 *R. G. D. I. P.* 945 (1977); H. G. Schermers, *International Institutional Law* 658-82 (1980); D. W. Bowett, *The Law of International Institutions* 147-51 (4th ed. 1982).

[47] These provisions are as follows.
(1) As to the ILO, in addition to a series of procedure relating to "complaint" provided in Articles 26-34, Article 37 provides as follows:
"1.   Any question or dispute relating to the interpretation of this Constitution ... shall be referred for decision to the International Court of Justice."
(2) As to the FAO, Article 17 (Interpretation of the Constitution and Settlement of Legal Questions) provides as follows:
"1.   Any question or dispute concerning the interpretaion of this Constitution, if not settled by the Conference, shall be referred to the International Court of Justice in conformity with the Statute of the Court or to such other body as the Conference may determine."
(3) As to the UNESCO, Article 14 in the section of "Interpretation" provides as follows:
"2.   Any question or dispute concerning the interpretation of this Constitution shall be referred for determination to the International Court of Justice or to an arbitral tribunal, as the General Conference may determine under its rules of procedure."
(4) As to the WHO, Article 75 in "Chapter 18 Interpretation" provides as follows:
"Any question or dispute concerning the interpretation or application of this Constitution which is not settled by negotiation or by the Health Assembly shall be referred to the International Court of Justice in conformity with the Statute of the Court, unless the parties concerned agree on another mode of settlement."
(5) As to the ICAO, Article 84 (Settlement of disputes) in "Chapter 18 Disputes and Default" provides as follows:
"If any disagreement between two or more contracting States relating to the interpretation or application of this Convention and its Annexes cannot be settled by negotiation, it shall, on the application of any State concerned

181

Firstly, these provisions deal with questions or disputes related to "interpretation" or "application". Some (those of the ILO, FAO, UNESCO) refer only to "interpretation", and the others refer to both of "interpretation" and "application". Since the ordinary usage of "interpretation", however, is wide enough to include "application", we find no legal significance to this difference.

Secondly, these provisions deal with "question" or "dispute" related to interpretations or applications of the constituent instruments. (That of the ICAO refers to "disagreement".) As to the concept of "dispute" under international law, the following definition given by the Permanent Court of International Justice in the *Mavrommatis Palestine Concessions* case (1924) is often referred to:[48]

---

in the disagreement, be decided by the Council. No member of the Council shall vote in the consideration by the Council of any dispute to which it is a party. Any contracting State may, subject to Article 85 [Arbitration prodecure], appeal from the decision of the Council to an *ad hoc* arbitral tribunal agreed upon with the other parties to the dispute or to the Permanent Court of International Justice. Any such appeal shall be notified to the Council within sixty days of receipt of notification of the decision of the Council."

(6) As to the UPU, Article 32 (Arbitration) in "Chapter 4 Settlement of Disputes" provides as follows:
"In the event of a dispute between two or more Postal Administrations of Member Countries concerning the interpretation of the Acts of the Union or the responsibility imposed on a Postal Administration by the application of those Acts, the question at issue shall be settled by arbitration."

(7) As to the ITU, Article 50 (Settlement of Disputes) provides as follows:
"1.   Members may settle their disputes on questions relating to the interpretation or application of this Convention or of the Regulations contemplated in Article 42, through diplomatic channels, or according to procedures established by bilateral or multilateral treaties concluded between them for the settlement of international disputes, or by any other method mutually agreed upon.
2.   If none of these methods of settlement is adopted, any Member party to a dispute may submit the dispute to arbitration in accordance with the procedure defined in the General Regulations or in the Optional Additional Protocol, as the case may be."

(8) As to the WMO, Article 29 in "Part 16 Interpretation and Disputes" provides as follows:
"Any question or dispute concerning the interpretation or application of the present Convention which is not settled by negotiation or by the Congress shall be referred to an independent arbitrator appointed by the President of the International Court of Justice, unless the parties concerned agree on another mode of settlement."

(9) As to the IMO, Articles in "Part 17 Interpretation" provide as follows:
"Article 65   Any question or dispute concerning the interpretation or application of the Convention shall be referred to the Assembly for settlement, or shall be settled in such other manner as the parties to the dispute may agree. Nothing in this Article shall preclude any organ of the Organization from settling any such question or dispute that may arise during the exercise of its functions.
Article 66   Any legal question which cannot be settled as provided in Article 65 shall be referred by the Organization to the International Court of Justice for an advisory opinion in accordance with Article 96 of the Charter of the United Nations."

(10) As to the WIPO, there is no relevant provision. WIPO adopted, however, Mediation, Arbitration, and Expedited Arbitration Rules in 1994. *See* for the text 34 *Int'l Legal Materials* 559 (1995).

(11) As to the IAEA, Article 17 (Settlement of disputes) provides as follows:
"(A)   Any question or dispute concerning the interpretation or application of this statute which is not settled by negotiation shall be referred to the International Court of Justice in conformity with the statute of the court, unless the parties concerned agree on another mode of settlement."

[48] *See, e.g., Parry and Grant Encyclopaedic Dictionary of International Law* 97 (C. Parry et al. eds. 1986).

"A dispute is a disagreement on a point of law or fact, a conflict of legal views or of interests between two persons."

This definition, however, is redundant. According to Minagawa,[49] a dispute arises where the opposing or confronting claims between the parties are established to exist in regard to a certain subject-matter; in short, it is a "conflict of will" between the subjects of international law. On the other hand, while the difference between a dispute and a conflict of legal views is only relative and not absolute, a legal dispute is a clash of legal claims, i.e. antithesis of two competing claims on the basis of law, a simple "disagreement" or "question" not being sufficient for a dispute to exist. In this sense, in most of the above-mentioned provisions, a wider scope of "question" than a traditionally defined concept of "dispute" under international law is open to the Court jurisdiction.[50]

(2) Mechanisms of Interpretation and Dispute Settlement

1.   All of the international organizations dealt with in the present section have, as a common characteristic, the structure that the interpretations or dispute settlements concerning their constituent instruments are attempted in an internal organ in the first instance, and are only secondarily referred to an outside judiciary organ.

2.   *The internal organ* in the first instance is ordinarily a political organ. Some of the provisions refer explicitly to the Assembly (the FAO, WHO, WMO and IMO) or the Council (the ICAO). In these cases, the designated organs will have the final say on the internal level of the organizations. In the other cases where no organ is designated, the organ concerned will, of course, attempt an interpretation or a dispute settlement in the first place. The following part of the final report of the San Francisco Conference relating to the Charter interpretation will, in principle, apply to any constituent instrument:

"In the course of the operations from day to day of the various organs of the Organization, it is inevitable that each organ will interpret such parts of the Charter as are applicable to its particular functions. This process is inherent in the functioning of any body which operates under an instrument defining its functions and powers. It will be manifested in the functioning of such a body as the General Assembly, the Security Council, or the International Court of Justice. Accordingly, it is not necessary to include in the Charter a provision either authorizing the normal operation of this principle."[51]

3.   *An outside judicial organ* will be used when the internal organ has failed to solve the question or dispute, or when a party is not content with the decision of the internal organ. Some of the provisions explicitly mention other possibilities based upon the parties' consent before the reference (the WHO, WMO, IMO and IAEA). There are three categories of outside judicial organs: the ICJ, an arbitral tribunal and other organs.

---

[49]   Minagawa, 'Various Aspects of Dispute in International Litigation --- Chiefly with Reference to Morelli's Construction', 9 *Hitotsubashi J. L. & Pol.* 1, 10-11 (1981).

[50]   Bindschedler, *supra* note 46, at 465-66.

[51]   *Supra* note 5.

4.	*The International Court of Justice* is available for a decision and for an advisory opinion.

As to the use of the Court for *a decision*, only States, not any international organization or individual, may be parties in cases before the Court (Article 34 (1) of the Statute). Consequently, the Court can be used only in the form of inter-State litigation. On the other hand, since the decision of the Court has no binding force except between the parties and in respect of that particular case (Article 59 of the Statute), the interpretation by the Court does not bind international organizations or other States.

Judging from the provisions concerned, the Court appears to have been given compulsory jurisdiction with respect to the questions or disputes among member States related to the constituent instruments of the following international organizations: the ILO (Article 37), FAO, UNESCO, WHO, ICAO and IAEA. For the cases of the ILO (Article 29) and ICAO, there already exist "the report of the Commission of Inquiry" (ILO) and "the decision of the Council" (ICAO), and the decision of the Court would make them definitive and render it impossible for any member State to contest their legality. Since the subject of appeal is "[a]ny of the Members"(ILO: Article 26) and "[a]ny contracting State" (ICAO: Article 84), these procedures are open to all member States.

As to the use of the Court for *an advisory opinion*, the authority to make a request for an advisory opinion is limited to certain organs of the United Nations and certain international organizations (Article 96 of the Charter of the United Nations and Article 65 of the Statute). The legal effect of the advisory opinion is, of course, not legally binding and is simply advisory unless otherwise provided by some other complementary provisions.

All of the international organizations dealt with in the present section except the UPU are authorized to request advisory opinions of the Court by an agreement with the United Nations. While some of the provisions mentioned above refer explicitly to this request of advisory opinions (the ILO, FAO, WHO, IMO and IAEA), lack of the reference does not affect this authority. The explicit reference in some provisions, however, appears, according to their terms, to imply that the reference is obligatory (the ILO and IMO). The scope of questions is limited to "legal questions arising within the scope of their activities" for these international organizations, while the General Assembly and the Security Council may request "on any legal question" (Article 96 of the Charter).

5.	*An Arbitral Tribunal* is referred to in the constituent instruments of the following five international organizations: the UNESCO, ICAO, UPU, ITU and WMO. These could, in terms of their usage, be classified as (a) the only means of settlement (UPU), (b) an alternative among other means (UNESCO, ITU and WMO) and (c) a tribunal of appeal (although as an alternative to the ICJ) (ICAO). In the context of our study, however, importance lies in whether the arbitral tribunal has compulsory jurisdiction when the questions are not solved by the means agreed upon by the parties concerned. According to the terms of the provisions concerned, compulsory jurisdiction appears to be given to the arbitral tribunal in cases of the UNESCO, ICAO, UPU and WMO. In case of the ITU, the provision is permissive and refers to the optional additional protocol for compulsory settlement of disputes. The provisions of the ICAO and ITU contain a detailed procedure for establishing an arbitral tribunal. Those of the UNESCO, UPU and WMO, however, simply refer to an arbitral tribunal, and could encounter difficulties particularly when the parties concerned disagree in their implementation.

6   *Other Organs* are referred to in the constituent instruments of the ILO and FAO. The Constitution of the ILO refers to "the appointment of a tribunal for the expeditious determination of any dispute or question relating to the interpretation of a Convention which may be referred thereto by the Governing Body or in accordance with the terms of the Convention" (Article 37 (2)). That of the FAO simply refers to "such other body as the Conference may determine" (Article 17 (1)). In either case, reference to these organs is, although an alternative to the ICJ, obligatory.

(3) Practice and Evaluation

(1) Non-Use of Judicial Organs

The mechanisms of interpretation and dispute settlement relating to the constituent instruments of the eleven international organizations dealt with in the present section could be summarized as follows. *Questions or disputes relating to an interpretation of the constituent instrument were, in most cases, dealt with in the internal organs of the organization concerned, and not submitted to an outside judicial organ.*[52] As far as we have surveyed,[53] there are only four cases,[54] excluding the cases relating to application for review of administrative tribunal judgments. These are the "Judgment of the Special Arbitral Tribunal set up by the Executive Board of UNESCO" (1949),[55] "Constitution of the Maritime Safety Committee of the Inter-Governmental

---

[52] *See* the articles listed in *supra* note 46.

[53] Our survey is based upon *The International Law Reports.*

[54] Apart from these four cases which were related to the interpretation of the constituent instrument of respective international organization, there are three cases related to UPU and decided by arbitral tribunals based upon a series of Postal Conventions before the present Constitution of UPU was adopted in 1964. The following three cases were not related to the interpretation of constitutional provisions (in the substantive sense of the term: *see* the definition of the term "constitution" in Chapter 5, Section 1 of the present study) of UPU: (1) Case of sea transit charges between the Postal Administration of the Netherlands and the Postal Administration of the United States of America with the Postal Administration of Switzerland and Canada as Arbitrators (1945) based upon a *Compromis* of 1934 in conformity with Article 25 of the UP Convention of Madrid of 1920; (2) Case of dues for reply coupons issued in Croatia and transit charge for Mails from occupied Yugoslavia between the Postal Administration of Portugal and the Postal Administration of Yugoslavia with the Postal Administration of the Netherlands and Denmark as Arbitrators (1956) under Article 31 of the UP Convention of Brussels of 1952; (3) Case between the Postal Administration of Turkey and the Postal Administration of Syria with the International Bureau of the UPU as Sole Arbitrator (1948) based upon a *Compromis spécial. See* for these cases 23 *Int'l L. Rep.* 585, 591, 596 (1956).

[55] Since differences arose on a subject relating to the interpretation of Article 5 of the Constitution of UNESCO, the Executive Board of UNESCO set up a Special Arbitral Tribunal (composed of three members: Rolin (President), Adolfo du Costa and Lachs) to decide on this question. *See* United Nations Educational, Scientific and Cultural Organization (Constitution) Case, 16 *Ann. Dig. & Rep. Pub. Int'l L. Cases* 331 (1949).

Maritime Consultative Organization (1960),[56] "Appeal relating to the Jurisdiction of the ICAO Council" (1972), and "Interpretation of the Agreement of 25 March 1951 between the WHO and Egypt" (1980). The latter three cases were analyzed in the previous chapter of our study.

(2) The Evaluation of the Mechanisms of Interpretation and Dispute Settlement

1.　　The analysis of the mechanisms of interpretation and dispute settlement leads to the conclusion that *outside judicial organs are available for all of the international organizations dealt with in the present section*. Firstly, member States are, of course, free to submit, based upon a compromis, a dispute to the ICJ. In many of them, furthermore, compulsory jurisdiction is given to an outside judicial organ: the ICJ for the ILO, FAO, UNESCO, WHO and WMO; an arbitral tribunal for the UNESCO, ICAO, UPU and WMO. Secondly, all of them, except the UPU, are authorized to request advisory opinions of the ICJ. Furthermore, in some cases (the ILO and IMO) a request for an advisory opinion is considered to be obligatory.

　　Consequently, as far as outside judicial organs are institutionally available, non-use of them would suggest that States were loath to make use of judicial organs for the purpose of interpretation and dispute settlement relating to the constitutent instrument of an international organization.

2.　　It will be desirable, on the other hand, to shed some light upon *the imperfect aspects of utilizing judicial organs*.

　　The first imperfection relates to *an initiative in this process*. In case of requesting an advisory opinion from the ICJ, the determination of this request will be made by a majority voting in the organ authorized to request. Consequently, the majority States in the organ concerned could adopt a resolution, and, furthermore, easily reject a proposal or an objection of the minority States to the effect that an advisory opinion upon its legality should be requested. Thus, advisory opinions appear to have been requested only when the question was not politically important and did not encounter any strong resistance of States, or when the majority States were confident in the legality of the resolution and wanted to take advantage of a judicial judgment for the purpose of justifying it and persuading the minority States of its legitimacy. It is not sure, moreover, whether provisions of obligatory request of advisory opinions have been interpreted and dealt with as such. It would be desirable both for the legal and political stability in the organization to enable a certain number of minority States to request an advisory opinion of the Court while an individual State or a quite small number of States should not be authorized to request an advisory opinion in order

---

[56]　The resolution adopted by the IMCO Assembly reworded Article 56 as follows: "Considering that the Convention provides in Article 56 that questions of law *may* be referred to the International Court of Justice for an advisory opinion." Schwarzenberger pointed out that the IMCO, in such a manner, did not treat its request for an advisory opinion as compliance with a legal duty in the case of a disagreement (Article 56 provides "shall be referred".) and that this provides further evidence for the reduced place of judicial organs in the United Nations system and the overriding position granted to political organs of international institutions. G. Schwarzenerger, 3 *International Law, Inernational Constitutional Law* 553 (1976).

to avoid abuse.[57]

The second imperfection is related to *the legal effect of a judicial judgment.* In the case of advisory opinions, such opinions are only advisory unless there exists (usually there does not exist) a provision that the parties concerned (i.e. the States concerned and the international organization itself) shall be bound by the opinions. The majority States would be easily (apart from its political implications and considerations) reject, by a majority voting, the acceptance of opinion favorable to the minority States. The minority States could also persist in their autointerpretation. In the case of litigation, on the other hand, the decision will only bind the parties. It is in fact probable that an international organization and member States will deal with the decision as an authoritative interpretation of the constituent instrument. Institutionally, however, a judicial decision does not guarantee an authoritative interpretation in the sense of binding the organization itself and all the member States.

3.   *Negative opinions have also been expressed against reference to outside judicial organs.* For example, *Legal Advisers and International Organizations* (1966), a report of the conference in which many legal advisers to international organizations participated, contains the following passage:

"In some organizations that could, if they wished, use the advisory opinion procedures of the International Court, one reason for reluctance to use them has been a concern that *the Court, being outside the mainstream of the organization's activity, might come to decisions not fully sensitive to the internal requirements for effective operation.* In other words, the detached objective legal view may not contribute to the actual effectiveness of the organization. Added to this is *the reluctance of all parties, even those in a minority position, to force an 'authoritative,' definite, and presumably enduring interpretation when compromise and flexibility may be more useful.* ('It does not help that the application of a legal rule is legally impeccable if it is politically impossible.') This is reflected in the practice of adopting informal legal decisions in those organizations that have a power of 'authoritative' interpretation."[58] [Italics ours]

Audéoud, in a similar vein, referred to the following five points for the negative attitude in international organizations toward the use of judicial organs: (a) the traditional reticence of States to the Court; (b) the divergence between the essentially legal considerations binding the Court and the economic, technical and political considerations preponderant for international organizations; their activities make it necessary to take into consideration non-legal elements such as the economic

---

[57] For example, Article 159 (10) of the United Nations Convention of the Law of the Sea provides as follows:
"Upon a written request ... sponsored by at least one fourth of the members of the Authority for an advisory opinion on the conformity with this Convention of a proposal before the Assembly on any matter, the Assembly shall request the Sea-Bed Disputes Chamber of the International Tribunal for the Law of the Sea to give an advisory opinion thereon and shall defer voting on that proposal pending receipt of the advisory opinion by the Chamber."

[58] *Legal Advisers and International Organizations* 10-11 (H. C. L. Merillat ed. 1966).

situation of a State, the political equilibrium in the organization and an adaptation of the organization to the economic, social or political evolution of its members; (c) certain questions need urgent solutions which could not be given rapidly by the Court; (d) procedures of settlement proper to international organizations have two advantages: firstly, members of an organ possess a better knowledge of the facts at the basis of the resolution than any international tribunal; secondly, any settlement will be more effective and respected if it is made in harmony with the parties. Audéoud, consequently, concluded as follows:

> "Il paraît donc plus efficient pour les Organisations intrnationales d'opter pour des modes de réglement adap[t]és à leurs contexes et à leurs activités; la Cour conservant son rôle de juridiction internationale, que nous qualifierons de ≪principale≫, mais peu appropriée aux domaines des Organisations internationles."[59]

(3) Toward Uniformity and Stability in Interpretations

1. The *raison d'être* of the constituent instrument establishing the legal framework for the operations and activities of an organization will be lost if its interpretations and applications are made arbitrarily by the organs or the memer States. Mechanisms for unifying different interpretations are, as analyzed above, available but not used in practice.

The question is, then, how uniformity is achieved, or not achieved, *in practice on the operational level of an internal organ*. In political organs consisting of governmental representatives of member States, political considerations of States or technical considerations of the organization will ordinarily prevail over legal considerations of a uniform and stable interpretation of the constituent instrument.

Consequently, some kind of means or procedures will be institutionally needed for making political organs take legal considerations into account in their operations and activities. In the international organizations dealt with in the present section, this necessity is, to some extent, satisfied by firstly, the existence of a legal counsel and secondly, the use of quasi-judicial organs.

2. In the United Nations and many other international organizations, there exists *a legal office or a legal counsel*.[60] "Legal Advisers and International Organizations" referred to above, pointed out that, despite great diversity in the nature and activities of various international organizations, the conference "demonstrated clearly that the common ground was spacious and common problems numerous".[61] The cases of the United Nations (which was analyzed in the previous section, but

---

[59] Audéoud, *supra* note 46, at 1005-06.
   "It appears therefore more efficient for international organizations to opt for the modes of settlement adapted to their context and activities; the Court conserves its role of international jurisdiction which we qualify as 'principal', but is not very proper to the fields of international organizations." [Our translation]

[60] It appears that there exists a legal counsel or a legal office at least in such organizations as the UN, ILO, FAO, UNESCO, WHO, ICAO, IAEA and WIPO. *See, e.g., Kokusaikikan Soran (General Survey of International Organizations)* (Ministry of Foreign Affairs of Japan ed. 1991) [in Japanese], *Encyclopedia of the United Nations and International Agreements* (E. J. Osmañczyk 2nd ed. 1991).

[61] *Legal Advisers and International Organizations, supra* note 58, at xi.

is also explained here for convenience) and the ILO will be taken up here.

As to *the United Nations legal office*, which is composed of the Legal Counsel as under-secretary-general and about fifty professional staff, the organizational manual of the Secretariat describes the functions of the Office of Legal Affairs as follows:

"[The Office of Legal Affairs] [s]erves as a unified central legal service for the Secretariat and other United Nations organs and, in this capacity, advises them on *constitutional and legal questions*; [d]eals with questions concerning privileges and immunities and the legal status of the Organization; [p]repares drafts of international conventions, agreements, rules of procedure of United Nations organs and conferences and other legal texts; ...

[The General Legal Division] [p]repares legal opinions and studies and provides advice to United Nations organs and bodies and their subsidiaries, as well as departments and offices of the Secretariat, on *the interpretation of the Charter*, rules of international law and treaties and United Nations resolutions and regulations, on legal aspects of programmes and activities in which the Organization is engaged and on the drafting of international conventions and agreements, resolutions and regulations; ..."[62] [Italics ours]

As for *the Office of the Legal Adviser of the ILO*, which is composed of a Legal Adviser and several lawyers, it is responsible for advising the International Labour Office and ILO meetings on legal questions relating to the status, membership, and activities of the Organization. Consultations in committees of the International Labour Conference are particularly frequent on points of law which arise during the drafting of Conventions and Recommendations. Particularly famous is the fact that requests by governments for opinions concerning the interpretation of provisions of International Labour Conventions are dealt with by the Office of Legal Adviser in close collaboration with the International Labour Standards Department. The International Labour Office has considered it to be its duty to assist governments in this manner, but has always pointed out that it has no special authority to interpret the texts of conventions and that the Court alone is competent to give an authentic interpretation. The practice of requesting the Office for its opinion has, however, developed to the point where there is a considerable "jurisprudence" of Office opinions upon disputed points of interpretation. The Office took the following position in 1938:

"[A]lthough the Constitution of the International Labour Organization does not confer upon the International Labour Office any special authority to interpret the texts of conventions adopted by the International Labour Conference, it would seem that, when an opinion given by the Office has been submitted to the Governing Body and published in the *Official Bulletin* and has met with no adverse comment, the Conference must, in the event of its subsequently including in another convention a provision identical with or equivalent

---

[62] Organization Manual: Section H, A Description of the Functions and Organization of the Office of Legal Affairs 1, 4, U. N. Doc. ST/SGB/Organization, Section H/Rev. 2, 18 April 1983. *See also* the recent edtion: ST/SGB/Organization, Section: OLA/Rev. 1, 14 November 1994.

to the provision which has been interpreted by the Office, be presumed, in the absence of any evidence to the contrary, to have intended that provision to be understood in the manner in which the Office has interpreted it."[63]

3. *Quasi-judicial organs* are sometimes made use of in the United Nations and many other international organizations.[64] The cases of the ILO and the ICAO will be taken up here.

As for *the ILO*, any Member has the right to file a complaint with the Office if it considers that any other Member is not securing the effective observance of any Convention which both have ratified; and the Governing Body may appoint a Commission of Inquiry to consider the complaint and to report thereon (Article 26). The Members agree that they will each place at the disposal of the Commission all the information in their possession which bears upon the subject-matter of the complaint (Article 27). The Commission shall prepare a report embodying its findings on all questions of relevant fact and containing recommendations to be taken (Article 28). Each of the governments concerned in the complaint shall within three months inform the Director-General whether or not it accepts the recommendations; if not, whether it proposes to refer the complaint to the ICJ (Article 29). In the event of any Member failing to carry out within the time specified the recommendations contained in the report of the Commission or in the decision of the Court, the Governing Body may recommend to the Conference such action as it may deem wise and expedient to secure compliance therewith (Article 33).

In the complaints filed by Ghana and Portugal in 1961, the Governing Body set up Commissions of Inquiry, each composed of three members who were appointed on the proposal of the Director-General of the ILO. These members were, it is said, personalities of the highest standing appointed in their personal capacity, and both the Governing Body and the Commissions themselves stressed their independent character and the judicial nature of their functions. Valticos commented on this point as follows:

"The chief characteristics of these procedures are the independent nature of the body appointed to consider the complaints, the steps taken to ensure impartiality, the thoroughness of the inquiries undertaken, the principle that the investigation of such complaints involves the public interest and that the Commissions must themselves take steps to obtain full and impartial information, and the provision made for regular follow-up procedure after the complaint as such has been disposed of.... The parties have accepted the Commission's recommendations in every case and have never appealed against them to

---

[63] International Labour Office, 23 (1) *Official Bulletin* 32, *cited in* Jenks,'The Interpretation of International Labour Conventions by the International Labour Office', 20 *Brit. Y. B. Int'l L.* 132, 133 (1939). *See also* Osieke, 'Exercise of the Judicial Function', *supra* note 27, at 322-24.

[64] It appears that there exists a legal (or similar) committee (commission) at least in such organizations as the UN, ILO, FAO, UNESCO, ICAO and IMO. *See, e.g., Kokusaikikan Soran (General Survey of International Organizations)* (Ministry of Foreign Affairs of Japan ed. 1991) [in Japanese], *Encyclopedia of the United Nations and International Agreements* (E. J. Osmañczyk 2nd ed. 1991).

the International Court of Justice." [65]

As for *the ICAO*, any disagreement between two or more contracting States relating to the interpretation or application of the International Civil Aviation Convention and it Annexes that cannot be settled by negotiation shall be decided by the Council (Article 84). The judicial principle of "Nemo judex in sua causa" is also realized since "[n]o member of the Council shall vote in the consideration by the Council of any dispute to which it is a party." The legal procedure in this process by the Council was strengthened by the adoption of "Rules of the Settlement of Differences" by the Council on 9 April 1957.[66] The Rules have a similar structure to the judicial procedure of the ICJ; particularly in the procedure of "disagreements", they regulate in detail a series of procedures such as the submission of an application with a memorial, submission of the counter-memorial, filing of a preliminary objection and action thereon, appointment of a Committee of five individuals not concerned in the disagreement, written proceedings related to the reply and the rejoinder, presentation of a report by the Committee to the Council, and decision by the Council containing the conclusions together with its reasons (any objecting Member may have its views recorded in the form of a dissenting opinion).

There also exists the Legal Committee in the ICAO. This Legal Committee was established in 1947 by the Assembly, is open to all contracting States, and is composed of legal experts appointed by member States. Its functions include advice to the Council on questions relating to the interpretation or amendment of the Convention.[67]

As briefly explained above, the Council of the ICAO plays a quasi-judicial role in the settlement of disputes between contracting States, and some consideration is taken for this quasi-judicial function. It is pointed out, however, that *there exists an inherent defect in a Council composed of governmental representatives performing a judicial function in the settlement of disputes.* In a comment upon the judgment of the ICJ in the *Appeal Relating to the Jurisdiction of the ICAO Council* case, FitzGerald, former legal officer of the ICAO, took up this point. "In spite of the fact that some individuals may be initially nominated by a State, they lose their character as mere nominees, become arbitrators or judges, and are expected to act judicially and impartially." FitzGerald continued as follows:

"In the case of the ICAO Council, the persons sitting on the bench are demonstrably the national representatives of the respective member states. They are not, for the purposes of considering disagreements or complaints, divested of their character as national representatives. Hence, there is at the outset a contradiction in the ICAO procedure for the settlement of disputes which provides that representatives of states sitting as such will be

---

[65] N. Valticos, *International Labour Law* 247 (1979). *See also* 35 *Int'l L. Rep.* 285 (1967).

[66] This "Rules of the Settlement of Differences" is found in the 'Memorial of the Government of India', Appeal Relating to the Jurisdiction of the ICAO Council, I. C. J. Pleadings 330 (1973). *See also* Mankiewicz, 'Pouvoir judiciaire du Conseil et règlement pour la solution des différends', 3 *A. F. D. I.* 383, 388-94 (1957).

[67] *See*, for details, FitzGerald, 'The International Civil Aviation Organization and the Development of Coventions on International Air Law (1947-1978)', 3 *Annals Air & Space L.* 51 (1978).

called upon to act in a judicial capacity. Indeed, a perusal of the minutes of the Council meetings of July 28-29, 1971, shows that some of the members wanted to defer decisions because they wished to await instructions from their governments.... But it is a contradiction in terms to say that one will act as a judge and yet receive instructions.... *[It points out] the inherent defect which exists in the machinery for the settlement of disputes contained both in the Chicago Convention and in the Transit Agreement, which require a state to act judicially in circumstances where it is practically impossible to divorce the state from its political context.*"[68] [Italics ours]

4. As was explained above, we have a legal counsel and quasi-judicial organs as means or procedures for making the political organs take legal considerations into account in their operations and activities. We must, however, pay due attention to the limitations of these means and procedures.

When we come back to the context of our study with the above analysis in mind, we could conclude as follows. As to the questions or disputes relating to interpretations of constituent instruments, outside judicial organs are available for all of the international organizations dealt with in the present section. These organs, however, have hardly been utilized and it is, rather, internal political organs which have in fact solved these questions and disputes. In the operations and activities of these internal political organs, some institutional devices are installed for making the political organs take legal considerations into account. In many cases, however, political considerations will inevitably prevail over legal considerations in the operations and activities of political organs. This aspect would become clearer as the issue becomes more important politically. This means that, *while the constituent instrument of an international organization will play an important normative role in establishing a legal framework for the structure and activities of the organization, this constituent instrument itself will inevitably change according to the will of the majority States dominant in the daily operations and activities of political organs of the organization.*

Section 4   Economic International Organizations[69]

(1) Introduction
In the present section, we will deal with economic international organizations, not only

---

[68] FitzGerald, 'The Judgment of the International Court of Justice in the Appeal Relating to the Jurisdiction of the ICAO Council', 12 *Canadian Y. B. Int'l L.* 153, 168-69 (1974).

[69] For the relevant bibliography of the present section, *see, e.g.,* Metzger, 'Settlement of International Disputes by Non-Judicial Methods', 48 *Am. J. Int'l L.* 408 (1954); Lambrinidis, 'The Emergence of Quasi Judicial Quasi Administrative Organ and Methods for the Settlement of International Disputes', 16 *Revue hellénique de droit international* 78 (1963); G. Malinverni, *Le réglement des différends dans les organisations internationales économiques* (1974); P. T. B. Kohona, *The Regulation of International Economic Relations through Law* (1985).

those of the specialized agencies, but also other economic international organizations. The latter are, however, limited to some important ones. In the light of their mechanisms of interpretation and dispute settlement, these organizations could be conveniently classified into the following three groups:

(a) *Money and Finance*: The International Monetary Fund (IMF), International Bank for Reconstruction and Development (IBRD), International Finance Corporation (IFC), International Development Association (IDA), International Fund for Agricultural Development (IFAD), Asian Development Bank (ADB), Inter-American Development Bank (IDB), African Development Bank (AfDB).

(b) *Commerce*: The International Trade Organization (ITO), General Agreement on Tariffs and Trade (GATT), European Free Trade Association (EFTA), International Commodity Organizations, Producers' Associations.

(c) *Others*: The Organization for Economic Co-operation and Development (OECD), United Nations Industrial Development Organization (UNIDO), Caribbean Community (CARICOM), Economic Community of the West-African States (ECOWAS), etc.

(2) Mechanisms of Interpretation and Dispute Settlement
(1) Money and Finance[70]

1.   We will first look at *the provisions relating to interpretation and dispute settlement in the constituent instrument*. Article 29 of the Articles of Agreement of the IMF provides as follows:

"(a) Any question of interpretation of the provisions of this Agreement arising between any member and the Fund or between any members of the Fund shall be submitted to the Executive Board for its decision.   If the question particularly affects any member not entitled to appoint an Exective Director, it shall be entitled to representation in accordance with [the regulations of the Board of Governors].

(b) In any case where the Executive Board has given a decision under (a) above, any member may require, within three months from the date of the decision, that the question be referred to the Board of Governors, whose decision shall be final....

(c) Whenever a disagreement arises between the Fund and a member which has withdrawn, or between the Fund and any member during liquidation of the Fund, such disagreement

---

[70] For the relevant bibliography of these organizations, *see, e.g.*, Gold, 'The Interpretation by the International Monetary Fund of the Articles of Agreement', 3 *Int'l & Comp. L. Q.* 256 (1954); Hexner, 'Interpretation by Public International Organizations of Their Basic Instruments', 53 *Am. J. Int'l L.* 341 (1959); Fawcett, 'The Place of Law in an International Organization', 36 *Brit. Y. B. Int'l L.* 321 (1960); Gold, 'Interpretation by the International Monetary Fund of Its Articles of Agreement - II', 16 *Int'l & Comp. L. Q.* 289 (1967); J. Gold, *Interpretation by the Fund* (1968, Pamphlet Series No. 11); Mann, 'The "Interpretation" of the Constitution of International Financial Organizations', 43 *Brit. Y. B. Int'l L.* 1 (1968-69); D. Carreau, *Le Fonds monetaire international* 97-109 (1970); J. Gold, *Legal and Institutional Aspects of the International Monetary System: Selected Essays* (1979).

shall be submitted to arbitration by a tribunal of three arbitrators ...."

Other organizations have also a similar provision: the IBRD (Article 9), IFC (Article 8), IDA (Article 10), IFAD (Article 11), ADB (Article 60), IDB (Article 13) and AfDB (Article 61).

2.   *Characteristics of the mechanisms of interpretation indicated by these provisions* could be summarized as follows:[71] (1) the function of authoritative interpretation rests with the ordinary executive organs of these institutions and not with any tribunal external to them; (2) the exercise of the interpretative function is not limited to decisions on actual disgreements, but is used also to resolve doubts in interpretation and thus to prevent controversies and to assure the uniform application of operative arrangements; (3) the executive organs have exclusive jurisdiction to decide on questions of interpretation of the instrument that may arise between the organization and its members or between members themselves; (4) the persons exercising the interpretative function represent interested parties and their votes are weighted according to certain defined criteria.

These points apply to "any question of interpretation" arising between actual members of the IMF and to the time period during which the IMF is in operation. "Disagreements" relating to members that have withdrawn or to issues arising during the period of liquidation of the IMF will be dealt with by arbitration tribunals.[72]

3.   The published records of the Bretton Woods Conference, at which the Articles of Agreement of the IMF and those of the IBRD were drafted, provide hardly any clue as to the reasons that led to the drafters to vest a power of final interpretation in the IMF and the IBRD themselves. It is pointed out, however, that there was a feeling at Bretton Woods that *frequent appeals to an external tribunal on questions of interpretation, particularly on matters in which the tribunal could not be expert, would impede their work.*[73] Hexner summarized this point concisely as follows:

"These arrangements for final interpretation by non-judicial bodies were the result of a give-and-take process carried out in a series of complex international negotiations. [The monetary experts who undertook the negotiations] wished to keep decision-making on delicate policy issues involving interpretation in the hands of financial experts. They also wished to create a framework within which the principal policies of the institutions could be evolved with due consideration to the balance of interests indicated by the different quotas. Furthermore, they aimed at the creation of a constitutional framework which would not preclude the adjustment of policies to changing political and economic circumstances. They believed that all these purposes would be impaired if the function of final interpretation was handed over to an external judicial authority."[74]

It is suggestive in this connection that both of the Articles of Agreement of the IMF and

---

[71] Hexner, *supra* note 70, at 343-44.

[72] The IMF, IBRD, IFC and IDA are authorized to request an advisory opinion from the ICJ on legal questions arising within the scope of their activities.

[73] *See, e.g.,* G. Gold, *Interpretation by the Fund* 2 (1968).

[74] Hexner, *supra* note 70, at 344.

those of the IBRD require, in their Article 1, that the IMF or the IBRD be guided in all its (policies and) decisions by the purposes set forth in this Article.

4.	Let us look at *the practice* on this point. Since the Articles of Agreement of the IMF is a complex, lengthy, and important instrument, a considerable number of interpretations have been necessary in order to enable the IMF to function efficiently. In practice, however, the overwhelming proportion of these interpretations have been adopted outside Article 29, though there is no essential difference between interpretations adopted under Article 29 and those not adopted under that provision, apart from the more formal and authoritative character of the former. In this connection, Gold, the General Counsel and Director of the Legal Deparment of the IMF, stated as follows:

> "The explanation may be that the adoption of interpretations outside Article [29] preserves a certain informality precisely because these interpretations are not given the stamp of final authoritativeness that they would have under Article [29]. The practice is thus more consistent with the spirit of consultation and collaboration which is the first declared purpose of the Fund and which is essential for its success."[75]

This provision was amended in 1969. After complicated negotiations in which the members of the EEC insisted that an internal power of final interpretation was unorthodox, the issue was resolved by a compromise that retained the internal procedure for interpretation but reinforced it with the following additional safeguards to be added after (b) cited above:

> "Any question referred to the Board of Governors shall be considered by a Committee on Interpretation of the Board of Governors. Each Committee member shall have one vote. The Board of Governors shall establish the membership, procedures, and voting majorities of the Committee. A decision of the Committee shall be the decision of the Board of Governors unless the Board of Governors, by an eighty-five percent majority of the total voting power, decides otherwise."[76]

5.	As for the other financial international organizations dealt with in the present part, it is not clear why a similar mechanism of interpretation was adopted. It would be reasonable, however, to assume that the same considerations as in the case of the IMF and the IBRD as well as the fact that this mechanism of interpretation had worked without any problem in those organizations had

---

[75] G. Gold, *Interpretation by the Fund* 3-16 (1968).

[76] J. Gold, *Legal and Institutional Aspects of the International Monetary System: Selected Essays* 302-06 (1979); Treves, 'Les décisions d'interprétation des Statuts du Fonds monétaire international', 79 *R. G. D. I. P.* 5 (1975). According to Gold (*id.* at 305),

> "The Board of Governors ahs not yet taken the decision contemplated by the First Amendment on membership, procedures, and voting majorities of the Committee on Interpretation. The delay has caused no inconvenience so far because throughout the history of the Fund requests for formal interpretations have been rare, and none has been requested since the Amendment became effective."

This seems to apply even to the present. *See* the small number of old items listed under "Interpretation under Article XXIX(a)" in *Selected Decisions and Selected Documents on the International Monetary Fund* (19th Issue, 1994) at XXXV.

some influence upon the drafters of the organizations later established.

(2) Commerce
(a) The International Trade Organization

1.   The Havana Charter for the International Trade Organization (ITO) did not enter into force, but Articles 92-96 of it provided as follows.

The Members shall not have recourse to any procedure other than the procedures envisaged in this Charter for complaints and the settlement of differences arising out of its operation (Article 92). If any Member considers that any benefit accruing to it under this Charter is being nullified or impaired, it may make representations or proposals, which shall be given sympathetic consideration, or the Members concerned may submit the matter to arbitration upon terms agreed between them (Article 93). Any matter not satisfactorily settled in accordance with the previous provisions may be referred to the Executive Board; the Executive Board shall promptly investigate the matter and shall decide whether any nullification or impairment exists; it shall take appropriate steps including, among others, releasing the Member(s) affected from obligations or the grant of concessions to any other Member(s) (Article 94). The Executive Board shall, if requested to do so within thirty days by a Member concerned, refer to the Conference for review any action taken by the Executive Board; the Conference shall confirm, modify or revcerse such action referred to it (Article 95). Any decision of the Conference under this Charter shall, at the instance of any Member whose interests are prejudiced by the decision, be subject to review by the International Court of Justice by means of an advisory opinion, which shall bind the Organization (Article 96). Any Member shall be free, not later than sixty days after such action is taken by the Conference or after such opinion has been delivered by the Court, to give written notice of its withdrawal from the Organization (Article 95).

2.   Among several characteristics of the mechanism of dispute settlement indicated by these provisions, we would like to draw attention, in contrast with the GATT analyzed next, to the fact that the possibility of judicial review by the ICJ was introduced in respect of legal questions in the decisions of the Executive Board or Conference. The judicial review of ITO decisions was an issue in the process of drafting the ITO Charter. Rubin explained as follows:

> "The issue may perhaps be usefully over-simplified by phrasing it as the issue of distrust of the ITO or distrust of the Court. The supporters of extensive Court review ... argued that *a body like the Conference of the ITO was always subject to political or other influences*, and that *judicial review was a useful check even if, as they predicted, it would be seldom resorted to*. The supporters of the other point of view ... felt that *unlimited access to the Court might be used to obstruct ITO action*. The issues which would come before the ITO would be mostly factual; ... On such issues, this school considered *the judgment of the ITO's experts more reliable than that of judges*."[77] [Italics ours]

---

[77] Rubin, 'The Judicial Review Problem in the International Trade Organization', 63 *Harvard L. Rev.* 78, 87 (1949).

It was concluded that the mechanism of dispute settlement realized for the ITO "appear to represent a reasonble balance between the desire for security and protection inherent in ample judicial review and the desire that an administrative agency dealing in complicated economic questions should have scope for the use of its *expertise*."[78] [Italics original]

(b) The General Agreement on Tariffs and Trade[79]

1.   While the GATT has many provisions relating to dispute settlement, its principal provisions are Articles 22 and 23. Article 22 provides, in paragraph 1, that each contracting party shall accord sympathetic consideration to, and consult regarding, such representation as made by another party, and, in paragraph 2, that the CONTRACTING PARTIES may, at the request of a contracting party, consult parties concerned in respect of any matter for which it has not been possible to find a satisfactory solution through consultation.

Paragraph 1 of Article 23 provides that if any contracting party should consider that any benefit accruing to it directly or indirectly under this Agreement is being nullified or impaired or that the attainment of any objectives of the Agreement is being impeded as the result of (a) the failure of another party to carry out its obligations under this Agreement, or (b) the application by another party of any measure, whether or not it conflicts with the provisions of this Agreement, or (c) the existence of any other situation, the contracting party may for the adjustment, make representations or proposals to the other parties concerned.

Paragraph 2 provides that if no satisfactory adjustment is effected within a reasonable time, the matter may be referred to the CONTRACTING PARTIES; the latter shall promptly investigate any matter so referred to them and shall make appropriate recommendations; if the latter consider that the circumstances are serious enough to justify such action, they may authorize parties to suspend the application to any other parties of such concessions or obligations under this Agreement as they determine.

2.   In the practice of paragraph 2 of Article 23, most of the questions referred to the CONTRACTING PARTIES were considered by a "panel". This long-standing practice was, in 1979, codified in "Understanding Regarding Notification, Consultation, Dispute Settlement and

---

[78] *Id.* at 96-97.

[79] For the relevant bibliography of the GATT, *see, e.g.*, Jackson, 'GATT as an Instrument for the Settlement of Trade Disputes', 61 *Proc. Am. Soc'y Int'l L.* 144 (1967); J. H. Jackson, *World Trade and the Law of GATT* 163-89 (1969); Hudec, 'The GATT Legal System: A Diplomat's Jurisprudence', 4 *J. World Trade L.* 615 (1970); Flory, 'Les Accords du Tokyo Round du G. A. T. T. et la réform des procédures de règlement des différends dans le système commercial interétatique', 86 *R. G. D. I. P.* 235 (1982); McGovern, 'Disputes Settlement in the GATT: Adjudication or Negotiation?', in *The European Community and GATT* 73 (M. Hilf et al. eds. 1986).

While we will not analyze the World Trade Organization (WTO) which came into existence on 1 January 1995, *see*, for its dispute settlement system *on paper, e.g.*, Kohona, 'Dispute Resolution under the World Trade Organization: An Overview', 28 *J. World Trade* 23 (1994), Petersmann, 'The Dispute Settlement System of the World Trade Organization and the Evolution of the GATT Dispute Settlement System since 1948', 31 *Common Mkt L. Rev.* 1157 (1994), Vermulst & Driessen, 'An Overview of the WTO Dispute Settlement System and its Relationship with the Uruguay Round Agreements', 29 *J. World Trade* 131 (1995), Dillon, 'The World Trade Organization: A New Legal Order for World Trade?', 16 *Michigan J. Int'l L.* 349 (1995).

Surveillance".[80]

3.   Among the characteristics of dispute settlement of the GATT, we would like to draw attention, in the context of our study, to the following points.

Firstly, *the adjustment through consultation between the parties concerned* constantly occupies a central position. Article 22 aims at the promotion of consultation. Article 23 makes the consultation of paragraph 1 a condition for opening the procedure of paragraph 2 (Article 6 of "Understanding"). Furthermore, parties concerned may request an appropriate body or individual to use their good offices (Article 8); they will be regularly consulted with by panels and given adequate opportunity to develop a mutually satisfactory solution (Article 15); and they will be given the report of the panel before its circulation to the CONTRACTING PARTIES (Article 18).

Secondly, *the non-legal requirements of the procedure* must be noted. Request for a consultation in Article 22 sets no particular requirement. Requirements for a representation in Article 23 are nullification or impairment of any benefit under the Agreement or impediment of attainment of any objective of the Agreement, and not necessarily violation of any legal obligations of the Agreement by a contracting party. This means that *the purpose of this procedure lies not in clarifying the rights and obligations of a contracting party by a strict application of the GATT provisions and, thereby, punishing the violating party, but in promoting mutually satisfactory solutions and, thereby, restoring any lost balance of interests between the parties concerned.*

Thirdly, however, *the panels in the core of the procedure have a quasi-judicial character.* While the Director-General will propose the composition of the panel after securing the agreement of the contracting parties concerned, any citizens of countries whose governments are parties to the dispute shall be excluded (Article 11); panel members would serve in their individual capacities and not as government representatives (Article 14); the objective assessment made by a panel of the matter before it shall include an objective assessment of the facts of the case and the applicability of and conformity with the Agreement (Article 16); and the report of the panel shall set out the rationale behind any findings and recommendations that it makes (Article 17).

(c)   The European Free Trade Association[81]

1.   Article 31 of the Convention Establishing the European Free Trade Association (EFTA) is titled "General consultations and complaints procedure" and contains the following provisions. If any Member State considers that any benefit under this Convention or any objective of the Association is being or may be frustrated and if no satisfactory settlement is reached between the Member States concerned, any of those Member States may refer the matter to the Council (paragraph 1); the Council shall promptly, by majority vote, make arrangements for examining the matter, including a reference to an examining committee (paragraph 2); in the light of such

---

[80]   26 *General Agreement on Tariffs and Trade, Basic Instruments and Selected Documents* 210 (1979).

[81]   For the relevant bibliography of the EFTA, *see, e.g.*, J. Lambrinidis, *The Structure, Function, and Law of a Free Trade Area, the European Free Trade Association* 202-38 (1965); Szokoloczy-Syllaba, 'EFTA: The Settlement of Disputes', 20 *Int'l & Comp. L. Q.* 519 (1971).

considerations as whether it has been established that an obligation under the Convention has not been fulfilled, and whether and to what extent any benefit under the Convention or any objective of the Association is being or may be frustrated, as well as of the report of any examining committee, the Council may, by majority vote, make recommendations to any Member State (paragraph 3); if a recommendation is not complied with and the Council finds, by majority vote, that an obligation under this Convention has not been fulfilled, the Council may, by majority decision, authorise any Member State to suspend to the Member State concerned the application of the obligations under the Convention (paragraph 4).

2.   In the context of our study, we would like to draw attention to the following points as the characteristics of the dispute settlement procedure of the EFTA.

Firstly, *the position of violation of an obligation under the Convention* is to be noted. While violation of the Convention is not a requirement for opening the procedure (paragraph 1) like in the GATT procedure, it is taken into consideration (paragraph 3), and constitutes a condition necessary for the decision by the Council to authorise suspension of the obligations under the Convention. The Council may make recommendations without any violation of the Convention, but may not authorise such a suspension without it, unlike in the GATT.

Secondly, *the procedure has a quasi-judicial characteristic.* The Council shall, before taking action under paragraph 3, refer the matter at the request of any Member State concerned to an examining committee (paragraph 2). In view of the safeguards for the independence, competence and integrity of the members of the Examining Committees which are prescribed in Article 33 of the Convention, the power of a Member State engaged in a dispute to force the hand of the Council in referring the matter to an Examining Committee provides a guarantee in favor of a Member State fearing prejudicial treatment of its case by the majority of the members of the Council.[82]

Thirdly, however, *the tendency, in practice, of searching for a compromise* must be emphasized. There were not many formal complaints raised under Article 31. It was pointed out that the Member States concentrated on finding a practical solution to the dispute and that the legal aspects of a dispute may be expected to take second place to practical considerations and to expediency aiming at the adjustment of interests with a view to securing the continuation of the operation of the Convention to the satisfaction of all Member States.[83]

(d) International Commodity Organizations[84]

1.   There are at the moment nine international commodity agreements: Wheat (1986); Sugar

---

[82] Lambrinidis, *supra* note 81, at 212.

[83] Szokoloczy-Syllaba, *supra* note 81, at 528-29.

[84] For the relevant bibliography of international commodity organizations, *see, e.g.,* Fischer, 'Le mode de règlement des différends adopté par l'accord international sur le blé', 1 *A. F. D. I.* 208 (1955); Fawcett, 'The Function of Law in International Commodity Agreements', 44 *Brit. Y.B. Int'l L.* 157 (1971); Clariana, 'Settlement of Disputes in International Commodity Agreements, 1949-1979', 63 *Rivista di diritto internazionale* 392 (1980); K.-R. Khan, *The Law and Organization of International Commodity Agreements* 373-77 (1982); P. M. Eisemann, *L'organisation internationale du commerce des produits de base* 342-57 (1982).

(1987); Tin (1981); Coffee (1982); Cocoa (1986); Olive Oil (1986); Natural Rubber (1987); Jute and Jute Products (1989) and Tropical Timber (1983). The procedures of dispute settlement of these agreements have many common aspects and could conveniently be explained as follows.[85]

2.   Many of them have the following common aspects.

Firstly, *a procedure of consultations* is found in such agreements as Coffee (1982) and Cocoa (1986). In this procedure, each member accords full consideration to any representation by another member concerning the interpretation or application of the Agreement and affords adequate opportunity for consultations. On the request of either party and with the consent of the other, the Executive Director shall establish an appropriate conciliation procedure (Cocoa) or an independent panel which shall use its good offices with a view to conciliating the parties (Coffee). Any unsolved matter may be referred to the Council.

Secondly, *a procedure of dispute settlement* is found in such agreements as Tin (1981), Sugar (1987) and Natural Rubber (1987) in addition to Coffee (1982) and Cocoa (1986). In this procedure, any dispute concerning the interpretation or application of the Agreement which is not settled by negotiation shall, at the request of any member party to the dispute, be referred to the Council for decision. A majority of members, or members holding not less than one-third of the total votes, may require the Council to seek *the opinion of the advisory panel* before giving its decision. The panel shall, in principle, consist of two persons (one having wide experience in matters of the kind in dispute and the other having legal standing and experience) nominated by the exporting (producing) members, and two such persons nominated by the importing (consuming) members and a chairman selected by the four persons nominated above or, if they fail to agree, by the Chairman of the Council. *Persons appointed to the advisory panel shall act in their personal capacities and without instructions from any Government.* The opinion of the advisory panel and the reasons therefor shall be submitted to the Council which, after considering all the relevant information, shall decide the dispute.

Thirdly, *a procedure of complaints* is found in the same five agreements as above. In this procedure, any complaint that any member has failed to fulfil its obligations under the Agreement shall, at the request of the member making the complaint, be referred to the Council which shall make a decision on the matter. No member shall be found to have been in breach of its obligations under the Agreement except by a distributed simple majority vote and by specifying the nature of the breach; if the Council so finds, however, it may, by a distributed two-thirds majority vote, suspend such member's voting rights in the Council.

---

[85] Some preliminary explanation about the organizations would be useful. An international commodity organization consists, in general, of the Council (the highest authority of the organization to carry out the provisions of the agreement) composed of all the members, Committees (responsible to the Council), and the Secretariat. As for the voting system in the Council, both the exporting (producing) members and the importing (consuming) members hold 1,000 votes respectively, which are distributed among the members in each category according to various criteria of different agreements. A decision of the Council requires more than half of the total votes of the exporting members and importing members respectively; this would exclude an arbitrary decision by either category of members. In practice, however, decisions are made by consensus.

3.   The others have different, but simple procedures. Those of Jute and Jute Products (1989) and Tropical Timber (1983) deal with complaints and disputes in the same manner. In this procedure, any complaint that a member has failed to fulfil its obligations under the Agreement and any dispute concerning the interpretation or application of the Agreement shall be referred to the Council for decision, which shall be final and binding.

In the procedure of Wheat (1986), any dispute concerning the interpretation or application of the Convention which is not settled by negotiation shall, at the request of any member concerned, be referred to the Council for decision. Any member which considers that its interests as a party to this Convention have been seriously prejudiced by actions of any member affecting the operation of this Convention may bring the matter before the Council, which shall immediately consult with, and may make recommendations to, the members concerned.

4.   In the context of our study, we would like to draw attention to the following points as characteristics of the procedures of the international commodity agreements.

Firstly, *negotiations and consultations* are given an important place. Even in those agreements in which a procedure of consultations is not separately provided, negotiations are generally a condition necessary for opening the procedure of dispute settlement, and the decision by the Council in the procedure of complaints is sometimes subject to prior consultation with the members concerned.

Secondly, *the power of final determination is conferred on the internal political organ, the Council.* Reference of a dispute to the ICJ or an arbitration is quite exceptional. While the special voting system adopted in the Council is useful in maintaining the balance of interests between the two categories of States, it would not guarantee the judicial character of the interpretation and application of the Agreement made by the Council.

Thirdly, however, *the tendency to make such an interpretation and application by the Council quasi-judicial* is to be noted. It is pointed out that the procedure of the advisory panel dates back to the negotiations for the revised International Wheat Agreement in 1953, and that it was adopted as a compromise between the claim for reference to outside arbitration or to decision by the ICJ and the claim for the Council's "Master in its own house" by deciding disputes by weighted voting.[86] It is to be added, however, that this procedure of the advisory panel has hardly been used.[87]

(e) Producers' Associations

1.   Producers' associations which are composed only of the producing (or exporting) developing countries of a certain commodity number more than ten and include such commodities as petroleum, cocoa, copper, natural rubber, bauxite, bananas, iron ore, sugar and pepper. Unlike the cases of

---

[86] Metzger, *supra* note 69, at 411-16.

[87] Rare examples are as follows: (1) The Report of the Advisory Panel under Article 61 of the International Coffee Agreement (1962) on the legality of a system for the selective adjustment of quotas was presented in 1965 (5 *Int'l Legal Materials* 195 (1966)); (2) The findings of Arbitration Panel under Article 44 of the International Coffee Agreement (1968) on Brasil-United States dispute on processed coffee was presented in 1969 (8 *Int'l Legal Materials* 564 (1969)).

international commodity agreements, it is difficult to analyze the objectives and functions of these organizations legally because of ambiguous provisions, confusion of ideas and poor drafting in their constituent instruments.[88]

2. Despite the variety among producers' associations, Pollard, the legal adviser to the International Bauxite Association, observed that they have some common features.[89] In the context of our study, we would like to draw attention to the following points.

Firstly, most of them do not provide for the settlement of disputes by independent judicial tribunals. Secondly, they have *the tendency to confer on the supreme policy-making organs of these bodies a power of decision in determining disputes relating to the interpretation and application of their constituent instruments*; it was pointed out that disputes likely to arise in these organizations would be of a conflict of interests nature, for which the ordinary judicial process and the existing body of international legal rules are inadequate to provide definitive and satisfactory solutions. Thirdly, some, if not many, of them have the practice of establishing appropriate commissions or resorting to legal counsel to advise competent policy-making organs on the discharge of their interpretative constitutional functions in order to avoid their acting *ultra vires*.

(3) Other Economic International Organizations[90]

International organizations are quite diverse. While those grouped organizations as explained above have some common patterns of dispute settlement, there are many others which have different mechanisms of dispute settlement. Let us look briefly at some of them.[91]

(a) The Organization for Economic Co-operation and Development (OECD), Council for Mutual Economic Assistance (CMEA, COMECON: dissolved in 1991), Council of Arab Economic Unity (CAEU), Amazonian Cooperation Council (ACC) and Union of Central African States (UEAC)

The constituent instruments of these organizations do not have a provision for the settlement of disputes concerning their interpretation and application. They do not provide, in detail, the objectives, functions, structures, implementation procedures, rights and obligations of member States and other important issues, but are confined to establishing *a forum or a framework for*

---

[88] *See, e.g.*, D. E. Pollard, *Law and Policy of Producers' Associations* 161 (1984).

[89] *Id.* at 242-71.

[90] As to the economic international organizations in Africa, *see, e.g.*, S. A. Akintan, *The Law of International Economic Institutions in Africa* (1977).

As to the COMECON, *see, e.g.*, R. Szawlowlski, *The System of the International Organizations of the Communist Countries* (1976); G Schiavone, *The Institutions of COMECON* (1981).

[91] As to the constituent instruments of these organizations, some are found in *Int'l Legal Materials* [ILM] (Union of Central African States: 7 ILM 725 (1968); Amazonian Cooperation Council: 17 ILM 1045 (1978); Central African Customs and Economic Union: 4 ilm 699 (1965); East African Community: 5 ILM 633 (1966), 6 ILM 932 (1967), 9 ILM 561 (1970).). For the rest, *see* II. B.- II. J. *International Organization and Integration: Annotated Basic Documents and Descriptive Directory of International Organizations and Arrangements* (R. J. G. Kapteyn et al. eds. 1983); *Les organisations régionales africaines, Recueil de textes et documents* (S. Belaouane-Gherari & H. Gherari eds. 1988).

economic cooperation among member States by providing *only principal structure and functions.* They, therefore, set wide objectives, each member State possesses one vote and resolutions are adopted by unanimity. Disputes arising in the planning and implementation of economic cooperation would be solved by negotiations and consultations in the Council which is composed of representatives of all the member States and is the supreme decision-making organ. It is submitted that *the constituent instruments of such organizations constitute only a starting point for the cooperation among member States and the actual organizations will develop in whatever direction in accordance with the subsequent agreement reached among them.* This is demonstrated by the case of the OECD which now constitutes a huge complex of diverse organs, far exceeding the scope of activities expected from its constituent instrument.

(b) The Latin American Economic System (LAES) and Central African Customs and Economic Union (CACEU)

The constituent instruments of these organizations are relatively concise and are confined to establishing a forum or a framework for economic cooperation among member States by providing only principal structure and functions as in the above cases. What is different is that they have an explicit provision to the effect that *the Council, the supreme organ, will decide on the interpretation and application of the constituent instrument.* However, since the Council in these organizations will decide this matter by consensus or unanimity, any interpretation of the constituent instrument is to be based upon the agreement among the member States.

(c) The United Nations Industrial Development Organization (UNIDO)

While the UNIDO could *prima facie* be classified as an economic organization, it is closer to the specialized agencies of the United Nations dealt with in the second section rather than the above economic organizations, in view of the fact that its primary objective is the promotion of industrial development in developing countries and its functions lie in providing various forms of techinical assistance. In fact, the following procedure of dispute settlement is considered to correspond with this character.

Any dispute among Members concerning the interpretation and application of the Constitution that is not settled by negotiation shall be referred to the Board. If the dispute is not settled there, any party to the dispute may refer the matter either (i) if the parties so agree, to the ICJ or to an arbitral tribunal, or (ii) otherwise, to a conciliation commission. The Conference and the Board are separately empowered to request the ICJ to give an advisory opinion on any legal question arising within the scope of the Organization's activities.

(d) The Latin American Integration Association (LAIA, ALADI: successor to the Latin American Free Trade Association (LAFTA)), and Andean Subregional Integration

The Treaty of Montevideo Establishing the Latin American Integration Association entered into force in 1981 and replaced the LAFTA. While the Treaty of Montevideo which established the LAFTA did not have a provision for dispute settlement concerning the interpretation and application of the Treaty, the Contracting Parties adopted the Protocol Establishing the Final Mechanism for the Settlement of Disputes within LAFTA in 1967. This Mechanism is composed of (1) obligatory direct negotiation, (2) obligatory conciliation by the Standing Executive

Committee, and (3) the compulsory Arbitration Court whose jurisdiction would extend to matters on a list formulated by the Council of Foreign Affairs Ministers concerned.

Andean Subregional Integration is an organization of economic integration for the Andean countries constituted by some members of the LAFTA. According to Article 23 of the Agreement, the Commission, the supreme organ comprising the Members States, shall carry out such procedures of negotiation, good offices, mediation and conciliation for differences concerning the interpretation or implementation of the Agreement. Should no agreement be reached, Member States shall submit to the procedures laid down in the above Protocol; they declare thereby that the procedures of compulsory arbitration shall extend to all matters covered by the Agreement and by the Decisions of the Commission.

(e) The Benelux Economic Union (BEU), East African Community (EAC), Economic Community of West African States (ECOWAS), and Caribbean Community (CARICOM)

The constituent instruments of these organizations have, in addition to organizational provisions concerning the organs, detailed provisions for creating a common market or integrating other economic matters. Each of them possesses its own court, which shall decide on differences concerning the interpretation and application of the constituent instrument.

In the Treaty Establishing the Benelux Economic Union, the College of Arbitrators shall settle the disputes arising between the parties concerning the application of the Treaty (Article 41), and a dispute which cannot be settled in the Committee of Ministers shall be submitted to the College of Arbitrators at the request of either of the parties to the dispute. The Treaty Concerning the Creation and the Statute of a Benelux Court of Justice provides that it shall be the Court's task to promote uniformity in the application of those legal rules common to three countires designated either by treaty or by a decision of the Committee of Ministers (Article 1) and that the Court shall deal with questions of the interpretation of legal rules designated above and arising in cases pending in a court of one of the three countries or in the College of Arbitrators (Article 6).

The Treaty for East African Co-operation pla s to establish the East African Common Market and provides that it shall be the responsibility of the Common Market Council to settle problems arising from the implementation of the Treaty (Article 30). It also provides, however, that the Common Market Tribunal shall ensure the observance of law and of the terms of the Treaty in the interpretation and application of so much of the Treaty as appertains to the Common Market, and that its reasoned decision shall be final and conclusive and not open to appeal.

The Treaty of the Economic Community of West African States provides that any dispute that may arise among the Member States regarding the interpretation or application of the Treaty shall be amicably settled by direct agreement, and that, in the event of failure to settle such disputes, the matter may be referred to the Tribunal of the Community by a party to such disputes and the decision of the Tribunal shall be final (Article 56). The Tribunal shall ensure the observance of law and justice in the interpretation of the provisions of the Treaty (Article 11).

The Treaty Establishing the Caribbean Community[92] provides that any dispute concerning the interpretation or application of the Treaty, unless otherwise provided for in Articles 11 and 12 of the Annex, shall be determined by the Conference (Article 19). Article 11 of the Annex provides that if any Member State considers that any benefit under the Annex or any objective of the Common Market is flustrated and if no satisfactory settlement is reached between the Member States concerned, any of them may refer the matter to the Council. The Council shall promptly make arrangements for examining the matter, including a reference to a Tribunal to be established (Article 12) of the matter at the request of any Member State concerned. If the Council or the Tribunal finds that any benefit or any objective is frustrated, the Council may, by majority vote, make recommendations, and, if such recommendation is not complied with, the Council may, by majority vote, authorise any Member State to suspend in relation to the Member State concerned the application of obligations under the Annex (Article 11).

(3) Evaluation : Economic International Organizations and Judicial Procedures
(1) General Trends in the Mechanisms of Interpretation and Dispute Settlement

As clearly demonstrated by the preceding category ((3) Other Economic International Organizations), the mechanisms of interpretation and dispute settlement of economic international organizations differ according to the purpose and character of each organization. It would be possible, however, to point out some characteristics common to principal, particularly universal, economic international organizations. In the context of our study, we would like to draw attention to the following three points.

Firstly, *use of a(n outside) judicial organ is exceptional.* Those organizations in which a judicial procedure forms a part of the mechanism of interpretation or dispute settlement are limited to the ITO, which did not come into existence, and certain regional organizations aimed at the creation of a common market among the member States. The latter organizations have purposes and characters closer to those of "organizations for integration" such as the European Union *vis-à-vis* "organizations for cooperation"; they can be regarded as exceptions even among the economic international organizations dealt with in the present section. In the many other economic international organizations, use of a judicial organ is limited to exceptional circumstances such as during the liquidation of the organization.

Secondly, *the de facto power of decision in interpretation or dispute settlement is generally conferred on internal political organs such as an executive council.* While it is exercised in a two-stage process of the Executive Board (Directors) and the Board of Governors in some organizations, it is exercised by the Council in others. While this decision in interpretation is legally final in some organizations, the *de facto* power of final decision is guaranteed by

---

[92] The Caribbean Free Trade Association (CARIFTA) was replaced by the CARICOM. Article 26 of the Agreement Establishing the CARIFTA, however, was similar to Article 31 of the Convention Establishing the EFTA. *See* 7 *Int'l Legal Materials* 938 (1968); Simmonds, 'The Caribbean Economic Community: A New Venture in Regional Integration', 23 *Int'l & Comp. L. Q.* 453 (1974).

authorizing suspension of the application of concessions or other obligations under the agreement in others. The weighted voting system is adopted in many, if not all, organizations.

Thirdly, *a tendency toward quasi-judicial interpretations* is to be noted. The advice or opinion of an independent impartial committee composed of expert members well experienced with the relevant problems and acting in their individual capacities is sometimes requested and usually becomes definitive.

Fourthly, importance is given to *the adjustment of interests by consultation and conciliation.* While consultation and conciliation are separate procedures in some organizations, they form a central position in the united procedure in other organizations. Stress is placed more on restoring the lost balance of interests or promoting the compromise among the parties concerned than on finding the violation of legal obligations or determining the legal interpretation of the constituent instrument by judicially interpreting its provisions.

(2) The Alleged Inadequacy of Judicial Procedures

1. The common characteristics of the mechanisms of interpretation and dispute settlement of economic international organizations as explained above could be summarized as follows: *The internal political organs assuming th. d. ily operation of provisions of the constituent instrument aim primarily to adjust interests among the member States through the procedures of consultation and conciliation in the light of the opinions of quasi-judicial organs, without referring the matter to a judicial organ.* The fundamental reason for this tendency lies in the allegation that judicial procedures are inadequate in the operation of economic international organizations. Why is this so ?

2. Such a claim dates back to the era of the League of Nations.[93] The Council of the League adopted rules of procedure in 1932 for the optional friendly settlement of economic disputes between States. The Economic Committee which drafted the rules considered that bodies composed of judges unacquainted with all the details of economic life and inclined to rely on legal criteria did not always appear to function in a satisfactory manner. According to these rules, a dispute can only be validly brought before the Experts by a joint application from the parties to the case (Article 2); the application shall state the subject of the dispute, the nature of the decision to be given (advisory opinion, conciliation or arbitration) as well as the number and names of the Experts to be selected (Article 6); and if the parties have requested an arbitral award, that fact shall involve the obligation on their part to submit to the award to be given and to carry it out in good faith (Article 11).

3. As many economic international organizations having the same kinds of the mechanisms as explained above were set up after the Second World War, the idea that judicial procedures are inadequate for the operation of economic international organizations has been increasingly put forward. Let us here outline the alleged grounds for this idea by reference to the articles of Metzger

---

[93] Hudson, 'The Friendly Settlement of Economic Disputes between States', 26 *Am. J. Int'l L.* 353 (1932).

and Lanbrinidis.[94]

Firstly, such *alleged reasons for non-use of judicial organs* are pointed out as follows: (1) States are, traditionally, unwilling to permit any important case taken to the Court. (2) States (particularly their economic experts) are reluctant to place confidence in the capacity of judicial bodies (legal minds) to decide disputes of a primarily economic, financial or commercial nature, the main preoccupation under a 'dispute' article always being the accommodation of interests. (3) Outsiders have limited knowledge of the negotiations that preceded the treaty, the operation (and corresponding responsibility) of the agreement, and the whole dynamic and complicated structure of mutual rights and obligations and the multiple interplay of interests involved in a multilateral context, all of which rest on a usually delicate balance and need constant, motherly supervision and adjustment; they are also unaware of, or indifferent to, the repercussions that their 'decisions' on a particular dispute might have on the future operation of the agree. ent in question. (4) Judicial procedures are time-consuming, and problems arising out of the operation of economic organizations require quick settlement. (5) Judicial procedures are overly formalistic, both in terms of procedure and substance, the legal, as distinct from the practical, considerations being overriding. (6) The remedies available through judicial procedures are too rigid since restoration of damages or satisfaction form only secondary considerations in the context of . conomic organizations. (7) Judicial procedures operate on a 'victory versus defeat' pattern.

Secondly, *the main characteristics of economic organizations* are pointed out as follows: (1) Judicial functions are entrusted to administrative organs and procedures are a mixture of judicial and administrative procedural patterns. Dispute-resolution is considered to be part of, not distinct from, the normal administration of the agreements. Weighed voting is considered to be rational in the sense that it reflects differences of interests. Deciding organs are composed not of third, impartial and disinterested persons, but of persons acting as a rule, as representatives of their respective States, and usually administrators rather than lawyers. (2) The main aim of this procedure is not so much to establish responsibility, assess damages and order reparation but, rather, to verify the existence of present or imminent embarrassments caused in the course of the operation of the treaty concerned and to restore the functional balance of the interests involved, without disturbing the overall balance of interests of all member States to the agreement in question or endangering the very existence of the institution concerned. (3) The approach adopted by these organs to the problems related to interpretation of treaties and the obligations of member States deriving therefrom will be much more liberal and flexible than that of traditional judicial institutions.

Thirdly, *the significance or implication of these mechanisms* could be pointed out as follows: (1) Expediency prevails over legal considerations. The legal aspect of a dispute, from both the substantial and procedural point of view, will lose importance and be played down. The underlying conflict of interests will be brought to the surface and the merits of a 'case' will be examined and the case ultimately resolved, in view of the need to compromise and accommodate

---

[94] Metzger, *supra* note 69; Lambrinidis, *supra* note 69.

interests of member States to these treaties and to secure the efficient and smooth operation, as well as the realisation of the goals, of the institution concerned. (2) *The impact on treaty interpretation*: Traditional and cherished methods, rules and habits of interpretation sanctioned by judicial judgment may become obsolete wherever the settlement of the disputes arising out of a treaty is entrusted to these quasi-administrative, quasi-judicial organs and 'methods'. This second point is quite suggestive for our study.

4.   These enumerated points were more systematically developed by Malinverni in 1974. Let us finally look briefly at his logically developed system. According to Malinverni, inadequacy of judicial settlement could be explained from the following three viewpoints: (1) the nature of disputes; (2) the framework in which disputes arise; and (3) the reserved attitude of States toward international courts.[95]

As to *the nature of disputes*: In the international economic relations to be regulated, economic notions are frequently difficult to define rigorously, and economic fluctuations are rapid, important and dynamic. The object to be regulated influences the nature of the rules themselves to the effect that economic rules are less abstract, less rigorous, and safeguard or derogation clauses would reduce the binding character of rules. The nature of disputes would be influenced by the nature of rules. Economic disputes are not always related to legally based protests. The element of damage is more important than the element of illegality which is not always possible to identify because of the vague rules. Disputes would often be related to the modification or elaboration of rules as well as to their interpretation, and to the potential damage. These differences are inadequate for judicial settlement for the reasons of competence (courts examine only legal disputes) and admissibility (courts require the existence of disputes and the interest of suing).

As to *the framework in which disputes arise*: The framework inevitably affects the character of disputes and the procedure of settlements. International organizations have an institutional element and a multilateral element. On the institutional element, one or two political organs in economic organizations hold the monopoly of functions and dispute settlements are considered part of the daily administration. On the multilateral element, States not parties to the dispute are frequently requested to participate in the procedure. Any member State is often able to request the intervention of the competent organ. The conditions for opening the procedure is wide enough. On these points, use of judicial procedures is inadequate and the organization itself is, in its nature and functions, in a better position to bring about a satisfactory solution in the light of the compromise between particular interests of member States and the general interests of the organization.

As to *the reserved attitude of States toward international courts*: It is generally believed, particularly among economists, that judges are unable to solve dynamic and complex economic disputes in a satisfactory manner. In the economic matters, rapid settlements are often in fact as important as correct settlements. Since economic disputes often contain non-legal conflicts of

---

[95] Malinverni, *supra* note 69, at 23-101.

interests and are too important, States refuse to submit such disputes to judicial procedures. States prefer the organization itself in cases where they are represented and could, by their votes, influence the decision.

(3) Evaluation

1.　　Does an inherent contradiction exist between judicial procedures and economic disputes? Malinverni, while presenting the argument explained above on the one hand, admits that this alleged compatibility is "manifestly exaggerated". A number of economic fields have been regulated by law as demonstrated by the many treaties governing international economic relations. The jurisprudence of internal courts and the Court of Justice of the EC proves the possibility that judges could appreciate economic notions. There does not exist, therefore, an intrinsic antinomy between judicial methods and economic matters.[96]

Kopelmanas, on the other hand, analyzed the case concerning the rights of United States nationals in Morocco (ICJ) and the case concerning Oscar Chinn (PCIJ), and pointed out that "the Court deliberately limited its action to the scope of the text in cause, even at the risk of failing to settle the dispute referred to it", and that "the Court was very reluctant to get involved beyond the extent of the strict interpretation of the texts and beyond purely juridical considerations". However, Kopelmanas also admits that negotiations alone cannot suffice to eliminate all the difficulties and that a power of decision must be given to a third and impartial body to whom the parties in cause will submit their difference. He ultimately proposed not a permanent court with a fixed number of judges, but a panel of judges from which the parties could choose those competent to resolve their particular difference, which is similar to that adopted by the League Council in the resolution explained above.[97]

2.　　It is an important question whether judicial procedures are appropriate methods for settling economic disputes.[98] We could not attempt to answer this question. We would, however, like to draw attention to the following point: the mechanisms of interpretation and dispute settlement analyzed in the present section deal with many questions and disputes, including those of a non-legal nature which cannot be received by courts, taking into account the good functioning of the organization.

3.　　Keeping in mind the analysis and evaluation relating to the mechanism of interpretation and

---

[96] *Id.* at 92-94.

[97] Kopelmanas, 'La notion de la liberté économique devant la Justice internationale', 81 *Journal du droit internal* 64, 89, 95-96, 103-04 (1954).

[98] Apart from the difficulties inherent in judicial procedures, it cannot be contended as a reason for this argument that judges are not expert in economics. The ICJ may, for example, entrust any individual, commission or other organization that it may select, with the task of carrying out an enquiry or giving an expert opinion (Article 50 of the ICJ Statute); in the settlement of disputes of the United Nations Convention of the Law of the Sea, a court or tribunal may, in any dispute involving scientific or technical matters, select scientific or technical experts to sit with the court or tribunal, but without the right to vote (Article 289).

Schwarzenberger, more directly, pointed out that the international economic lawyer has to learn as much of the economic substratum of his chosen subject as is required to cope intelligently with its normative aspects ('The Principles and Standards of International Economic Law', 117 *Recueil des cours* 1, 11 (1966)).

dispute settlement concerning the constituent instruments of economic international organizations, we would like to conclude as follows.

In most of these economic organizations, interpretations and dispute settlements are not under the judicial control of outside tribunals, but are decided legally or in a *de facto* manner by internal political organs. While some measures of quasi-judicial procedures are installed to restrain arbitrary political interpretations to some extent, *the power of internal political organs to decide interpretations and disputes will increase the authority of the internal political organs themselves and, together with the emphasized tendency of adjustment of interests through consultation and conciliation, will reduce the normative constraint of the constituent instruments and ease their transformation through practice.* This means that an analysis of practice is indispensable for the interpretation or determination of the actual meaning of any given provision of the constituent instruments of economic international organizations.

Section 5   Other International Organizations

(1) Introduction
In the present section, we will analyze some of the important international organizations not dealt with in the previous sections: some principal regional organizations, two satellite organizations (the International Telecommunication Satellite Organization (INTELSAT) and the International Maritime Satellite Organization (INMARSAT)) and the International Sea-Bed Authority expected in the United Nations Convention on the Law of the Sea.

As for the regional organizations, it would be convenient to classify them, in the light of their purposes and functions, into the following three groups: (1) those for maintaining peace, (2) those for comprehensive purposes and (3) those for promoting cooperation.

(2) Regional International Organizations
(1) Regional International Organizations for Maintaining the Peace

1.   For this group, we analyze *the North Atlantic Treaty Organization* (NATO) and *the Warsaw Treaty Organization* (WTO: dissolved in 1991). Both of these were military alliances created in the political context of the Cold War: NATO in 1949 and WTO in 1955. Both organizations were based upon the collective self-defence recognized in Article 51 of the UN Charter, and provisions for collective self-defence are at the core of both treaties (Article 5 in NATO and Article 4 in WTO).

2.   In the context of our study, we would like to draw attention to the following points. The constituent instruments of these organizations are very concise (14 articles for NATO and 11 articles for WTO), and only provide for the establishment of organs (the Council for NATO and the Joint Command of the Armed Forces and the Political Consultative Committee for WTO) and some fundamental principles such as the peaceful settlement of disputes, cooperation among

member States, consultation, and collective self-defence against armed attack. By the nature of the organizations, a decision is not made by a vote, by unanimous agreement pursued through consultations. The provision for the peaceful settlement of disputes in Article 1 of both treaties is aimed generally at disputes involving member States and includes disputes concerning the interpretation and application of the constituent instrument

Consequently, *the constituent instruments of these organizations only provide for the engagement of collective self-defence and the forum for consultations among the member States.* Tthe actual organization could develop in whatever way in accordance with the agreements among the member States based upon consultations. In fact, while the NATO has seen considerable constitutional developments and many organs created in the light of experience, the WTO developed very little by comparison.[99]

(2) Regional International Organizations for Comprehensive Purposes

1.   For this group, we analyze the Western European Union (WEU), Organization of American States (OAS), League of Arab States (LAS) and Organization of African Unity (OAU). These organizations have, in general, those functions for maintaining peace as well as for promoting regional cooperation in political, economic and cultural matters.

2.   The Treaty of Economic, Social and Cultural Collaboration and Collective Self-Defence, which is the constituent instrument of *the Western European Union*, is a concise treaty like those of the NATO and WTO, and only provides for the establishment of the "Council of Western European Union", the Agency for the Control of Armaments and the Assembly in addition to the fundamental principles of cooperation in political, economic and cultural matters and the engagement of mutual assistance in the case of an armed attack.

The Council is the executive body of the organization. Its basic voting rule is unanimity, although either a qualified or a simple majority suffices for certain matters specified in the Protocols adopted later. The provision for the peaceful settlement of disputes (Article 10) concerns disputes involving member States in general.

Consequently, it could be concluded that *the Treaty establishing the WEU is also confined to providing the basic principles and establishing some organs, leaving much room for development by later agreements and practice among the member States.* In fact, it has developed through four Protocols and the Charter of the Assembly of the Western European Union.

3.   *The Organization of American States* (OAS) is based upon the Charter of the OAS (which entered into force in 1951), the Inter-American Treaty of Reciprocal Assistance (Rio Treaty: entered into force in 1948), and the American Treaty on Pacific Settlement (Pact of Bogotá: entered into force in 1955). The Charter of the OAS is a detailed constituent instrument of 150 articles whose constitution is similar to that of the UN Charter, and the Pact of Bogotá is a developed version of Chapter 5 (Pacific settlement of disputes) of the OAS Charter. Chapter 6 (Collective security) of the OAS Charter refers to the elaborate mechanism established by the Rio

---

[99] D. W. Bowett, *The Law of International Institutions* 182, 239 (4th ed. 1982).

Treaty; Chapter 5 of the OAS Charter and the Pact of Bogotá provide for detailed procedures for pacific settlement of the disputes in general between American States.

The Charter of the OAS could be described as an American version of the UN Charter, including detailed provisions concerning the functions, powers, constitution and activities of the organs (such as the General Assembly and the Councils) as well as the purposes, principles, members, fundamental rights and duties of States, pacific settlement of disputes, collective security and economic, social, educational, scientific and cultural standards. While a mechanism of interpretation or dispute settlement concerning the constituent instrument would be important in such an organization, there is no relevant provision in the Charter as there is in the case of the UN Charter. Since the sovereign equality and independence of States are, however, given great importance, the reasons by which any relevant provision was not inserted in the UN Charter would *a fortiori* apply to the OAS Charter. Consequently, the analysis in Section 1 would also apply here.

The OAS thus appears to be the most comprehensive regional organization outside Europe. It is pointed out, however, that it is more impressive structurally than in practice.[100]

4.   The Pact of *the League of Arab States* (which entered into force in 1945) is a concise constituent instrument of 20 articles in total. It is confined to those provisions relating to the purposes (collective defense and various forms of cooperation among member States), the Council (functions, voting procedure and effect of decisions), special Committees for each of various forms of cooperation, and other minor points. The collective defense and economic cooperation is strengthened by the Joint Defense and Economic Co-operation Treaty between the States of the Arab League (which entered into force in 1952).

There is no provision relating to interpretation. Article 5 (settlement of disputes), however, provides that if the two contending parties apply to the Council for the settlement of a dispute that does not involve the independence of a State, its sovereignty or its territorial intergrity, the decision of the Council shall be effective and obligatory.

It could be concluded in general, however, that *the Pact of LAS is also confined to providing basic principles for cooperation and establishing organs for them, leaving much room for development through later agreements and practice.* In fact it is said that the cultural and economic activities of the League have developed considerably.[101]

5.   The Charter of *the Organization of the African Unity* (which entered into force in 1963) is also a concise constituent instrument of 33 articles. It provides for, among other things, comprehensive purposes, principles and membership as well as functions, constitutions and voting rules of the organs (the Assembly of Heads of States and Government, the Council of Ministers, the General Secretariat and the Commission of Mediation, Conciliation and Arbitration). As for the latter Commission, the Protocol of the Commission of Mediation, Conciliation and Arbitration (signed in 1964) was made and is an integral part of the OAS Charter.

---

[100] *Id.* at 224. *See also* O. C. Stoetzer, *Organization of American States* (2nd ed. 1993).

[101] *Id.* at 232.

Article 27 of the OAS Charter relating to the interpretation of the Charter provides that any question which may arise concerning the interpretation of the Charter shall be decided by a vote of two-thirds of the Assembly of Heads of State and Government. In the early stages of the drafting of this article, provision was made for a reference to the ICJ, but it was considered that disputes as to the interpretation of any of the provisions of the Charter would be best disposed of within the framework of the Organization itself, rather than by an authority external to it because the majority of the member States of the Organization had yet to accept the compulsory jurisdiction of the ICJ.[102]

(3) Regional International Organizations for Promoting Cooperation

1.   For this group, we analyze the Council of Europe and the Association of South·East Asian Nations (ASEAN).

2.   The Statute of *the Council of Europe* (which entered into force in 1949) is a constituent instrument of 42 articles in total. It provides for, among other things, the extended area (except matters relating to National Defense) of purposes and membership as well as functions, constitutions, voting rules, activities and other matters of two organs (the Committee of Ministers and the Consultative Assembly). The former Committee is composed of government representatives, and the latter Assembly's members are elected by each Member Parliament. While both organs have a wide area of activities, their powers are limited, the medium of pursuing the broadly phrased aims being discussion and agreement.[103]

There is no provision relating to interpretation. In view of the nature of the organization, such questions are expected to be solved through discussions and agreements.

3.   *The Association of South East Asian Nations* is a unique organization which developed from the ASEAN Declaration (Bangkok Declaration) in 1967, and was strengthened by the Zone of Peace, Freedom and Neutrality Declaration in 1971, the Declaration of ASEAN Concord in 1976, the Treaty of Amity and Co-operation in Southeast Asia in 1976, and the Agreement on the Establishment of the ASEAN Secretariat in 1976. Having seen previous efforts towards regional cooperation fail, the founding members, it is said, opted for a cautious and gradual functionalist approach during the first stages of ASEAN's existence.[104]

The ASEAN Declaration refers only to various aims and purposes and the establishment of organs (the Annual Meeting of Foreign Ministers, the Standing Committee and others). The Declaration of ASEAN Concord adopted a programme of action as a framework for cooperation in the political, economic, social, cultural and information, and security fields. The Treaty of Amity contains provisions for fundamental principles of amity and cooperation, and for pacific settlement of disputes. The latter provisions provide for the establishment of a High Council and its

---

[102]   Elias, 'The Charter of the Organization of African Unity', 59 *Am. J. Int'l L.* 243, 267 (1965). *See also* Elias, 'The Commission of Mediation, Conciliation and Arbitration of the Organization of African Unity', 40 *Brit. Y. B. Int'l L.* 336 (1964).

[103]   Bowett, *supra* note 99, at 171. *See also* J.-J. Burban, *Le Conseil de l'Europe* 18-23 (Que sais-je?, 1985).

[104]   Syatauw, '*Directory: ASEAN*', in II. B - II. J. *International Organization and Integration* II. F. 2 - 1, 6 (1983).

conciliatory activities upon agreement by the parties in dispute.

Judging from the above, disputes concerning the constituent instruments and activities of ASEAN would be dealt with as part of the disputes in general anticipated in the provisions for pacific settlement of disputes. ASEAN would also develop in whatever direction in accordance with later agreements and practice among member States.

(4) Evaluation

Since diverse organizations are included in the above regional organizations, it would be difficult to reach any concise conclusion. It seems possible, however, to point out some tendencies from the perspective of our study.

Firstly, there is no provision for settlement of disputes concerning the interpretation of the constituent instruments of these regional organizations. As a result, such a dispute, it is submitted, is expected to be dissolved through negotiations or consultations, or as a part of the disputes in general between the member States to be dealt with in the procedures of dispute settlement of the organization, where the voting rule of unanimity or consensus is usually adopted. Consequently, the *consent of individual member States plays a greater role in these organizations.*

Secondly, the constituent instruments of these regional organizations are generally concise (that of OAS being an exception), which is quite contrary to those of such regional organizations dealt with in the previous section which aim at creating a common market. Since they are confined to providing for the purposes, fundamental structures of the organs and a forum for cooperation, *the actual organizations will be greatly influenced by later agreements and practice among the member States.*

(3) The International Telecommunication Satellite Organization and International Maritime Satellite Organization[105]

(1) Introduction

Here we analyze two special international organizations: INTELSAT and INMARSAT. These two are different from other international satellite organizations in that a competent private entity can participate in the operating agreement and that a weighted voting system is partly adopted. Let us look first at some of other international satellite organizations.

(1) The International System and Organization of Space Communications (INTERSPUTNIK) was established by the USSR and other socialist countries in 1972. There is no provision for the interpretation or dispute settlement concerning the constituent instrument. It is considered that the Board composed of representatives of each Member having one vote shall examine and decide on such questions (Article 12 (6-(20)) of the Agreement); the decisions of the Board shall be adopted by two-thirds vote, but they will not be binding on dissenting Members.

(2) The European Space Agency (ESA) was established by European countries in 1980.

---

[105] *See in general Manual on Space Law,* 4 Vols. (N. Jasentuliyana & R. S. K. Lee eds. 1979); Courteix,'Organisations internationales à vocation mondiale ou régionale dans le domaine des télécommunication par satellites', in 1 *Juris-classeur de droit international* (1985) Fascicule 141.

Article 17 (Disputes) of the Convention provides for the compulsory jurisdiction of the Arbitration Tribunal in relation to any dispute between two or more Member States, or between any of them and the Agency, concerning the interpretation or application of the Convention or its Annexes.

(3)   The Arab Corporation for Space Communications (ARABSAT) was established by a group Arab States. Article 19 (Settlement of Disputes) provides that the General Body, the supreme authority composed of the member States, of the Corporation shall adjudicate upon disputes between the Corporation and one or more members or among the members.

(2) The International Telecommunication Satellite Organization (INTELSAT)[106]

1.   Article 18 (Settlement of Disputes) of the Agreement Relating to INTELSAT and Article 20 (Settlement of Disputes) of the Operating Agreement Relating to INTELSAT provide, in essence, as follows.

Firstly, all legal disputes arising in connection with the rights and obligations under the Agreement *between (State) Parties* or *between INTELSAT and (State) Parties,* if not settled within a reasonable time, shall be submitted to arbitration in accordance with Annex C to the Agreement. Secondly, all legal disputes arising in connection with the rights and obligations under the Agreement or the Operating Agreement *between (State) Parties and Signatories* may be submitted to the above arbitration, provided that the (State) Parties and the Signatories involved agree to such arbitration. Thirdly, all legal disputes arising in connexion with the rights and obligations under the Agreement or the Operating Agreement *between Signatories* or *between INTELSAT and Signatories,* if not settled within a reasonable time, shall be submitted to arbitration in accordance with Annex C to the Agreement. (Annex C provides for a tribunal of three arbitrators.)

2.   We would like to draw attention to the following points as characteristic of the dispute settlement procedure of INTELSAT. Most of the disputes relating to the interpretation and application of the Agreement and the Operating Agreement are to be submitted to the compulsory jurisdiction of the arbitral tribunal; "disputes arising in connection with the rights and obligations under the Agreement and and the Operating Agreement" would be largely the same with the above-mentioned disputes. Excepted from the compulsory jurisdiction of the arbitral tribunal are those legal disputes between (State) Parties and Signatories (either (State) Parties or the telecommunication entities, public or private, designated by Parties), which could be a dispute between a State and a private enterprise, quite different from ordinary inter-State disputes.

---

[106] INTELSAT is composed of four organs. The Assembly of Parties composed of all the State Parties is "the principal organ" of INTELSAT. The Meeting of Signatories is composed of State Parties, or the telecommunications entities (public or private) designated by each State Party, which signed the Operating Agreement. (In these organs, each Party (Signnatory) has one vote and decisions are taken by a majority (two-thirds for substantive matters and simple for procedural matters) of votes casted.) The Board of Governors is composed of Governors appointed on the basis of investment shares and an equitable geographical distribution, and while a weighted voting system is adopted, it is also provided that the Board of Governors shall endeavour to take decisions unanimously. There is, finally, an executive organ responsible to the Board of Governors.

(3) The International Maritime Satellite Organization (INMARSAT)[107]

1. Article 31 of the Convention on INMARSAT and Article 16 of the Operating Agreement on INMARSAT, in essence, provide as follows. Firstly, disputes arising *between (State) Parties, or between (State) Parties and INMARSAT,* relating to rights and obligations under the Convention, if not settled by negotiation between the parties concerned, and if within one year of the time any party has requested settlement, a settlement has not been reached, the dispute may, if the parties concerned consent, be submitted to arbitration in accordance with the Annex to the Convention. Secondly, disputes arising *between (State) Parties and Signatories in their capacity as such,* relating to rights and obligations under the Agreement or the Operating Agreement may be submitted to the above arbitration if the (State) Parties and the Signatories involved agree to such arbitration. Thirdly, such disputes arising *between Signatories,* or *between Signatories and INMARSAT* if not settled by negotiation between the parties concerned, if within one year of the time any party to the dispute has requested settlement a settlement has not been reached, and unless otherwise mutually agreed, the dispute shall be submitted to arbitration in accordance with the Annex to the Convention at the request of any party to the dispute. (The Annex provides for an arbitral tribunal of three members.)

2. We would like to draw attention to the following points as characteristic of the dispute settlement procedure of INMARSAT. Unlike the case of INTELSAT, the disputes relating to the interpretation of the constituent instrument are not to be submitted to the compulsory jurisdiction of the arbitral tribunal except those disputes between Signatories or between Signatories and INMARSAT. In the case of disputes in which one party is a (State) Party, the jurisdiction of an arbitral tribunal is optional and depends on a prior agreement between the parties. This mixture is explained as a compromise between the United States and Western European States, who argued for a compulsory arbitration, and the Soviet Union and the socialist countries, who argued against it.[108]

(4) Evaluation

We could conclude from the above analysis that *there is no mechanism of interpretation or dispute settlement proper to the constituent instruments of international satellite organizations.* While, with the participation of private entities, there could certainly arise a dispute between a State and a private enterprise, mechanisms of interpretation or dispute settlement of these satellite organizations seem to correspond rather to *the composition of member States.* In the cases of the socialist countries (INTERSPUTNIK) and the Arab countries (ARABSAT), it is decided by the political supreme organ composed by the representatives of the member States; in the case of the Western States occupying a large majority (INTELSAT and ESA), it is to be submitted to the compulsory jurisdiction of an arbitral tribunal; in the case of a mixture of western

---

[107] The explanation of INTELSAT (note 106) applies equally to INMARSAT except for the names (the Assembly, the Council and the Directorate) and the non-existence of a Meeting of Signatories.

[108] Jasentuliyana, 'International Maritime Satellite System *(INMARSAT)*, in *supra* note 105, at 439, 453-54.

States and socialist countries, it is subject to an optional arbitral tribunal.

(4) The International Sea-Bed Authority[109]

(1) Introduction

The United Nations Convention on the Law of the Sea adopted in 1982 is a huge instrument composed of 17 parts (320 articles) and 9 annexes and deals with comprehensive problems of the law of the sea. Part 11 (The Area)[110] provides for the establishment of the International Sea-Bed Authority to organize and control activities in the Area.

The International Sea-Bed Authority is composed of the Assembly, the Council (36 members), the Secretariat and the Enterprise as the organ to carry out activities in the Area directly. While the Assembly is "considered the supreme organ of the Authority" (Article 160 (1)), the substantive powers are exercised by the Council. The composition, procedure and voting of the Council is provided in a complex and detailed manner. The Enterprise is composed of the Governing Board (15 members acting in their personal capacity), the Director-General and the staff. The relationship between the Authority and the Enterprise is not clear; while the Enterprise shall be the organ of the Authority and act in accordance with this Convention and the rules, regulations and procedures of the Assembly, as well as the general policies established by the Assembly, and shall be subject to the directives and control of the Council (Article 170 (2)), it shall enjoy autonomy in the conduct of its operations and operate in accordance with sound commercial principles (Articles 2 (2) and 1 (3)).

Which part of the Convention on the Law of the Sea is considered to be the constituent instrument of the International Sea-Bed Authority? From a formal viewpoint, the Convention constitutes an integral unity as a legal instrument, does not permit reservations or exceptions and was drafted on package deals; these would suggest that the whole Convention be considered the constituent instrument. From a substantive viewpoint, however, that the constituent instrument governs the structure and activities of the organization, Part 11 (The Area) and Annex 4 (Statute of the Enterprise) could be considered the principal part of the constituent instrument of the Authority.[111]

(2) The Mechanisms for Settlement of Disputes Concerning the Interpretation or Application of Part 11 and Annex 4.

1.   The mechanisms for settlement of disputes concerning the interpretation or application of

---

[109]   For the relevant bibliography of the International Sea-Bed Authority, *see, e.g.*, Sohn, 'Settlement of International Disputes relating to Deep Sea-Bed Mining', in *Festshrift für Rudolf Bindschedler* 443 (E. Diez et al. eds. 1980); Caflisch, 'The Settlement of Disputes relating to Activities in the International Seabed Area', in *The New Law of the Sea* 303 (C. L. Rozakis & C. A. Stephanou eds. 1983); Paolillo, 'The Institutional Arrangements for the Interanational Sea-Bed and Their Impact on the Evolution of International Organizations', 188 *Recueil des cours* 134 (1984).

[110]   While some provisions in Part 11 are modified by the Agreement relating to the Implementation of Part XI of the United Nations Convention on the Law of the Sea of 10 December 1982, it is considered that this Agreement has little impact on the point dealt with in our analysis. For the text of this Agreement, *see* 33 *Int'l Legal Materials* 1309 (1994).

[111]   For our discussion on this point, *see* Chap. 5, Sec. 1.

Part 11 and Annex 4 are provided for in Section 5 (Settlement of Disputes and Advisory Opinions) of Part 11, and Part 15 (Settlement of Disputes) is also applicable. Consequently, Section 1 of Part 15 regulating a voluntary settlement of disputes by peaceful means will first be applied (Article 285). This includes, among other things, the settlement of disputes by any peaceful means chosen by the parties (Article 280), obligation to exchange views (Article 283), and conciliation (Article 284). When the dispute is not solved by these voluntary procedures of peaceful means, compulsory procedures with binding decisions will be applied. Here we analyze the mechanisms for settlement of disputes concerning the interpretation or application of Part 11 and Annex 4 in the light of the subject of a dispute.

2.   The first category is *disputes between States Parties.* Article 187 (a) provides that the Sea-Bed Dispute Chamber (of the International Tribunal for the Law of the Sea), composed of 11 members selected by a majority of the 21 members of the Tribunal from among them, shall have jurisdiction under Part 11 and the Annexes relating thereto in disputes between States Parties concerning their interpretation or application. On the other hand, Article 188 (1) provides that disputes between States Parties referred to in Article 187 (a) may be submitted (i) at the request of the parties to the dispute, to a special chamber (composed of 3 or more of the members of the Tribunal, determined by the Tribunal with the approval of the parties) of the International Tribunal for the Law of the Sea, or (ii) at the request of any party to the dispute, to an *ad hoc* chamber of the Sea-Bed Disputes Chamber (composed of 3 of the members of the Chamber, determined by the Chamber with the approval of the parties). These provisions would lead to the conclusion that a mechanism of the compulsory jurisdiction of a judicial tribunal is established, while a choice of three kinds of judicial tribunals remains.

Furthermore in Section 2 of Part 15, Article 286 provides that any dispute concerning the interpretation or application of the Convention shall be submitted at the request of any party to the disputes to the court or tribunal having jurisdiction, which are (i) the International Tribunal for the Law of the Sea, (ii) the International Court of Justice, (iii) an arbitral tribunal (composed of 5 members, 2 appointed by each party, 3 appointed by agreement between the parties) and (iv) a special arbitral tribunal (composed of 5 members, each party appointing 2 members, the President of the tribunal appointed by agreement between the parties). Article 287 (2) provides, in addition, tha, a declaration of choice among these tribunals shall not affect or be affected by the obligation of a State Party to accept the jurisdiction of the Sea-Bed Disputes Chamber of the International Tribunal for the Law of the Sea.

Consequently, in the case of inter-State disputes concerning the interpretation or application of the constituent instrument, States to the dispute would have, depending on the nature of the dispute and the agreement between the parties, a choice of 7 tribunals mentioned above. Since these tribunals will have different members and characteristics, they might reach a different conclusion on the same matter. To this extent, uniformity in the interpretation of the Convention is restricted.[112]

3.   The second category is *disputes between States Parties and the Authority*. Article 187 (b) provides that the Sea-Bed Chamber shall have jurisdiction in disputes between a State Party and the Authority concerning (i) acts or omissions of the Authority or of a State Party alleged to be in violation of that Part or the Annexes relating thereto or of rules, regulations and procedures of the Authority adopted in accordance therewith, or (ii) acts of the Authority alleged to be in excess of jurisdiction or a misuse of power. These definitions appear wide enough to encompass all non-contractual disputes which could arise between a State Party and the Authority.[113]

Article 187 (b) must be read together with Article 189 (Limitation on jurisdiction with regard to decisions of the Authority), which provides, in essence, (i) that the Sea-Bed Dispute Chamber shall have no jurisdiction with regard to the exercise by the Authority of its discretionary powers in accordance with that part, (ii) that without prejudice to Article 191 (Advisory opinion), it shall not pronounce itself on the question of whether any rules, regulations and procedures of the Authority are in conformity with the Convention, nor declare invalid any such rules, regulations and procedures and (iii) that its jurisdiction shall be confined to deciding claims that the application of any rules, regulations and procedures of the Authority in individual cases would be in conflict with the contractual obligations of the parties to the dispute or their obligations under the Convention, claims concerning excess of jurisdiction or misuse of power, and to claims for damages to be paid or other remedy to be given to the party concerned for the failure of the other party to comply with its contractual obligations or its obligations under the Convention.

It was pointed out that Article 189 was contradictory and confusing.[114] Firstly, while the wording of Article 189 implies that the Convention has explicitly attributed discretionary powers on some matters to the Authority, no explicit attribution of such powers has been made with regard to any particular matter. Furthermore, Part 11 and the related Annexes leave the Authority little discretion by providing a legal framework that eliminates or at least considerably reduces the Authority's freedom of action. Secondly, it would be impossible for the Chamber to "decide" any such claim without "pronouncing itself", at least incidentally, on the legality of the rules, regulations and procedures which may be involved. It could be concluded that the vagueness of Article 189 was intentional and designed to conceal the substantive divergences between the Group of 77, who glorified the sanctity and intangibility of the powers of the Authority, and developed countries, who claimed the protection of the rights and interests of those involved in

---

[112] The applicability of Section 2 of Part 15 is not clear. While some (Caflisch, *supra* note 109, at 308-10; Paolillo, *supra* note 109, at 275-76) are negative on this point, the natural and ordinary interpretation of the relevant text appears to lead to a positive conclusion. The *travaux préparatoires* might lead to the negative one. Here we take the positive conclusion.

[113] Caflisch, *supra* note 109, at 310.

[114] Caflisch, *supra* note 109, at 315; Paolillo, *supra* note 109, at 285-90. *See also* Makarczyk, 'Contribution to the Problem of the Sttlement of Disputes concerning the Exploitation of Seabed Resources', in *Le règlementdes différends sur le nouvelles ressources naturelles* 53, 58-63 (R.- J. Dupuy ed. 1983).

the activities against any illegal acts of the Authority.

While the above procedure of judicial review is an *ex post* examination of the legality of action taken by the Authority, advisory opinions by the Chamber could be a *prior* procedure for preventing an illegal action. Article 191 provides that the Sea-Bed Disputes Chamber shall give advisory opinions at the request of the Assembly or the Council on legal questions arising within the scope of their activities. Article 159 (10) provides that upon a written request addressed to the President and sponsored by at least one-fourth of the members of the Authority for an advisory opinion on the conformity with the Convention of a proposal before the Assembly on any matter, the Assembly shall request the Chamber to give an advisory opinion thereon and shall defer voting on that proposal pending receipt of the advisory opinion.

4.   The third category is *disputes in which a subject other than a State and the Authority is involved.* Article 187 (c), (d) and (e) provide that the Chamber shall have jurisdiction in disputes between parties to a contract, being States Parties, the Authority or the Enterprise, state enterprises and natural or juridical persons concerned. Disputes may, depending on their nature, belong to the exclusive jurisdiction of the Chamber (Article 187 (c)(ii), (d) and (e)), may, unless both parties agree to settle the dispute by other means, be submitted to binding commercial arbitration by either party (Article 187 (c)(i), Article 188 (2)(a), Annex 3 Article 13 (15)), or may be submitted by either party to binding commercial arbitration (Annex 3 Article 4).

Some disputes concerning the interpretation or application of a contract shall be submitted not to the Sea-Bed Chamber, but to a commercial arbitral tribunal. Article 188 (2) (a) provides, however, that the tribunal shall have no jurisdiction to decide any question of interpretation of the Convention and that, when the dispute involves a question of the interpretation of Part 11 and the related Annexes, with respect to activities in the Area, that question shall be referred to the Chamber for a ruling. It could be said that uniformity in the interpretation of the constituent instrument of the International Sea-Bed Authority is assured by the Chamber *via* Article 188 which has borrowed the system of preliminary rulings of Article 177 of the Treaty establishing the EEC.

(3) Evaluation

1.   Any dispute concerning the interpretation or application of Part 11 and Annex 4, which could be considered the principal part of the constituent instrument of the International Sea-Bed Authority, shall be submitted to a judicial court at the request of any party to the dispute. This is in contrast with Part 15 (settlement of disputes for the whole Treaty) in which applicability of compulsory procedures with binding decisions is limited or excluded on important matters (Section 3).

A special system for the settlement of disputes concerning activities in the Area, which includes its own principles, organs and procedures, was established separately from the general system for the settlement of disputes in Part 11, as a means of adapting settlement procedures to the following *special characteristics of such disputes*: (1) activities in the Area are subject to a special legal order, based on the principle of the common heritage of mankind; (2) as a result, any such dispute affects the interests of all States; (3) such disputes will involve other entities in addition to States and (4) since the Authority will have a leading role, some procedure was considered essential for challenging its acts when questions of legality arise.[115] The compromise formula embodied in Article 188 allows the parties to a dispute the option of resorting to (i) the Sea-Bed Chamber, (ii) a special chamber of the Tribunal, (iii) an *ad hoc* chamber of the Sea-Bed Chamber (the intentions of the States parties to the dispute would be reflected on the composition of (ii) and (iii)), and (iv) a commercial arbitral tribunal. However, the members of the former three chambers are selected from among the members of the International Tribunal for the Law of the Sea. In the case of a commercial arbitral tribunal, questions of interpretation of Part 11 and Annex 4 will be referred to the Chamber for a ruling *via* Article 188 (2). We could conclude, therefore, that *the procedures of Section 5 of Part 11 have established a system in which uniformity in the interpretation of the constituent instrument of the Authority is, in principle, assured by a judicial court.*

As to the disputes between an international organization and its member States, two categories of procedures for dispute settlement could be distinguished. The first category is the same procedures provided for in the settlement of disputes between States; their purpose is to end the dispute. The second category is a special procedure whereby a judicial body conducts a legal review of the act to preserve the unity and coherence of a particular legal order by eliminating any acts contrary to it; it is rather exceptional as seen in Articles 173-176 of the Treaty establishing the EEC. In the drafting process of the Convention on the Law of the Sea, both approaches were examined. While the system incorporated in the Convention is a combination of elements of the two approaches, the former seems to be dominant in the following two points: (1) control of the legality of acts of the Authority is exercised by the Chamber not directly, through the review of act with a view to obtaining its invalidation, but indirectly by ruling on the dispute to which the act has given rise; and (2) the Chamber may decide claims based on the illegality of the Authority's decisions, but has no power to declare those decisions null and void.[116]

2.   Keeping the above analysis in mind, we would like to make the following statement in the light of the context of our study. *Any dispute concerning the constituent instrument of the International Sea-Bed A. thority is subject to the compulsory jurisdiction of a judicial court with a binding decision, which would assure uniformity in the interpretation of the constituent instrument. These judicial interpretations would be less evolutionary than those purpose-oriented interpretations by the organs of an international organization.* The problem remains, however, as to what extent this system of judicial control will work in the actual operation of the Authority.

Section 6   Conclusion

1.   **The Variety in Interpretative Procedures**: The examination of specific relevant provisions

---

[115] Paolillo, *supra* note109, at 274-75.

[116] *Id.* at 280-84.

of various constituent instruments indicates that the procedures provided by these provisions are diverse. In other words, the interpretative procedures differ in accordance with the functions and nature of each international organization, and do not permit a single conclusion. It is necessary, therefore, to analyze, from one organization to another, the possible influence exerted by the organs as interpreters.

In the United Nations, there is no provision related to interpretation of the Charter. However, the final report in the San Francisco Conference indicates that the competence of authoritative interpretation was not given to any State member or any organ, and that the procedure to assure a unified interpretation of the Charter was left unresolved. This situation has not been changed in actual practice and is to be entrusted to the procedures under general international law, namely agreement and acquiescence.

In the Specialized Agencies and IAEA (excluding economic international organizations), an institutional procedure has been adopted that interpretation or conflict resolution with regard to the constituent instruments are first attempted by the internal political organs and only secondly referred t. an external judicial organ. A compulsory jurisdiction is imposed upon the member States in some cases, but recourse to an advisory opinion by the Court is available in all of them except the UPU.

In economic international organizations --- in particular, universal ones --- some features could be pointed out. First, the legal or *de facto* competence to make a binding decision upon interpretation or conflict resolution with regard to the constituent instruments is attributed to the internal political (executive) organs. Secondly, they tend to assure a quasi-judicial interpretation by utilizing an independent impartial committee composed of expert members well experienced with the relevant problems and acting in their individual capacities.

In other international organizations, the procedures are quite diverse. In many of the regional organizations, constituent instruments are generally concise and only define their purposes and fundamental structures. In international satellite organizations, an arbitration procedure (compulsory or voluntary) is provided in some but not in others. In the International Sea-Bed Authority, a unified interpretation by a judicial organ is provided in the Convention.

2.   **Non-Recourse to Judicial Organs and the Superiority of Political Organs**: The interpretative procedures provided in constituent instruments differ, as summarized above, in accordance with the functions and nature of each organization. When the actual operation of these procedures is analyzed, however, one common feature becomes clear: non-recourse to judicial organs in this process and the phenomenon of the superiority of political organs.

In the United Nations, unification in the interpretation of the Charter is not institutionally assured. Their resolutions have, in principle, only recommendatory effect except in relation to internal matters. Furthermore, dissenting member States, in many cases, submit objections and use a variety of devices of protest against the decisions of the organs. In these circumstances, it is certainly impossible from a strictly legal viewpoint to attribute a status of authoritative interpretation of the Charter to the interpretation involved in those decisions to which objections

222

and protests are attached.

In spite of this legal state of affairs, it must be emphasized that the interpretation and application of the Charter by the organs continue to be made in the operation of the United Nations as if the interpretation had an authoritative effect at least within the United Nations. Judicial judgment or restraint by the advisory opinion of the Court has hardly been utilized. Therefore, the practice of the organs tends to have full effect within the United Nations except in those circumstances where the positive cooperation of the dissenting member States is indispensable for its implementation. This means that, in most of the actual operations of the United Nations, the problem of legal validity would be replaced by the problem of to what extent the will and capacity of the dissenting member States could be maintained. In a rare case, their will and capacity might cause a crisis in the United Nations as a result, but in most cases, the practice of the organs continues to be adopted, implemented and accumulated by overcoming the objections of minority member States. In ordinary treaties, interpretative confrontations would destabilize or obstruct the application of the treaties; the interpretation and application of the Charter, however, continues to be made at least within the United Nations. This means that, in the actual operation of the Charter, the interpretation by the internal political organs will occupy a dominant and superior position.[116]

In the Specialized Agencies and IAEA (excluding economic international organizations), judicial procedures are, although provided institutionally to some extent, hardly utilized in practice. The interpretation and conflict resolution with regard to their constituent instruments are deemed to have been dealt with, in most cases, in their internal political organs and rarely referred to an outside judicial organ. In fact, it is asserted that recourse to an outside judicial organ would be harmful to the effective activity and efficient functioning of the organization because of the delay involved, undue reliance upon legal elements, lack of sensitivity to the internal requirement for effective operation, and lack of understanding of the necessity for compromise and flexibility. Legal advisors and quasi-judicial committees have been provided in many organizations so that legal aspects are taken into consideration institutionally in the activities of political organs. These procedures do not seem, however, to control sufficiently the superiority of political considerations in political organs.

In many economic international organizations, the above tendency is conspicuous. Recourse to judicial organs is fundamentally excluded even on the instititonal level provided in the constituent instruments. There is certainly a tendency to assure a quasi-judicial interpretation by utilizing quasi-judicial committees (the Committee on Interpretation, panels, advisory panels,

---

[116] Rosenne, in this connection, pointed out that a majority vote in effect controls the application of the Charter, rendering abstract interpretation of it of little real interest, and added as follows (Rosenne, *supra* note 1 in Chap. 1, at 230):

"[I]n the absence of special stipulations providing for some sort of recourse to a disinterested third party, [the] emphasis on the political factors in the interpretation, and hence in the application, of the constituent instrument of an international organization reflects the fact that here *the process of interpretation is a different kind of process from that encountered daily in the interpretation of treaties, whether bilateral or multilateral, including multilateral treaties of universal scope.*" [Italics ours]

the Examining Committee and others). However, the status of, and recourse to, these committees are, in principle, secondary. Furthermore, adjustment of interests through consultation and conciliation is given great importance in the operation of the political organs. As shown by the fact that a breach of treaty by a State is not a condition for the procedure of an organ to be commenced or that the competence to make a legally binding decision is given to an internal political organ, the emphasis is placed not upon a legally appropriate interpretation from the strictly judicial viewpoint, but upon restoration of the balance of benefits and promotion of compromise.

In other international organizations as well, recourse to judicial procedures are hardly utilized. In many regional organizations, however, disputes regarding interpretation and application of the constituent instruments are expected to be resolved by negotiations or conciliation as part of the general procedure of conflict resolution, and, as a result of voting procedures aimed at unanimity or agreement among all the member States, the individual will of member States will be given precedence over the wishes of political organs.

3. **Implications**: As is clear from the foregoing analysis, judicial procedures are hardly utilized and have little actual significance in the interpretation of constituent instruments. This situation would support the following statement by Morgenstern.

"[T]he most important reason why there has not been greater recourse to judicial interpretation probably is that *such interpretation could inhibit, rather than advance, the growth of the law.* The amendment of the constituent instruments of the various organizations, except for such matters as the enlargement of elected organs, is difficult; if every issue of legality were submitted for judicial determination, there could be a risk of serious stultification. As Professor Ciobanu puts it: 'The broad majority of Members of the United Nations ... share the opinion of Judge Hudson that "*no great international instrument could be completely self-explanatory, and meaning should be given to its provisions, not so much by the rulings of judges on the bench of the Court, as by the experience of those who have the responsibility of making the instrument work*".'"[117] [Italics ours]

As a result of this situation, the practice (and the interpretation implied in it) of the internal political organs will have, *de facto* or legally as the case may be, a decisive influence upon the determination of the meanings to be given to the provisions concerned in the constituent instruments. This means, on the other hand, that if recourse to judicial procedures are not provided or sufficiently utilized, the operation and activiti. s of most of the universal international organizations where a majority rule of voting procedure is adopted will not be sufficiently controlled by a minority of member States *via* judicial machineries, but will be continually oriented

---

[117] Morgenstern, 'Legality in International Organizations', 48 *Brit. Y. B. Int'l L.* 241, 254-5 (1976-77). *See also* Campbell, 'The Attitudes and Practices of the Specialized Agencies and U. N. Organs and the Interpretation of Their Basic Constitutions', *The Juridical Review* 177, 181 (1986).

by the organs which are governed by a majority of member States. In other words, the legal rights and interests of minority States guaranteed by the constituent instruments will not necessarily be respected by their operation and activities. In this connection, Rosenne made a suggestive statement.

"[I]nstances of deliberate and isolated interpretation by the organ declared competent are rare, and *it is the ensemble of the action of the organ in question, or indeed of the Organization as a whole, rather than a series of deliberate interpretative decisions, that constitutes the living interpretation of the constituent instrument, the 'established practice of the organization' in the words of the 1986 Vienna Convention....*

... [M]ost interpretation of the constituent instruments of international organizations is, on the international plane, performed by political organs and is, in consequence, a reflection of the views of the majority in the organ in question at the given moment ... [Fundamental changes from the conceptions believed to have been in the minds of the authors of the Charter] may be defended as reflecting political realities and the real nature of the process of interpreting the constituent instrument of an animated international organization."[118] [Italics ours]

We do not contend that the previous conclusion is desirable.[119] To the contrary, it is a matter of *raison-d'être* for the constituent instruments which provide for the legal foundations and frameworks for the structures and activities of international organizations that these instruments will be interpreted and applied in a more or less unified manner and not in accordance with political whims. Several proposals attempting re-vitalization of judicial procedures were made in the 1950s with respect to the interpretation of the U.N. Charter. It is notorious that international organizations have a multiplying tendency in terms of both finance and institution as organizations generally have.

We only assert that the previous conclusion is obtained from an examination of the relevant provisions and their actual operation, and that this conclusion means that *the practice of the organs will affect, and is necessary to be taken into consideration when one is to interpret, the*

---

[118] Rosenne, *supra* note 1 in Chap. 1, at 241-2.

[119] In this connection, Rosenne lamented as follows (Rosenne, *id.* at 244-5):

"The overall picture of interpretation of the Charter of the United Nations and of the constituent instruments of international organizations which do not contain special provisions, or where there are not established practices for interpretation, is an unhappy one. Provisions of the Charter itself, let alone the rules of procedure, are 'establish. d' or 'destablished' at the behest of the majority of the day or at the whim of a politically determined President confident that a challenge to any ruling of his will be rebuffed....

... The way in which the Charter of the United Nations and many other comparable constituent instruments deal with interpretation has the effect of excluding two of the most essential features of interpretation, namely consistency and predictability. *A constituent instrument which deliberately excludes or minimizes the role of these factors cannot, in terms of legal science, be equated with an international agreement for which some measure of control over the interpretative process to ensure consistency of application, such as a treaty, is inherent in the nature of things.*" [Italics ours]

meaning of provisions in the constituent instruments. It might be a trite saying, but still an important point in the present context, that an interpretation based upon the text of constituent instruments could be different from that given to it in their actual operation. In the light of the fact that the practice developed by organs not subject to judicial control in the interpretation will, in most cases, be directed to *the effective performance of the purposes and functions of the organizations* rather than to strict conformity with the constituent instruments, the previous conclusion indicates that *the purpose-oriented practice of the organs will bring an evolutionary tendency into the interpretation of the constituent instruments.*

Chapter Five

The Emerging Doctrine
of
Interpretation of Constituent Instruments
as
the Constitutions
of International Organizations

Section 1 Constituent Instruments as the Constitutions of International Organizations

(1) The Concept of Constitutions

1. On a formal level, constituent instruments are agreements (treaties). Constituent instruments come into existence by being negotiated, signed, and ratified by States in the same manner as ordinary treaties. Constituent instruments are, therefore, treaties from the viewpoint of formal sources of international law. This means that constituent instruments are, in principle, governed by the law of treaties.[1]

2. On a substantive level, the constituent instruments of international organizations contain their *constitutions defined as those provisions that provide for the legal foundations and frameworks for the structures and activities of international organizations.* Among the various provisions, a distinction can be drawn between organizational provisions which "essentially relate, as their name implies, to the structure and operation of the institution" and substantive provisions which "are independent, in the sense that they would have a legal content even if the organization did not exist (albeit that the organization may have an important role to play in securing their observance)."[2]

According to the above definition of constitutions, *organizational provisions in the constituent instruments are certainly their core provisions as the constitutions of international organizations.* But it must also be pointed out that "not all provisions contained in these treaties are constitutional in nature, nor need all constitutional rules relating to an international institution be contained in such a document."[3]

The question whether, among the various provisions in the constituent instruments, only organizational provisions are constitutional or some of the substantive provisions having a close relationship with the organizations are also constitutional is a difficult one. The answer would depend upon the exact meaning given to the term "constitutions." In our study, we are attempting to clarify the interpretative framework of the constituent instruments of international organizations characterized as their constitutions from the viewpoint of "caractère constitutionnel (constitutional nature)." Consequently, the answer could be given only in the manner relative to what this constitutional nature is and whether a provision concerned has such a nature. It would be better, therefore, to reserve the possibility that some of the substantive provisions could be constitutional.

---

[1] The relevant provision, in this connection, in the Vienna Convention on the Law of Treaties is Article 5 (cited later in the text of Chap. 5, Sec. 2, (3)). The point of this article is the content of "relevant rules of the organization." It is only outside the content and scope reserved by the relevant rules of the organization that the constituent instrument is governed by this Convention on the law of treaties.

[2] Mendelson, 'Reservations to the Constitutions of International Organizations', 45 *Brit. Y. B. Int'l L.* 137, 145-6 (1971).

[3] Hahn, 'Constitutional Limitations in the Law of the European Organisations', 108 *Recueil des cours* 196 (1963).

(2) The "Caractère Constitutionnel (Constitutional Nature)" of Constituent Instruments

The task of constituent instruments as the constitutions of international organizations is to provide for the legal foundations and frameworks for their structures and activities. Various characteristics have been pointed out as the constitutional nature possessed by constituent instruments.[4] *The core of the constitutional nature of constituent instruments, however, is the fact that constituent instruments provide the legal foundations and framework for the structures and activities of international organizations on the basis of their evolutionary and teleological interpretations so that, despite changing international relations, international organizations can continue to function efficiently and perform effectively their given purposes and functions.* International organizations have been created because their purposes and functions cannot be achieved by the creation of simple norms of conduct by means of treaties, including multilateral law-making treaties. Their purposes and functions can be achieved only by the permanent operation of organizational entities. This implies that constituent instruments will always need to be adapted to the changing circumstances for the purposes of the efficient functioning and effective activities of international organizations.[5] Simon pointed out, quite accurately, that it is

---

[4] Monaco, for example, points out the following characteristics possessed by the constituent instruments as being of a constitutional nature: (1) Unlimited Continuity: Their objectives pursued are not only of continual nature, but are also able to be attained only by means of a common action carried on for an indefinite period of time; (2) The Necessity and Capacity of Adaptation: The unlimited continuity exposes constituent instruments to the erosive factors accompanying the lapse of time during which the constituent instruments are intended to be applied, thus subjecting them to the necessity of adaptation to an evolution of circumstances; (3) The Necessity of Uniform Interpretation: The organs of international organizations as well as the contracting States interpret and apply, and at the same time are obliged to respect their constituent instruments; here it is necessary to establish a uniform interpretation; (4) The Interpretation Method: One must reconcile the conventional origin of international organizations with their irresistible institutional tendency and, as a result, make reference to their purposes; (5) Their Superior Position: Constituent instruments tend to have a superior position to other treaties as is exemplified by Article 20 of the Pact of the League of Nations and Article 103 of the Charter of the United Nations. Monaco, *supra* note 24 in Chap. 1. *See also* the bibliography mentioned in *supra* note 32 in Chap. 1.

[5] It is submitted that this point of the core of the constitutional nature of constituent instruments is generally supported by the scholars mentioned in note 1, except Skubiszewski who is more cautious and says (Skubiszewski, *supra* note 1 in Chap. 1, at 892-3):

> "[The similarities to the national constitutions] do not suffice to make it possible to approach the interpretation of the Charter along the lines and according to the patterns of national constitutions. The Charter remains a treaty concluded by States, and what pertains to its interpretation is governed by the law of treaties, unless the Charter itself lays down rules that deviate from that law. Analogies ... call for great caution. The United Nations is composed of States which represent various views on the function of the constitution in their national spheres, in particular the adaptation, through interpretation, of the constitutional framework to the changing circumstances and exigencies of life.... The meaning of the word 'constitution' changes when transposed from the domestic to the international scene; it does not automatically carry with it the introduction of domestic patterns into the interpretation of the law of international organization."

It is the argument of the present author that practice of States, international organizations and the Court is gradually moving away from the very conservative and State-centric position of Skubiszewski, which is quite similar to that of Tunkin referred to in the text, and that it is now necessary to modify the interpretative framework of constituent instruments so that the dynamic operations of international organizations could be fully explained and

the evolutionary nature of constituent instruments which determines most clearly the irreducible specificity of constituent instruments and that the function of interpretation is to promote the institutional growth inscribed in the very logic of the organization.[6]

(3) The Interpretative Framework of Constituent Instruments as the Constitutions of International Organizations

1.　Constituent instruments are, on a formal level, to be understood as treaties and, therefore, to be interpreted within the interpretative framework regulated by the law of treaties as codified by the Vienna Convention on the Law of Treaties (Articles 31 and 32). On the other hand, constituent instruments are, on a substantive level, the constitutions of international organizations and, therefore, subject to the influences of their dynamism. These two different interpretative frameworks could be contrasted in the following way.

2.　Within the interpretative framework as treaties, the interpretation of constituent instruments understood as treaties has two characteristics. First, constituent instruments are interpreted as treaties within the textual framework embodied by Articles 31 and 32. Here the teleological approach can be used only within the four corners of the text. Secondly, constituent instruments interpreted in such a manner will provide the foundations of, and control the structures and activities of, international organizations. This is a one-way relationship from the constituent instruments toward the international organizations.

3.　Within the interpretative framework as the constitutions of international organizations, the interpretation of constituent instruments understood as constitutions has two characteristics in contrast to those mentioned above. First, taking into consideration the structures and activities of international organizations understood as autonomous and dynamic entities of international law, *constituent instruments are interpreted within the teleological framework so that their efficient functioning and effective activities can be assured and promoted.* Here *paramount consideration is given to the "efficiency" and "effectiveness" of international organizations to the extent that the teleological reasoning deviates from the textual interpretative framework in the law of treaties.* It will have the harmful effect of destroying the regulating functions for legal stability which the textual interpretative framework now possesses for ordinary treaties to pretend that those teleological interpretations are still within the textual framework. We should frankly admit that those teleological interpretations deviate quantitatively from the framework of "interpretation" and rather belong to the realm of "modification."

　　Secondly, there is a two-way relationship between the constituent instruments and the international organizations. On the one hand, the meanings of constituent instru-

---

controlled within it, although he does not intend to underestimate the fundamental role and importance of member States, as has been clearly indicated by the recent "crises" in several international organizations.

[6] Simon, *supra* note 1 in Chap. 1, at 157-66. Despite his excellent analysis on the constitutional nature of constituent instruments based upon various doctrines, Simon attempted to construct a sweeping doctrine which he calls "interprétation systématique." For a brief introduction of it, *see* my article, *supra* note 1 in Chap. 1, at 9-10.

ments interpreted in such a teleological manner will certainly provide the foundations of, and control the structures and activities of, international organizations. On the other hand, however, *the practice of international organizations affects, in feedback, the interpretations of constituent instruments, thus giving them an evolutionary nature*. The practice of international organizations (particularly that of political organs) which is based upon their constituent instruments will, to the contrary, have a legal value to be taken into consideration in their very interpretations. *"Subsequent practice" of the organs of international organizations is given the legal value which deviates qualitatively from the textual interpretative framework in the law of treaties*. On the one hand, "subsequent practice" admitted in the law of treaties is the one which is clearly based upon the understanding of all the parties; on the other hand, however, in the operation of constituent instruments, weight is given not to the consent of all the member States but to the practice (activities) of international organizations. And this unilateral practice of international organizations will gradually be given the status of criterion in the evolutionary interpretation of their constituent instruments and later form "the rules of the organization" considered to be part of the constitutions. It will also have the harmful effect of bringing "modification" into the framework of "interpretation" and destroying the regulating functions for legal stability which the interpretative framework now possesses for ordinary treaties to pretend that such a legal value given to the practice of the organs of international organizations is the same as that admitted in the law of treaties.

4.   The constitutional nature of constituent instruments will be realized by means of a mechanism which combines the two characteristics explained above. In other words, the doctrine of constituent instruments as the constitutions of international organizations will, by means of teleological and evolutionary interpretations derived from the two characteristics, gradually actualize the dynamism inherent in international organizations.

Section 2   The Legal Significance of the Practice of International Organizations

The interpretative framework of constituent instruments as the constitutions of international organizations recognizes that subsequent practice of their organs affects, in feedback, the interpretation of their constituent instruments, and has a legal value to be taken into consideration in their interpretation. The legal value given to the subsequent practice of the organs is qualitatively different from that given to the subsequent practice of State parties in the interpretative framework in the law of treaties analyzed above. The practice of the organs is given a legal value which is more than an auxiliary means in the interpretation, and is not necessarily confined to those which signify the implied consent of all the State parties of the constituent instruments.

In this part, we will first examine to what extent this phenomenon can be explained under general international law. Secondly, we will analyze some cases in which the status of criterion in the interpretation of constituent instruments has been given to the practice of the organs. Thirdly, we will see some law-making treaties in which the practice of the organs forms "the rules of the organization" considered to be part of the constitution. Finally, procedural rules of the interpretation provided in constituent instruments will be examined to see what role the practice of the organs could actually have in the determination of their meanings.

(1) Analysis under General International Law

1.   In some economic international organizations, as was analyzed in Chapter Four, Section 4, the competence of authoritative interpretation of their constituent instruments is expressly given to the internal political organs. In these cases, therefore, the mechanism that the practice of the organs would determine the meaning of their constituent instruments is furnished in advance. In other words, it is legally recognized by the State members that the practice of the organs affects their constituent instruments.

2.   The problem remains for cases where, as is in most international organizations, the competence of authoritative interpretation is not given to an internal organ political or judicial, and the practice of the organs does not constitute an implied agreement or form a customary international law within international organizations. Some useful elements, although insufficient, could be suggested in these cases.

The first point is *the presumption of validity of the practice (resolutions) of the organs.* The Court, in the *Certain Expenses* case and in the *Namibia* case, stated as follows:

"[W]hen the Organization takes action which warrants the assertion that it was appropriate for the fulfillment of one of the stated purposes of the Organization, the presumption is that such action is not *ultra vires* the Organization."[7]

"A resolution of a properly constituted organ of the United Nations which is passed in accordance with that organ's rules of procedure, and is declared by its President to have been so passed, must be presumed to have been validly adopted."[8]

The legal foundation for this position might not be clear and rather only "purely jurisprudential."[9] In the activities of international organizations, however, this presumption of validity will play a great role in their smooth operation.

The second point is *the relevance of judicial review.* Where there is a compulsory and exclusive machinery of review, the practice of the organs should be treated as legal by all the

---

[7]   Advisory Opinion on Certain Expenses of the United Nations (Article 17, Paragraph 2, of the Charter), [1962] I. C. J. 168.

[8]   Advisory Opinion on Legal Consequences for States of the Continued Presence of South Africa in Namibia (South West Africa) Notwithstanding Security Council Resolution 276 (1970), [1971] I. C. J. 22.

[9]   Thierry, 'Les résolution des organes internationaux dans la jurisprudence de la Cour internationale de Justice', 167 *Recueil des cours* 385, 422 (1980).

member States.[10] Because any State which considers otherwise is competent to have recourse to the court, it is reasonable to regard non-recourse as recognition of the validity of the practice concerned. Where there is no such machinery, however, there will remain the above-mentioned presumption of validity.

The third point is *acquiescence, estoppel and lapse of time*.[11] These are not the same concepts, but they all work in such a way as to prevent dissenting member States from submitting objections to the validity of the practice concerned. Acquiescence and lapse of time, in particular, would play a major role in those cases where controversies are not serious enough to cause a dispute among member States.

By means of these factors, such practice of the organs as not to constitute an agreement or a customary rule among the member States will have certain legal significance in the determination of meanings of constituent instruments. This means, on the contrary, that the problem still remains in those cases where the practice is adopted against some member States which submit objections and protest if not withdraw from the organization.

(2) The Practice of the Organs of International Organizations as a Criterion in the Interpretation of their Constituent Instruments[12]

1.   The growing value attached to the actual practice of the organs of international organizations was one of the points at issue in the *Certain Expenses* case. In this Advisory Opinion, the majority opinion relied upon the practice of the United Nations in interpreting such concepts as "budget," "expenses" and "action."[13] Judge Spender, in his separate opinion, criticized

---

[10] Lauterpacht, 'The Legal Effect of Illegal Acts of International Organizations', in *Cambridge Essays in International Law: Essays in Honour of Lord McNair* 88, 115 (1965).

[11] *Id.* at 117-20.

[12] *See* generally Lauterpacht, 'The Development of the Law of International Organization by the Decisions of International Tribunals', 152 *Recueil des cours* 379 (1976); Reuter, 'Quelques réflexions sur la notion de 'pratique internationale,' spécialement en matière d'organisations internationales, in *Studi in Onore di Giuseppe Sperduti* 187 (1984); Abou-El-Wafa, 'La pratique ultérieure des organisations internationales', 45 *Revue Egyptienne de Droit International* 29 (1989).

[13] According to the summary of Lauterpacht (*id.* at 451-52), the Court referred to the practice of the United Nations in the following seven contexts.

(1) The practice of the Organization was entirely consistent with the plain meaning of the word "budget" as used in the Charter in a sense unqualified by limiting adjectives;

(2) There was no basis for challenging the legality of the settled practice of including the expenses of functions entrusted to the Secretary-General by the various organs of the United Nations in the budgetary amounts apportioned by the General Assembly among the members of the United nations;

(3) The practice of the Organization bears out the interpretation of the word "action" in Article 11 (2) of the Charter as authorizing the General Assembly to make recommendations in specific cases for the maintenance of international peace and security;

(4) The practice of the Organization, in the form of concurrence by the General Assembly in the description of the functions of UNEF outlined by the Secretary-General, provided no evidence that the Force was to be used for purposes of enforcement action under Chapter VII of the Charter;

(5) The practice of the General Assembly from year to year had been to treat the expenses of UNEF as expenses

this reference:

> "[I]t is not possible to equate 'subsequent conduct' with the practice of an organ of the United Nations. Not only is such an organ not a party to the Charter but the inescapable reality is that both the General Assembly and the Security Council are but the mechanisms through which the Members of the United Nations express their views and act. *The fact that they act through such an organ, where a majority rule prevails and so determines the practice, cannot, it seems to me, give any greater probative value to the practice established within that organ than it would have as conduct of the Members that comprise the majority if pursued outside of that organ.*"[14] [Italics ours]

Judge Spender analyzed some relevant cases and elaborated his position on this problem of "Practice within the United Nations --- Its effect on or value as a criterion of interpretation" in

---

of the Organization within the meaning of Article 17 (2) of the Charter;

(6) "[I]n the light of ... [the] record of reiterated consideration, confirmation, approval and ratification by the Security Council and by the General Assembly of the actions of the Secretary-General in implementing the resolution of [the Security Council of] July 14, 1960 [relating to United Nations operation in the Congo], it is impossible to reach the conclusion that the operations in question usurped or impinged upon the prerogatives conferred by the Charter on the Security Council";

(7) "[T]he General Assembly has twice decided that even though certain expenses are 'extraordinary' and 'essentially different' from those under the 'regular budget', they are none the less 'expenses of the Organization' to be apportioned in accordance with the power granted to the General Assembly by Article 17, paragraph 2."

[14] *Certain Expenses* case, *supra* note 7, at 192.

Judge Spender recognized that it is a general principle of international law that the subsequent conduct of the parties to a bilateral --- or a multilateral --- instrument may throw light on the intention of the parties at the time the instrument was entered into and thus may provide a legitimate criterion of interpretation. However, he pointed out, an element of artificiality existing in this principle is greatly magnified when the principle is sought to be extended from the field of bilateral instruments to that of multilateral instruments of an organic character and where the practice (or subsequent conduct) relied upon is that, not of the parties to the instrument, but of an organ created thereunder. Judge Spender continued as follows (*id.* at 189-92):

> "I find difficulty in accepting the proposition that a practice pursued by an *organ* of the United Nations may be equated with the subsequent conduct of *parties* to a bilateral agreement and thus afford evidence of intention of the parties to the Charter (who have constantly been added to since it came into force) and in that way or otherwise provide a criterion of interpretation. Nor can I agree with a view sometimes advanced that a common practice pursued by an organ of the United Nations, though *ultra vires* and in point of fact having the result of amending the Charter, may nonetheless be effective as a criterion of interpretation....
>
> In the case of multilateral treaties the admissibility and value as evidence of subsequent conduct of one or more parties thereto encounter particular difficulties.... *If ... only one or some but not all of [the parties] by subsequent conduct interpret the text in a certain manner, that conduct stands upon the same footing as the unilateral conduct of one party to a bilateral treaty. The conduct of such one or more could not of itself have any probative value or provide a criterion for judicial interpretation....*
>
> However this may be, it is not evident on what ground *a practice consistently followed by a majority of Member States not in fact accepted by other Member States* could provide any criterion of interpretation which the Court could properly take into consideration in the discharge of its judicial function. The conduct of the majority in following the practice may be evidence against them and against those who in fact accept the practice as correctly interpreting a Charter provision, but could not, it seems to me, afford any in their favor to support an interpretation which by majority they have been able to assert." [Italics mostly ours]

the following way.

"An organ of the United Nations, whether it be the General Assembly, the Security Council, the Economic and Social Council, the Secretariat or its subsidiary organs, has in practice to interpret its authority in order that it may effectively function. So, throughout the world, have countless governmental and administrative organs and officials to interpret theirs. The General Assembly may thus in practice, by majority vote, interpret Charter provisions as giving it authority to pursue a certain course of action. It may continue to give the same interpretation to these Charter provisions in similar or different situations as they arise. In so doing action taken by it may be extended to cover circumstances and situations which had never contemplated by those who framed the Charter. But this would not ... necessarily involve any departure from the terms of the Charter

On the other hand, the General Assembly may in practice construe its authority beyond that conferred upon it, wither expressly or impliedly, by the Charter. It may, for example, interpret its powers to permit it to enter a field prohibited to it under the Charter or in disregard of the procedure prescribed in the Charter. Action taken by the General Assembly (or other organs) may accordingly on occasions be beyond power.

The Charter establishes an Organization. The Organization must function through its constituted organs. *The functions and authorities of those organs are set out in the Charter. However the Charter is otherwise described the essential fact is that it is a multilateral treaty, It cannot be altered at the will of the majority of the Member States, no matter how often that will is expressed or asserted against a protesting minority and no matter how large be the majority of Member States which assert its will in this manner or how small the minority....*

The question of constitutionality of action taken by the General Assembly or the Security Council will rarely call for consideration except within the United Nations itself, where a majority rule prevails. In practice this may enable action to be taken which is beyond power. *When, however, the Court is called upon to pronounce upon a question whether certain authority exercised by an organ of the Organization is within the power of that organ, only legal considerations may be invoked and de facto extension of the Charter must b[e] disregarded.*" [Italics ours]

2. E. Lauterpacht analyzed in depth the jurisprudence of the Court on this point. Based upon an exhaustive analysis of the jurisprudence,[15] Lauterpacht reached the following conclusion:

---

[15] Lauterpacht, *supra* note 12, at 447-65. The relevant parts of the jurisprudence of the Court which Lauterpacht mentioned are, in addition to some statements in the *Certain Expenses* case (1962) referred to in the text, and several other less important cases omitted here, the following.

(1) *Conditions of Admission* case, [1948] I. C. J. 63. While pointing out that because the text was sufficiently clear there was no reason to resort to preparatory work, the Court, nevertheless, added as follows: "The Court furthermore observes that Rule 60 of the Provisional Rules of Procedure of the Security Council is based on this interpretation."

"It is probably necessary to recognize that recourse to the practice of international organizations now stands on *an independent legal basis*; that is to say, that there exists *a specific rule of the law of international organization* to the effect that recourse to such practice is admissible and that States, on joining international organizations, impliedly accept the permissibility of constitutional development in this manner."[16] [Italics ours]

---

(2) *Reparation* case, [1949] I. C. J. 179. In connection with the question of whether the United Nations possesses international personality, the Court stated as follows: "Practice --- in particular the conclusion of conventions to which the Organization is a party --- has confirmed this character of the Organization, which occupies a position in certain respects in detachment from its Members.... The 'Convention on the Privileges and Immunities of the United Nations' of 1946 creates rights and duties between each of the signatories and the Organization. It is difficult to see how such a convention could operate except upon the international plane and as between parties possessing international personality."

(3) *Competence of the General Assembly* case, [1950] I. C. J. 9. After reaching a conclusion by a textual approach, the Court added as follows: "The Organs to which Article 4 entrusts the judgment of the Organization in matters of admission have consistently interpreted the text in the sense that the General Assembly can decide to admit only on the basis of a recommendation of the Security Council. In particular, the Rules of Procedure of the General Assembly provide for consideration of [an application and the decision upon it] only 'if the Security Council recommends the applicant State for membership' (Article 125). The Rules merely state that if the Security Council has not recommended the admission, the General Assembly may send back the application to the Security Council for further consideration (Article 126). This last step has been taken several times...."

(4) *Judgment of the ILO Administrative Tribunal* case, [1956] I. C. J. 91. The Court acknowledged the existence of a practice related to the employment of staff as follows: "In the practice of Unesco --- as well as in the practice of the United Nations and of the Specialized Agencies --- fixed-term contracts are not like an ordinary fixed-term contract between a private employer and a private employee.... The fact is that there has developed in this matter a body of practice to the effect that holders of fixed-term contracts, although not assimilated to holders of permanent or indeterminate contracts, have often been treated as entitled to be considered for continued employment, consistently with the requirements and the general good of the organization, in a manner transcending the strict wording of the contract. [Reference was made to a document entitled 'Personnel Recruitment Standards and Methods' and a statement upon it by the Director-General.] The practice as here surveyed is a relevant factor in the interpretation of the contracts in question. It lends force to the view that ...."

(5) *IMCO* case, [1960] I. C. J. 167-70. As a ground for adopting the registered tonnage of a flag State as a test for determining the respective size of ship-owning nations, the Court, firstly, examined Article 60 (entry into force of the Convention) and Article 17 (c) (election of two members of the Council by the Assembly) by stating as follows: "An examination of certain Articles of the Convention and the actual practice which was followed in giving effect to them throws some light on the Court's consideration of the question." Secondly, the Court referred to such conventions as the Load Line Convention of 1930 by stating as follows: "Moreover, the test of registered tonnage is that which is most consonant with international practice and with maritime usage."

(6) *Namibia* case, [1971] I. C. J. 22. In connection with Article 27, paragraph 3, of the Charter, the Court stated as follows: "[T]he proceedings of the Security Council extending over a long period supply abundant evidence that presidential rulings and the positions taken by members of the Council, in particular its permanent members, have consistently and uniformly interpreted the practice of voluntary abstention by a permanent member as not constituting a bar to the adoption of resolutions. By abstaining, a member does not signify its objection to the approval of what is being proposed; in order to prevent the adoption of a resolution requiring unanimity of the permanent members, a permanent member has only to cast a negative vote. This procedure followed by the Security Council, which has continued unchanged after the amendment in 1965 of Article 27 of the Charter, has been generally accepted by Members of the United Nations and evidences a general practice of that Organization."

[16] Lauterpacht, *id.* at 460 (1976).

237

It is said that this proposition rests on two grounds. The first is the fact that the courts and the organizations themselves accept practice in this way. The second ground is that consideration of the traditional bases such as subsequent practice, particular modes of change (agreement, acquiescence and estoppel) and general modes of change (development of a customary law of the organization) on which reference to such practice might otherwise be justified produces no satisfactory answer. This being so, Lauterpacht says, one arrives in a situation in which one must conclude either --- as does Judge Spender --- that there is no legal basis for reference to the practice of organs of an organization; or that such reference rests on an independent legal basis.[17]

3.   This question, in our opinion, must be approached with caution by examining the nature of the practice concerned. First, what is the nature of the competence which the organ concerned has with regard to the content of the practice concerned. Secondly, *whether the practice concerned is a collective practice of the organ itself or can be reduced to the sum of individual practice of the member States of the organ.*

With respect to the first point, it is widely recognized that resolutions concerned with the internal working of international organizations can have legally binding or other full legal effects.[18] Therefore, as far as concerning the sphere of internal working, the legal value attached to the practice of the organs could mostly be based upon the competence of the organs to make decisions of legally binding or other full legal effects.

With respect to the second point,[19] the examples of the jurisprudence concerned require a careful examination.

In some cases, the Court seems to emphasize the aspect of *individual practice of the member States.* In the relevant part of the *Namibia* case, the Court stated that members of the Council, in particular its permanent members, "have consistently and uniformly interpreted ..." and that "[t]his procedure ... has been generally accepted by Members of the United Nations and evidences a general practice of that Organization." These expressions would suggest that *the*

---

[17] *Id.* at 460-4.

[18] Virally, 'La valeur juridique des recommandations des organisations internationales', 2 *A. F. D. I.* 66, 70-7 (1956); Skubiszewski, 'Enactment of Law by International Organizations', 41 *Brit Y. B. Int'l L.* 198, 226-32 (1965-66); di Qual, *Les effets des résolutions des Nations Unies* 62-70 (1967); J. Castañeda, *Legal Effects of United Nations Resolutions* 22-69, esp. 30-48 (A. Amoia trans. 1969). *See also* generally B. Sloan, *United Nations General Assembly Resolutions in Our Changing World* (1991).

[19] In this connection, Charpentier admits the formation of a customary rule in the institutional framework which is different from that of an interstate customary rule. Because States intervene here, says Charpentier, as component of the competent organ and not as subjects of interstate juridical order, it would be to misunderstand the logic of the organization to regard the custom formed by the precedents coming from organs of the organization as being interstate. However, he also admits that, so far as the customary rule formed in such a manner is in contradiction with the constituent instrument, the consent of the member States must be sought, although the scope of them will be loosened to that of Article 108 of the Charter. Charpentier, 'Tendances de l'élaboration du droit international public coutumier', in *L'élaboration du droit international public* 105, 119-23 (1975). *See also* Ferrari Bravo, 'Méthodes de recherche de la coutume internationale dans la pratique des États', 192 *Recueil des cours* 233, 297-9 (1985).

Court, in recognizing the existence of a customary rule in the Organization, based its finding upon the individual practice of member States of the United Nations, in particular the permanent members of the Council rather than upon the practice of the Council as a collective practice of an organ.[20]

Even in the *Certain Expenses* case, there are certain cases where *the distinction is not clear between the collective practice of an organ and the individual practice of member States.* As is shown by such expressions as the Financial Regulations of the United Nations "adopted by unanimous vote," a statement "adopted without opposition," a resolution "adopted without a dissenting vote" and a description of the functions of UNEF concurred in by the General Assembly "without a dissenting vote," the Court seems to emphasize the support of all the member States as far as possible.

On the other hand, there are certainly *other cases where it is impossible to reduce the practice of the organs to that of member States.* In such cases as adoption of rules of procedure, conclusion of conventions by the United Nations, decisions by the organs in matters of admission, a document submitted under the authority of, and a statement made by the Director-General with respect to the contract of employment, election of two Council members by the Assembly upon registered tonnage and adoption of the budget including various items and expenses, these various practices could be only regarded as a collective practice of the organs.

It is important in this connection, however, that *most of these practices are concerned with the internal working of the organizations concerned.* In the last analysis, the principal cases among these are those in the *Certain Expenses* case.[21] This is why Judge Spender criticized the

---

[20] *See also* Reuter, *supra* note 12, at 203 (1984).

[21] How should one appreciate the practice of the organs in the *Certain Expenses* case? The majority opinion is presumed to have considered that the United Nations has, by Article 17 of the Charter, the competence to assign the expenses that it regards to be those of the U.N. to the member States. With regard to the scope of "expenses" as well, it seems to have recognized the competence of the General Assembly for their decision because it seems to have judged the legality of PKO (and of their expenses) in the light of the will of the General Assembly. The following criticism will be useful here (Gross, *supra* note 66, at 391-2).

"In relying on the 'practice' of the Assembly the Court assumed that both budget and expenses can be defined generally and ad hoc by a two-thirds majority of the Assembly with binding effect for all Members. The Assembly could thus require all Members to pay for the execution of resolutions which, as was recognized by the Court, were themselves lacking binding force ....

[However i]t is the consensus of the membership which determines what is the budget and what are the expenses of a particular organization at any given time, and not the majority vote of a representative body."

The situation developed after this Advisory Opinion in the following way. Those States which had refused the assignment of the expenses concerned by the Assembly refused to accept the Advisory Opinion and continued to refuse the payment. While, as a result, the application of sanction provided in Article 19 became possible, the Assembly took an exceptional step of deciding not to take votes in the 19th session from the political consideration. The problem was "solved" only when, in the Special Committee on Peace-keeping Operations, an agreement was reached that the question of the applicability of Article 19 would not be raised with regard to the UNEF and the ONUC, and others. This series of developments seems to indicate that the criticism of Gross cannot be easily rejected. *See* United Nations, *Repertory of Practice of United Nations Organs, Supplement No. 3, Volume 1, Articles 1-22 of the Charter* 395-9 (1972). *See*

majority opinion so severely.

If it is accepted that the legal value, as a criterion in the interpretation of constituent instruments, is given to the collective practice of the organs in the sphere outside the internal working of the organizations, as seems to be the case in the *Certain Expenses* case, this will lead to *the existence of a customary rule inherent to international organizations, which recognizes a constitutional development in such a manner*. Although this has become a central issue in the Court, the Court and the organizations themselves seem to accept this manner of reasoning.

(3) The Evolutionary Practice of International Organizations Reflected in Some Law-Making Treaties --- With Particular Reference to the Notion "Relevant Rules of the Organization"

1. It has been gradually recognized in the law-making treaties with regard to international organizations that subsequent practice of the organs of international organizations could affect, in feedback, the interpretation of their constituent instruments, and has a legal value to be taken into consideration in their interpretation. Here, it is not merely a constituent instrument which constitutes the legal foundation of an international organization, but also the "constitution" comprising the rules in force in the organization. And "relevant rules of the organization" which form part of the constitution have been considered to include an evolutionary practice of the international organization.[22]

2. The Vienna Convention on the Law of Treaties (1969) contains Article 5 (Treaties constituting international organizations and treaties adopted within an international organization) which provides as follows:

> "The present Convention applies to any treaty which is the constituent instrument of an international organization and to any treaty adopted within an international organization without prejudice to any relevant rules of the organization."

The commentary attached to this article in the final draft articles adopted by the International Law Commission succinctly explains the *raison-d'être* of this article as follows:

> "The draft articles, as provisionally adopted ..., contained a number of specific reservations with regard to the application of the established rules of an international organization.... [The Commission considered that insertion of a general reservation provision of the same sense in the present place] was desirable in case the possible impact of rules of international organizations in any particular context of the law of treaties should have been inadvertently

---

also Castañeda, *supra* note 97, at 48; T. M. Franck, *Nation Against Nation* 259 (1985). *But see* Zoller, 'The 'Corporate Will' of the United Nations and the Right of the Minority', 81 *Am. J. Int'l L.* 610, 615-20 (1987).

[22] *See*, for details of this sub-section, Sato, 'Status of Constituent Instruments of International Organizations in the Law of Treaties --- With Particular Reference to the Notion 'Relevant Rules of the Organization" , 16 *Hitotsubashi J. L. & Pol.* 25 (1988).

overlooked."[23]

In the Vienna diplomatic conference, it was emphasized by the observers of some international organizations that "relevant rules" should include "the practice" or "the established practices." Waldock (Expert Consultant), in a related discussion, stated that the Commission had considered that *the words "any relevant rules" were intended to include both rules laid down in the constituent instrument and rules established in the practice of the organization as binding.*[24] This position was accepted by the conference.

3.   The Vienna Convention on the Representation of States in their Relationship with International Organizations of a Universal Character (1975) contains Article 3 (Relationship between the present articles and the relevant rules of international organizations) which provides as follows:

"The application of the present articles is without prejudice to any relevant rules of the organization."

In the Vienna diplomatic conference, El-Erian (Expert Consultant) explained the *raison d'être* of this article by stating that the Commission was concerned *not to hamper in any way the development of their own rules by international organizations, bearing in mind that the law of international organizations was in constant evolution.*[25] Furthermore, at the final stage of the conference, it was decided that an express definition should be given to the term "rules of the Organization." Article 1, (34) of the Convention provides as follows:

"[R]ules of the Organization" means, in particular, the constituent instruments, relevant decisions and resolutions, and established practice of the Organization."

4.   The Vienna Convention on the Law of Treaties between States and International Organizations or between International Organizations (1986)[26] contains Article 6 (Capacity of

---

[23]   Report on the International Law Commission to the General Assembly, U.N.Doc. A/6309/Rev.1., [1966] 2 *Y. B. Int'l L. Comm'n* 169, 191.

[24]   Summary Records of the 10th meeting, at 57, para. 40, in *United Nations Conference on The Law of Treaties, Official Records, First Session, 1968.*

[25]   Summary Records of the 3d meeting, at 81, para. 62, in 1 *United Nations Conference on The Representation of States in their Relations with International Organizations, Official Records, 1976.*

[26]   Some of the bibliography concerning this convention are the following: Zemanek, 'The United Nations Conference on the Law of Treaties Between States and International Organizations or Between International Organizations: The unrecorded history of the "general agreement"', in *Völkerrecht, Recht der Internationalen Organisationen, Weltwirtschaftsrecht, Festschrift für Ignas Seidl-Hohenveldern* 665 (K.-H. Böckstiegel, H.-E. Folz, J. M. Mössner, K. Zemanek eds. 1988); Reuter, 'La conference de Vienne sur les traités des organisations internationales et la sécurité des engagements conventionnels', in *Du droit international au droit l'integration, Liber amicorum Pierre Pescatore* 545 (F. Capotorti, C.-D. Ehlermann, J. Frowein, F. Jacobs, R. Joliet, T. Koopmans, R. Kovar eds. 1987); Riphagen, 'The Second Round of Treaty Law', *id.* at 565; Morgenstern, 'The Convention on the Law of Treaties between States and International Organizations or between International Organizations', in *International Law at a Time of Perplexity, Essays in Honour of Shabtai Rosenne* 435 (Y. Dinstein & M. Tabory eds. 1989); do Nascimento e Silva, 'The 1969 and the 1986 Conventions on the Law of Treaties: A Comparison', *id.* at 461.

international organizations to conclude treaties) which provides as follows:

"The capacity of an international organization to conclude treaties is governed by the rules of that organization."

The commentary attached to this article in the final draft articles explains the *raison-d'être* of this article as follows:

"It should be clearly understood that *the question how far practice can play a creative part, particularly in the matter of international organization's capacity to conclude treaties, cannot be answered uniformly for all international organizations.* This question, too, depends on the 'rules of the organization'.... [I]t must be admitted that international organizations differ greatly from one another as regards the part played by practice and the form which it takes, inter alia in the matter of their capacity to conclude international agreements.... For these reasons, practice as such was not specifically mentioned in article 6; practice finds its place in the development of each organization in and through the 'rules of the organization,' as defined in article 2, subparagraph 1 (j), and that place varies from one organization to another.

.... In matters such as the capacity to conclude treaties, which are governed by the rules of each organization, there can be no question of fixing those rules as they stand at the time when the codification undertaken becomes enforceable against each organization. *In reserving the practice of each organization in so far as it is recognized by the organization itself, what is reserved is not the practice established at the time of entry into force of the codification but the very faculty of modifying or supplementing the organization's rules by practice to the extent permitted by those rules.* Thus, without imposing on the organizations the constraint of a uniform rule which is ill-suited to them, article 6 recognizes the right of each of them to have its own legal image."[27]

The term "rules of the organization" was originally defined in Article 2, para. 1, (j) as follows; "'rules of the organization' means, in particular, the constituent instruments, relevant decisions and resolutions, and established practice of the organization." The commentary adds the following explanation concerning the significance of practice.

"[B]y referring to 'established' practice, the Commission seeks only to rule out uncertain or disputed practice; it is not its wish to freeze practice at a particular moment in an organization's history."[28]

In the Vienna diplomatic conference,[29] the conflict between the socialist countries which revealed their distrust of international organizations and the western countries led to a compromise

---

[27] Report of the International Law Commission on the Work of Its Thirty-Fourth Session (3 May-23 July 1982), U.N. Doc. A/37/10, [1982] 2-2 *Y. B. Int'l L. Comm'n* 1, 24.

[28] Id. at 21.

[29] *See* Vienna Convention on the Law of Treaties between States and International Organizations or between International Organizations, U.N.Doc. A/CONF. 129/15.

based upon two amendments: the insertion of the following statement in the preamble; and the addition, in the definition of rules of the organization" of Article 2, para. 1, (j), of "adopted in accordance with the constituent instruments" after "decisions and resolutions."[30]

"Recognizing that the practice of international organizations in concluding treaties with States or between themselves should be in accordance with their constituent instruments,".

5.   With respect to these conventions, two observations could be made. First, in drafting conventions regulating the status and activities of international organizations, the necessity has been consistently recognized that *the relevant rules of the organization should be taken into account* and that *they should prevail over the general rules to be adopted*. The *raison-d'être* of those provisions explained above was to safeguard the relevant rules of the organization and to avoid hampering the development of the rules by each organization, keeping in mind that the law of international organizations is in constant evolution.

Secondly, the focus in the present context is on whether *"relevant rules of the organization" can include practice in the process of being established, in other words the very faculty of supplementing the organization's rules by practice*. In contrast to the 1969 Convention and the 1975 Convention which do not seem to be clear on this point, the 1986 Convention could be considered to give a positive reply. The Commission made it clear that *it was not its wish to freeze practice at a particular moment in an organization's history*. This position seems to have been basically maintained in the diplomatic conference.

Section 3   In Search of the Theoretical Foundations of the Interpretative Framework as the Constitutions of International Organizations

The two characteristics explained in detail above which correspond to the teleological and evolutionary interpretations are important elements of the constitutional nature of constituent instruments. In advocating an emerging doctrine of the interpretative framework of constituent instruments as the constitutions of international organizations, the most important point is to clarify the *limit* of this framework within which this doctrine can be developed in accordance with the dynamism inherent in international organizations. Because the doctrine will set the constituent instruments free from the regulating restrictions of the interpretative framework in the law of treaties, it is indispensable to present an alternative framework which will put the constituent instruments under its clear control.

We will, in the first section, seek the theoretical foundations of this doctrine in the four

---

[30] Yachi, 'United Nations Conference on the Law of Treaties between States and International Organizations or between International Organizations' [in Japanese], 85 *Kokusaiho Gaiko Zassi (The Journal of International Law and Diplomacy)* 374, 376 (1986).

theories which have been referred to by various scholars in this connection: (1) the theory of interpretation in the European Communities, (2) the theory of interpretation in the federal constitution of the U.S.A., (3) the theory of institution developed in France, and (4) the theory of inter-temporal law. Then, in the second section, we will present several important elements in clarifying the interpretative framework of the doctrine of constituent instruments as the constitutions of international organizations.

(1) The Theory of Interpretation in the European Communities

1. *Introduction:* In the interpretation of the constituent instruments of the European Communities (hereinafter cited as the EC) by the Court of Justice of the EC, the teleological and dynamic approach of interpretation has been, it is submitted, often used to promote the purpose of integration. It is generally understood that the EC is an organization promoting integration different from an ordinary organization promoting cooperation,[31] and this difference of structure is said to influence to a certain degree the methods of interpretation.[32] If so, the characteristics of constituent instruments as the constitutions might present themselves more clearly in the case of the EC.

2. *Factors for the Dynamism:* As Degan pointed out, the nature of the treaties interpreted and the nature of the court interpreting them seem to determine the methods used in their interpretation.[33] These two will be examined below.

The first is the nature of the constituent instruments of the EC. The constituent instruments of the EC are, on a formal level, inter-state treaties, but, on a substantial level, the constitutions of the EC, international organizations for integration. In analyzing the reasons why the objectives given the EC have become an extremely fertile directive of interpretation, Pescatore pointed out first, that their constituent instruments are entirely full of teleology, that is, they are entirely founded upon the notion of objectives to attain; secondly, that, on the level of the means of realization, the implementation of the objectives thus defined is entrusted to the institutions which operate in a large measure of independence and autonomy in the formation of their will. In his

---

[31] Virally, 'Definition', *supra* note 2 in Chap. 1, at 54.

[32] Ch. de Visscher, *Problèmes d'interprétation judiciaire en droit international public* 154 (1963).

For some useful bibliography with regard to the interpretation in the Court of Justice of the EC, *see* Monaco, 'Les principes d'interprétation suivis par la Cour de Justice des Communautés européennes', in *Mélanges offerts à Henri Rolin, Problèmes de droit des gens* 217 (1964); Chevallier, 'Methods and Reasoning of the European Court in Its Interpretation of Community Law', 1 *Comm'n Mkt L. Rev.* 21 (1964); Degan, 'Procédés d'interprétation tirés de la jurisprudence de la Cour de Justice des Communautés européennes', 2 *Revue trimestrielle de droit européen* 189 (1966); A. Green, *Political Integration by Jurisprudence* 416-33 (1969); Pescatore, 'Les objectifs de la Communauté européenne comme principes d'interprétation dans la jurisprudence de la Cour de Justice', 2 *Miscellanea W. J. Ganshof van der Meersch* 325 (1972); A. Bredimas, *Methods of Interpretation and Community Law* (1978).

[33] V. Degan, *L'interprétation des accords en droit international* 160-2 (1963). *See also* Degan, *supra* note 32, at 190-1.

opinion, the teleological method is particularly appropriate to the characteristics proper to the treaties instituting the EC.[34]

The second is the nature of the interpretative organs.   It is quite important, in this connection, that the competence of authoritative interpretation is exclusively given to the Court of Justice. By means of the preliminary rulings, the Court of Justice has a final and exclusive competence of interpretation and guarantees the uniformity of the EC's legal order. As a result, the Court of Justice is expected to exercise various functions such as those of an international tribunal, of a constitutional tribunal and of an administrative tribunal.[35]

3.   *The Development of Dynamism in Interpretation:* The problem of the treaty-making power is taken up here as a typical example in this connection.[36] The criteria in recognizing treaty-making powers of the EC have drastically evolved in the past from a restrictive to a flexible understanding.[37]

In the early years up to the 1960s, the jurisprudence of the Court of Justice with respect to the treaty-making powers indicated a restrictive understanding[38] which could be based upon the

---

[34] Pescatore, *supra* note 32, at 327-8.

[35] *See, e.g.*, W. Feld, *The Court of the European Communities* (1964); Bogaert, 'Le caractère juridique de la Cour de Justice des Communautés européennes', in *Mélanges offerts à Henri Rolin, Problèmes de droit des gens* 449 (1964); Bebr, 'Judicial Policy of the Court of Justice in Developing the Legal Order of the European Communities', in *Toward World Order and Hunam Dignity* 293, 294 (W. Reisman & B. Weston eds. 1976).

 Chevallier stated as follows (Chevallier, *supra* note 32, at 34):

 "[The] Court is beginning to decide cases in the spirit of a national court and no longer of international court. In other words, the Court, instead of confining itself to noting in a mechanical way the wishes of the authors of the Treaties, seems now to consider the Common Market as a fact, of the existence of which it takes judicial notice and from which observation it draws the necessary consequences."

[36] Pescatore, 'Les relations extérieures des Communautés européennes', 103 *Recueil des cours* 1 (1961); Costonis, 'The Treaty-Making Power of the European Economic Community: The Perspectives of a Decade', 5 *Comm'n Mkt L. Rev.* 421 (1968); Malawer, 'Treaty-Making Competence of the European Communities', 7 *J. World Trade L.* 169 (1973); Leopold, 'External Relations Power of EEC in Theory and in Practice', 26 *Int'l & Comp. L. Q.* 54 (1977); Boulouis, 'La jurisprudence de la Cour de Justice des Communautés européennes relative aux relations extérieures des Communautés, 160 *Recueil des cours* 335 (1978); Pescatore, 'External Relations in the Case-Law of the Court of Justice of the European Communities', 16 *Comm'n Mkt L. Rev.* 65 (1979); *Division of Powers between the European Communities and their Member States in the Field of External Relations* (C. Timmermans & E. V lker eds.1981); Kovar, 'La contribution de la Cour de justice au développement de la condition internationale de la Communauté européenne', *Cahier de droit européenne* 527 (1978).

[37] Giardina, 'The Rule of Law and Implied Powers in the European Communities', 1 *Italian Y. B. Int'l L.* 99, 103-4 (1975).

[38] The Court, in the *Fédération Charbonnière de Belgique* case (1956), stated (Case 8/55, [1955-56] ECR 292, at 299):

 "The Court considers that without having recourse to a wide interpretation it is possible to apply a rule of interpretation generally accepted in both international and national law, according to which rules laid down by an international treaty or a law presuppose the rules without which that treaty or law would have no meaning or could not be reasonably and usefully applied."

 See also Case 20/59, [1960] ECR 325, at 336.

 McMahon made the following comment on this case (McMahon, 'The Court of the European Communities Judicial Interpretation and International Organization', 37 *Brit. Y. B. Int'l L.* 320, 342 (1961)):

following two factors. (1) The "principe de l'attribution des compétences," which means that the EC cannot exercise any authority, substantive or functional, except where and to the extent that such authority has been expressly conferred on it; and the method of defining general tasks, which is primarily analytical: taking the problem one by one and laying down in each case *ad hoc* what are the powers of the EC or, rather, of its institutions.[39] (2) Those provisions such as EEC Article 235, EURATOM Article 203 and ECSC Article 95 (1)[40] were said to grant the power to act in a case where such action is necessary to attain, within the framework of the common market, one of the objectives of the EC, but this power is lacking. Here a new, independent "pouvoir d'action" is created beside the existing ones. On the other hand, the theory of implied powers can only relate to existing "pouvoir d'action," and cannot fill a gap in the totality of the specific powers conferred on the institutions for the activities of the EC.[41]

It was in the *AETR* case (1971) that the Court of Justice changed its attitude to a flexible one. The Court showed an understanding of the broad notion of implied treaty-making powers by stating:

"To determine in a particular case the Community's authority to enter into international agreements, regard must be had to the whole scheme of the Treaty no less than to its substantive provisions.

Such authority may arise not only from an explicit conferment by the Treaty --- as is the case with Articles 113 and 114 for tariff and trade agreements and with Article 238 for association agreements --- but may equally flow from other provisions of the Treaty and from measures adopted, within the framework of those provisions, by the Community institutions.

In particular, each time the Community, with a view to implementing a common policy envisaged by the Treaty, adopts provisions laying down common rules, whatever form these may take, the Member States no longer have the right, acting individually or

---

"It will be noticed that the Court here is formulating a limited and severely circumscribed doctrine of implied powers. There in no attempt to impute a new power to the Organization. Powers will only be implied to implement a power already expressed in the Treaty and then only to achieve the limited purpose of that express power and to permit it a reasonable and useful application. In two recent cases [Case 20/59 and Case 25/59] the Court has again referred to the above view and it is submitted that the attitude of the Court is to be welcomed. Subject to and within the above limitations, the doctrine of implied powers will always be necessary for the effective functioning of any international organization."

See also P. Hay, *Federalism and Supranational Organizations* 190-1 (1966); Bredimas, *supra* note 32, at 117-8; C. Mann, *The Function of Judicial Decision in European Economic Integration* 293-4 (1972).

[39] P. Pescatore, *The Law of Integration* 37-8 (C. Dwyer trans. 1974).

[40] *See e.g.* Marenco, 'Les conditions d'application de l'article 235 du Traité C.E.E.', 13 *Revue de marché common* 147 (1970); Lesguillons, 'L'extension des compétences de la C.E.E. par l'article 235 du Traité de Rome', 20 *A. F. D. I.* 886 (1974); Schwartz, 'Article 235 and Law-Making Powers in the European Community', 27 *Int'l & Comp. L. Q.* 614 (1978); Kapteyn, 'Article 235' in 6 *The Law of the European Economic Community, A Commentary on the EEC Treaty* 6-269 (H. Smit & P. Herzog eds. 1981).

[41] P. Kapteyn & P. van Themaat, *Introduction to the Law of the European Communities* 73 (1973).

even collectively, to undertake obligations towards third countries which affect those rules....

With regard to the implementation of the provisions of the Treaty the system of internal Community measures may not therefore be separated from that of external relations."[47]

The reasoning based upon in the *AETR* case has been developed in a series of later cases. The conditions for the implied treaty-making powers have been loosened from the prior institution of internal rules on matters coming within the scope of the agreement (the *AETR* case) to the adoption of measures on the basis of which internal rules could be instituted (the *Kramer* case),[43] and finally to the parallelism of internal and external Community powers (the *Rhine* case).

The Court, in the *Rhine* case, stated as follows:

"[T]he power to bind the Community vis-à-vis third countries nevertheless flows by implication from the provisions of the Treaty creating the internal power and in so far as the participation of the Community in the international agreement is, as here, necessary for the attainment of one of the objectives of the Community."[44]

4.   *Some Comments:* The dynamic development of the EC powers has not been limited to the area of treaty-making powers but has been realized in most other areas. Based upon its thirty years of development, Tizzano referred to a considerable expansion of the EC powers by virtue of an extremely dynamic practice, and pointed out two ways for it: (1) by developing principles and techniques of interpretation (symbolized by the doctrine of implied powers), especially judicial, that made clear the full potential of the rules known as Community law; and (2) by making continually wider and more frequent use of the clauses in the Treaties which lay down formal procedures to supplement the powers of the Community institutions (such as EEC Article 235). Although formally and logically distinct, these two ways are actually closely connected at a functional level, in the sense that both tend toward the development of the EC powers.[45]

It is certainly true that both the Court of Justice[46] and such articles as EEC Article 235[47] have played a major role in the dynamic development of the EC powers. These elements do not,

---

[42] Case 22/70, [1971] ECR 263, at 274. *See also* Kovar, 'L'affaire de l'A.E.T.R. devant la Cour de Justice des Communautés européennes et la compétence internatinale de la C.E.E.', 17 *A.F.D.I.* 386 (1971).

[43] *See* Joined Cases 3, 4 and 6/76, [1976] ECR 1279, at 1309. *See also* Koers, 'The External Authority of the EEC in Regard to Marine Fisheries', 14 *Comm'n Mkt L. Rev.* 269 (1977).

[44] Opinion 1/76, [1977] ECR 741, at 755. *See also* Hardy, 'Opinion 1/76 of the Court of Justice: The Rhine Case and the Treaty-Making Powers of the Community',14 *Comm'n Mkt L. Rev.* 561 (1977); Groux, 'Le parallélisme des compétences internes et externes de la Communauté économique européenne', *Cahier de droit européen* 3 (1978).

[45] Tizzano, 'Chapter III - The powers of the Community', in *Thirty Years of Community Law* 43, 46 (The Commission of the European Communities ed. 1981).

[46] Rasmussen, 'Chapter VII - The Court of Justice', in *Thirty Years of Community Law* 151, 190 (The Commission of the European Communities ed. 1981).

[47] Tizzano, *supra* note 45, at 50 et seq.

however, exist in the ordinary constituent instruments of international organizations for cooperation.

It is rather the teleological nature of the constituent instruments of the EC which is common to the ordinary constituent instruments. Although the EC is an organization for integration rather than cooperation, essential parts of the provisions would be dedicated to the definition of the purposes and the structures and procedures for their implementation, which can provide the foundations of the dynamism for integration. This common feature would suggest that constituent instruments for both integration and cooperation have a similar constitutional nature for dynamism, although they might be slightly different in terms of degree.[48]

(2) The Theory of Interpretation in the Federal Constitution of the U.S.A.

1. *Introduction:* What is influential among international lawyers in the U.S.A. in connection with the interpretation of constituent instruments is the theory of interpretation in the federal constitution of the U.S.A.[49] Cohen, for example, explains as follows:

"The Charter, like our Constitution, sets forth a few basic principles and leaves to those who will live under it the responsibility of finding suitable means of carrying out those principles. Some means are specified in the Charter but these are not necessarily exclusive. The Charter is not a code of legal procedure to be strictly construed. I know no better canon of construction to be used in determining charter power than that laid down by Chief Justice Marshall in *McCulloch v. Maryland* for determining constitutional power: 'Let the end be legitimate, let it be within the scope of the Constitution, and all means which are appropriate, which are plainly adapted to that end, which are not prohibited, but consist with the letter and spirit of the Constitution, are constitutional.' Member States have the right and responsibility to find means which are appropriate, which are not prohibited but consist with the letter and spirit of the Charter, to carry out the purpose of the Charter."[50]

---

[48] The following statement of Pescatore seems to support this point (Pescatore, 'International Law and Community Law ------ A Comparative Analysis', 7 *Comm'n Mkt L. Rev.* 167, 173 (1970).):

"The technique used by the drafters of the European Treaties in a number of areas is to establish more or less precisely defined objectives as opposed to specific ends. This technique calls in its turn for a process of interpretation which may be called dynamic because it is primarily a function of the common objectives set by the member States, of a particular vision of the future --- a 'prospective' approach to use a current term."

[49] Vallat, 'The Competence of the United Nations General Assembly', 97 *Recueil des cours* 203, 248-50 (1959); W. Friedmann, *The Changing Structure of International Law* 154 (1964); C. W. Jenks, *The Prospects of International Adjudication* 461 (1964); Engel, '"Living" International Constitutions and the World Court (The Subsequent Practice of International Organs Under Their Constituent Instruments)', 16 *Int'l & Comp. L. Q.* 865, 909 (1967); ditto, 'The Changing Charter of the United Nations', *Y. B. World Affairs* 71 (1953); Schick, 'Towards a Living Constitution of the United Nations', 2 *Int'l L. Q.* 1 (1948).

[50] B. Cohen, *The United Nations, Constitutional Developments, Growth, and Possibilities* 6 (1961).

Goodrich, in referring to the formula made by Marshall, also stated (L. Goodrich, *The United Nations in a Changing World* 36 (1974)) that it "provides a reasonable standard for determining the powers of United Nations

2.   *Marshall and Holmes:* The concept of "implied power" mentioned in the constitutional law of the U.S.A. is generally understood to date back to *McCulloch v. Maryland* (1819),[51] in which Chief Justice Marshall stated as follows:

> "[The nature of a constitution requires] that only its great outlines should be marked, its important objects designated, and the minor ingredients which compose those objects be deduced from the nature of the objects themselves.... In considering [the present] question, then, we must never forget that it is a constitution we are expounding."[52]

It was in *Missouri v. Holland* (1920) that Justice Holmes made the following statement which is, again, frequently referred to in connection with the interpretation of constituent instruments.

> "[W]hen we are dealing with words that also are a constituent act, like the Constitution of the United States, we must realize that they have called into life a being the development of which could not have been foreseen completely by the most gifted of its begetters.... The case before us must be considered in the light of our whole experience, and not merely in that of what was said a hundred years ago."[53]

3.   *Recent Arguments:* The problem of constitutional interpretation has been debated, in particular, since the 1970s in the U.S.A. This has taken the form of controversy between the "originalists" and "nonoriginalists."[54] The originalists argue that the Court must confine itself to norms clearly stated or implied in the language of the Constitution and that constitutional language, understood in light of the substantive intentions or values behind its enactment, is the sole proper source for constitutional interpretation. On the other hand, the nonoriginalists argue that the Court may protect norms not mentioned in the Constitution's text or its pre-ratification

---

organs."   *See also* L. Goodrich, E. Hambro, and A. Simons, *Charter of the United Nations, Commentary and Documents* 25, n.25 (1969).

The American oral statement in the *Certain Expenses* case referred to the passages of Chief Justice Marshall and Justice Holmes quoted in the text and contended that the same idea should be applied to the interpretation of the Charter. Oral Statement of Mr. Chayes, Advisory Opinion on Certain Expenses of the United Nations (Article 17, paragraph 2, of the Charter), I. C. J. Pleadings 413, 425-7 (1962). Reference to Chief Justice Marshall is found in the dissenting opinion of Judge Jessup in the South West Africa cases (1966). South West Africa Cases, Second Phase, [1966] I. C. J. 353, n.1. It was already contended in 1923 that the previous idea of Marshall concerning interpretation should be applied to the interpretation of the Covenant of the League of Nations. Gregory, 'The Neutralization of the Aaland Islands', 17 *Am. J. Int'l L.* 63, 75 (1923).

[51] *See, e.g.,* R. Chandler, R. Enslen and P. Renstrom, 1 *The Constitutional Law Dictionary* 424 (1985).

[52] McCulloch v. Maryland, 4 Wheat. 316 (1819). *See also* Plous and Baker, 'McCulloch v. Maryland, Right Principle, Wrong Case', 9 *Stanford L. Rev.* 710 (1957); Dodd, 'Implied Powers and Implied limitations in Constitutional Law', 29 *Yale L. J.* 137 (1919); Kruse, 'Implied Powers und Implied Limitations', 4 *Archiv des Völkerrechts* 169 (1953-54).

[53] Missouri v. Holland, 252 U.S. 416, 433 (1920).

[54] *See, e.g.,* the following bibliography and others listed there: Sandalow, 'Constitutional Interpretation', 79 *Michigan L. Rev.* 1033 (1981); Bennett, 'Objectivity in Constitutional Law', 132 *Univ. Pennsylvania L. Rev.* 445 (1984); Simon, 'The Authority of the Framers of the Constitution: Can Originalist Interpretation Be Justified?', 73 *California L. Rev.* 1482 (1985); E. Chemerinsky, *Interpreting the Constitution* (1987).

history and that it is legitimate for judges to look beyond text and original intention in interpreting constitutional language.

While it is not necessary to explain these controversies further, let us indicate a point which this series of arguments has made abundantly clear up to the present. This is that constitutional interpretation requires a substantial theory of interpretation. Unlike the case of contract or will in which the drafter's intention is supreme and binding, constitutional interpretation needs a substantial theory of interpretation accompanying rational reasons with regard to why the drafter's intention must be considered binding, or if not, then why other methods of interpretation included in the nonoriginalist's approach should be adopted. It is only in the light of this substantial theory of interpretation that the propriety of an interpretation can be judged.

4.   *Criticism:* Criticisms have certainly been made against the analogy of the theory of constitutional interpretation. The toughest critic would be Gross, who presented the following contention: the Charter of the United Nations is not a constitution in the sense of the American Constitution; the U.N. is not like the United States even in its infancy. The possibility, of course, cannot be excluded that after a century, the U. N. will acquire the degree of integration which will make the comparison with the federalism of the United States more tenable. However, if the Constitution of the United States is very flexible, even its ends must be achieved *in conformity with its letter and spirit,* as was pointed out by Chief Justice Marshall. Great and dynamic as the principle of effectiveness may be as a method of interpretation, effectiveness is in general a principle of good faith.[55]

5.   *Some Comments:* The basic idea underlying the analogy is that both the Constitution of the United States as a constituent act and the Charter of the United Nations as a constituent instrument have created an organism. As the expression "constituent" common to them indicates, they have created *an institution capable of life and growth the development of which could not*

---

[55] Thus, Gross contended as follows ('The International Court of Justice and the United Nations', 120 *Recueil des cours* 313, 403-4 (1967)):

> "The Court's jurisprudence leaves no doubt that as an organ of the United Nations and as an interpreter of its Charter it will carry forward the purposes and principles of the Organization. But there are limits to what a Court can expect to, and what can legitimately be expected that it should, accomplish and these are set by its role as a Court and the environment in which it, as well as the United Nations, functions.
>
> Methods of interpretation, by whatever designation they go, are but tools in the hand of the interpreter.... Rules of interpretation are not so much 'roads to right legal solutions' as 'footholds for struggling for these solutions.'"

This anxiety based upon the realistic understanding of the power structure in the international society is to some extent shared by those invoking the analogy. Friedmann, for example, stated as follows (Friedmann, *supra* note 49, at 158):

> "It is, of course, always uncertain how far the court's judicial interpretation will stand the strains of political tension. Like the constitutional courts of federal states, the court has a certain policy function in trying to move forward but not so fast as to break up the United Nations in its formative phase. In the mixture of legal and policy considerations, the court only reflects the typical dilemma of any constitutional court. But its task, and the scope of its molding powers, is far more severely circumscribed by the fragility of the society which has set it up."

be completely foreseen. It is, therefore, pointed out that they must be interpreted in the light of our whole experience, and not merely in that of what was said two hundred or fifty years ago. Furthermore, as a constitution provides great outlines and important objects, other minor ingredients being deduced from the nature of the objects, constitutional interpretation should, they claim, be flexible in accordance with the formula indicated by Marshall.

The validity of the analogy seems to be related to two elements. The first is the fact that, in international law, there are rules of interpretation accepted as positive law, whereas, in the American constitutional law, any method of constitutional interpretation must be justified by a substantial theory of interpretation, as was clarified by the recent controversy. To the extent that the constituent instruments of international organizations deviate from the interpretative framework in the law of treaties, a substantial theory of interpretation needs to be constructed.

The second element is related to the appreciation of the difference between the national foundation for the U.S. federal constitution and the international foundation for the U.N. Charter. There is presumed to be some difference in terms of effectiveness which the interpretations by the court and organs (of a State and an international organization) can have between national integration on the one hand and international organization, which depends on the voluntary cooperation of sovereign States, on the other. This difference ultimately depends upon how one appreciates the fragility of international society where, nowadays, international law has developed from a law of coexistence to one of cooperation and society is gradually being transformed to a community, while its members still remain sovereign States. And this appreciation could be attempted only in parallel with a comprehensive appreciation of the effectiveness of international organizations.

(3) The Theory of Institution

1.   *Introduction:* What is influential among the international lawyers in France is the theory of institution established around 1930s by M. Hauriou and G. Renard in France.[56] Lesguillons, for example, stated as follows:

> "[L]'analyse formelle d'un acte constitutif est insuffisante pour le caractériser: de ce point de vue, un contrat, un traité laisseraient apparaître en première place l'autonomie et l'accord des volontés, alors que dans l'institution c'est la cause qui l'emporte et la cause n'est pas révélée par l'analyse formelle de l'acte. L'origine conventionnelle d'une institution n'est pas déterminante pour son développement: c'est que d'autres éléments le sont. 'Toutes les fois', écrit le doyen Hauriou, 'que d'un contrat, d'un pacte, d'un traité, résulte la création d'un corps constitué quelconque, il convient d'admettre qu'une opération de fondation s'est

---

[56]   The theory of institution is said to have been created by Hauriou, developed by Renard and later adopted by Desqueyrat (*see, e.g.*, A. Desqueyrat, *Le droit objectif et la technique positive* (1933)) and Delos (*see, e.g.*, J. Delos, *La société internationale et les principes du droit public* (2d ed. 1950)) in France, and Romano (*see, e.g.*, S. Romano, *L'ordinamento giuridico* (3d ed. 1977)) in Italy.

mêlée à l'opération contractuelle'."[57]

In an indirect manner, Pescatore, among others, referred to a similar idea when he stated: "En effet, le statut constitutif de toutes les organisations internationales est représenté, à l'origine, par une convention multilatérale; dans la suite, à partir de la mise en place des institutions, ce caractère contractuel s'estompe et c'est désormais le caractère institutionnel qui prime. La convention multilatérale se mue alors, pour ainsi dire, en constitution."[58]

2. *The Theory of Institution:* Hauriou, one of the founding fathers, defined the concept of institution as follows:

"[U]ne institution est une idée d'oeuvre ou d'entreprise qui se réalise et dure juridiquement dans un milieu social; pour la réalisation de cette idée, un pouvoir s'organise qui lui procure des organes; d'autre part, entre les membres du groupe social intéressé à la réalisation de l'idée, il se produit des manifestations de communion dirigée par les organes du pouvoir et

---

[57] H. Lesguillons, *L'application d'un traité-fondation: Le traité instituant la C.E.E.* 65-6 (1968). ("The formal analysis of a constitutive act is not sufficient to characterize it: from this viewpoint, a contract, a treaty will allow to appear in the first place the autonomy and the agreement of the intentions, although, in the institution, it is the cause which prevails and the cause will not be revealed by the formal analysis of the act. The conventional origin is not determinant for its development: it is other elements which are determinant. Hauriou writes, 'Every time that a creation of some corporate body results from a contract, a pact or a treaty, it should be admitted that a founding operation was mixed with a conventional operation.'" [Our translation])

[58] Pescatore, 'Les relations extérieures des Communautés européennes, 103 *Recueil des cours* 1, 152-53 (1961). ("In fact, the constitutive statute of all the international organizations is, in the beginning, represented by a multilateral convention; subsequently, as soon as the institutions are established, this contractual nature shades off and it is from now on the institutional nature that prevails. The multilateral convention will then be transformed into constitution." [Our translation])

The basic idea of the theory of institution seems to have, more or less, influenced a wide range of scholars. Focsaneanu, for example, stated as follows in connection with the internal law of the United Nations (Focsaneanu, 'Le droit interne de l'organisation des Nations Unies', 3 *A.F.D.I.* 315, 320 (1957)):

"Ce n'est qu'en prenant comme fondement ces idées empruntées à la théorie de l'institution que l'on peut atteindre à une compréhension exhaustive et systématique du droit interne des organisations internationales, en général, et du droit interne de l'O.N.U., en particulier, pour arriver à une explication qui embrasse le phénomène dans toute son ampleur et le situe correctement dans l'ensemble de la réalité juridique."

("It is only by taking as foundation these ideas borrowed from the theory of institution that one can reach an exhaustive and systematic comprehension of the internal law of international organizations, in general, and the U.N., in particular, in order to arrive at the explanation which covers the phenomenon in all its width and places it correctly in the entirety of juridical reality." [Our translation])

With regard to the reference to the theory of institution, *see also* Monaco, 'Les principes régissant la structure et le fonctionnement des organisations internationales, 156 *Recueil des cours* 79, 196, n.10 (1977), reprinted in R. Monaco, *Scritti di diritto delle organizzazioni internazionali* 459, 478, n.10 (1981); Lachs, 'Le role des organisations internationales dans la formation du droit international', in *Mélanges offerts à Henri Rolin, Problèmes de droit des gens,* 161, n.9, 10 (1964); Mestre, 'Les traités et le droit interne', 38 *Recueil des cours* 233, 301-2 (1931).

Dupuy, in explaining the transformation of international society and the nature of international organizations, used the concepts of "le droit relationnel" and "le droit institutionnel." Dupuy, 'Communauté internationale et disparités de développement', 165 *Recueil des cours* 9, 45-114 (1979). Based upon these concepts, Simon attempted to apply the theory of institution to the interpretation of constituent instruments in his original manner. Simon, *supra* note 1 in Chap. 1, at 473-89. For a criticism, *see* the review by Combacau (109 *Journal du droit international* 752, 754-5 (1982)).

réglées par des procédures."[59]

Therefore, the three elements of every institution are (1) the idea of the work or enterprise to be realized in a social group; (2) the organized power put at the service of this idea for its realization; and (3) the manifestations of communion that occur within the social group with respect to the idea and its realization.

Renard, another founding father, did not develop his doctrine in a systematic manner and is difficult to understand. However, with respect to the concept of institution, he made the following statement:

"La *fondation*, c'est l'acte de la personnalité humaine qui donne naissance à une *institution*.... Fonder une famille, fonder un Etat, fonder une religion, fonder un établissment charitable ou une entreprise, --- c'est d'abord porter en soi-m me une *Idée*, et puis c'est vouloir ne pas l'emporter avec soi dans la tombe; c'est l'envelopper de *Voies et Moyens* appropriés un perpétuel renouvellement.... Fonder, c'est enfermer dans une oeuvre l'étincelle --- presque d'une vie --- d'un développement qui se poursuivra longtemps après que le fondateur ne sera plus."[60]

According to Renard, institution is contrasted with contract in various points.[61] In contract, what is supreme is the accord of wills, whereas, in institution, it is the cause. Contract is static, immobile; it will be executed as it has been concluded. Institution operates by a constant readaptation of the means to the purposes pursued, and the purposes pursued to the variations of social milieu. Without such a development, there is no continuity.

3. *Some Comments:* It was Bastid who analyzed the theory of institution from the viewpoint of international organizations. She reached a negative conclusion with regard to both Hauriou and Renard for respective reasons which will not be discussed here. However, based upon the concept of institution two principal elements of which are the nature of continuity and the organic nature, Bastid thought the theory of institution useful and reached the following conclusion.

---

[59] M. Hauriou, 'La théorie de l'institution et de la fondation (Essai de vitalisme social)'(originally appeared in 1925), in *Aux sources du droit* 89-128 (1933). ("[A]n institution is an idea of a work or enterprise that is realized and endures juridically in a social milieu; for the realization of this idea, a power is organized that equips it with organs; on the other hand, among the members of the social group interested in the realization of the idea, manifestations of communion occur that are directed by the organs of the power and regulated by procedures." [translation cited from *The French Institutionalists* 99 (A. Broderick ed., M. Welling trans. 1970)])

[60] G. Renard, *L'institution, fondement d'une rénovation de l'ordre social* 45-6 (1933). ("The *foundation*, it is the act of a human personality which gives birth to an *institution*.... To found a family, to found a State, to found a religion, to found a charitable institution or an enterprise --- it is first of all to carry an *idea* within oneself, and then to intend not to bring it with oneself to the tomb; it is to clothe it with the *ways and means* appropriate to a perpetual renewal.... To found, it is to keep in the work the spark --- almost of the life --- of a development which continues for a long time after the founder ceases to exist." [Our translation])

[61] *Id.* at 147-90. *See also* G. Renard, *La théorie de l'institution, essai d'ontologie juridique* 360 et seq. (1930); ditto, *La philosophie de l'institution* (1939); ditto, 'Les bases philosophiques du droit international et la doctrine du "Bien commun"', 3-4 *Archives de philosophie du droit et de sociologie juridique* 465 (1931).

"La notion d'institution juridique permet de rendre compte de ce complexe de règles inhérent à toute organisation internationale et du développement organique et normatif qui se greffe ou surgit du mécanisme primitif. Mais sous peine de méconnaître les bases fondamentales de la société internationale, il convient de ne pas oublier la place du contractuele et pour la définition des pouvoirs des organes, soit pour apprécier la nécessité de l'assentiment permanent et agissant des Etats participants....

Dans ces limites et en se gardant de vouloir forcer les analogies ... la notion d'institution juridique peut aider à construire une théorie générale des organisations internationales."[62]

In the final analysis, the theory of institution is directed to the theory of society rather than to the theory of law as the sub-titles indicate such as "Essai de vitalisme social" (Essay of social vitalism) attached to Hauriou's article and "Essai d'ontologie juridique" (Essay of juridical ontology) attached to Renard's book. Stone made the following suggestive comment:

"The French institutionalists thought that the very existence of an institution imports the existence of constitutional principles of a 'juridical' nature concerning its organisation and operation, principles which emerge from its activities.... [T]he sense in which personality and constitutional law necessarily spring from institutions, is not that of positive law, but rather the sense that these results are warranted by the 'nature of social life'.... Their personality and the norms which spring from them are (for the natural lawyer) part of *le droit*, whether they are part of *la loi* or not; though from the positive lawyers' standpoint this is merely a demand that this *droit* should be made into *la loi*."[63]

From this viewpoint, the *raison-d'être* of the theory of institution consists in indicating the existence of the dynamism inherent in the institutional phenomenon and the necessity for law to take this dynamism into consideration. This is suggestive because, as international organizations are established and regulated by constituent instruments, they tend to be appreciated in the light of constituent instruments understood in the law of treaties without sufficiently taking the inherent dynamism and stability into consideration.

On the other hand, the theory of institution has an inherent limitation in appreciating legally the phenomenon of international organizations because it is not a theory of positive law. First,

---

[62] Bastid, 'Place de la notion d'institution dans une théorie générale des organisations internationales', in *Études en l'honneur d'A. Mestre* 50-1 (1956). ("The notion of juridical institution allows to account for the complex of rules inherent in every international organization and for the organic and normative development which will be grafted on or will appear from the original mechanism. But in order not to disregard the fundamental basis of the international society, one should not forget the place of the contractual for the definition of the powers of the organs, or for appreciating the necessity of the permanent and effective consent of the participating States.... Within these limits and by taking care not to force the analogies ... the notion of juridical institution can help construct a general theory of the international organizations." [Our translation])

[63] J. Stone, *Social Dimensions of Law and Justice* 525 (1966). *See also* Stone, 'Two Theories of "The Institution"', in *Essays in Jurisprudence in Honor of Roscoe Pound* 296-338 (R. A. Newman ed. 1962); W. Friedmann, *Legal Theory* 239 (5th ed. 1967).

because of the decentralized structure of international society, the conventional basis among the member States of international organizations must be duly emphasized in the legal appreciation of their structures and operation, as was indicated by Bastid.

Secondly, the problem is how to make an appropriate balance in the legal appreciation between the importance of the conventional basis and the necessity of taking into consideration the inherent dynamism as an institution. The answer to this delicate question does not seem to be given by the theory of institution.

(4) The Theory of Inter-Temporal Law[64]

1.   *Introduction:* In the *Namibia* case (1971), there was a difference of opinion between the majority of judges and Judge Fitzmaurice over the applicability of inter-temporal law. The majority opinion, in applying Article 22 of the Covenant of the League of Nations and the Mandate, stated:

> "All these considerations [such as events subsequent to the adoption of the instruments in question and the subsequent development of international law in regard to non-self-governing territories] are germane to the Court's evaluation of the present case. Mindful as it is of the primary necessity of interpreting an instrument in accordance with the intentions of the parties at the time of its conclusion, the Court is bound to take into account the fact that the concepts embodied in Article 22 of the Covenant ... were not static, but were by definition evolutionary ....   The parties to the Covenant must consequently be deemed to have accepted them as such. That is why, viewing the institutions of 1919, the Court must take into consideration the changes which have occurred in the supervening half-century, and its interpretation cannot remain unaffected by the subsequent development of law .... Moreover, an international instrument has to be interpreted and applied within the framework of the entire legal system prevailing at the time of the interpretation."[65]

On the other hand, Judge Fitzmaurice contended that what must be sought is the original intention of the parties at the time of the conclusion of the Covenant and the mandate, and stated:

> "My reading of the situation is based --- in orthodox fashion --- on what appears to have been the intentions of those concerned at the time. The Court's view, the outcome of a different, and to me alien philosophy, is based on what has become the intentions of new

---

[64] For some of the useful bibliography, *see* Yasseen, 'L'interprétation des traités d'après la convention de Vienne sur le droit des traités', 151 *Recueil des cours* 1, 62-70 (1976); do Nascimento e Silva, 'Le facteur temps et les traités', 154 *Recueil des cours* 215, 265-70 (1977); Elias, 'The Doctrine of Intertemporal Law', 74 *Am. J. Int'l L.* 285 (1980); I. Sinclair, *The Vienna Convention on the Law of Treaties* 124-6, 138-40 (2d ed. 1984); P. Reuter, *Introduction au droit des traités* 87-8 (2d ed. 1985); P. Tavernier, *Recherches sur l'application dans le temps des actes et des régles en droit international public (Problèmes de droit intertemporel ou de droit transitoire)* 205-7 (1970).

[65] *Namibia* case, *supra* note 8, at 31.

and different entities and organs fifty years later."[66]

The point at issue here is how the legal nature of Article 22 of the Covenant and the Mandate should be understood. Judge Fitzmaurice relied on their conventional (contractual) aspect, whereas the majority opinion relied on their institutional aspect. The inter-temporal law applied by the majority opinion in this way seems to have a useful suggestion in finding the theoretical foundations of the constitutional nature of constituent instruments.

2.   *Article 31, Paragraph 3 (c) of the Vienna Convention on the Law of Treaties:* The Third Report submitted to the International Law Commission by Waldock in 1964 contained the following draft article entitled "The inter-temporal law":[67]

"1. A treaty is to be interpreted in the light of the law in force at the time when the treaty was drawn up.

2. Subject to paragraph 1, the application of a treaty shall be governed by the rules of international law in force at the time when the treaty is applied."

Waldock, in drafting this article, relied heavily upon the formulation by Judge Huber in the *Island of Palmas* arbitration (1928), which was as follows:

"[A] juridical fact must be appreciated in the light of the law contemporary with it, and not of the law in force at the time when a dispute in regard to it arises or falls to be settled....

As regards the question which of different legal systems prevailing at successive periods is to be applied in a particular case (the so-called intertemporal law), a distinction must be made between the creation of rights and the existence of rights. The same principle which subjects the act creative of a right to the law in force at the time the right arises, demands that the existence of the right, in other words its continued manifestation, shall follow the conditions required by the evolution of law."[68]

Therefore, in corresponding to the distinction between the creation and the continuation of rights, Waldock set the distinction between the interpretation which is to be made in the light of the law in force at the time of the conclusion and the application which is to be governed by the law in force at the time of the application.[69]

This manner of drafting was supported by the majority of the members in the Commission. The majority considered that whether a change in the law will have this effect depends on the initial intention of the parties in using the terms and that the effect of the change in the law should be regarded as a matter of the application of the law rather than of a rule of interpretation. They preferred to confine the statement of the rules of interpretation to those dealing with the

---

[66]   *Id.* at 223.

[67]   Waldock, 'Third Report on the Law of Treaties', [1964] 2 *Y. B. Int'l L. Comm'n* 5, 8-9, U. N. Doc. A/CN. 4/167 and Add. 1-3.

[68]   Island of Palmas Case (Netherlands, United States), 2 *R. Int'l Arb. Awards* 831, 845.

[69]   Waldock, *supra* note 67, at 9.

establishment of the initial meaning of the terms.[70] However, this manner of drafting was reexamined in 1966 partly because of the critical comments submitted by governments.[71] The Commission seemed generally disinclined to deal with the problem of intertemporal law in the draft articles. It was understood that the question whether the terms used were intended to have a fixed content or to change in meaning with the evolution of the law could be decided only by interpreting the intention of the parties.[72] Thus, the Commission, in the final draft articles of 1966, referred to "(c) Any relevant rules of international law applicable in the relation between the parties" as to be taken into consideration, together with the context in paragraph 3 of the draft article 27, which became Article 31 of the present Convention on the Law of Treaties by being adopted without change in the diplomatic conferences in 1968 and 1969.

The attitude of the Commission on this point is explained as follows in the commentary :
"[The Commission] considered that ... the relevance of rules of international law for the interpretation of treaties in any given case was dependent on the intentions of the parties, and that to attempt to formulate a rule covering comprehensively the temporal element would present difficulties. It further considered that correct application of the temporal element would normally be indicated by interpretation of the term in good faith. The Commission therefore concluded that it should omit the temporal element and revise the reference to international law so as to make it read 'any relevant rules of international law'."[73]

3.   *The Resolution Adopted by l'Institut de Droit International:* L'Institut adopted a resolution entitled "The Intertemporal Problem in Public International Law" in 1975[74] after consideration of the reports submitted by Sørensen since 1968.[75] This resolution consists of a preamble and six articles of the following content:

The preamble refers, among others, to the necessity that any solution of an intertemporal problem in the international field must take account of the dual requirement of promoting the development of the international legal system and preserving the principle of legal stability which is an essential part of any juridical system. Article 1 indicates a fundamental principle: unless otherwise indicated, the temporal sphere of application of any norm of public international law shall be determined in accordance with the general principle of law by which any fact, action or situation must be assessed in the light of the rules that are contemporaneous with it. Article 3

---

[70] Report of the Commission to the General Assembly, [1964] 2 *Y. B. Int'l L. Comm'n* 173, 202-3, U. N. Doc. A/5809. *See* the arguments in the 765th and the 769th meetings, [1964] 1 *Y. B. Int'l L. Comm'n* 275 et seq. and 308 et seq.

[71] Especially the Netherlands. *See* Waldock, 'Sixth Report on the Law of Treaties', [1966] 2 *Y. B. Int'l L. Comm'n* 51, 92 U. N. Doc. A/CN. 4/186 and Add. 1-7.

[72] Statement of Waldock in the 872d meeting, [1966] 1 *Y. B. Int'l L. Comm'n* 199, para. 9.

[73] Report of the Commission to the General Assembly, [1966] 2 *Y. B. Int'l L. Comm'n* 169, 222, U.N. Doc. A/6309/Rev. 1. *See also* the similar statement of Yasseen, a member of the Commission at that time. Yasseen, *supra* note 64, at 66-7.

[74] 56 *Annuaire de l'Institut de Droit International* 36 (1975).

[75] Sørensen, 'Le problème dit du droit intertemporel dans l'ordre international', 55 *A.I.D.I.* 1 (1973).

provides the freedom of States to make this indication: States and other subjects of international law shall have the power to determine by common consent the temporal sphere of application of norms. Article 4 refers to the significance of interpretation: wherever a provision of a treaty refers to a legal or other concept without defining it, it is appropriate to have recourse to the usual methods of interpretation in order to determine whether the concept concerned is to be interpreted as understood at the time when the provision was drawn up or as understood at the time of its application.

Based upon the three reports by Sørensen and the comments by the members concerned, it is possible to emphasize the important role given to the interpretation in the actual, concrete application of the theory of inter-temporal law. In the final report, Sørensen states that an international legal norm, conventional or customary, very frequently employs expressions and notions whose meanings and scopes are not defined by the norm itself, and that the question of whether to take the meaning which the notion or the term had at the time when the norm was established is related to whether the norm concerned contains "un renvoi à contenu fixe ou un renvoi mobile" (reference to a fixed content or mobile reference).[76] From this viewpoint, Sørensen reached the following conclusion:

"De l'avis du rapporteur, il résulte de la pratique judiciaire et arbitrale internationale ... qu'il n'est pas possible de répondre à cette question par une formule générale qui en toute circonstance donnerait la préférence soit au sens originaire, soit au sens ultérieur. Au contraire, la nature de la réponse dépend des circonstances de l'espèce. C'est à la suite d'une interprétation de la norme qu'il faut trancher la question dans le cas d'espèce et cette opération d'interprétation particulière doit porter plus précisément sur le choix entre les deux possibilités. En ce qui concerne une disposition conventionnelle, quelle était l'intention des parties contractantes? A-t-on voulu un renvoi fixe ou un renvoi mobile? Si l'intention des parties à cet égard ne peut pas être établie, quelle est la solution qui s'impose par l'objet et le but du traité?"[77]

4. *Some Comments:* From the above analyses, it is possible to give the following comments to the theory of inter-temporary law. First, the fundamental principle of the theory of inter-temporary law is that a juridical fact must be appreciated in the light of the law contemporary with it. Secondly, despite this principle, the States parties have the power to decide the law to be applied to the fact concerned, and consequently, the problem becomes a matter of interpretation

---

[76] *Id.* at 90.

[77] *Id.* at 90-1. ("In the opinion of the rapporteur, it results from the international judicial and arbitral practice ... that it is not possible to respond to this question by a general formula which would in any circumstances give the preference either to the original meaning or the subsequent meaning. To the contrary, the nature of the response depends upon the circumstances of the case. It is as a result of an interpretation of the norm that one must solve the question in individual cases and this individual operation of interpretation must precisely bear on the choice between the two possibilities. With regard to a conventional provision, what was the intention of the contracting parties? If the intention of the parties in this regard cannot be established, what is the solution which is imposed by the object and purpose of the treaty?" [Our translation])

in search of the intentions of the parties. Thirdly, when the applicable law is a treaty, the nature of a treaty indicated in its object and purpose could have a certain effect of presumption in the interpretation in search of whether the intentions of the parties were a reference to a fixed content or a mobile reference.

These comments would lead us to the following conclusions with regard to the interpretation of constituent instruments. First, because constituent instruments are reasonably considered to contain many concepts and provisions of mobile reference, the provisions concerned will, unless the intentions of the parties are proved to be reference to a fixed content upon the examination, be regarded to be based upon a mobile reference and will be so interpreted. To this extent, the evolutionary nature of constituent instruments will be supported by the theory of inter-temporary law and their evolutionary and teleological interpretation will have a legitimacy. Secondly, we could consider in the same way the fact that subsequent practice of the organs of international organizations has an influence upon the determination of the content of provisions of constituent instruments and also functions as a criterion of interpretation. The theory of inter-temporary law would give a legitimacy to this phenomenon by attributing a legal foundation to the mechanism of mobile reference thought to be contained in the many provisions of constituent instruments.[78]

Section 4 Toward the Determination of the Interpretative Framework as the Constitutions of International Organizations

Some of the important elements in clarifying the doctrine of the interpretative framework of constituent instruments as the constitutions of international organizations will be developed here.

(1) With Regard to the Criterion of "Necessity"

1.   The interpretative framework of constituent instruments as constitutions, as has been developed above in detail, exceeds the interpretative framework in the law of treaties in both: (1) the quantitative aspect of teleological extent admitted and (2) the qualitative aspect of legal significance possessed by the practice of the organs of international organizations. These two aspects are, although theoretically distinct, intertwined in the actual activities of international organizations. The following two views are worth citing as pointing out, respectively, these two aspects.

As to the first aspect, Bindschedler explained:

---

[78]   de Visscher seems to support this idea based upon the theory of intertemporal law. Ch. de Visscher, *Théories et réalités en droit international public* 321-2 (3d ed. 1960); ditto, *Theory and Reality in Public International* Law 261 (rev. ed. P.E. Corbett trans. 1968).

"Dans son application, le principe d'interprétation de l'effet utile aboutit à reconnaître aux organisations internationales des *compétences tacites ou implicites* ("implied powers"). Qui veut la fin veut les moyens: dans la mesure où des moyens indispensables à la réalisation d'un but ne sont pas prévus par le statut, ils doivent être déduits...."[79]

As to the second aspect, Higgins stated:

"[T]he point I wish to make is that U.N. political organs have at least an initial discretion to decide what actions are necessary to carry out their functions --- whether it be an Interim Committee, a Peace Observation Committee, the right to hold prisoners of war, or whatever --- and upon that practice its implied powers will be built."[80]

The actual activities of international organizations are considered to be the synthesis of these two aspects. *The implied powers founded on the principle of effectiveness will be built upon the practice of international organizations, but will, at the same time, legitimize their new practice.* Thus, these two in combination would actualize the evolutionary nature of international organizations.

2.   In determining the inherently evolutionary interpretative framework as the constitutions of international organizations as pointed out in the two views mentioned above, it is important to make some clarifications with regard to the criterion of "necessity".

First, as was pointed out by the Court in the *Reparation* case, the organization must be deemed to have those powers which are conferred upon it "by necessary implication as being essential to the performance of its duties." The criterion of "necessary" or "essential" indicated here signifies not only that such powers are conferred upon the organization, but also that the powers conferred upon it are limited to only such powers. International organizations have, unless expressly provided, only those powers necessary or essential to the performance of their duties.[81]

---

[79]   Bindschedler, 'La délimitation des compétences des Nations Unies', 108 *Recueil des cours* 307, 327-30 (1963). ("In its application, the principle of interpretation called effectiveness leads to the recognition of international organizations' 'implied powers.' Who wants the end wants the means: insofar as the means indispensable for the achievement of the purpose are not provided for by the statute, they must be deduced...." [Our translation])

[80]   Higgins, 'The Development of International Law by the Political Organs of the United Nations', 59 *Proc. Am. Soc'y Int'l L.* 116, 123 (1965). In connection with the *Reparation* case, Higgins stated "[w]hereas it is arguable that the seeds of international personality are in the Charter itself, the authority to use it to bring claims was given to the United Nations not by the Charter but *by the Members, subsequently*". [Italics original] *Id.*

[81]   This concept of "necessity" will play a great role in practice since constituent instruments establish only the fundamental structures of international organizations and reserve the room for continual developments in accordance with the appearance of new functional needs. Because the *raison d'être* of an organization is the function to perform which it has been established, the concept of "necessity" is to be applied in connection with the function. Virally, for example, pointed out (Virally, 'La notion de fonction dans la théorie de l'organisation internationale', in *La communauté internationale: Mélanges offerts à Charles Rousseau* 277, 293 (1974)):

"[L]a fonction ne confère pas seulement une habilitation, elle impose une mesure: c'est seulement ce qui lui est 'nécessaire' qui peut être fait. La théorie des pouvoirs impliqués, consacrée par la Cour internationale de Justice dans son avis consultatif du 11 avril 1949 (Rec., p. 174) et qui représente la meilleure systématisation du caractère normatif de la finalité fonctionnelle, en retient ces deux aspects."

("[T]he function not only confers a qualification but it imposes a limit: it is only that which is 'necessary' for it which can

Secondly, the following points could be made by the comparison between the majority opinion and that of Judge Hackworth in the advisory opinions by the Court in the *Reparation* case and the *Effect of Awards* case. "Essential" is something more than "important", but it does not mean "absolutely essential" or "indispensable." The existence of an alternative mode of achieving the objective envisaged in the attribution of the basic power does not, by itself, diminish the essential need for the implied power,[82] nor does it exclude its exercise in the manner of restricting the express powers of other organs.

Thirdly, the significance of the presence of express powers in the constituent instruments must be taken into consideration. On the one hand, the implied powers contradictory to express provisions cannot in principle be admitted even if they prove to be necessary. Otherwise, the *raison-d'être* of the constituent instruments will be questioned. But it does not mean that a contradictory practice will not be made. If the express provisions are ignored and do not cause a protest by other member States, an implicit consent --- *de facto* modification --- could be considered to exist with regard to those provisions concerned. On the other hand, when the relevent provisions do not exist or only partially exist, could they be considered to exclude the relevant implied powers? The principle *expressio unius est exclusio alterius* will not necessarily be applied as is shown by the practices concerning treaty-making capacities and legislating capacities of internal law, although this point could be an issue. (For example, Judge Hackworth applied this principle by referring to Article 22 of the Charter in the *Effect of Awards* case.)

(2) With Regard to the Nature of the Provisions in the Constituent Instruments

1.   The interpretative framework as the constitution applied to a concrete case of activities of an international organization will inevitably be influenced by the specific nature of the relevant provisions in the constituent instrument. In this sense, the distinction between organizational provisions and substantive provisions cannot be, although useful to understand the constitutional nature *as a whole*, sufficient to clarify the interpretative framework as the constitution applied to a concrete case. *A case-by-case examination of the specific nature of relevant provisions* will be indispensable for this purpose.

From this perspective, Schachter justly emphasized that it is essential in considering the criteria of interpretation to bear in mind *the great differences that exist in the various provisions with regard to their degree of generality and the nature of the choices they require*. He introduced, for convenience, four categories: "rules", "principles", "standards" and "doctrine" (or

---

be done. The theory of implied powers recognized by the International Court of Justice in its advisory opinion of 11 April 1949 (Rep., p. 174) and which represent the best systematization of normative nature of functional finality, retains these two aspects." [Our translation])

[82] Lauterpacht, 'The Development of the Law of International Organization by the Decisions of International Tribunals', 152 *Recueil des cours* 379, 430-2, 434-6 (1976).

"general theory"). They are worth citing briefly.[83]

"Rules" refer to the norms which have relatively precise and explicit terms and which are generally intended to be applied without discrimination as to individual characteristics. In these "rules" such as those concerning procedure and organizational activities, key terms and expressions have generally accepted definitions taken for granted in almost all cases which arise.

"Principles", such as the broadly stated precepts of Article 2 of the Charter, have much greater generality, and their key terms are often highly abstract, thus leading to a clash with one another in specific cases. The opposition and indeterminancy of the principles call for a frame of reference that is quite different from that required in deciding the issues presented by specific rules. Here emphasis shifts from a dictionary and ordinary meaning to an assessment of a complex factual situation and a consideration of the consequences of a decision in the light of more basic values that are regarded as implicit in the constituent instruments.

"Standards", such as "good faith", "peace-loving" and "with due regard to equitable geographical distribution", refers to highly general prescriptions which involve evaluating the individual features of events, in contrast to "rules" (and to some degree "principles") which assume a relatively uniform application irrespective of individual characteristics. They are used to judge conduct of a kind which does not seem susceptible of treatment under more specific criteria and requires that each case be judged largely on its own facts. Their application necessarily requires consideration of the basic aims of the constituent instruments and of the perceived necessities of time and place.

"Doctrine" or "general theory", such as those in the great constitutional debates in the United Nations in 1950s and 1960s, comes into play particularly in cases of conflict between competing principles and in giving concrete meaning to broad concepts. Constitutions are generally considered to have certain underlying and implicit premises, which are literally extra-constitutional since they are not formulated in the constituent instruments, but which provide a higher-law rationale to justify choices between competing principles.

These four categories of legal provisions could be refined by further logical and syntactical analysis and replaced by more precise classification. But they clearly demonstrate that it is essential for the clarification of the interpretative framework as the constitution applied to a concrete case to examine the specific nature of relevant provisions in the constituent instruments.

2.   Based upon the previous analyses in the present article, several points could be added to the case-by-case examination of the specific nature of relevant provisions explained above.

First, practices of member States and of the organs of international organizations which could contain their interpretation of relevant provisions must be also analyzed in this examination. As was previously analyzed, the nature of relevant provisions will be influenced by these practices.

Secondly, the applicability of the theory of inter-temporal law requires that the intentions of the member States crystallized in the relevant provisions should be clarified: Have the member

---

[83] Schachter, 'The Relation of Law, Politics and Action in the United Nations', 109 *Recueil des cours* 165, 188-96 (1963). *See also* Dillard, 'Some Aspects of Law and Diplomacy', 91 *Recueil des cours* 445, 477 (1957).

States embodied in the relevant provisions such concepts or norms which anticipate various changes and developments and intend their adaptations to them after the establishment of the organization?

Thirdly, the relevancy of the provisions to the restriction of State sovereignty of member States must be analyzed. It is said that a pole in the general theory of international organizations is the State sovereignty and that their development will always constitute a dynamic equilibrium between the exigencies of their functions which find their source in the recognition on the part of their member States of certain common interests on the one hand and the resistence of certain member States with a view to protecting their other interests on the other.[84] Consequently, it will be necessary to distinguish between the provisions which could enhance the autonomy and efficiency of international organizations without directly involving the restriction of State sovereignty of member States and those which could promote their effectiveness only with the restriction and sacrifice of State sovereignty.

Fourthly, the purpose-oriented nature of organizational provisions should be duly taken into consideration. Because international organizations are considered as instruments, all of their structures are designed with a view to enabling them to achieve their functions most effectively and efficiently. Consequently, it will be reasonable to assume that organizational provisions have, in contrast to substantive provisions or ordinary treaties, a strong purpose-oriented nature which plays an important role in the constitutional interpretation.[85]

(3) With Regard to the Determination of the Guiding Principle in the Interpretative Framework as Constitutions

It is clear from the foregoing that the constitutional nature of constituent instruments and the interpretative framework as the constitutions have been, to a considerable extent, accepted by both the doctrines and the Court. However, it should also be pointed out that they are not generally accepted by all of the member States, particularly some great powers.[86] In such a situation, how should the applicability of the interpretative framework as the constitutions to a concrete case be appreciated? The following points should be taken into consideration.

First, the question will be *to reconcile the need to allow international organizations to evolve in adaptation to the constant changes with safeguarding individual States against having completely novel obligations imposed upon them merely as a result of being outvoted.*[87] The *raison-d'être* of the constituent instruments consists not only of establishing international organizations but also of protecting the reserved legal rights and interests of minority States by putting the activities of international organizations under their proper control. The general

---

[84] Virally, *supra* note 81, at 296.

[85] *Id.* at 291-2.

[86] *See supra* note 5 and 36 in Chap. 1.

[87] Waldock, 'General Course on Public International Law', 106 *Recueil des cours* 1, 34-5 (1962).

applicability as law requires that any interpretation of constituent instruments could be applicable even in other cases where the majority States and the minority States change their places: the prohibition of double standards. Satisfaction of this necessity demands a high statesmanship based upon a perspective for long-term development of international organizations on the part of the political organs as principal interpreters of the constituent instruments.[88]

Secondly, due attention must be paid to *the inherent fragility proper to international organizations in the present international society.* In the present state of organization of international society, cooperation on the part of member States will be necessary for the implementation of politically important resolutions. It might be possible to argue that such a consideration on the level of fact should be excluded from the legal analysis of constitutional interpretation. However, so far as there is some room left for discretion in the interpretation process, it would be reasonable and legitimate to take into consideration as legally relevant the element of whether international organizations could have actual effectiveness. De Visscher referred to this point as follows:

"Cette recherche de l'effectivité comporte une limite évidente. Si enclin que l'on soit à envisager les organisations internationales dans leurs perspectives d'avenir, dans ce qu'on appelle parfois leur 'dynamique', rien de solide ne peut se faire si, dans cette voie, on dépasse ce qu'autorise le degré de solidarité, réelle entre les Etats qui les ont instituées. Du maintien de cette solidarité, de l'assentiment continu qui en est l'expression, dépendent l'effectivité et finalement le sort de toute organisation internationale."[89]

---

[88] Rosenne stated this point as follows (Sh. Rosenne, 'Is the Constituent Instrument of an International Organization an International Treaty?', in ditto, *Developments in the Law of Treaties 1945-1986,* 181, 233 (1989)):

"[E]specially for questions involving the interpretation of a constituent instrument, there frequently occurs an inversion of what is often thought to be the process of interpretation, since the question is not so much one of textual exegesis for the purpose of applying the text in a concrete case, but rather one of the concrete circumstances to be carefully and comprehensively analysed, appraised and understood before determining how the constituent instrument as a whole, or some individual provision in it, is to be applied (or whether it was correctly applied in the past). This is an operation calling for the highest qualities of statesmanship and judicial and legal skill....

Unlike the interpretation of treaties where the fine-tuning has been supplied by a plethora of judicial decisions and arbitral awards extending over a long period of time, the development of any comprehensive and coherent pattern for the methodology of the interpretation of the constituent instrument is, on the whole, the outcome --- the intended outcome --- of political and not of judicial or arbitral action."

See also Gross, 'On the Degradation of the Constitutional Environment of the United Nations', 77 *Am. J. Int'l L.* 569 (1983), *reprinted in* L. Gross, 2 *Essays on International Law and Organization* 661 (1984).

[89] Ch. de Visscher, *Les effectivités du droit international public* 159 (1967).
("This search for effectiveness comprises an evident limit. How inclined one may be to envisage the international organizations in their perspective of future, in what one sometimes calls their 'dynamism', nothing solid can be created if, in this way, one exceeds what the degree of actual solidarity among the States which have established them authorizes. Upon the maintenance of this solidarity, the continuous consent which is its expression, depends the effectiveness and ultimately the destiny of every international organization." [Our translation]) *See also* a similar statement of Robinson. Robinson, 'Metamorphosis of the United Nations', 94 *Recueil des cours* 493, 580 (1958).

Chapter Six

Conclusion

Conclusion

We have demonstrated, as the interpretative framework of constituent instruments, an emerging doctrine of "the constitutions of international organizations", which differs from that of ordinary treaties in both: (1) the quantitative aspect of teleological extent admitted (2) the qualitative aspect of the legal significance possessed by the practice of the organs of international organizations. The analysis of various legal theories and materials in which we searched for the possible theoretical foundations of this emerging doctrine revealed that although each of them contains *a useful suggestion* (for example, that the constituent instruments contain teleological elements sufficient for the evolution of dynamism inherent in the international organizations; that they are considered to create an organism capable of life and growth, the development of which cannot be foreseen completely by the begetters; that they are to be considered to contain the dynamism and stability inherent in the institutional phenomena; that they are considered to contain many concepts and provisions of mobile reference to the temporal elements), none of them would be satisfactory for the refined and systematic construction of this emerging doctrine. It should, however, also be pointed out that they clearly demonstrate that *it has always been an important preoccupation, irrespective of time and place, that collective organisms could only be legally regulated by giving their inherent dynamism an appropriate place.*

Contrary to the interpretative framework of treaties which is based upon a large number of judicial decisions and arbitral awards extending over a long period of time, *this doctrine of constituent instruments as the constitutions is a product of recent phenomena in mainly universal international organizations.* As the present analysis has clarified, the present level of doctrines and actual practices seems to allow only the construction of *a solid but basic framework of interpretation.* In the operation of the international organizations, much seems to depend upon a high statesmanship based upon a perspective for their long-term development on the part of the member States constituting the political organs as principal interpreters of their constituent instruments. However, in spite of these limitations, we are convinced that *this doctrine could provide a useful perspective for the present and future evolution of international organizations in the dynamically changing international relations.*

The present study has left some problems. The doctrine of the constitutions of international organizations as the interpretative framework of their constituent instruments needs to be further examined, modified and improved by concrete analyses of the structures and activities of different organizations. These analyses must include examinations with regard to, among other things, (1) to what extent this doctrine has actually been accepted by the member States of various international organizations, (2) in what manner this doctrine has been applied to the different constituent instruments, and (3) what is the criterion to distinguish those provisions to which this doctrine could be applied from other provisions to which it could not.

Bibliography

and

Index

Bibliography

The authors in bold type indicate that their works are particularly useful for our study.

Books

Abi-Saab, G. (ed.), *The Concept of International Organization* (1981).

Akehurst, M. B., *The Law Governing Employment in International Organizations* (1967).

Akintan, S. A., *The Law of International Economic Institutions in Africa* (1977).

Alvarez, A., *Le droit international nouveau dans ses rapports avec la vie actuelle des peuples* (1959).

Bastid, P., *Cours de droit international public: Le droit des organisations internationales (Les cours de droit, 1968-69).*

Bedjaoui, M., *The New World Order and the Security Council, Testing the Legality of its Acts* (1994).

Belaouane-Gherari, S., & H. Gherari (eds.), *Les organisations régionales africaines, Recueil de textes et documents* (1988).

Bettati, M., *Le droit des organisations internationales* (Que sais-je ?, 1987).

Blum, Y., *Eroding the United Nations Charter* (1993)

Bowett, D. W., *United Nations Forces, A Legal Study of United Nations Practice* (1964).

Bowett, D. W., *The Law of International Institutions* (4th ed. 1982).

Bredimas, A., *Methods of Interpretation and Community Law* (1978).

Broderick, A. (ed.), *The French Institutionalists* (M. Welling trans. 1970).

Burban, J.-J., *Le Conseil de l'Europe* (Que sais-je?, 1985).

Carreau, D., *Le Fonds monetaire international* (1970).

Castañeda, J., *Legal Effects of United Nations Resolutions* (A. Amoia trans. 1969).

Chandler, R., R. Enslen and P. Renstrom, *The Constitutional Law Dictionary*, Vol. 1 (1985).

Chemerinsky, E., *Interpreting the Constitution* (1987).

Ciobanu, D., *Preliminary Objections Related to the Jurisdiction of the United Nations Political Organs* (1975).

Cohen, B. V., *The United Nations: Constitutional Developments, Growth, and Possibilities* (1961).

Combacau, J., & S. Sur, *Droit international public* (1993).

Cot, J. - P. & A. Pellet (ed.), *La Charte des Nations Unies* (2d ed. 1991).

de Visscher, Ch., *Theory and Practice in Public International Law* (Rev. ed. P. E. Corbett trans. 1968) [corresponding to the French third edition].

de Visscher, Ch., *Théorie et réalités en droit international public* (4th ed. 1970).

de Visscher, Ch., *Problème d'interprétation judiciaire en droit international public* (1963).

271

de Visscher, Ch., *Les effectivités du droit international public* (1967).

Degan, V. D., *L'Interprétation des accords en droit international* (1963).

Delos, J., *La société internationale et les principes du droit public* (2d ed. 1950).

Desqueyrat, A., *Le droit objectif et la technique positive* (1933).

di Qual, L.,*Les effets des résolutions des Nations Unies* (1967).

Dinh, N. Q., P. Daillier & A. Pellet, *Droit international public* (5th ed. 1994).

Dugard, J., *The South West Africa / Namibia Dispute* (1973).

Dupuy, R.-J., *Manuel sur les organisations internationales* (1988).

Dupuy, P.-M., *Droit international public* (2d ed. 1993).

Eisemann, P. M., *L'organisation internationale du commerce des produits de base* (1982).

Feld, W., *The Court of the European Communities* (1964).

Fitzmaurice, Sir G., *The Law and Procedure of the International Court of Justice*, 2 Vols. (1986).

Franck, T. M., *Nation Against Nation* (1985).

Friedmann, W., *Legal Theory* (5th ed. 1967).

Friedmann, W., *Changing Structure of International Law* (1964).

Gold, J., *Interpretation by the Fund* (1968, Pamphlet Series No. 11).

Gold, J., *Legal and Institutional Aspects of the International Monetary System: Selected Essays* (1979).

Goodrich, L. M., *The United Nations in a Changing World* (1974).

Goodrich, L. M., E. Hambro, and A. Simons, *Charter of the United Nations, Commentary and Documents* (3d rev. ed. 1969).

Goodrich, L. M., *The United Nations* (1960).

Green, A., *Political Integration by Jurisprudence* (1969).

Gross, L., *Essays on International Law and Organization*, 2 Vols. (1984).

Haraszti, G., *Some Fundamental Problems of the Law of Treaties* (1973).

Hay, P., *Federalism and Supranational Organizations* (1966).

Hussain, I., *Dissenting and Separate Opinions at the World Court* (1984).

International Monetary Fund, *Selected Decisions and Selected Documents on the International Monetary Fund* (19th Issue, 1994).

Jackson, J. H., *World Trade and the Law of GATT* (1969).

Jasentuliyana, N., & R. S. K. Lee (eds.), *Manual on Space Law*, 4 Vols. (1979).

Jenks, C. W., *The Prospects of International Adjudication* (1964).

Kahn, R., *Implied Powers of The United Nations* (1970).

Kaptayn, P. & P. van Themaar, *Introduction to the Law of the European Communities* (1973).

Kapteyn, R. J. G., et al.(eds.), *International Organization and Integration: Annotated Basic Documents and Descriptive Directory of International Organizations and Arrangements*, 5Vols. (1983).

Kelsen, H., *Pure Theory of Law* (2d ed. M. Knight trans. 1967).

Kelsen, H., *The Law of the United Nations: A Critical Analysis of Its Fundamental Problems* (1950). With Supplement *Recent Trends in the Law of the United Nations* (1951).

Khan, K.-R., *The Law and Organization of International Commodity Agreements* (1982).

Kohona, P. T. B., *The Regulation of International Economic Relations through Law* (1985).

Kopelmanas, L., *L'Organisation des Nations Unies* (1947)

Lambrinidis, J., *The Structure, Function, and Law of a Free Trade Area, the European Free Trade Association* (1965).

Lauterpacht, H., *The Development of International Law by the International Court* (1958).

Lesguillons, H., *L'application d'un traité-fondation: Le traité instituant la C.E.E.* (1968).

Malinverni, G., *Le réglement des différends dans les organisations internationales économiques* (1974).

Mann, C., *The Function of Judicial Decision in European Economic Integration* (1972).

McWhinney, E., *Conflict and Compromise: International Law and World Order in a Revolutionary Age* (1981).

Merillat, H. C. L. (ed.), *Legal Advisers and International Organizations* (1966).

Meyers, H., *The Nationality of Ships* (1967).

Ministry of Foreign Affairs of Japan (ed.), *Kokusaikikan Soran (General Survey of International Organizations)* (1991) [in Japanese].

Miyazaki, S. (ed.), *Kihon Hanrei Sôsho Kokusaiho (Basic Cases on International Law)* (1981).

Ninčić, D., *The Problem of Sovereignty in the Charter and in the Practice of the United Nations* (1970).

O'Connor, J. F., *Good Faith in International Law* (1991).

Osmañczyk, E. J. (ed.), *Encyclopedia of the United Nations and International Agreements* (2d ed. 1991).

Parry, C. et al. (eds.), *Parry and Grant Encyclopaedic Dictionary of International Law* (1986).

Pescatore, P., *The Law of Integration* (C. Dwyer trans. 1974).

Pollard, D. E., *Law and Policy of Producers' Associations* (1984).

Reisman, W. M., & A. R. Willard, *International Incidents, The Law That Counts in World Politics* (1988).

Renard, G., *La philosophie de l'institution* (1939).

Renard, G., *La théorie de l'institution, essai d'ontologie juridique* (1930).

Renard, G., *L'institution, fondement d'une rénovation de l'ordre social* (1933).

Reuter, P., *Introduction au droit des traités* (2d ed. 1985).

Rideau, J., *Juridictions internationales et contrôle du respect des traités constitutifs des organisations internationales* (1969).

Romano, S., *L'ordinamento giuridico* (3d ed. 1977).

Rosenne, Sh., *The Law and Practice of the International Court* (2d rev. ed. 1985).

Rouyer-Hameray, B., *Les compétences implicites des organisations internationales* (1962).

Schermers, H. G., *International Institutional Law* (1980).

Schiavone, G., *The Institutions of COMECON* (1981).

Schwarzenerger, G., *International Law, Vol. 3, Inernational Constitutional Law* (1976).

Simma, B. (ed.), *The Charter of the United Nations, A Commentary* (1994).

273

Simon, D., *l'interprétation judiciaire des traités d'organisations internationales* (1981).

Sinclair, I., *The Vienna Convention on the Law of Treaties* (2d ed. 1984).

Sloan, B., *United Nations General Assembly Resolutions in Our Changing World* (1991).

Slonim, S., *South West Africa and the United Nations: an International Mandate in Dispute* (1972).

Stoetzer, O. C., *Organization of American States* (2d ed. 1993).

Stone, J., *Social Dimensions of Law and Justice* (1966).

Sur, S., *L'interprétation en droit international public* (1974).

Szawlowski, R., *The System of the International Organizations of the Communist Countries* (1976).

Takano, Y. (ed.), *Hanrei Kenkyu Kokusaishihosaibansho* (*The Jurisprudence of the International Court of Justice*) (1965).

Tavernier, P., *Recherches sur l'application dans le temps des actes et des régles en droit international public (Problèmes de droit intertemporel ou de droit transitoire)* (1970).

Thierry, H., J. Combacau, S. Sur & Ch. Vallée, *Droit international public* (5th ed. 1986).

Timmermans, C., & E. V lker (eds.), *Division of Powers between the European Communities and their Member States in the Field of External Relations* (1981).

Tunkin, G., *Theory of International Law* (W. E. Butler trans. 1974).

Valticos, N., *International Labour Law* (1979).

Verzijl, J. H. W., *The Jurisprudence of the World Court*, 2 Vols. (1965 & 1966).

Virally, M., *L'organisation mondiale* (1972).

Voïcu, I., *De l'interprétation authentique des traités internationaux* (1968).

Weissberg, G., *The International Status of the United Nations* (1961).

Yambrusic, E. S., *Treaty Interpretation* (1987).

Articles

Abou-El-Wafa, A., 'La pratique ultérieuredes organisations internationales', 45 *Revue Egyptienne de Droit International* 29 (1989).

Akehurst, M., 'The Hierarchy of the Sources of International Law', 47 *Brit. Y. B. Int'l L.* 273 (1974-1975).

Amerasinghe, C. F., 'The United Nations Expenses Case --- A Contribution to the Law of International Organization', 4 *Indian J. Int'l L.* 177 (1964).

Anand, R. P.,'The Role of Individual and Dissenting Opinions in International Adjudication', 14 *Int'l & Comp. L. Q.* 788 (1965).

Audéoud, O., 'La Cour internationale de Justice et le règlement des différends au sein des organisations internationales', 18 *R. G. D. I. P.* 945 (1977).

Bastid, P., 'Place de la notion d'institution dans une théorie générale des organisations internationales', in *Études en l'honneur d'A. Mestre* 50 (1956).

Bastid, P., 'La théorie de l'acte constitutif des organisations internationales', in P. Bastid, *Cours de droit international public: Le droit des organisations internationales* 50 (Les cours de droit, 1968-69).

Bebr, G., 'Judicial Policy of the Court of Justice in Developing the Legal Order of the European Communities', in *Toward World Order and Hunam Dignity* 293 (W. Reisman & B. Weston eds. 1976).

Bennett, R. W., 'Objectivity in Constitutional Law', 132 *Univ. Pennsylvania L. Rev.* 445 (1984).

Berlia, G., 'Admission d'un État aux Nations Unies (Charte art. 4)', 53 *R. G. D. I. P.* 481 (1949).

Bernhardt, R., 'Interpretation and Implied (Tacit) Modification of Treaties, Comments on Arts. 27, 28, 29 and 38 of the ILC's 1966 Draft Articles on the Law of Treaties', 27 *Zeitschrift für auslandisches öffentliches Rechts und Völkerrecht* 491 (1967).

Bindschedler, D., 'Le règlement des différends relatifs au statut d'un organisme international', 124 *Recueil des cours* 453 (1968).

Bindschedler, R. L., 'La délimitation des compétences des Nations Unies', 108 *Recueil des cours* 307 (1963).

Bollecker, B., 'L'avis consultatif du 21 Juin 1971 dans l'affaire de la Namibie (Sud-Est Africain), 17 *A. F. D. I.* 281 (1971).

Boulouis, J., 'La jurisprudence de la Cour de Justice des Communautés européennes relative aux relations extérieures des Communautés, 160 *Recueil des cours* 335 (1978).

Bowett, D. W., 'International Incidents: New Genre or New Delusion?', 12 *Yale J. Int'l L.* 386 (1987).

Caflisch, L. C., 'The Settlement of Disputes relating to Activities in the International Seabed Area', in *The New Law of the Sea* 303 (C. L. Rozakis & C. A. Stephanou eds. 1983).

Campbell, A. I. L., 'The Attitudes and Practices of the Specialized Agencies and U. N. Organs and the Interpretation of Their Basic Constitutions', *The Juridical Review* 177 (1986).

Charpentier, J., 'Tendances de l'élaboration du droit interntional public coutumier', in *L'élaboration du droit international public* 105 (1975).

Chaumont, Ch. M., 'La signification du principe de spécialitè des organisations internationales', in *Probléme de droit des gens: Mélanges offerts à Henri Rolin* 55 (1964).

Chevallier, R. - M., 'Methods and Reasoning of the European Court in Its Interpretation of Community Law', 1 *Comm'n Mkt L. Rev.* 21 (1964).

Chiu, H., 'Succession in International Organizations', 14 *Int'l & Comp. L. Q.* 83 (1965).

Ciobanu, D., 'Impact of the Characteristics of the Charter upon Its Interpretation', in *Current Problems of International Law: Essays on U. N. Law and the Law of Armed Conflict* 3 (A. Cassese ed. 1975).

Clariana, G. G., 'Settlement of Disputes in International Commodity Agreements, 1949-1979', 63 *Rivista di diritto internazionale* 392 (1980).

Colliard, C. A., 'Avis Consultatif relatif à la composition du Comité de Sécurité maritime de l'Orgnisation intergouvernementale consultatative de la Navigation maritime du 8 juin 1960', 6 *A. F. D. I.* 338 (1960).

Colliard, C. A., 'Le règlement des différends dans les organisations intergouvernementales de caractère non politique', in *Hommage d'une génération de juristes au Président Basdevant* 152 (1960).

Combacau, J., Review of 'Simon, D., l'interprétation judiciaire des traités d'organisations internationales (1981)', 109 *Journal du droit international* 752 (1982).

Combacau, J., 'La question du transfert du Bureau régional de l'O. M. S. devant la Cour international de Justice', 26 *A. F. D. I.* 225 (1980).

Conforti, B., 'Le rôle de l'accord dans le système des Nations Unies', 142 *Recueil des cours* 203 (1974).

Costonis, J. J., 'The Treaty-Making Power of the European Economic Community: The Perspectives of a Decade', 5 *Comm'n Mkt L. Rev.* 421 (1968).

Cot, J. - P., 'La conduite subséquente des parties à un traité', 70 *R. G. D. I. P.* 632 (1966).

Courteix, S. 'Organisations internationales à vocation mondiale ou régionale dans le domaine des télécommunication par satellites', in 1 Juris-classeur de droit international (1985) Fascicule 141.

de Lacharrière, R., 'Cour international de Justice --- Jugement du Tribunal administratif de l'O. I. T. sur requêtes contre l'U. N. E. S. C. O., Avis consultatif du 23 octobre 1956', 2 *A. F. D. I.* 383 (1956).

de Visscher, Ch., 'L'interprétation judiciaire des traités d'organisation internationale', 41 *Rivista di diritto internazionale* 177 (1958).

Degan, V. D., 'Attempts to Codify Principles of Treaty Interpretation and the South-West Africa Case', 8 *Indian J. Int'l L.* 9 (1968).

Degan, V. D., 'Procédés d'interprétation tirés de la jurisprudence de la Cour de Justice des Communautés européennes', 2 *Revue trimestroelle de droit européen* 189 (1966).

Dehaussy, J., 'Le problème de la classification des traités et le projet de convention établi par la Commission du Droit international des Nations Unies', in *Recueil d'études de droit international en hommage à Paul Guggemheim* 305 (1968).

Dillard, H. C., 'Some Aspects of Law and Diplomacy', 91 *Recueil des cours* 445 (1957).

Dillon, Jr., Th. J., 'The World Trade Organization: A New Legal Order for World Trade?', 16 *Michigan J. Int'l L.* 349 (1995).

do Nascimento e Silva, G. E., 'The 1969 and the 1986 Conventions on the Law of Treaties: A Comparison', in *International Law at a Time of Perplexity, Essays in Honour of Shabtai Rosenne* 461 (Y. Dinstein & M. Tabory eds. 1989).

do Nascimento e Silva, G. E., 'Le facteur temps et les traités', 154 *Recueil des cours* 215 (1977).

Dodd, W. F., 'Implied Powers and Implied limitations in Constitutional Law', 29 *Yale L. J.* 137 (1919).

Dugard, J., 'The Opinion on South West Africa (Namibia): the Teleologists Triumph', 88 *South African L. J.* 467 (1971).

Dugard, J., 'Namibia (South West Africa): The Court's Opinion, South Africa's Response, and Prospects for the Future', 11 *Columbia J. Transna'l L.* 14 (1972).

Dupuy, R. J., 'Communauté internationale et disparités de développement', 165 *Recueil des cours* 9 (1979).

Dupuy, P. - M., 'Editorial: Sécurité collective et organisation de la paix', 97 *R. G. D. I. P.* 617 (1993).

Eagleton, C., 'International Organization and the Law of Responsiblity', 76 *Recueil des cours* 319 (1950).

Elias, T. O., 'The Doctrine of Intertemporal Law', 74 *Am. J. Int'l L.* 285 (1980).

Elias, T. O., 'The Commission of Mediation, Conciliation and Arbitration of the Organization of African Unity', 40 *Brit. Y. B. Int'l L.* 336 (1964).

Elias, T. O., 'The Charter of the Organization of African Unity', 59 *Am. J. Int'l L.* 243 (1965).

Engel, S., '"Living International Constitutions and the World Court (the Subsequent Practice of International Organs under Their Constituent Instruments)', 16 *Int'l & Comp. L. Q.* 865 (1967)

Engel, S., 'The Changing Charter of the United Nations', 7 *Y. B. World Aff.* 71 (1953).

Engel, S., 'Procedures for the de facto Revision of the Charter', *Proc. Am. Soc'y Int'l L.* 108 (1965).

Fawcett, J. E. S., 'The Function of Law in International Commodity Agreements', 44 *Brit. Y. B. Int'l L.* 157 (1971).

Fawcett, J. E. S., 'The Place of Law in an International Organization', 36 *Brit. Y. B. Int'l L.* 321 (1960).

276

Feinberg, N., 'L'admission de nouveaux Membres à la Société des Nations et à l'Organisation des Nations Unies', 80 *Recueil des cours* 293 (1952).

Ferrari Bravo, L., 'Méthodes de recherche de la coutume internationale dans la pratique des États', 192 *Recueil des cours* 233 (1985).

Fischer, G., 'Le mode de règlement des différends adopté par l'accord international sur le blé', 1 *A. F. D. I.* 208 (1955).

FitzGerald, G. F., 'The International Civil Aviation Organization and the Development of Coventions on International Air Law (1947-1978)', 3 *Annals Air & Space L.* 51 (1978).

FitzGerald, G. F., 'The Judgment of the International Court of Justice in the Appeal Relating to the Jurisdiction of the ICAO Council', 12 *Canadian Y. B. Int'l L.* 153 (1974).

Fitzmaurice, Sir G., 'Judicial Innovation --- Its Uses and Its Perils --- as Exemplified in Some of the Work of the International Court of Justice during Lord McNair's Period of Office', in *Cambridge Essays in International Law, Essays in Honour of Lord McNair* 24 (1965).

Fitzmaurice, Sir G., 'The Law and Procedure of the International Court of Justice: General Principles and Substantive Law', 27 *Brit. Y. B. Int'l L.* 1 (1950), *reprinted in* Sir G. Fitzmaurice, 1 *The Law and Procedure of the International Court of Justice* 1 (1986).

Fitzmaurice, Sir G., 'The Law and Procedure of the International Court of Justice: Treaty Interpretation and Certain Other Treaty Points', 28 *Brit. Y. B. Int'l L.* 1 (1951), *reprinted in* Sir G. Fitzmaurice, 1 *The Law and Procedure of the International Court of Justice* 42 (1986).

Fitzmaurice, Sir G., 'The Law and Procedure of the International Court of Justice: International Organizations and Tribunals', 29 *Brit. Y. B. Int'l L.* 1 (1952), *reprinted in* Sir G., Fitzmaurice, 1 *The Law and Procedure of the International Court of Justice* 70 (1986).

Fitzmaurice, Sir G., 'The Law and Procedure of the International Court of Justice 1951-4: Treaty Interpretation and Other Treaty Points', 33 *Brit. Y. B. Int'l L.* 203 (1957), *reprinted in* Sir G. Fitzmaurice, 1 *The Law and Procedure of the International Court of Justice* 337 (1986).

Flory, Th., 'Les Accords du Tokyo Round du G. A. T. T. et la réform des procédures de règlement des différends dans le système commercial interétatique', 86 *R. G. D. I. P.* 235 (1982).

Focsaneanu, L., 'Le droit interne de l'organisation des Nations Unies', 3 *A. F. D. I.* 315 (1957).

Giardina, A., 'The Rule of Law and Implied Powers in the European Communities', 1 *Italian Y. B. Int'l L.* 99 (1975).

Gold, J., 'The Interpretation by the International Monetary Fund of the Articles of Agreement', 3 *Int'l & Comp. L. Q.* 256 (1954).

Gold, J., 'Interpretation by the Internaional Monetary Fund of Its Articles of Agreement - II', 16 *Int'l & Comp. L. Q.* 289 (1967).

Goodrich, L. M., 'The Changing United Nations', in *Transnational Law in a Changing Society, Essays in Honor of Philip C. Jessup* 259 (W. Friedmann et al. eds. 1972).

Gordon, E., 'Old Orthodoxies amid New Experiences: The South West Africa (Namibia) Litigation and the Uncertain Jurisprudence of the International Court of Justice', 1 *Denver J. Int'l L. & Policy* 65 (1971).

Gordon, E., 'The World Court and the Interpretation of Constitutive Treaties', 59 *Am. J. Int'l L.* 794 (1965).

Gregory, Ch. N., 'The Neutralization of the Aaland Islands', 17 *Am. J. Int'l L.* 63 (1923).

Gros, A., 'Concerning the Advisory Role of the International Court of Justice', in *Transnational Law in a Changing Society, Essays in Honor of Philip C. Jessup* 313 (W. Friedmann et al. eds. 1972).

Gros, A., 'The Problem of Redress against the Decisions of International Organizations', 36 *Transactions of the Grotius Soc'y Int'l L.* 30 (1950).

277

Gross, L., 'Underutilization of the International Court of Justice', 27 *Harvard Int'l L. J.* 571 (1986).

Gross, L., 'States as Organs of International Law and the Problem of Autointerpretation', in *Law and Politics in the World Community: Essays on Hans Kelsen's Pure Theory and Related Problems in International Law* 59 (G. A. Lipsky ed. 1953), *reprinted in* L. Gross, 1 *Essays on International Law and Organization* 367 (1984).

Gross, L., 'Election of States to United Nations Membership', *Proc. Am. J. Int'l L.* 37 (1954), *reprinted in* L. Gross, 1 *Essays on International Law and Organization* 585 (1984).

Gross, L., 'Progress towards Universality of Membership in the United Nations', 50 *Am. J. Int'l L.* 791 (1956), *reprinted in* L. Gross, 2 *Essays on International Law and Organization* 607 (1984).

Gross, L., 'Expenses of the United Nations for Peace-Keeping Operations: The Advisory Opinion of the International Court of Justice', 17 *Int'l Organization* 1 (1963), *reprinted in* L. Gross, 2 *Essays on International Law and Organization* 753 (1984).

Gross, L., 'Domestic Jurisdiction, Enforcement Measures and the Congo', *Australian Y. B. Int'l L.* 137 (1965), reprinted in L. Gross, 2 *Essays on International Law and Organization* 1173 (1984).

Gross, L., 'The International Court of Justice and the United Nations', 120 *Recueil des cours* 313 (1967), *reprinted in* L. Gross, *Essays on International Law and Organization* 845 (1984).

Gross, L., 'On the Degradation of the Constitutional Environment of the United Nations', 77 *Am. J. Int'l L.* 569 (1983), *reprinted in* L. Gross, 2 *Essays on International Law and Organization* 661 (1984).

Groux, J., 'Le parallélisme des compétences internes et externes de la Communauté économique européenne', *Cahier de droit européen* 3 (1978).

Gutiérrez Posse, H., 'La maxime ut res magis valeat quam pereat (Interprétation en fonction de l''effet utile'), Les Interprétation "extensives'"et "restrictives"', 23 *Österreichische Zeitschrift für öffentliches Recht* 229 (1972).

Hahn, H., 'Constitutional Limitations in the Law of the European Organisations', 108 *Recueil des cours* 196 (1963).

Hambro, E., 'Dissenting and Individual Opinions in the International Court of Justice', 17 Zeitschrift für ausländiches öffentliches Recht und Völkerrecht 229 (1956-57).

Hardy, M., 'Opinion 1/76 of the Court of Justice: The Rhine Case and the Treaty-Making Powers of the Community',14 *Comm'n Mkt L.* Rev. 561 (1977).

Hardy, M. J. L., 'Jurisdiction of the Administrative Tribunal of the I. L. O., The Advisory Opinion of the International Court of Justice of October 23, 1956', 6 *Int'l & Comp. L. Q.* 338 (1957).

Hardy, M. J. L., 'Claims by International Organizations in Respect of Injuries to Their Agents', 37 *Brit. Y. B. Int'l L.* 516 (1961).

Harvard Law School, 'Research in International Law', 29 *Am. J. Int'l L., Supp.* 966 (1935).

Hauriou, M., 'La théorie de l'institution et de la fondation (Essai de vitalisme social)', in *Aux sources du droit* 89 (1933).

Hevener, N. K., 'The 1971 South-West African Opinion, A New International Judicial Philosophy', 24 *Int'l & Comp. L. Q.* 791 (1975).

Hexner, E. P., 'Teleological Interpretation of Basic Instruments of Public International Organizations', in *Law, State, and International Order, Essays in Honor of Hans Kelsen* 119 (S. Engel ed. 1964).

Higgins, R., 'The Advisory Opinion on Namibia: Which UN Resolutions Are Binding under Article 25 of the Charter?', 21 *Int'l & Comp. L. Q.* 270 (1972).

Higgins, R., 'The Development of International Law by the Political Organs of the United Nations', 59 *Proc. Am. Soc'y Int'l L.* 116 (1965).

Hirose, Y., 'The Right of Self-Determination of Peoples and the Powers of the United Nations [in Japanese]', 204 *Meiji*

278

Gakuin L. Rev. 1 (1973).

Hogg, J. F., 'Peace-Keeping Costs and Charter Obligations --- Implications of the International Court of Justice Decision on Certain Expenses of the United Nations', 62 *Colum. L. Rev.* 1230 (1962).

Honig, F., 'The International Court of Justice 1947-50', *Zeitschrift für ausländisches öffentliches Recht und Völkerrecht* 407 (1952).

Hudec, R. E., 'The GATT Legal System: A Diplomat's Jurisprudence', 4 *J. World Trade L.* 615 (1970).

Hudson, M. O., 'Admission to the United Nations: Advisory Opinion of World Court as to Conditions', 34 *Am. B. A. J.* 652 (1948).

Hudson, M. O., 'The Friendly Settlement of Economic Disputes between States', 26 *Am. J. Int'l L.* 353 (1932).

Humber, P. O., 'Admission to the United Nations', 24 *Brit. Y. B. Int'l L.* 90 (1947).

Huntzinger, J., 'L'affair de l'appel concernant la compétence de Conceil du l'O. A. C. I. devant la Cour international de Justice (arrét du aout 1972)', 78 *R. G. D. I. P.* 975 (1974).

International Law Commission, 'Report of the International Law Commission to the General Assembly', [1966] 2 *Y. B. Int'l L. Comm'n* 169, 218, U.N. Doc. A/6309/Rev. 1.

Jackson, J. H., 'The Legal Framework of United Nations Financing: Peacekeeping and Penury', 51 *California L. Rev.* 79 (1963).

Jackson, J. H., 'GATT as an Instrument for the Settlement of Trade Disputes', 61 *Proc. Am. Soc'y Int'l L.* 144 (1967).

Jacobs, F. G., 'Varieties of Approach to Treaty Interpretation: with Special Reference to the Draft Convention on the Law of Treaties before the Vienna Diplomatic Conference', 18 *Int'l & Comp. L. Q.* 318 (1969).

Jacqué, J. - P., 'Rapport général, Le Consta', in *Les organisations internationales contemporaines* 3 (1988).

Jacqué, J. - P., 'L'avis de la Cour International du Justice du 21 Juin 1971', 76 *R. G. D. I. P.* 1046 (1972).

Jenks, C. W., 'The Interpretation of International Labour Conventions by the International Labour Office', 20 *Brit. Y. B. Int'l L.* 132 (1939).

Jennings, Sir R., 'The International Court's Advisory Opinion on the Voting Procedure on Questions Concerning South-West Africa', 42 *Transactions of the Grotius Society* 85 (1957).

Johnson, D. H. N., 'Review of Books: Le Droit international nouveau dans ses rapports avec la vie actuelle des peuples. By Alejandro Alvarez', 35 *Brit. Y. B. Int'l L.* 274 (1959).

Kahn, E., 'The International Court's Advisory Opinion on the Internatinal Status of South-West Africa', 4 *Int'l L. Q.* 78 (1951).

Kano, T., 'Revision of the IMCO Convention and Flags of Convenience [in Japanese]', 28(4) *Kobe L. J.* 369 (1979).

Kapteyn, R. J. G., 'Article 235' in 6 *The Law of the European Economic Community, A Commentary on the EEC Treaty* 6 (H. Smit & P. Herzog eds. 1981).

Koers, A. W., 'The External Authority of the EEC in Regard to Marine Fisheries', 14 *Comm'n Mkt L. Rev.* 269 (1977).

Kohona, P. T. B., 'Dispute Resolution under the World Trade Organization: An Overview', 28 *J. World Trade* 23 (1994).

Kopelmanas, L., 'La notion de la liberté économique devant la Justice internationale', 81 *Journal du droit internal* 64 (1954).

Kovar, R., 'La contribution de la Cour de justice au développement de la condition internationale de la Communauté européenne', *Cahier de droit européenne* 527 (1978).

Kovar, R., 'L'affaire de l'A.E.T.R. devant la Cour de Justice des Communautés européennes et la compétence internatinale de la C.E.E.', 17 *A. F. D. I.* 386 (1971).

279

Kraus, H., 'Système et fonction des traités internationaux', 50 *Recueil des cours* 311 (1934).

Kruse, H., 'Implied Powers und Implied Limitations', 4 *Archiv des Völkerrechts* 169 (1953-54).

Lachs, M., 'Les conventions multimaterales et les organisations internationales', 2 *A. F. D. I.* 334 (1956).

Lachs, M., 'Le role des organisations internationales dans la formation du droit international', in *Mélanges offerts à Henri Rolin, Problèmes de droit des gens* 161 (1964).

Lachs, M., 'Le développment et les fonctions des traités multilateraux', 92 *Recueil des cours* 229 (1957).

Lambrinidis, J. S., 'The Emergence of Quasi Judicial Quasi Administrative Organ and Methods for the Settlement of International Disputes', 16 *Revue hellénique de droit international* 78 (1963).

Lang, W., 'Les régles d'interprétation codifiés par la Convention de Vienne sur le Droit des Traités et les divers types de traités', 24 *Österreichische Zeitschrift für öffentlishes Recht* 113 (1973).

Lauterpacht, E., 'The Legal Effect of Illegal Acts of International Organizations', in *Cambridge Essays in International Law: Essays in Honour of Lord McNair* 88 (1965).

Lauterpacht, E., 'The Development of the Law of International Organization by the Decisions of International Tribunals', 152 *Recueil des cours* 379 (1976).

Lauterpacht, H., 'Restrictive Interpretation and the Principle of Effectiveness in the Interpretation of Treaties', 26 *Brit. Y. B. Int'l L.* 48 (1949).

Leopold, P. M., 'External Relations Power of EEC in Theory and in Practice', 26 *Int'l & Comp. L. Q.* 54 (1977).

Lesguillons, H., 'L'extension des compétences de la C.E.E. par l'article 235 du Traité de Rome', 20 *A. F. D. I.* 886 (1974).

Liang, Y. - L., 'Notes on Legal Questions Concerning the United Nations, Reparation for Injuries Suffered in the Service of the United Nations', 43 *Am J. Int'l L.* 460 (1949).

Liang, Y. - L., 'Notes on Legal Questions Concerning the United Nations', 43 *Am. J. Int'l L.* 288 (1949).

Lissitzyn, O. J., 'International Law and the Advisory Opinion on Namibia', 11 *Columbia J. Transna'l L.* 50 (1972).

Macdonald, R. St. J., 'The United Nations Charter: Constitution or Contract ?', in *The Structure and Process of International Law* 889 (R. St. J. Macdonald & D. M. Johnston eds. 1983).

MacGibbon, I. C., 'The Scope of Acquiescence in International Law', 31 *Brit. Y. B. Int'l L.* 143 (1954).

Makarczyk, J., 'Contribution to the Problem of the Sttlement of Disputes concerning the Exploitation of Seabed Resources', in *Le règlementdes différends sur le nouvelles ressources naturelles* 53 (R.- J. Dupuy ed. 1983).

Malawer, S. S., 'Treaty-Making Competence of the European Communities', 7 *J. World Trade L.* 169 (1973).

Manin, A., 'Appel concernant la compétence du Conceil de l'O. A. C. I. ', 19 *A. F. D. I.* 290 (1973).

Mankiewicz, R. H., 'Pouvoir judiciaire du Conseil et règlement pour la solution des différends', 3 *A. F. D. I.* 383 (1957).

Mann, F. A., 'The "Interpretation" of the Constitution of International Financial Organizations', 43 *Brit. Y. B. Int'l L.* 1 (1968-69).

Marenco, G., 'Les conditions d'application de l'article 235 du Traité C.E.E.', 13 *Revue de marché common* 147 (1970).

McDougal, M. S., 'The International Law Commission's Draft Articles upon Interpretation: Textuality redivivus', 61 *Am. J. Int'l L.* 992 (1967).

McGovern, E., 'Disputes Settlement in the GATT: Adjudication or Negotiation ?', in *The European Community and GATT* 73 (M. Hilf et al. eds. 1986).

McMahon, J. F., 'The Court of the European Communities Judicial Interpretation and International organizations', 37 *Brit. Y. B. Int'l L.* 320 (1961).

McNair, Lord, 'The Functions and Differing Legal Character of Treaties', 11 *Brit. Y. B. Int'l L.* 100 (1930), *reprinted in* Lord McNair, *The Law of Treaties* 739 (1961).

Mehrish, B. N., 'Travaux Préparatoires as an Element in the Interpretation of Treaties', 11 *Indian J. Int'l L.* 39 (1971).

Mendelson, M. F., 'Reservations to the Constitutions of International Organizations', 45 *Brit. Y. B. Int'l L.* 137 (1971).

Meron, Th., 'Budget Approval by the General Assembly of the United Nations: Duty or Discretion ?', 42 *Brit. Y. B. Int'l L.* 91 (1967).

Merrills, J. G., 'Sir Gerald Fitzmaurice's Contribution to the Jurisprudence of the International Court of Justice', 48 *Brit. Y. B. Int'l L.* 183 (1976-77).

Mestre, A. 'Les traités et le droit interne', 38 *Recueil des cours* 233 (1931).

Metzger, S. D., 'Settlement of International Disputes by Non-Judicial Methods', 48 *Am. J. Int'l L.* 408 (1954).

Minagawa, T., 'Various Aspects of Dispute in International Litigation --- Chiefly with Reference to Morelli's Construction', 9 *Hitotsubashi J. L. & Pol.* 1 (1981).

Minagawa, T., 'The Principle of Domestic Jurisdiction and the International Court of Justice', 8 *Hitotsubashi J. L. & Pol.* 9 (1979).

Monaco, R., 'Les principes régissant la structure et le fonctionnement des organisations internationales, 156 *Recueil des cours* 79 (1977), *reprinted in* R. Monaco, *Scritti di diritto delle organizzazioni internazionali* 459 (1981).

Monaco, R., 'Les principes d'interprétation suivis par la Cour de Justice des Communautés européennes', in *Mélanges offerts à Henri Rolin, Problèmes de droit des gens* 217 (1964).

Monaco, R., 'Le caractère constitutionnel des actes institutifs d'Organisations internationales, in *La communauté internationale: Mélanges offerts à Charles Rousseau* 153 (1974).

Morawiecki, W., 'Legal Regime of the International Organization', 15 *Polish Y. B. Int'l L.* 71 (1986).

Morawiecki, W., 'Les fonctions des Nations Unies et leur efficacité', 4 *Polish Y. B. Int'l L.* 69 (1971).

Morgenstern, F., 'The Convention on the Law of Treaties between States and International Organizations or between International Organizations', in *International Law at a Time of Perplexity, Essays in Honour of Shabtai Rosenne* 435 (Y. Dinstein & M. Tabory eds. 1989).

Morgenstern, F., 'Legality in International Organizations', 48 *Brit. Y. B. Int'l L.* 241 (1976-77).

Mushkat, M., 'De quelques problèmes relatifs à l'interprétation de la Charte et aux transformations de structure des Nations-Unies', 17 *Revue hellénique de droit international* 240 (1964).

Note, 'The IMCO Opinion: A Study in Treaty Interpretation', *Duke L. J.* 288 (1961).

Ogawa, Y., 'The International Court of Justice and Law-making (1) [in Japanese]', 15 (4) *J. L. & Pol. (Hotoseiji)* 619 (1964).

Opsahl, T., 'An "International Constitutional Law"?', 10 *Int'l & Comp. L. Q.* 760 (1961).

Osieke, E., 'Unconstitutional Acts in International Organizations: The Law and Practice of the International Civil Aviation Organization (ICAO)', 28 *Int'l & Comp. L. Q.* 1 (1979).

Osieke, E., 'The Legal Validity of Ultra Vires Decisions of International Organizations', 77 *Am. J. Int'l L.* 239 (1983).

Osieke, E., 'Admission to Membership in International Organizations: The Case of Namibia', 51 *Brit. Y. B. Int'l L.* 189 (1980).

Osieke, E., 'The Exercise of the Judicial Function with Respect to the International Labour Organization', 47 *Brit. Y. B. Int'l L.* 315 (1974-75).

Osieke, E., '"Ultra-Vires" Acts in International Organizations --- The Experience of the International Labour Organization', 48 *Brit. Y. B. Int'l L.* 259 (1976-77).

Paolillo, F. H., 'The Institutional Arrangements for the Interanational Sea-Bed and Their Impact on the Evolution of

International Organizations', 188 *Recueil des cours* 134 (1984).

Pescatore, P., 'Les objectifs de la Communauté européenne comme principes d'interprétation dans la jurisprudence de la Cour de Justice', 2 *Miscellanea W.J.Ganshof van der Meersch* 325 (1972).

Pescatore, P., 'External Relations in the Case-Law of the Court of Justice of the European Communities', 16 *Comm'n Mkt L. Rev.* 65 (1979).

Pescatore, P., 'International Law and Community Law --- A Comparative Analysis', 7 *Comm'n Mkt L. Rev.* 167 (1970).

Pescatore, P., 'Les relations exté rieures des Communautés européennes', 103 *Recueil des cours* 1 (1961).

Petersmann, E. - U., 'The Dispute Settlement System of the World Trade Organization and the Evolution of the GATT Dispute Settlement System since 1948', 31 *Common Mkt L. Rev.* 1157 (1994).

Pharand, A. D., 'Analysis of the Opinion of the International Court of Justice on Certain Expenses of the United Nations', 1 *Canadian Y. B. Int'l L.* 272 (1963).

Plous H. J., and G. E. Baker, 'McCulloch v. Maryland, Right Principle, Wrong Case', 9 *Stanford L. Rev.* 710 (1957).

Pollux, 'The Interpretation of the Charter', 23 *Brit. Y. B. Int'l L.* 54 (1946).

Prandler, Á., 'Compentence of the Security Council and the General Assembly', in *Questions of International Law* 153 (G. Haraszti ed. 1977).

Rama Rao, T. S., 'The Expenses Judgment of the International Court of Justice --- A Critique', 12 *Indian Y. B. Int'l Aff.* 134 (1963).

Rama-Montaldo, M., 'International Legal Personality and Implied Powers of International Organizations', 44 *Brit. Y. B. Int'l L.* 111 (1970).

Rapisardi-Mirabelli, A., 'La classification des traités internationaux', 4 *Revue de droit international et de législation comparée* 653 (1923).

Rasmussen, H. 'Chapter VII - The Court of Justice', in *Thirty Years of Community Law* 151 (The Commission of the European Communities ed. 1981).

Renard, G., 'Les bases philosophiques du droit international et la doctrine du "Bien commun"', 3-4 *Aachives de philosophie du droit et de sociologie juridique* 465 (1931).

Reuter, P., 'Quelques réflexions sur la notion de 'pratique internationale,' spécialement en matière d'organisations internationales, in *Studi in Onore di Giuseppe Sperduti* 187 (1984).

Reuter, P., 'La conference de Vienne sur les traités des organisations internationales et la sécurité des engagements conventionnels', in *Du droit international au droit l'integration, Liber amicorum Pierre Pescatore* 545 (F. Capotorti, C. - D. Ehlermann, J. Frowein, F. Jacobs, R. Joliet, T. Koopmans, R. Kovar eds. 1987).

Riphagen, W., 'The Second Round of Treaty Law', *id.* at 565

Robinson, J., 'Metamorphosis of the United Nations', 94 *Recueil des cours* 493 (1958).

Rosenne, Sh., 'Is the Constituent Instrument of an International Organization an International Treaty ?', in Sh. Rosenne, *Developments in the Law of Treaties 1945-1986* 181 (1989).

Rosenne, Sh., 'Interpretation of Treaties in the Restatement and the International Law Commission's Draft Articles: A Comparison', 5 *Colum. J. Transnat'l L.* 205 (1966).

Rosenne, Sh., 'Is the Constituent Instrument of an International Organization an International Treaty ?', 12 *Comunicazioni e Studi* 21 (1966).

Rosenne, Sh., 'On the Non-Use of the Advisory Competence of the International Court of Justice', 39 *Brit. Y. B. Int'l L.* 1 (1963).

Rosenne, Sh., 'Notes, Travaux Préparatoires', 12 *Int'l & Comp. L. Q.* 1378 (1963).

Rovine, A. W., 'The World Court Opinion on Namibia', 11 *Columbia J. Transna'l L.* 203 (1972).

Rubin, S. J., 'The Judicial Review Problem in the International Trade Organization', 63 *Harvard L. Rev.* 78 (1949).

Russell, R. B., 'United Nations Financing and "The Law of the Charter"', 5 *Colum. J. Transnational L.* 68 (1966).

Ruzié, D., 'L'avis consultatif de la Cour international de Justice du 20 juillet 1982 dans l'affaire de la demande de réformation du jugement n° 273 du Tribunal administratif des Nations Unies', 100 *Journal du Doit International* 76 (1983).

Ruzié, D., 'L'avis consultatif de la Cour international de Justice du 12 juillet 1973 dans l'affaire de la demande de réformation du jugement n° 158 du tribunal administratif des Nations Unies', 19 *A. F. D. I.* 320 (1973).

Samore, W., 'The New International Law of Alejandro Alvarez', 52 *Am. J. Int'l L.* 41 (1958).

Sandalow, T., 'Constitutional Interpretation', 79 *Michigan L. Rev.* 1033 (1981).

Sato, T., 'Constituent Instruments of International Organizations and Their Interpretative Framework --- Introduction to the Principal Doctrines and Bibliography', 14 *Hitotsubashi J. L. & Pol.* 1 (1986).

Sato, T., 'Status of Constituent Instruments of International Organizations in the Law of Treaties --- With Particular Reference to the Notion "Relevant Rules of the Organization"', 16 *id.* 25 (1988).

Sato, T., 'An Emerging Doctrine of the Interpretative Framework of Constituent Instruments as the Constitutions of International Organizations', 21 *id.* 1 (1993).

Schachter, O., 'Interpretation of the Charter in the Political Organs of the United Nations', in *Law, State, and International Order, Essays in Honor of Hans Kelsen* 269 (S. Engel ed. 1964).

Schachter, O., 'Review, The Law of the United Nations', 60 *Yale L. J.* 189 (1951).

Schachter, O., 'The Relation of Law, Politics and Action in the United Nations', 109 *Recueil des cours* 165 (1963).

Schick, F. B., 'Towards a Living Constitution of the United Nations', 2 *Int'l L. Q.* 1 (1948).

Schreuer, C. H. 'The Interpretation of Treaties by Domestic Courts', 45 *Brit. Y. B. Int'l L.* 255 (1971).

Schwartz, I. E., 'Article 235 and Law-Making Powers in the European Community', 27 *Int'l & Comp. L. Q.* 614 (1978).

Schwarzenberger, G., 'The Principles and Standards of International Economic Law', 117 *Recueil des cours* 1 (1966).

Schwarzenberger, G., 'Review of the Charter of the United Nations', 47 *Int'l L. A.* 64 (1957).

Seidl-Hohenveldern, I., 'The Legal Personality of International and Supranational Organizations', 21 *Revue égyptienne de droit international* 35 (1965).

Seyersted, F., 'Objective Inernational Personality of Intergovernmental Organizaions, Do Their Capacities Really Depend upon the Conventions Establishing Them ?', 34 *Nordisk Tidsskrift for International Ret, Acta Scandinavica Juris Gentium* 1 (1964).

Seyersted, F., 'United Nations Forces, Some Legal Problems', 37 *Brit. Y. B. Int'l L.* 351 (1961).

Sharma, S. P., 'The ILC Draft and Treaty Interpretation with Special Reference to Preparatory Works', 8 *Indian J. Int'l L.* 367 (1968).

Simmonds, K. R., 'The Caribbean Economic Community: A New Venture in Regional Integration', 23 *Int'l & Comp. L. Q.* 453 (1974).

Simmonds, K. R., 'The UN Assessments Advisory Opinion', 13 *Int'l & Comp. L. Q.* 854 (1964).

Simmonds, K. R., 'The Constitution of the Maritime Safety Committee of IMCO', 12 *Int'l & Comp. L. Q.* 56 (1963).

Simon, L. G., 'The Authority of the Framers of the Constitution: Can Originalist Interpretation Be Justified ?', 73 *California L. Rev.* 1482 (1985).

Simon, D., 'L'interprétation de l'accord du 25 mars 1951 entre l'O. M. S. et l'Égypte', 85 *R. G. D. I. P.* 793 (1981).

Skubiszewski, K., 'Implied Powers of International Organizations', in *International Law at a Time of Perplexity, Essays in Honour of Shabtai Rosenne* 855 (Y. Dinstein & M. Tabory eds. 1989).

Skubiszewski, K., 'Remarks on the Interpretation of the United Nations Charter', in *Völkerrecht als rechtsordnung, Internationale Gerichtsbarkeit, Menchenrecht: Festschrift für Herman Mosler* 891 (1983).

Skubiszewski, K., 'Enactment of Law by International Organizations', 41 *Brit Y. B. Int'l L.* 198 (1965-66).

Sloan, B., 'The United Nations Charter as a Constitution', 1*Pace Y. B. Int'l L.* 61 (1989).

Sloan, B., 'General Assembly Resolutions Revisited (Forty Years Later)', 58 *Brit. Y. B. Int'l L.* 39 (1987).

Sohn, L. B. (Chairman), J. P. Chamberlain and L.H. Woolsey, 'Report of Special Committee on Reference to the International Court of Questions of United Nations Competence', 44 *Proc. Am. Soc'y Int'l L.* 256.

Sohn, L. B., 'Settlement of International Disputes relating to Deep Sea-Bed Mining', in *Festshrift für Rudolf Bindschedler* 443 (E. Diez et al. eds. 1980).

Sørensen, M., 'Le problème dit du droit intertemporel dans l'ordre international', 55 *A. I. D. I.* 1 (1973).

Stone, J., 'Two Theories of "The Institution"', in *Essays in Jurisprudence in Honor of Roscoe Pound* 296 (R. A. Newman ed. 1962).

Stone, J., 'Non Liquet and the Function of Law in the International Community', 35 *Brit. Y. B. Int'l L.* 124 (1959).

Stone, J., 'Fictional Elements in Treaty Interpretation --- A Study in the International Judicial Process', 1 *Sydney L. Rev.* 344 (1955), *reprinted in* J. Stone, *Of Law and Nations: Between Power Politics and Human Hopes* 167 (1974).

Suy, E., 'The Constitutional Character of Constituent Treaties of International Organizations and the Hierarchy of Norms', in *Recht zwischen Umbruch und Bewahrung, Festschrift für Rudolf Bernhardt* 267 (U. Beyerlin et al. eds. 1995).

Szokoloczy-Syllaba, A., 'EFTA: the Settlement of Disputes', 20 *Int'l & Comp. L. Q.* 519 (1971).

Tammes, A. J. P., 'Decisions of International Organs as a Source of International Law', 94 *Recueil des cours* 261 (1958).

Tavernier, P., 'L'avis consultatif de la Cour international de Justice du 20 juillet 1982 dans l'affaire de la demande de réformation du jugement n° 273 du Tribunal administratif des Nations Unies (affaire Mortished)', 28 *A. F. D. I.* 392 (1982).

Thierry, H., 'Les résolution des organes internationaux dans la jurisprudence de la Cour internationale de Justice', 167 *Recueil des cours* 385 (1980).

Thierry, H., 'Avis consultatif de la Cour International de Justice de 20 juillet 1962, Certaines dépenses des Nations Unies (Article 17 paragraphe 2 de la Charte)', 8 *A. F. D. I.* 247 (1962).

Tizzano, A., 'Chapter III - The Powers of the Community', in *Thirty Years of Community Law* 43 (The Commission of the European Communities ed. 1981).

Treves, T., 'Les décisions d'interprétation des Statuts du Fonds monétaire international', 79 *R. G. D. I. P.* 5 (1975).

Tunkin, G., 'International Law in the International System', 147 *Recueil des cours* 1 (1975).

Tunkin, G., 'The Legal Nature of the United Nations', 119 *Recueil des cours* 1 (1966).

Uchida, H., 'International Status of South-West Africa [in Japanese]', in *Hanrei-Kenkyu-Kokusaishihosaibansho* (*The Jurisprudence of the International Court of Justice*) 332 (Y. Takano ed. 1965).

Vallat, Sir F., 'The Competence of the United Nations General Assembly', 97 *Recueil des cours* 203 (1959).

Vallat, Sir F., 'The General Assembly and the Security Council of the United Nations', 29 *Brit. Y. B. Int'l L.* 63 (1952).

van der Meersch, Ganshof., 'L'ordre juridique des Communautés européennes et le droit international', 148 *Recueil des cours* 21 (1975).

van Bogaert, E., 'Le caractère juridique de la Cour de Justice des Communautés européennes', in *Mélanges offerts à Henri Rolin, Problèmes de droit des gens* 449 (1964).

Vermulst, E., & B. Driessen, 'An Overview of the WTO Dispute Settlement System and its Relationship with the Uruguay

Round Agreements', 29 *J. World Trade* 131 (1995).

Virally, M., 'La valeur juridique des recommandations des organisations internationales', 2 *A. F. D. I.* 66 (1956).

Virally, M., 'Sur la classification des traités à propos du projet d'articles de la Commission du droit international', 13 *Comunicazione e Studi* 15 (1969).

Virally, M., 'La notion de fonction dans la théorie de l'organisation internationale', in *La communauté internationale: Mélange offerts à Charles Rousseau* 277 (1974).

Virally, M., 'Definition and Classification of International Organizations: a Legal Approach', in *The Concept of International Organization* 50 (G. Ab-Saab ed. 1981).

Waldock, Sir H., 'General Course on Public International Law', 106 *Recueil des cours* 1 (1962).

Weissberg, G., 'The Role of the International Court of Justice in the United Nations System: the First Quarter Century', in *The Future of the International Court of Justice* 131 (L. Gross ed. 1976).

Wengler, W., 'Recours judiciaire à instituer contre les décisions d'organes internationaux', 44-I *Annuaire de l'Institut de Droit International* 224 (1952); 45-I *id.* at 265 (1954); 47-I *id.* at 5 (1957); 47-II *id.* at 274, 488 (1957).

Wright, Q., 'The Interpretation of Multilateral Treaties', 23 *Am. J. Int'l L.* 94 (1929).

Wright, Q., 'The Jural Personality of the United Nations', 43 *Am. J. Int'l L.* 509 (1949).

Wright, Q., 'The Strengthening of International Law', 98 *Recueil des cours* 1 (1959).

Yachi, S., 'United Nations Conference on the Law of Treaties between States and International Organizations or between International Organizations' [in Japanese], 85 *Kokusaiho Gaiko Zassh* (*The Journal of International Law and Diplomacy*) 374 (1986).

Yasseen, M. K., 'L'interprétation des traités d'après la Convention de Vienne sur le droit des traités', 151 *Recueil des cours* 1 (1976).

Zacklin, R., 'The Problem of Namibia in International Law', 171 *Recueil des cours* 227 (1981).

Zemanek, K., 'The United Nations Conference on the Law of Treaties Between States and International Organizations or Between International Organizations: The unrecorded history of the "general agreement"', in *Völkerrecht, Recht der Internationalen Organisationen, Weltwirtschaftsrecht, Festschrift für Ignas Seidl-Hohenveldern* 665 (K. - H. Böckstiegel, H. - E. Folz, J. M. Mössner, K. Zemanek eds. 1988).

Zoller, E., 'The "Corporate Will" of the United Nations and Rights of the Minority', 81 *Am J. Int'l L.* 610 (1987).

Index of Subjects

288

Index of Cases

The page numbers in bold type indicate the pages where the case is discussed, and the other page numbers indicate the pages where it is cited.

International Court of Justice

Index of International Treaties

Index of International Organizations

Index of Names

The page numbers in bold type indicate the pages where his/her work is discussed, and the other page numbers indicate the pages where it is cited.

Abou-El-Wafa, A. 234
Ago, R. 78, 131, **135**, 136, 137, 146, 152, 153, 249, 251
Akehurst, M. 138, 166
Akintan, S. A. 202
Alvarez, A. **34**, 36, 42, 43, 47, 48, **50**, 51, 52, 60, 64, 80, 84, 90, 150, 155
Amerasinghe, C. F. 65, 75
Ammoun, F. 109, 124, 141, 152
Anand, R. P. 41
Aréchaga, E. Jiménez de 109, 124, **127**, 128, 141, **145**, 152
Armand-Ugon, E. C. 59, 90, 94, **97**, **98**, 118, 138
Audéoud, O. 181, **187**, **188**
Azevedo, Ph. 42, 43, 47, 48, 50, 52, 80, 150, 155

Badawi (Pasha), A. H. 42, 48, 52, 57, 59, 65, 80, 84, 90, 94, **97**, **98**, 100, 118, 138, 150-52
Basdevant, J. 43, **44**, 48, 52, 65, 80, 90, 94, **97**, **98**, 100, 118, 138, 150-52, 181
Bastid, P. 7, **253-55**
Bebr, G. 245
Bedjaoui, M. 14, 146, 153
Belaouane-Gherari, S. 202
Bengzon, C. 109, 124, 141
Bennett, R. W. 249
Berlia, G. 42
Bernhardt, R. 12, 26
Bettati, M. 11
Bindscheler, D. 181, 183
Bindschedler, R. 216, **259**, 260
Bollecker, B. 115
Boulouis, J. 245
Bowett, D. W. **35**, 36, 41, 181, 211, 213

Bredimas, A 244, 246
Broderick, A. 253
Bustamante y Rivero, J. L. 65, 100

Caflisch, L. C. 216, 218, 219
Campbell, A. I. L. 224
Carreau, D. 193
Castañeda, J. 165
Chamberlain, J. P. 177
Chandler, R. 249
Charpentier, J. **238**
Chaumont, Ch. M. 3
Chemerinsky, E. 249
Chevallier, R.- M. 244, **245**
Chiu, H. 89
Ciobanu, D. 3, 9, 164-67, **171**, 177, 178, 224
Clariana, G. G. 199
Cohen, B. V. 9, **248**
Colliard, C. A. 118, 123, 181
Combacau, J. 11, 130, 134, 252
Conforti, B. 164, 168, 174, **175**
Córdova, R. 90, 94, 118, 138, **140**, 152
Costonis, J. J. 245
Cot, J.- P. 32
Courteix, S. 214

Degan, V. D. 22, 26, 244
Dehaussy, J. 7
Delos, J. 251
Desqueyrat, A. 251
de Castro, F. 109, **117**, **118**, 124, **127**, **129**, **130**, 141, 152
de Lacharrière, G. L. 138, 146
de Visscher, Ch. **6**, 7, 25, 30, 42, 46, **48**, 52, 63, 80, 84, **85**, **86**, **89**, 90, 150, 151, **154**, 155, 244, 259, **264**
Dillard, H. C. 109, 124, 127, 141, 152, 262
Dillon, Jr, Th. 197
Dinh, N. Q. 11

297

299

International Law in Japanese Perspective

1. S. Oda & H. Owada: *Japanese State Practice 1971-1975.* (forthcoming)
    ISBN 0-7923-1405-0
2. M. Miyoshi: *Considerations of Equity in the Settlement of Territorial and Boundary Disputes.* 1993   ISBN 0-7923-2217-7
3. T. Sato: *Evolving Constitutions of International Organizations.* 1996
    ISBN 90-411-0202-7

KLUWER LAW INTERNATIONAL – THE HAGUE / LONDON / BOSTON